Chantell Ilbury / Clem Sunter

THE FOX Trilogy

Imagining the unimaginable and *dealing* with it

HUMAN & ROUSSEAU / TAFELBERG

Published jointly by Human & Rousseau and Tafelberg,
both imprints of NB Publishers,
A division of Media24 Boeke (Pty) Ltd
40 Heerengracht, Cape Town

Design and cover by Nazli Jacobs
Typeset in 11.5 on 14pt Palatino
Printed and bound in South Africa

ISBN: 978-0-624-07555-4 (Second softcover edition 2015)
ISBN: 978-0-624-05296-8 (First softcover edition 2011, Fifth
impression 2014)

Also available as ebooks (refer to the last page)

THIS BOOK IS DEDICATED TO

Our families who are our foundation;
Our friends who stand by us in good
  and bad times;
Our colleagues who assisted us in producing
  the book in such a professional manner;
  and
The fox within you – whoever you are,
  wherever you are and whatever you do.

Contents

Socrates & the Fox   337

Prologue

Method

Defining the Game

Foreword

About ten years ago in June 2001, the two of us co-authored a book entitled *The Mind of a Fox*. We chose the title to contrast our way of thinking about the future with what was conventionally being taught at American business schools and in the most popular management textbooks. The idea being widely imparted at the time was the hedgehog approach.

What are foxes and hedgehogs? A Greek poet called Archilochus wrote the following line of verse in 650 BC: "The fox knows many things, but the hedgehog knows one big thing". Why he chose these animals, heaven only knows, but it is certainly relevant for business. For the conventional approach to the future is to formulate a vision (the hedgehog big idea), support it with a mission statement, align everybody to the vision and mission, and march collectively towards them. Focus is the key to hedgehog-style leadership, the mantra being: do not allow yourself to be distracted by side issues, in particular issues which somehow contradict your vision.

The hedgehog concept has merit, but with one huge proviso: the future has to turn out to be more or less like the one assumed in the vision. Then hedgehogs can sweep the board. However, if the future goes off in an entirely different direction, they can lead a company collectively over the edge of a cliff. They either win or lose big time; which is the cue for the foxes to come into play in designing corporate strategy.

Foxes believe that the future is unpredictable and many elements are beyond the control of the individual or the organisation thinking about the future. The key is therefore to prepare yourself for anything the future can throw at you, be it a shift in economies or markets, a breakthrough in technology, a political revolution or a natural calamity. In other words, you have to road-test the vision and strategy against a range of scenarios. This will ensure that you know in advance what adaptations you have to make if any of the possible futures that you entertain emerge as reality.

The quality and speed of your response will thus be enhanced to cope with even the most extreme course of events. As we put it, you will have imagined the unimaginable and learned of ways to deal with the opportunities and threats contained therein. You will have a grasp of the drills to survive the black swan scenarios and thrive in the white swan scenarios. Charles Darwin would have approved of this foxy approach, given that markets change much faster and more dramatically than Nature. Just ask yourself: how many businesses are around a century after they were established? Very few because the vast majority did not have the foresight to adapt to the changing times. So they went extinct or were taken over.

Incidentally, we stress that the scenarios do not have to capture the future exactly. They need to open the minds of the individuals making the decisions to the fact that there are other paths and other options. As the legendary scenario planner, Pierre Wack, once said: "It is much better to be vaguely right than precisely wrong!"

Moreover, foxes do not just write scenarios. They also want to make decision makers aware of the clues that the future always has on offer to signify imminent change. They therefore put as much effort into identifying the flags which would indicate that one is moving from one scenario to another. They are continually searching for the tipping points or beginnings of something new that might usher in a completely changed environment. Then, based on the disposition of the flags, they attach subjective probabilities to the scenarios. When the probabilities rise, they connect the dots by calculating the impact of the scenario on the organisation concerned and what it should do about it – now and in the future. After all, scenarios without a plan of action are just daydreams or academic fantasies lacking substance.

In short, foxy leaders reduce the risks inherent in volatile markets and uncertain times by having many ideas about how the future can pan out. They constantly watch the flags to see which idea is about to come into play. They are as necessary to any business as visionary hedgehogs and it is the debate between the two that produces the optimum strategy in the long run.

Examples of how we ourselves have used the technique that we advocate are as follows:

1. The publishing of a 'High Road' scenario for South Africa in mid-1987. The theme was that the ruling government would negotiate a political settlement with the genuine black leaders, and South Africa would re-enter the global economy as a full-blown democracy. The flag was the release of Nelson Mandela. It went up in February 1990 and democratic elections were held four years later. At the time the scenario was published, it was considered a fairy tale. Within seven years, the miracle happened.

2. The incorporation of a 'Gilded Cage' scenario into our letter to George W Bush in *The Mind of a Fox* in June 2001. In this scenario, a massive terrorist attack on a Western city was anticipated which would precipitate among other things a security clampdown on immigration into the US. The flags were the rise of Fundamental Islam (see the postscript in the book); the better organisation of terrorist organisations in places like Saudi Arabia; and the two attacks on US embassies in Africa in 1998 which could be regarded as a dry run for the real thing. The 9/11 attack on New York occurred three months after we published the warning to Mr Bush in our book;

3. The inclusion of a 'Hard Times' global recession scenario in our second book *Games Foxes Play* that hit the bookshelves in April 2005. The flag was a decline in property values in the US causing American consumers to stop borrowing and curtail spending. After all, a middle class American's house is his or her biggest asset. The resultant drop in consumer expenditure would trigger a crash in the US economy followed by one in the world at large. The flag went up in January 2007 when the property index declined for the first time in 20 years. The rest is history; and

4. The listing of major smacks from Mother Nature as a breaking future for 2011 in an article written for the website News24.com in December 2010. So far this year we have had the floods in Australia and the earthquakes in New Zealand and Japan. The flags for the severe consequences of these events were the increasing density of population in places at risk together with the growing interdependence of the global economy.

During the last ten years, we have done numerous sessions world-wide using this methodology to test the viability of an organisation's strategy against the various extreme futures hypothesised. We often say to people that we cannot make their fears disappear, but we can structure them in a way that makes them easier to handle. The global financial crisis undoubtedly boosted the popularity of our approach because of the anxieties created by it in the minds of those who plot strategy. The latter now recognise the need to be open-minded and flexible in a way that was not apparent before the crisis. They want to diminish the chance of failure and hedgehog-sized losses.

We have also written two further books which are featured in this fox trilogy. The second is called *Games Foxes Play* because we feel the metaphor of a game is a useful one to apply to business. Like sport, business has competitors, rules and game-changing uncertainties; and just as you win, lose or draw in sport, you make money, lose money or break even in business.

However the most important thing is to choose the right game. As we remark with a wry smile, it is no good being world badminton champion because very few people watch the sport on television. You are the best in the world but you don't make much money. So one of the questions we ask a business is: "Do you play badminton?" on the grounds that changes in consumer behaviour can cause product obsolescence and thereby empty the profit out of any game.

The title of the third book, *Socrates & the Fox*, we selected to showcase the great Athenian philosopher and the Socratic Method that he passed on as his legacy. If Socrates were alive today and pursued a career as a management consultant, he would not have asked a company about its targets, key performance indicators and budgets. He would have asked: "Why do you exist and is anything happening out there to undermine the reason for your existence?" This has recently become a sharp question in light of the recession driving consumers toward the cheaper alternative. Those companies that have provided such an option have been winners, while those that haven't have been fighting to maintain their relevance.

In the second and third books we evolved the Conversation Model that we currently use when facilitating strategy sessions with top executive teams. It has no frills or gadgets; and the agenda is easily understandable and logical. Nevertheless, it does promote a conversation that most businesses have never had before. For this reason we know of many institutions that have used our model without using us. Moreover our website, www.mindofafox.com, from which the model can be downloaded, has become one of the most popular of its kind on the internet. Just google the two words 'mind fox' to see how many hits we must be getting around the world to be No1 for that phrase.

Another welcome development for us is the enthusiastic endorsement of our model by the investment community. After all, they have lived for years in the fickle universe of stock market booms and crashes. Hence a measured response to events that can be game-changers in the markets is critical to any successful investment strategy. Our argument is that it is more sensible to make decisions based on the balance of evidence around different economic scenarios than to bet the whole shop on a single forecast. In this connection, one of the important questions to ask is whether the market indices reflect the probabilities that you as an investor are giving to the good and the bad scenarios. Where the answer is no, there is probably an opportunity to make money or protect what you have, as long as you are fleet-footed.

When we initially collaborated on the first book, we had no idea where the road would lead us. Like good foxes, we have adapted along the way. This trilogy is a record of that adaptation. Indeed, we are still adapting our model by trying to improve our techniques of assessing how far up a flag has gone; and what probability should be assigned to a scenario in light of the position of the flag. We hope you, the readers, will be tempted to explore the future along similar lines. However if, in the process, you discover that you really are a hedgehog, get yourself a foxy adviser!

Chantell Ilbury
Clem Sunter

The Mind of a
FOX

Scenario Planning in *Action*

Introduction to the Third Impression

We normally associate 911 with an emergency call. It also represents September 11. At 8:45 am (New York time) on that day in 2001, the world changed forever. This was the moment when the first of two hijacked planes slammed into the World Trade Center. Another one hit the Pentagon and a fourth crashed in Pennsylvania. No terrorist attack has ever caused such a shock. The *unthinkable* had happened – and it wasn't a movie.

When we wrote this book in the first part of 2001, we included a letter to President Bush. In it, we warned him that the key uncertainty during his tenure was nuclear terrorism, more specifically the possibility of terrorists planting a nuclear device in a Western city. While the tools of destruction and method of delivery were different to what we had envisaged, the impact was just as devastating. Nothing could have demonstrated the power of scenario planning more effectively than this terrible tragedy. We could never have captured it in a forecast, but it was possible to provide a warning in the form of a scenario.

Indeed, the logic contained in our two scenarios – "Friendly Planet" and "Gilded Cage" – is now more pertinent than ever. The natural temptation for the "rich old millions" in the West must be to batten down the hatches and isolate themselves in a Gilded Cage. We all know that security is the most basic of all human needs. However, this could lead to an even more divided world as the gap between the "rich old millions" and the "poor young billions" widens further. The increasing tension and stress associated with this scenario will ironically make it more likely than before that another evil act of the same – or perhaps even greater – magnitude will be perpetrated by terrorists. No advances in technology, no improvements in intelligence and security management systems can render an individual nation impregnable against attack. The terrorist will always find a chink in the bars of the cage, however thick you make them, to pass through and commit his foul deed. Moreover, the knowledge of how to manufacture weapons of mass destruction is itself indestructible. And it will continue to spread. Meanwhile, inside the cage, a superabundance of soft targets awaits the terrorist. The growing interdependencies and networks of a modern society make it increasingly vulnerable to dislocation and attack, particularly by people who are prepared to die in the process.

The only way to minimise – not entirely eliminate – the threat of further outrages is for America to take the lead in building a Friendly Planet. This involves more than a military victory over the terrorists. The realisation has to dawn that to be a secure winner, you cannot be surrounded by resentful losers. The preferred scenario is therefore one in which, as we say in the book, "the rich old millions resolve to find common ground with the poor young billions to eradicate poverty and disease, to tackle problems of the environment, to bring international criminal syndicates to justice and to root out dangerous terrorist organisations." Otherwise, the future is bleak. Anything goes. And it would be unwise to dismiss *any* 911 call as a hoax.

Chantell Ilbury
Clem Sunter
September 2001

Eye of the tiger or fox of the fairway?

Have you ever watched the world's finest golfer blast the ball effortlessly from a tee, then follow his crisp iron shot at the pin with a perfect putt and think "he really needs to jack up his game"? Of course you don't, but he does, even when he is about to win the 2001 Masters and have all four Major trophies sitting on his mantelpiece at the same time. This is Tiger Woods – the fox of the fairway. Why a fox? He is cunning, bright, curious and he reacts with his environment. The *New York Times* once described foxes as "the most beautiful and interesting animals to observe".

The common fox in Europe has reddish fur with black patches behind the ears and a light tip to its brush-like tail. Underneath, it sports a white waistcoat and dark leggings. Including the tail, the animal is just over a metre long. It is a small but beautiful wild dog, the eyes having a watchful gleam quite different to a domesticated dog. The whole demeanour of the animal is one of alertness, as if it would be up and off at the first sign of danger.

Beautiful – yes; but interesting? Foxes have many dens, sometimes called earths, within their territory. They use them to their best advantage because dens give them options. Foxes normally choose the most secure den in which to give birth to and nurture their young, but they maintain the other dens in case the secure one is put at risk. They are continually foraging for new sources of food and eat almost anything – rodents, rabbits, birds and insects as well as fruit and berries in season. They are highly adaptable to different terrains, ranging from dense forests to cultivated farmland. In fact, they can adapt easily to urban environments and change their eating habits accordingly. Scavenging from refuse bins is an urban pastime. They are so resourceful that the landed gentry in England find them fun to hunt; but maybe not for much longer if the politicians have their way. Foxes have extraordinarily sensitive noses that can pick up an interesting scent a mile off. Even the spiky exterior of the humble hedgehog can't protect it from a hungry fox.

Which brings us to hedgehogs. They, on the other hand, live in one burrow all their lives. For them a single home is their security – nice and warm and cosy, and generally quite big. Hedgehogs hibernate during winter, effectively cutting themselves off from the outside world. They have plump little bodies with very short legs that hardly raise them from the ground. They are all of thirty centimetres long, covered with sharp, greyish brown spikes and blessed with a pig-like snout. Unlike foxes, hedgehogs like to live where there is certainty in the availability of food. Their favourite fare includes insects, but they are also partial to snails and slugs, which are slow enough for them to catch. Hedgehogs are generally non-confrontational. Whereas foxes will readily enter a fight, hedgehogs prefer to roll up in a ball and use their protective spikes to deter any challenge, especially from foxes. Nevertheless, foxes are carnivorous and are not unknown to make a tasty meal of sleepy hedgehogs. And gypsies have been known to bake them in a covering of clay.

Foxes? Hedgehogs? What have these got to do with golf? And more importantly, what can we learn from distinguishing between them? This book attempts to uncover the mind of a fox. What makes someone a fox? How does a fox manoeuvre not only through the game of business, but also through the game of life? In order to gain an insight into the versatile mind of the fox, we need to compare it to the stiffer persona of the staid hedgehog.

In brief, a hedgehog is a person who believes that life revolves around one big idea, one ultimate truth and that if only we can get at that idea or truth, everything else will come right. Once programmed or hooked on an idea, or even worse an ideology, a hedgehog cannot shake it off. Alternatives are irrelevant. As opposed to searching for a hypothesis which most closely fits the facts, a hedgehog will shoehorn the facts into something which will support his ideology, however much the arguments have to be distorted.

A fox, in contrast to a hedgehog, is someone who believes that life is all about knowing many things. Foxes are people who embrace uncertainty and believe that experience – doing things – is an essential source of knowledge. Action sorts out the sheep from the goats! Moreover, like good golfers know that an excellent sub-par round is only built up one shot at a time, foxes depend upon an incremental approach to change the status quo. Life very rarely confronts you with life-changing experiences. Rather, the transformation of your prospects is the result of many small steps taken one at a time, with little knowledge in advance of what the next step will be until it presents itself. Hence, foxes understand that it is a waste of time trying to delineate an exact path into the long-term future. Crossroads upon crossroads upon crossroads await you. You take the turning you like at the time, and you never look over your shoulder. Consequently, while hedgehogs like to bury themselves in certainty and cloister themselves from disruptive influences, foxes enthusiastically forage for new ideas and explore new routes in the quest of developing a wider range of options for nourishment. In pursuing this course, foxes rely as much on intuition and imagination as they do on their reason and senses. James Dyson, a well-known and very foxy British inventor, puts his success down to his obsession for detail and never-say-die approach to problem-solving: "Once you begin to break down a problem into little bits and tackle each one you find a solution." Voilà – he has completely redesigned the vacuum cleaner, the wheelbarrow and the washing machine and is worth £500 million.

Returning to the world of golf, how would a hedgehog-like golfer differ from Tiger Woods? Firstly, he would have a pre-tournament press conference at which he would expand at great length on his vision and strategic plan for the event. If conditions during the tournament were exactly as predicted in his plan and he played the course exactly as he had anticipated, he might win it. But if the weather was different, the course tougher, and things did not go according to plan, he would end up with a series of lousy scores and his name way down the list. He might even call a post-tournament conference to complain how things totally beyond his control had led to his demise: for example, the state of the greens, the newness of his clubs or the unruly nature of the spectators. Hedgehogs can be bad losers cum laude!

Resilience is where Tiger has such an advantage over his fellow competitors, and permits him to win by such large margins in tournaments. For the reality is that things seldom go according to plan for any player, however consistent he is; and Tiger is more consistent than most. Where Tiger puts clear blue water between himself and the rest of the field is his ability to turn adversity into opportunity. When he hits a wayward shot, his powers of recovery are sublime. If his drive ends up behind a tree, he can hook or slice his iron shot so that the ball bends in flight and lands on the green. From "unplayable" lies just off the putting surface, he invents a chip shot which leaves his ball centimetres from the hole. He holes long putts when he needs to. He can stop a shot in mid-swing when he hears the inopportune click of a spectator's camera shutter.

Tiger has the strength, the touch and the imagination to be the champion. In addition, he possesses the vital characteristic of BMT or big match temperament. None of these qualities is spontaneously acquired. Admittedly, in Tiger's case, he always had the potential; his father spotted it at the age of three. However, his current prowess has arisen from years of preparation, hard physical training and focus. He can make those minor adjustments to his game which are crucial to his victories precisely because, more than any other mortal on earth, he has achieved mastery over what he can control – his shot-making. He has the flexibility because he has the focus. This may sound contradictory! Nevertheless, we are going to show you later in the book that focusing one's energy is a prerequisite for the capacity to manoeuvre out of difficult situations.

Two boardroom species

As in golf, so in business there are plenty of hedgehog CEOs. Some achieve spectacular results in terms of earnings-per-share growth and capital appreciation for shareholders. But their companies have invariably been fortunate enough to experience business conditions in line with their own wishes or reflecting the assumptions contained in their strategic plans. It is only when the future branches off in an unexpected and undesired direction that the mettle of a CEO is tested and you can tell whether he is a fox or a hedgehog.

An obvious indicator of a hedgehog CEO is that he shoots the equivalent of a golf score in the upper 90s when he experiences the unexpected. Then he explains in the annual report and to members at the annual general meeting how the mess is due to adverse factors beyond his control; but the company is doing something about it! When things go badly on the golf course, cheating hedgehogs have been known to move their balls surreptitiously to better lies by employing the "foot wedge" – another name for an adroit little kick. The other tactic is to replace the ball nearer the hole on the green after cleaning it. In competition, hedgehog "ringers" might even enter a better score on their cards than they actually achieved; or bolster their handicaps beforehand by logging in artificially high scores. In business, the hedgehog equivalent is to use strong-arm tactics to retain market share, be unmerciful towards suppliers, bully the employees or subtly embroider the accounts. In the short term, hedgehogs have lots of ways of covering up bad track records! The amazing thing is that hedgehog CEOs can still come out smelling like roses and pay themselves huge bonuses with the full support of the board's remuneration committee. A recent UK study showed that there is no correlation whatsoever between CEOs' pay and performance.

On the other hand, Tiger Woods has to perform within the rules to be paid. If he didn't regularly shoot rounds in the 60s, if his name wasn't regularly at the top of the leader board, he wouldn't get the sponsorship fees or prize money. Tiger cannot bamboozle anyone with fine statements of intent about strategic restructuring or repositioning. His clubs do the talking and the results speak for themselves!

The examples chosen from golf and business highlight how different a hedgehog is from a fox. Hedgehogs are inflexible and slow to move. However, once they start on a course, they don't deviate. Inertia sets in. Because so many hedgehogs in the animal kingdom have been flattened by cars, they now have their own tunnels excavated for them under motorways by caring preservation societies. Colin Powell, the American secretary of state who was previously an army man, makes it clear in his autobiography that he despises military people in the hedgehog mould. They are immaculately dressed but make little practical contribution. According to Powell, all they do is "break starch", namely put on trousers that have been starched to perfection. In other words, hedgehogs are conspicuous at military parades, bristling with importance and marching to the thump of the big bass drum. But they are seldom seen in the trenches doing the actual fighting and showing courage under fire.

By contrast, foxes are quick to make changes in their actual behaviour. Occasionally, these are large changes, as when Reynard the fox leaps out of the chicken coop when he sees Farmer Giles coming out of the farmhouse door with his shotgun! Their intuitive response is what allows them to survive in a changing environment. One point which is constantly missed by management text books and business school courses is that 80 per cent of the success of world-class companies is due to excellence in implementation and delivery under a variety of conditions. They are simply brilliant at reaching their goals even when things crop up which they were not registering on their radar screens. At the most, 20 per cent of their success is attributable to the quality of their original plans or the conceptual part of the management process that the majority of management gurus write big tomes about. In the real world, the adaptations along the way are the ones that count. The trick is not the inventive idea: discoveries which will set the world alight are a dime a dozen. The trick is co-ordinating the 101 little things that make the idea happen. Think of the percentage of boardroom decisions that never get further than the minute book.

World-class companies tend therefore to be run by foxy CEOs who are not obsessed with the "vision" thing. They are prepared to contemplate views that are contrary to their company's conventional wisdom and "official future". They seek to attract people who are lateral thinkers and who can negotiate the rapids if necessary. As one foxy CEO said: "It's the bombshell you don't expect that can do you in. The best protection is to have commanders under you who can make split-second decisions under enemy fire. Each decision may not be for the best, but the next one corrects what's bad about the previous one. So the chain of decisions holds up in the end." Clearly, this has not been the case with the way mad cow disease has been handled in Europe. Ministers have had to resign because at first they didn't take the issue seriously enough and responded with denials that there was a problem. Now the pendulum has swung the other way, and governments are trying to make up lost ground with draconian laws which could jeopardise the beef industry. As if that is not enough, European farmers' misery has been compounded by the outbreak of foot-and-mouth disease. The latter is so contagious that strong measures are a necessity to halt it. All in all, a cool, foxy head is required to steer any country affected through these shoals of uncertainty.

Sam Walton, the founder of Wal-Mart Stores, which is now the largest retailer in the world with over one million employees, was a fox. He spent most of his time away from his office visiting the stores, checking standards and more importantly inspiring his staff to think of ways of doing things differently and better. He walked the walk. He had a good nose for business and was forever sniffing out promising innovations developed at store level which could be applied throughout the group. This is in marked contrast to hedgehog leaders who hibernate in their penthouse suites surrounded by their equally aloof, hedgehog-like assistants. They seldom venture out of the cloistered calm of their offices to meet real people in the real world – but then they feel it is unnecessary to do so since they've already worked out the grand solution. To all intents and purposes, hedgehog leaders are invisible except for the odd photograph and ceremonial function. They rule by remote control.

Have you seen the movie *Brassed Off* ? It's about a brass band from a Yorkshire colliery winning the national championships against the background of the closure of the colliery. In one scene, a young female executive asks the managing director whether he has read her viability study into ways of keeping the pit open. He says no, the decision to close was taken two years ago and coal is history. Her retort is that clearly reports have to be seen to be written rather than written to be seen. That's the way sleek head-office hedgehogs like it!

The unnatural, inward-looking and incestuous atmosphere of a hedgehog lair resembles that of a royal court of old plagued by intrigue and infighting among the courtiers. The only measure of success is how favourable a courtier's standing is with the king or queen. In the resulting competition in which each courtier is vying for the eye of the monarch, the hedgehog species show their expertise at stabbing their rivals in the back. They have so many spikes to do it with! Conspiracy theories abound, and any questioning of the party line laid down by the ruler is viewed as treachery. Niccolò Machiavelli, the sixteenth-century Florentine philosopher who promoted the use of unscrupulous statecraft to preserve power, would have been quite at home in the company of modern, smooth-talking hedgehogs. The only thing he would find unfamiliar in today's world is the speed of travel and communication which has reduced us to a global village. Unfortunately, it has also produced a superclass of globe-trotting hedgehogs with no fixed abode and no fixed commitments to any community or country. Their entire time is spent chasing the bucks across national boundaries, cooped up in the intensive care of a 747's first-class cabin. You can be sure that if Machiavelli had been alive at the beginning of the 21st century, he would have had multiple passports, several aliases and would be clocking up millions of air miles. Even as the prince of hedgehogs, he had respect for the fox. He had this to say about his rival: "As a prince must be able to act just like a beast, he should learn from the fox and the lion; because the lion does not defend himself against traps, and the fox does not defend himself against wolves. So one has to be a fox in order to recognise traps, and a lion to frighten off wolves."

It goes without saying that hedgehogs are natural centralisers who want to achieve change from the top down. They are conceited enough to think they have all the answers for the working classes. Development – with a capital "D" – should radiate out from the centre. Foxy executives, on the other hand, support the idea of change from the bottom up. Decentralisation, without losing all control, is the name of the game for the business fox. On a slightly different note but in the same context, foxy monarchs in the old days used to employ court jesters with the aim of the latter bending the royal ear with unorthodox opinions on matters of state. As they say, there's many a truth that lies in jest. Nevertheless, the court jester had to invest considerable humour in putting across his contrarian views in order to make the sovereign laugh and thus minimise his chances of being beheaded! We naturally choose friends that we agree with, but we learn something new from people with whom we don't. An old Spanish adage goes as follows: "He who advises is not the traitor." So, in plain English, don't shoot the messenger.

A lesson from Mother Nature, flying frogs and sea-foxes

You needn't have salt water coursing through your veins to imagine the following analogy: an angling hedgehog, if there ever was one, would prefer to fish within the known, protective waters of a cove where the effects of tide and winds are relatively certain and controllable. In contrast, a sea-fox would prefer to investigate other fishing grounds beyond the protective waters of the cove and be willing to operate in the uncertain and uncontrollable elements of the open sea.

Thus, an essential element in the difference between the mind-set of the fox and the hedgehog is the fox's preparedness to strike out for the unknown. This in turn means an acceptance that mistakes do happen. What is more, mistakes are not just golden opportunities for learning; they are, in fact, sometimes the *only* opportunity for learning something truly new and making progress. In 1928, Alexander Fleming discovered penicillin accidentally when he saw that a bit of mould, which had fallen from a culture plate in his laboratory, had destroyed bacteria around it. Basically, he won the Nobel Prize, and a knighthood into the bargain, for a mistake which he had the intelligence to follow up on.

Hedgehogs balk at this approach because it may well expose them to peer ridicule. Indeed, they view mistakes in two possible lights. If it is somebody else's, that person is to blame because somebody has to be held responsible and punished. If the mistake is their own, no-one is to blame because it was the result of circumstances beyond anyone's control. In the latter case, hedgehogs are very good at producing an expression of injured innocence, reminding one of professional footballers about to be given a yellow or red card for a foul. Either way, mistakes are perceived by hedgehogs as aberrations which don't advance you up the learning curve. Failure has the same penalty attached to it as drawing the "chance" or "community chest" card in a game of Monopoly that says: do not pass go, do not collect £200, move directly to jail! Better be right all the time is the maxim of the cautious hedgehog; or at least don't be caught out if you're wrong.

Foxes can take solace from the fact that their approach to learning and problem-solving has been used successfully for many years by the world's most powerful and foxy CEO – Mother Nature. As pointed out by Professor Daniel C. Dennet, the Director of Cognitive Studies at Tufts University in Medford, Massachusetts: "For evolution, which knows nothing, the leaps into novelty are blindly taken by mutations, which are copying 'errors' in the DNA. Most of these are fatal errors, in fact. Since the vast majority of mutations are harmful, the process of natural selection actually works to keep the mutation rate very low. Fortunately for us, it *does not achieve perfect success*, for if it did, evolution would finally grind to a halt, its sources of novelty dried up."

This is particularly evident in the enigmatic rain forests of Borneo which boast one of the largest concentrations of gliders – at least thirty different species of animals as diverse as lizards, squirrels, lemurs or colugos, snakes, geckos and frogs – that have changed their physiological structure over the years to allow them to glide from tree to tree. Why is this island so rich in gliding species while other rain forests like the Amazon have none? The answer – Mother Nature and evolution. The rain forests of South East Asia are dominated by giant dipterocarp trees which tend to crowd out other trees and, to add insult to injury, offer hungry residents infrequent and unpredictable bounties of fruit. To work within this context of inconsistent and non-controllable food sources, the frogs and other animals that lived within the area took to an ingenious way of moving from one arboreal restaurant to another – jumping large distances. A creative strategy indeed! They realised that this provided the most effective way of getting around without excessive climbing and exposure to the danger of predators. Gradually they evolved to a more manageable mode of movement – *gliding*. Understandably this didn't happen overnight, nor without its fair share of bruised and battered little bodies. But it was all part of the learning experience.

The point of the gliding, flying frogs? The mind-set of making mistakes and learning from them to expand one's knowledge, so intrinsic to the mind of the fox, is nothing new. It is a natural process, and it has been around for millions of years. The other important lesson to derive from this example is: *think the unthinkable*. A frog that glides? You're pulling my leg. But it's a fact like the flying hedgehogs in the previous section – except that the latter travel first class! Mind you, in the world of political affairs, the Florida recount in the US presidential election was also unthinkable until it happened in 2000.

How else can the advance in the forest gliders be construed to be of relevance to the global economy? How can those blessed with a higher cognitive function than a flying lizard benefit from this insight? Humans have the tendency to try and pre-empt a future to which they link adverse consequences by taking actions to head it off. To a risk-averse person there is nothing wrong with this strategy. Ironically, however, such restrictive thinking was not the type that laid the foundations for, and made possible, a global economy. The great explorers of the past, like Marco Polo, David Livingstone and Christopher Columbus were all foxes who were responsible for establishing trade routes and the exchange of ideas and cultures. The hedgehogs followed in their tracks as settlers. Much of the time these pioneering foxes didn't know where they were going. Columbus thought he was heading for Asia, but intercepted America by chance.

Indeed, in determining their position at sea, the early navigators implemented a learn-from-mistakes philosophy. They would first make a guess about where they were. Next, they estimated – to the nearest nautical mile – their latitude and longitude. After that, they worked out how high in the sky the sun would reach at midday if, by some incredible coincidence, that *was* their actual position. They would then measure the actual elevation of the sun, compare the figures and adjust their initial estimate accordingly. If they were still wrong, they would indulge in a process of iteration till they obtained an answer that was approximately correct. Today, on the same principle of taking the plunge and then revising one's position in light of further information, the global economy is being significantly reshaped by the new-age sea-foxes – the Internet pioneers. Take Amazon.com and eBay. The former, even with its ups and downs, has revolutionised retailing with its on-line marketing of books. The other set up a website which has changed the nature of auctioneering forever. Have you ever heard of cyber-fleas? Probably not, but eBay is the world's biggest cyber-fleamarket. You can sell or buy almost anything on the site. At the heart of eBay's success is that nobody in the world of bricks and mortar can imitate it. Its uniqueness lies in its virtuality.

A philosophical interlude
and moment for introspection

Pause here for a second and ponder: "OK, what am I? A hedgehog or a fox?" Whether we like it or not, most senior business people are more likely to be of the prickly variety. Hedgehogs, according to Isaiah Berlin in his celebrated essay *The Hedgehog and the Fox*, "relate everything to a central vision, one system less or more coherent or articulate, in terms of which they understand, think and feel". The twentieth-century accent on strategic planning with rigid structures and objectives has made employees march unquestioningly to the same tune. But managerial hedgehogs shouldn't worry; they share the same characteristics as writers and philosophers of the likes of Dante, Plato, Hegel, Dostoevsky, Nietzsche and Proust. You may ask why there is such a preponderance of hedgehogs in the senior ranks of business today. Well, most senior managers are middle-aged folk who belong to a generation where lifetime employment was *the idea*. Back in the last century, parents would send their children to respectable schools so that they could qualify to go to respectable universities and thereafter join respectable organisations – for life. From womb to tomb, twentieth-century man was programmed to be a hedgehog. The fact that this world is vanishing fast is leading to a much higher proportion of the younger generation becoming foxes. The 21st century belongs to them.

Nevertheless, what cannot be denied is that, over the last few hundred years, business has owed a great deal to the foxes. These, according to Berlin, "pursue many ends, often unrelated and even contradictory. Their thought is often scattered or diffused, moving on many levels, seizing upon the vast variety of experiences." In the world of philosophy and literature, full foxy points go to the likes of Shakespeare, Aristotle, Molière and Goethe but, in the commercial sphere, we must not overlook foxy families like the Medicis, the Rothschilds and the Rockefellers.

Bertrand Russell, a fox of considerable stature in British philosophy in the last century, gave a delightful description of how differently hedgehog and foxy philosophers arrive at the truth. Hedgehogs, like the German philosopher Gottfried Leibniz, produce a vast edifice of deduction pyramided upon a pinpoint of logical principle. Foxes draw comparatively modest conclusions from a broad survey of many facts. If a principle proposed by a hedgehog "is completely true and the deductions are entirely valid, all is well; but the structure is unstable, and the slightest flaw anywhere brings it down in ruins". As against this, a philosophical fox such as John Locke or David Hume makes sure that the base of the pyramid "is on the solid ground of observed fact, and the pyramid tapers upward, not downward; consequently the equilibrium is stable, and a flaw here or there can be rectified without total disaster".

Interestingly, Immanuel Kant, the greatest philosopher in modern times who died at the ripe old age of eighty in 1804, was a hybridised version of the two creatures we are talking about – in other words he was a "hedgefox". In his masterly book, *The Critique of Pure Reason*, he combined the pronouncements of the rational and empirical schools of philosophy. The former states that, through pure reasoning, you can derive the meaning of existence and everything else in the world from first principles (hedgehog stuff). The other maintains that the only source of knowledge is experience (foxy stuff). Kant drew on both perspectives to come up with his theory of synthetic *a priori* propositions like "every event has a cause". He argued that this belief could not be divorced from experience but neither could it be derived from experience. It was part of our inherent nature to believe that every cause has an effect (and vice versa) in that it gives coherence to our perceptions. Hence, the concept of cause and effect transcended experience.

The greatest mind of the twentieth century, Albert Einstein, was also a hedgefox. Like Plato, he believed that you could shed light on the mysteries of the universe by sitting in an armchair and contemplating the problem in a single-minded manner. You could even play thought experiments in your mind and see where they led. However, unlike Plato and like a true fox, he believed that all theories had to be grounded in fact and confirmed by observation. For example, in 1905 he presented his special theory of relativity, which included the famous equation $E = mc^2$. It was only in 1945 with the detonation of the atom bomb that the equation was verified. Likewise, in 1916, when he introduced the general theory of relativity, it contained the entirely new concepts of space being curved and light rays being bent in a gravitational field. These were subsequently confirmed in 1919 by observations of how starlight curved around an eclipsed sun. In brief, his two famous quotes sum up his philosophy of life: "God may be sophisticated, but He is not malicious" and "God does not play dice". As he grew older, his hedgehog side came to the fore with his attempt to develop a unified field theory which explained everything. Then, when he failed, he tried to prove it was impossible. And when he failed to do that either, he worried that no-one else would ever lay the matter to rest!

Einstein's example implies that, if you are going to be a hedgefox, the prime time to be one is between the ages of 25 and 40. On the one hand, you still retain the arrogance of youth to challenge mainstream orthodoxies; on the other hand, you have experienced something of the world at large to see how diverse it is. Einstein was 26 when he announced the special theory of relativity and 37 when he launched the general theory. It is no coincidence that most of the great advances in physics and mathematics were achieved by relatively young geniuses. The Nobel Prize comes much later on, once the idea has become generally accepted. It must be hard to live with yourself if you were so much cleverer when you were young!

Moving to the East, foxes make use of the Chinese philosophy of Yin and Yang in that they understand the need for balance between the many opposing elements we face in this world. We live in a state of permanent contradiction, wondering whether to be just or merciful; tough or gentle; bold or cautious; competitive or co-operative. Indeed, we're perfectly happy to carry completely conflicting beliefs in our mind, skipping from one to the other. For instance, when tragedy strikes, we believe in predestination – what will be, will be. At other times, we believe that life is about what we decide to do of our own free will. Is the universe infinite in time and space, or did it start with a big bang and its boundaries are now expanding? One or other view must be right, but they can't both be right at the same time. Kant called these paradoxes "antinomies". He used them to justify his rejection of pure rationalism on the one hand and pure empiricism on the other. For a more homely antinomy, consider the wisdom contained in these two old saws: "birds of a feather flock together" and "opposites attract". We accept both of them! And then there is the antinomy which lies at the heart of capitalism. Individual companies want to crush the competition in order to maximise their own profits. Yet competition is good for society as a whole.

Foxy judges and juries in particular have to keep opposites in mind as they listen to the persuasive arguments of the prosecution and defence. It is only when they've heard all sides of the case that they make a judgement of "guilty" or "not guilty". Two-party democracies like the American one are supposed to offer alternative versions of the political truth to electors. Lately, the Republicans and Democrats have been awfully alike in their policies. It is only when you have disputes like the Florida recount that the knives really come out with the lawyers in tow. A foxy CEO of Coca-Cola Enterprises had this to say at a university commencement address several years ago: "Imagine life as a game in which you are juggling five balls in the air. You name them – work, family, health, friends and spirit – and you're keeping all of these in the air. You will soon understand that work is a rubber ball. If you drop it, it will bounce back. But the other four balls – family, health, friends and spirit – are made of glass. If you drop one of these, they will be irrevocably scuffed, marked, nicked or even shattered. They will never be the same. You must understand that and strive for balance in your life." But here's the rub: success in work usually comes with single-mindedness. Another contradiction! As *Business Week* said in a recent issue: "The fundamental task of today's CEO is simplicity itself: get the stock price up. Period."

In contrast to foxes, hedgehogs view the world through ideologically tinted spectacles which let in no other light besides that which is on the same wavelength as their idea. They're excellent at selective reporting of the facts. Moreover, because they focus on their idea in isolation, they ignore the critical interdependencies that make up complete systems. Hence, they will often press so hard for an idea that they mess up the workings of the system as a whole. They don't see the trade-offs, and so they run into the law of unintended consequences where the world is worse off than if they had not intervened at all. This happens particularly with hedgehog-like development agencies who impose their own solutions on local communities rather than finding out what they want in the first place. Ignorance of

cultural differences is often at the heart of costly development mistakes. A classic case of the aforementioned law in
action was the establishment of irrigation schemes in the
Sudan which immediately led to an increase in diseases associated with water-borne bugs. The way the colonial powers drew the boundaries in Africa is hard to beat. On a different front, everybody said that casinos in South Africa
would create jobs. They've had precisely the opposite effect. Wherever they've been erected, they've drained the local economy of money as poor people – seduced by the
dream of becoming instant millionaires – have frittered
away their hard-earned, meagre incomes on the slot machines. Consequently, local businesses and shops have suffered and have had to lay off staff.

Nowhere can a hedgehog's blinkered approach better be
illustrated than in the environmental field. We all know that
we cannot allow the environment to be destroyed – it must
be preserved for future generations. Equally, we know that
economic development is crucial for the improvement in
life of the masses of poor people on this Earth. So, somewhere there has to be a compromise, as the phrase "sustainable development" implies. Neither deeply green hedgehogs who only press the environmental button nor dark
blue hedgehogs only interested in economic growth have
the answer. In fact, the best definition of sustainable development comes from a Norwegian fox, Gro Harlem Brundtland, who popularised the phrase in the first place. Not
only was she Prime Minister of Norway, she also chaired
the World Commission on Environment and Development
which published the Brundtland Report in 1987 entitled
Our Common Future. In it, sustainable development was defined as: "Development which meets the needs of the present generation without compromising the ability for future
generations to meet their needs." Beguilingly simple, but it

says it all. Subsequently, more detailed definitions have been published, but they do not come close to this single pearl of wisdom. However, when all is said and done in the environmental debate, foxes acknowledge that extremists can advance the boundaries of knowledge through the Hegelian approach of thesis and antithesis leading to synthesis. Somebody has to push the edge of the envelope on either side to set new standards for the middle ground.

Tiger Woods, for a different reason, can also be nominated as a philosophical fox. He is a student of what the Japanese call *Kaizen* – a striving for continual improvement to the extreme point of testing something until it breaks and then analysing *why* it broke. The results are thereafter assimilated into future designs and applications. In a similar way and like the navigators of old, the scientific method demands that a scientist, after establishing a hypothesis, continually tests it to *disprove* or reject it. If the hypothesis survives the trauma of testing, it is embraced as probable fact. As Sir Arthur Conan Doyle's famous detective, Sherlock Holmes, once remarked to his faithful assistant Dr Watson: "How often have I said to you, that when you have eliminated the impossible, whatever remains, however improbable, must be the truth?" What he was possibly suggesting is that eliminating what one can't do provides a more revealing insight into what is possible. By approaching the cognitive process in the Sherlock Holmes way, we will not only be more accurately informed but also make more effective decisions. Often the best way of choosing your favourite person or thing is to start at the bottom and reject your obvious dislikes. Then you gradually work upwards until you're comparing your top two preferences to make your final decision.

Cluedo, the popular detective game, illustrates Holmes's point perfectly. The way to win the game and identify the

41

murderer of the owner of Tudor Close is to eliminate all the other suspects. If Colonel Mustard didn't do it with the candlestick in the conservatory, then it might have been Miss Scarlett with the dagger in the study – and so on. Another example is this well-known riddle: if you come to a crossroads and meet two locals, one of whom always tells the truth and the other one always tells lies, and you don't know which is which, what question do you ask to ensure that you get to St Ives? The answer is: "What would the other fellow say if I asked him?" Whichever person you asked, you would know that the answer is false, discard it and take the opposite route. As Holmes would say: "It's elementary, my dear Watson." In the quiz show *Who Wants To Be A Millionaire?* it is as important to be adept at eliminating wrong answers as it is to have a feel for the right one, especially when you're close to the million!

Foxy parents get their young children to do something by telling them *not* to do it. In a similar vein, Nelson Mandela once gave a very foxy definition of leadership: "A leader is like a shepherd. He stays behind the flock, letting the most nimble go on ahead, whereupon the others follow, not realising that all along they are being directed from behind." So once again, are you a hedgehog or a fox? Or maybe a bit of both? If you're the last, you're lucky to be so special. In the business world, hedgefoxes play the crucial role of bridging the gap between hedgehogs to whom they easily relate and foxes for whom they act as corporate crusaders.

Tiger and the *Titanic* provide clues

As Tiger, the fox of the fairway, navigates the hallowed greens of the world's greatest golf courses, the philosophy of *Kaizen* has equipped him to optimise on every bit of fortune and misfortune that comes his way. He is an obsessive student of both the game and his play. He continually reviews video footage of old tournaments – even those he has won – to criticise his play and to look for any information, no matter how trivial or apparently contradictory, that will allow him to make more accurate decisions when playing any course, under any conditions and against any other player.

The result: as he prepares for a tournament, he has a firm understanding of what lies inside and outside his control. For a start, he has a thorough knowledge of the rules of the game of golf and any recent revisions governing not only play but also the range of equipment that can be used. Obviously, he knows that he has no control whatsoever over the content of the rulebook: it controls him. No individual golfer, however awesome, has the power to change the rules. He can submit a proposal for a change if he thinks a particular rule is ridiculous; but until the relevant governing body in golf has considered it, he must abide by what's laid down in the book. So what Tiger does control is his knowledge of the rules: what he doesn't control is the content of the rules themselves.

The same applies to the layout of the course. Tiger can't change that. But he can play practice rounds to get a feel for each hole; and he and his caddie can measure the yardages and decide on the optimum strategy to be adopted for each hole. Again, he has no control over the strengths and the weaknesses and the overall capabilities of the other players. However, he can make himself familiar with their style of play; and he knows that, on the last day of the tournament, if he is breathing down their necks going into the final stretch, many of them will wilt under pressure! The weather: that's an important element during a tournament that is outside everybody's control. Tiger may have a general idea of the kind of conditions that will probably prevail; but he certainly won't know until the actual day, and sometimes only at the time of his actual shot, whether the wind is blowing or not and in what direction; whether it's sunny or raining; and what the temperature is.

Broadly, in the lead-up to the tournament, he classifies everything into those things he can control: his swing, his selection of clubs, his state of mind, his knowledge of the course; and those things that he cannot control: the rules of the tournament, the layout of the course, the quality of the other players, the weather conditions. Equally, he divides all factors into those of which he is certain and those of which he is uncertain. Of the things he doesn't control, he can be certain of the rules and the layout of the course; but he can't be certain about the weather and the level at which the other players will perform on the actual day. Of the things over which he has control, he can be certain of the number of clubs that he will have in his bag; but he won't know the actual club that he will choose for a shot until he has examined all the options before he plays the shot. More importantly, he doesn't know in advance what score he is going to shoot because there's many a slip between cup and lip. The decision he takes for each shot after weighing up the various scenarios may or may not have the desired outcome. There are no guarantees, even for Tiger Woods. He is sometimes in the rough and sometimes even out of bounds.

Hopefully, this exposition on Tiger's cognitive processes is giving you a clue as to where our thoughts are leading us when we explore the mind of the fox. But, like the good foxes we are, in order to make the trail even clearer, we want to provide a negative example – something which exhibits all the worst traits of hedgehogs. We can think of nothing better than the events which led up to the sinking of the *Titanic* at 2:20 am on 15 April 1912. It was the ship's maiden voyage; and the disaster, which occurred at the zenith of Britain's imperial authority on the world stage, was never entertained as a scenario by the company that owned the ship, the engineers who constructed it or the captain who sailed it. The ship was deemed unsinkable. After all, it had a double-bottomed hull that was divided into sixteen watertight compartments; and for the ship to sink, more than four of these compartments had to be flooded. It followed from this overambitious reasoning that the *Titanic* was not equipped with a sufficient number of lifeboats, and the crew did not properly conduct lifeboat drills for the passengers at the beginning of the voyage. Moreover, at the time of the disaster, the ship was steaming too fast in view of the fact that the bridge had been warned of icebergs in the vicinity. The consequence: five of the *Titanic*'s compartments were ripped open in a glancing blow with an iceberg; 1 513 souls went to a watery grave; and a terrible price was paid for the conceit of the imperial hedgehogs who literally believed that Britannia ruled the waves.

In retrospect, the participants in the *Titanic* project should have done an analysis of what they could and could not control. No way could they control the state of the ocean; yet they definitely controlled the safety features of the ship. Secondly, while they could be certain about the performance parameters of the liner under normal conditions, they couldn't be certain about all the possible conditions which the ship might meet on its voyages. Hence, all those eminent minds fell into the trap of ignoring the unthinkable – and that's how accidents happen. Today, a growing number of companies are hiring risk management experts, with the specific objective of painting "unthinkable" scenarios for the SHE (safety, health and the environment) aspects of their business. Four key questions are normally asked. What are the types of accidents that can happen? What is their probability of occurrence? What will the severity of the impact be if they do? And what are we reasonably going to do to minimise or eliminate the risk of those accidents? In light of tougher SHE legislation being introduced everywhere in the world to hold companies and individuals accountable for their actions, answers to these questions are as important as the examination of the risks of fraud, corruption and theft in the financial area, which is usually done by internal audit departments. The silly thing is that there is no trade-off between good SHE practice and the bottom line. When workers believe management care, they work harder.

Our foxy matrix

This brings us to the essential purpose of this book which is to analyse how a fox thinks and acts. If, after the brief bout of introspection we recommended you undertake earlier on, you decided you were a 24-carat hedgehog, the material that follows attempts to persuade you to become a fox. If, however, all things considered, the mirror responded that you were already a fox, don't stop reading – chances are that we can improve your mental processes so that you become an even more effective fox.

You may well ask: can you ever turn a hedgehog into a fox? The answer is: retrench him and see! But, seriously, in this day and age of more and more people having to work for themselves, necessity is the mother of invention and even the most stolid hedgehogs have to change. And it's never too late, as the large preponderance of silver foxes who would otherwise have been retired can testify. The more interesting question is whether any foxes become hedgehogs. The answer is plenty, for – as you will see – it's much harder staying at the top than getting there in the first place. Entrepreneurs who are foxy whilst they are building up their businesses turn into the most reprehensible hedge-hogs once they've accumulated the money, the power and the prestige. The trouble comes when a fox starts believing too much in his own judgement and in his own press. Hunger is replaced by laziness. Overconfidence ousts self-questioning and self-criticism. Success breeds complacency and complacency breeds hedgehogs. Thus, the humble fox who took nothing for granted in the beginning becomes an arrogant hedgehog in the end who has delusions of gran-deur and knows he's right. And we all know pride comes before the fall. That's why so few businesses last fifty years. Those that start out as losers go bankrupt first; and the ma-jority of those that start out as winners are subsequently killed by their success. Besides being sophisticated, God is also a Great Equaliser!

Long-term success in the commercial sphere is therefore a rarity. You can see the truth of this statement also in the field of sport and the arts, where you can count the truly great in any category on one hand. They are individuals who don't just make it to the summit – they stay there for a long time because they never lose the edge. Examples are Pele in football; Gareth Edwards in rugby; Donald Brad-man in cricket; Mohammed Ali in boxing; Carl Lewis in athletics; Pete Sampras and Martina Navratilova in tennis; Jack Nicklaus in golf; Margot Fonteyn and Rudolf Nureyev in ballet; Charles Dickens in literature; John Gielgud in films and Picasso in art. Then there were The Beatles: they not only dominated the 1960s but are still No. 1, which hap-pens to be the title of their latest album of original hits. Be-ing a champion does not exclude going through a bad patch. But you bounce back – like André Agassi and come-back kid Jennifer Capriati who both won the 2001 Aus-tralian Open tennis championship. Will Tiger Woods join this star-studded cast of foxes? Only time will tell.

Before introducing our foxy matrix, a word of caution. We do not want this book to be lumped in the same category as all those heavy management treatises incorporating matrices which offer the ultimate solution for the readers' happiness. Our matrix is neither the be-all and end-all of business, nor is it a shatteringly brilliant new concept to take your breath away. Rather, as we will demonstrate, it sets out in a simple fashion how human beings naturally think in their pristine, foxy state – before they've been conned into accepting some artificially rigid thinking device marketed as the new way to plan strategically ahead.

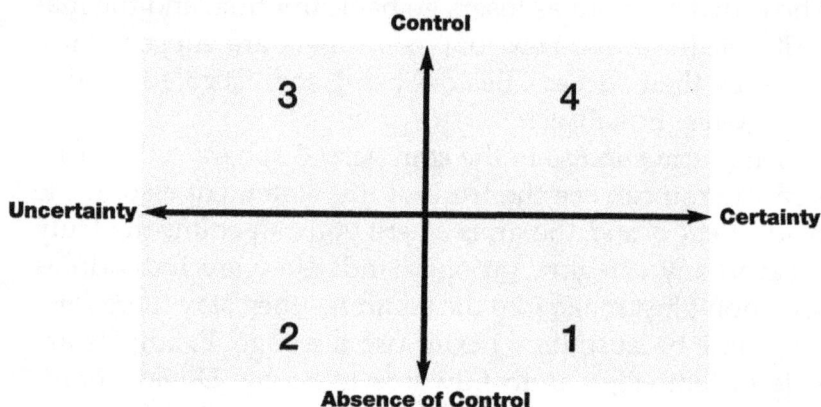

Our matrix has two axes: the horizontal one portrays certainty and uncertainty and the vertical one control and the absence of control. These two axes yield four quadrants: the bottom right-hand one represents things that are certain but outside our control. Then going clockwise, the bottom left-hand one encompasses things that are both uncertain and outside our control; the top left-hand one things which are uncertain but within our control; and the top right-hand one things which are certain and within our control.

Quite a large number of people never stray from a particular quadrant. Those who restrict themselves to the first quadrant tend to be *fatalists* who know what's going to happen, but feel they cannot do anything about it. People keeping to the second quadrant are *dice-rollers* who believe that everything in life happens purely by chance. The third quadrant is inhabited by *fence-sitters* who feel a certain sense of control, but are eternally ambivalent. They meet themselves coming the other way in arguments. The fourth and last quadrant is occupied by the *control freaks* who know exactly what is going to happen because they believe that they are totally in control. This is where most of the hedgehogs sit.

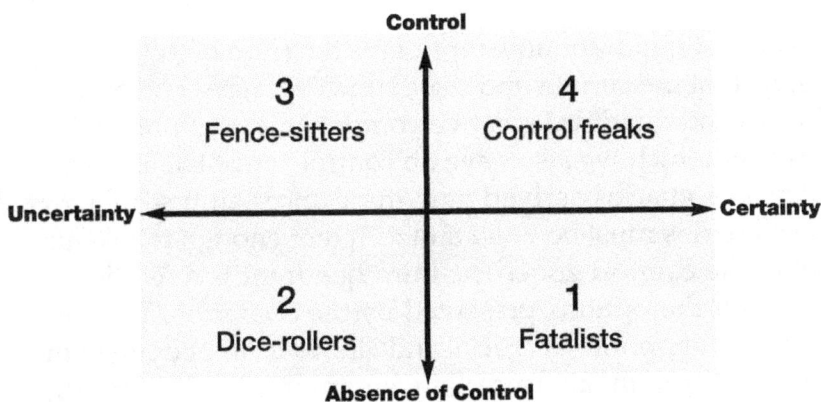

Foxes are none of these species but borrow from all of them. You can't box a fox! Hence, the matrix has to be modified to the one shown on the next page.

The most important aspect of the newly constituted matrix follows Sherlock Holmes's line of thinking: first eliminate the impossible before concentrating on the possible. To put it slightly differently, if you want to be truly in charge of your destiny, you first require to know your limitations and be humbler than you think. Hence, the lower layer of the matrix which many people ignore lays a solid foundation for effective thinking in the upper part.

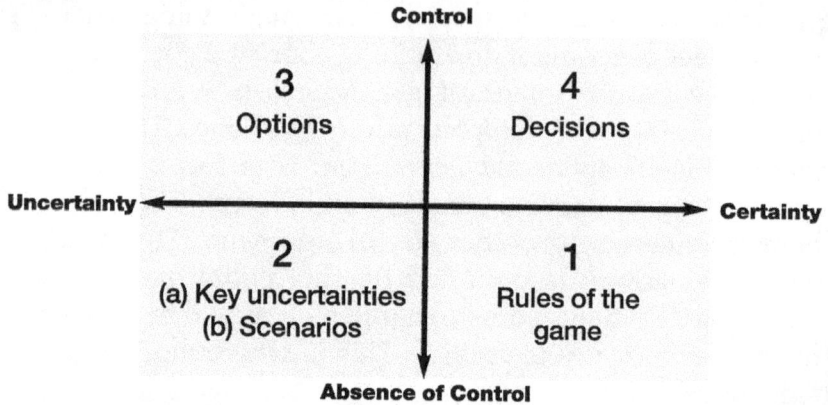

```
                          Control
                            ▲
                            │
         3                  │            4
      Options               │        Decisions
                            │
Uncertainty ◄───────────────┼───────────────► Certainty
                            │
         2                  │            1
  (a) Key uncertainties     │       Rules of the
     (b) Scenarios          │          game
                            │
                            ▼
                    Absence of Control
```

The first quadrant now represents the rules of the game –
things that are certain and over which we have no control.
The second quadrant has two components: key uncertainties over which we also have no control; and plausible and
relevant scenarios derived from these uncertainties, though
the scenarios must be vivid and different enough to take us
out of the comfort zone. The third quadrant is now identified with the options presented by the scenarios. The formulation of options is crucial and allows us to operate with
more control in an uncertain environment. The fourth
quadrant is the area where decisions are made based on the
preferred scenario and linked to the preferred option. It is
also the quadrant where strategic plans and programmes of
action should be located, as these are really decision paths
formulated in advance. The term "scenario planning" normally denotes the processes one goes through in the first
two quadrants. "Rules of the game" are sometimes called
"predetermined elements" and "key uncertainties" are
"driving forces". Otherwise, nothing is different in terms
of the methodology.

Instead of the more restrictive, cognitive model used by
hedgehogs that operates solely on the right-hand side of the

matrix, this model goes beyond such linear thinking. Handling uncertainty in a systematic and realistic manner provides a real competitive advantage to companies that want to be imaginative; it paves the way for a strategic conversation about the future without reams of paperwork and computer runs being required in advance; it serves up strategic insights without getting mired down in too much detail and it is comprehensive without being pretentious.

Our matrix, in essence, represents the mind of the fox. The model also partially answers the question why scenario planning has failed to catch on in the corporate world in the same way that strategic planning has. CEOs abhor uncertainty. They can't stand ambiguity and ambivalence. Their attitude is encapsulated in that famous phrase "give me a one-armed economist that doesn't say 'on the one hand and on the other'". However, the fault also lies with the scenario planners themselves who sometimes come across as intellectuals in an ivory tower, using precious language which is out of touch with the shop floor.

The model may sound complicated with plenty of bells and whistles: but it's not. In practice, we work through the matrix and draw scenarios every day of our lives. Imagine the following situation: you are driving down a main road and there is a crossroads ahead. You are on the main road, and logic and law dictate that you have the right of way. This can be referred to as the *rule of the game*. However, on the minor road travelling at right angles to you and towards the intersection is another vehicle that, theoretically, should stop. This action is out of your control, cannot be guaranteed and is, therefore, uncertain. This is a *key uncertainty*. In your mind you play out different *scenarios*:

1. The driver of the other car sees you and slows to a halt, allowing you to travel through safely.

2. The driver of the other car doesn't see you, drives

straight through the intersection, and you have a near miss.

3. The driver of the other car doesn't see you, drives straight through the intersection and you crash.

Based on the scenarios, you have a number of *options*:

1. Maintain your speed on the assumption that the driver is eventually going to see you.

2. Slow down because you worry that the driver is not going to see you.

3. Speed up in the hope that you may get through the intersection before the other car arrives.

Options 1 and 3 may result in a crash, whereas option 2 won't. These options will influence your *decision*. In a matter of seconds, you have just worked through the matrix. If you have a cautious temperament, you'll choose option 2. If you don't, you'll go for 1 or 3.

Another situation we have all been in when we were young, and when the matrix is definitely used, is the telephone call asking someone out on a first date. The rules of the game are simple: you have no chance at all if you don't talk to your intended date; if you come on too strong, you may put him/her off; but if you act too casual, you may not get the message across. The key uncertainty is simple: you don't know how the person on the other end of the phone is going to react to anything you say. The scenarios are infinite because the conversation can go in any direction. The options are to take the leap and ask up front; or start cautiously, see how the land lies and possibly pop the question of a date later on. And then you decide, intellectually or impulsively, what to do. It brings to mind rose-petal scenarios of the type "she loves me, she loves me not" as a young lover pulls each petal off the flower!

Further down the line, the matrix is an excellent way of judging whether you want to enter into matrimony with the lady or gentleman in question. The rules of the game can be summed up in the wedding vow you make to your partner "to have and to hold from this day forward, for better for worse, for richer for poorer, in sickness and in health, to love and to cherish, till death do us part". The key uncertainty is whether you do indeed continue to love each other or grow estranged. In the first case, you don't have to consider options for you *will* stay together. In the second case, the options are clear: stick together and make the marriage work or part company with possible repercussions on the kids if any. Couples in the second category have to decide for themselves which course of action is right. And they often reverse their decisions.

Memories of the future

Because scenarios are stories that unfold in a sequentially organised manner, they can be viewed as multiple pathways into the future. Each path denotes a hypothetical condition of the environment to which an option for action can be attached: if the future turns out this way, I will do that. According to David Ingvar, the head of the Neurobiology Department at the University of Lund in Sweden, these paths are stored in the prefrontal lobes of our brain. The more we walk down them in our minds, the more we remember them. In other words, we are continually forming a "memory of the future" in our imagination and revisiting it time and again.

In his research, David Ingvar addresses the question as to what function this "memory of the future" might serve and why it would have evolved. Apart from giving us a filter to help us deal with the mass of information that we encounter, it prepares us for action once one of the visited futures materialises. In other words, it gives us the best possible leverage in advance to deal with a wide range of future developments and outcomes. A good example of where this theory is applied in practice is the use of simulators to train pilots to fly aircraft. By the time they pass the final exam, it must be second nature to them what to do in all situations but especially emergency ones. In the latter case, they won't have time to scroll through an instruction manual like the one they have for landing. The rules of the game for flying, the key uncertainties during flight, the range of scenarios that you may have to face as a pilot, the options open to you to respond and the selection of the correct option must be ingrained. It's a pity that CEOs don't go through simulator training before they fly their businesses into the future. Of the largest 100 companies in the world in the 1950s, 70 have disappeared without a trace. Imagine taking a flight where there was only a 30 per cent probability of landing safely!

Few things are certain in this life, but especially in business. In many ways uncertainty, the natural field of operations of the fox, offers a real challenge for business, but it also opens up the doors for development. It is sad, therefore, that big business today is a century behind the physicists who in 1900 embraced uncertainty in that most "certain" branch of science – physics. The study of elementary particles has given rise to the exciting field of quantum physics that takes the deterministic picture of the universe offered by Isaac Newton and blows it wide open. According to Paul Davies, a theoretical physicist and Professor of Natural Philosophy at the University of Adelaide in Australia, even the common-sense rule of cause and effect that we referred to earlier is suspended at the atomic level. The rule of law is replaced by a sort of anarchy or chaos where things happen spontaneously and without certainty. Particles of matter may simply pop into existence without warning, and then equally abruptly disappear again. Or a particle in one place may suddenly materialise in another place, or reverse its direction of motion. If you think this is odd, please answer the question: do you believe in miracles? If you do, then you also believe that things occasionally happen for no earthly reason.

In contrast, modern-day business is positively Newtonian in its outlook and trails behind science in its rate of development. Business still takes a deterministic view of the world. It pictures it running like clockwork. As long as one can analyse the inner workings of the clock in minute detail, one can predict exactly what the mechanism is going to do in the foreseeable future. Actually, there is so much competition, so much discontinuity in the markets and so many new horizons that are opening up as a result of technological change that the only thing that is certain is uncertainty. Businesses therefore have to work within this uncertainty and require a complexity-reduction process to do so. In this respect, our foxy matrix offers an ideal way to gather all the relevant information, sift it like sand running through an hourglass and use it to focus on the most realistic options available at any one time. The final decision is more informed; but if it proves to be wrong, the decision maker can return to the matrix for another round.

SWOT – a nuts and bolts explanation

Readers may well ask where SWOT analysis (strengths, weaknesses, opportunities and threats) fits into our matrix. The answer is that the matrix now changes the sequence to OTSW: opportunities and threats are outside our control whereas we can do something about our strengths and weaknesses. Opportunities and threats therefore belong to the first two quadrants on the lower deck, and strengths and weaknesses to the last two quadrants on the upper deck.

Let us consider the example of a proud owner of a hardware store in a small country town. We'll call him John. The opportunity may well be that the only other hardware store in town is about to close because the owner has made it known that he is going to retire. If John is certain about this information, it is a rule of the game. If it is a rumour it is a key uncertainty. Either way, it offers John an opportunity to expand his business. The converse is that John has heard that a big supermarket chain is intending to establish a new branch in the town. It will have a hardware section which will offer considerable discounts and a variety of goods to customers. That is a threat. Again, depending on the credibility of the source of this news, its appropriate place is in the first or the second quadrant of the matrix.

John now considers his strengths and weaknesses and his options in light of them. One of his strengths is customer loyalty because his shop has been around a long time and he likes to chat to his customers; and they like to chat to him. His option in the "opportunity" scenario just outlined is to persuade these customers to speak to those who have frequented the other shop and tell them what a decent deal they can get at his shop. Word of mouth may suffice. Another option may be to drop leaflets in their letter boxes. John also realises that one of his weaknesses is that he doesn't carry some of the brand names that the other shop does. His option is to expand his range of hardware and correct this situation or stick to his traditional lines and try and convince his new customers to switch brands.

In the "threat" scenario of a retail giant arriving in town, John may opt to build on his strong customer loyalty by making his shop even more welcoming – by putting say a little coffee stall inside. If he pursues this strategy, he will be going out of his way to differentiate himself from the impersonal surroundings of the supermarket. However, John may decide to close up shop because, in analysing his weaknesses such as comparatively higher prices and a narrower range, he realises that he's too vulnerable and he should quit while the going is good. Fishing in the local dam becomes an overwhelmingly attractive alternative.

Reversing the order of SWOT analysis makes it no less effective and, as the example shows, it can form an integral part of our matrix.

The principle of irresistible temptation and tobogganing in the dark

As you will by now have realised, the matrix builds on the well-tried methodology of scenario planning. It adds a third and fourth quadrant to represent the two final stages of decision-making – option formulation and choice – after the scenarios have been compiled. For this reason, we have subtitled the book "scenario planning in *action*". It completes the loop, so to speak. Before moving on to a more detailed analysis of the four quadrants, we would like to relate one story and two quotes from a trio of internationally acclaimed and very foxy futurists. They all worked for Royal Dutch Shell which is considered the holy grail of scenario planning. Then we'll close the section with a cautionary tale.

Pierre Wack headed Shell's scenario planning department during the 1970s and acted as consultant to Anglo American's scenario team during the construction of the High Road/Low Road scenarios in the 1980s. He was assisted by Ted Newland, another scenario giant who used to work at Shell. Pierre is considered the pathfinder of scenario planning along with Herman Kahn who wrote the

1962 bestseller *On Thermonuclear War: Thinking About the Unthinkable*. One of Pierre's favourite forms of flattery was to call you a remarkable person. He was, as the following story indicates, one of the most remarkable men of all. In the mid-1970s, Pierre nominated two rules of the game governing the future of the oil business. The first rule was that the supply of oil would decline because, as Arab countries received a higher price per barrel, they wouldn't need to sell so much oil to meet their domestic commitments. The second rule was that demand for oil would continue to rise, even at higher prices, because Western countries could not put in conservation measures fast enough to reduce consumption. The key uncertainty was at what point in time the downward sloping supply curve would intersect the upward sloping demand curve. If sooner, the scenario was a second oil price shock (the first one occurred in the early 1970s when the price went from $3 to $12 a barrel). This would be caused by the market entering a "zone of anxiety" in which the "principle of irresistible temptation" prevailed. Rotterdam spot traders would see the tightening of the market and ramp the price skywards. If the intersection was later, the price would remain firm at $12. Shell had two options – base their strategy on the "second shock" scenario or on business as usual. In the event, they chose the "second shock" scenario, the oil price soared to over $30 a barrel and Shell scored mightily, moving up to pole position among the oil giants. Pierre always looked for the points of greatest leverage in terms of bang for the buck: and this was a perfect illustration.

Pierre's successor at Shell was Peter Schwartz who went on to establish the Global Business Network in California and wrote *The Art of the Long View: Planning for the Future in an Uncertain World*. Along with Pierre's two-part article in the *Harvard Business Review* of September/October, 1985 entitled "The Gentle Art of Reperceiving", this book must rate as the best in scenario literature. The memorable quote from it is: "An old Arab proverb says that he who predicts the future lies even if he tells the truth."

The third person is Arie de Geus, who was co-ordinator of group planning at Shell and has, since his retirement from Shell, concentrated on showing how managers and organisations actually learn to do new things. In a piece entitled "Planning as Learning" he made what at first blush may appear to be a surprising statement: "A child who is playing with a doll learns a great deal about the real world at a very fast pace." However, based on this principle, business executives on management courses in Europe participate in a game called Lego Serious Play. They apparently use the blocks to demonstrate in a practical way their vision for the company. Then they demolish their models and start afresh, thus learning the importance of being adaptable. Arie's point is that lengthy lectures from planners seldom lead to a change of behaviour in an audience of experienced executives. Games do and scenarios in a sense are a series of "what if" games.

Now we come to the cautionary tale. One of us (no prize for hazarding a guess!) was visiting Boston in the mid-1980s to give a guest lecture on scenario planning at the Harvard Business School. It was February and bitterly cold. The professor in charge of the course, Bruce Scott, invited Pierre Wack and the said author to his weekend retreat in the hills some miles outside the city. The countryside was covered in snow, which had been falling all week. In the evening, after a splendid meal, the host decided this was a good moment to go tobogganing down the local country lane. It was a long thin toboggan which at a pinch could accommodate three people, in this case three scenario planners. So, in the pitch dark with Bruce lighting our way with a torch, we walked to the top of the lane dragging the toboggan. Bruce sat down on it at the front, with Pierre in the middle and the said author in the rear position. Bruce pointed the torch down the lane and we set off.

Now the first rule of the game for tobogganing is that on a steep slope, when the snow is beginning to turn to ice, the toboggan will gather speed extremely quickly. Friction to retard the motion is not a factor. The second rule of tobogganing is that the route that you intend taking should be visible to the naked eye. The third rule is that at speed a torch is not effective to light up the way at night. The key uncertainty in this situation is not whether or not you are going to arrive at the bottom, but at which corner you are going to part company with the road. The options were simple: embark on this risky venture or sensibly stay at home in front of a blazing log fire nestling a nice glass of brandy. The decision was never at issue, given that male bravado rises by the power of the number of males present (in this situation it was cubed) and the quantity of wine imbibed (substantial).

The result was a sudden exit from the lane, but later than expected by the rear member of the toboggan since we made it miraculously through the early curves. None of us sustained critical injuries, as we had plunged deeply into a soft snowdrift. After dusting the snow off our clothes, we tramped back to the house with the toboggan in tow. There our spirits were revived by the log fire and brandy associated with the second option. The moral of this tale: even scenario planners have their comeuppance!

Rules of the game

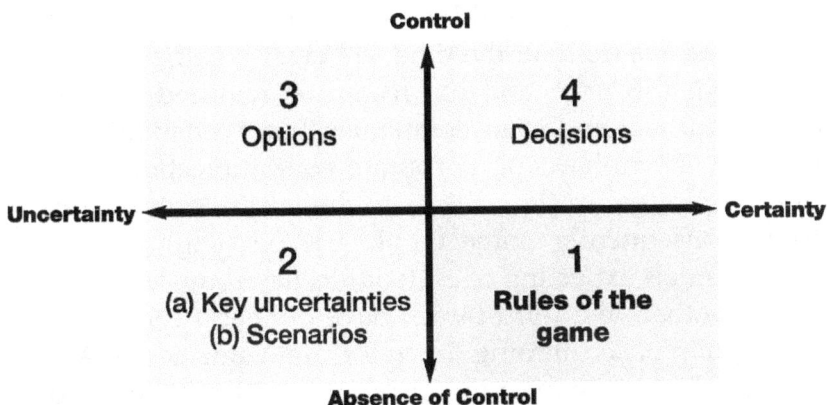

Control

3 Options	**4** Decisions
2 (a) Key uncertainties (b) Scenarios	**1** **Rules of the game**

Uncertainty ◄————————————————————► Certainty

Absence of Control

Apollo 13, Plato and chess

If you want to see how the rules of the game are applied with fox-like energy, you need do no more than microwave some popcorn, kick off your shoes, take the phone off the hook and watch *Apollo 13* on video. Your ambition to pursue the merger with another company or beat your family doctor over eighteen holes at golf will shrivel against the challenge of bringing home three astronauts hurtling out of control through space. The rules of their game include some of the most powerful and unchangeable rules in the universe – the rules of gravity, time and distance. Separated by thousands of kilometres from the Earth and faced with an unanticipated problem in their capsule, the only thing of which they are certain is a lonely, slow and horrible death if they make a mistake. They work through the matrix by starting with an examination of the astrophysical rules of the game. There'll be more on the fate of our astronauts later.

Plato said that the unexamined life is not worth living. In business, you might say that the unexamined game is not worth playing. Consider sending a team of rugby players on to a hockey field without sticks and expecting them to play hockey. They couldn't. They would neither know the rules of the game nor would they be properly equipped. Yet in business we do it all the time. We enter a game without examining the rules and the resources required to play. Worse, you will find some companies that, even in this day and age of emphasising corporate communication, keep their employees in the dark as to the nature of the game itself. Consequently, some employees pitch up wearing white flannels expecting cricket; others have studded boots on for football; the third bunch have donned headgear in anticipation of scrumming down for rugby and so on. And then the directors expect to mould an effective team out of their workforce! Whew!

But how do foxes and hedgehogs view the rules of the game? On the one hand, we believe that foxes embrace the rules and use them to gain advantage. They understand the boundaries of the game and that there are games within a game. They are like chess players who are thinking several moves ahead. On the other hand, hedgehogs can't see beyond the present. They are constantly breaking the rules of the game either through ignorance or through the misbegotten belief that while the rules apply to others, *they* can wilfully break them. And if they don't break them, they can bend them to suit themselves.

Snakes, bombs and Scottish caddies

The R&A (Royal and Ancient Golf Club of St Andrews) is the governing authority for the Rules of Golf outside the United States of America and its territories. One of the most unusual judgements the R&A Rules Committee has been asked to make in recent years concerned the dramatic experience of a golfer in Africa. As he was approaching the top of his back swing for a shot from the light rough, a dangerous snake slithered between his feet. With a fine adjustment to his downswing he delivered a fatal blow to the snake's head. Should it be counted as a stroke? After much deliberation the golfer was given a "not guilty" verdict. It was thought that the intention to strike the ball ceased at the moment he spotted the snake.

During the Second World War, many people clung to normality by continuing to play golf, and a special set of wartime rules was drawn up by Major G.L. Edsell. He generously allowed players to take shelter without penalty during gunfire or while bombs were falling. The positions of known delayed-action bombs were marked by red and white flags, which the small print added were "placed at reasonably, but not guaranteed, safe distances from the bombs". A ball moved by enemy action could be replaced. If lost or destroyed another ball could be dropped without penalty. But a player whose stroke was affected by the simultaneous explosion of a bomb or shell, or by the sound of machine-gun fire, could play another ball only under penalty of one shot.

Although we may shake our heads and chuckle at the idiosyncrasies of the game of golf that sees the rules respected and adhered to in such extremes, the fact is that in golf, as indeed in life, there are rules that are certain, cannot be broken, are out of our control and therefore should be respected. As we have already intimated, the rules of any game cannot be changed unless the relevant and recognised authority has agreed that they should. Moreover, rules are necessary: otherwise games, which are just one manifestation of organised human behaviour, would not be possible. The rules of golf will no doubt be cursed by the frustrated hacker who has had a spectacularly "off" day and single-handedly redesigned the course with his six-iron – but they *are* necessary. There was an occasion when an American tourist, playing extraordinarily bad golf at St Andrews, re-marked to his caddie that this was not his usual game. With the customary dry wit of a Scot, the caddie replied: "What then, sir, is your usual game? Tennis, baseball, ten-pin bowling . . . ?"

The last story does raise an important pair of guidelines for budding entrepreneurs. First, study the rules of the game of the industry you intend going into very carefully. Does it provide a real opportunity of making money? Or could you be condemned to a life of slogging your guts out trying to get blood out of a stone? So many people do this, it's not funny. Second, ask yourself whether you have a natural ability to succeed in that sector. The last thing you want to do is stumble in because you, or your parents or your friends, thought it was a good idea at the time. It's no good being a gunslinger with a slow hand in a game where you're quick or you're dead. It may sound very obvious but at the outset the question is: "Am I in the right game – for me?"

Narrowing the cone of uncertainty

Far from being *prescriptive*, the rules of the game should be viewed as *descriptive*, as they shape the parameters within which we can operate. They show how the system ticks. Imagine the future opening up like a cone of uncertainty, as illustrated in the accompanying diagram. What the rules of the game do is to reduce that cone within reason and limit the number of outcomes. Hence, the inner cone with the three little discs on the rim (indicating possible scenarios). For instance, given the rules of soccer, you will hardly ever have a score at the final whistle as high as in a rugby game. Pierre Wack once said that, in making a good decision, it is as informative to know which futures are excluded by the rules of the game as it is to know which ones lie within the rules. In fact, a facilitator in a scenario workshop should squeeze the cone to as narrow a funnel as possible so that his group can concentrate their energy on handling the range of futures they plausibly face. Remember, business –

The UNIVERSE of possibilities
a reduction within reason

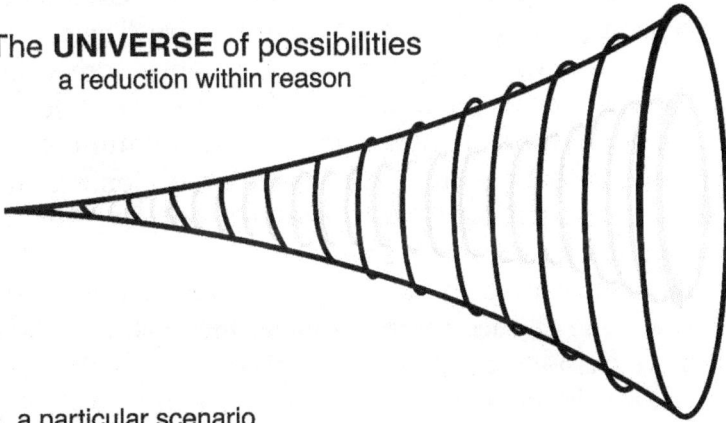

a particular scenario

time

as well as politics – is the art of the possible. It undoubtedly causes frustration to dwell at length on the rules of the game when people are eager to discuss proposals for action. But it's like drawing back a bow. You have to make it as tight as you can before releasing the arrow. Then you have a chance of hitting the target.

Moreover, without first establishing what you don't control, you will not achieve a firm understanding of what you do control. And you may be surprised by how much you do control. For the most inspiring examples of this principle, you only have to look at invalids who lead normal lives under the harshest of circumstances. They are not restricted. On the other hand, action programmes without rules of the game preceding them are merely "wish lists" where nothing ever gets done. Often lack of money is the reason, because no-one has worked out beforehand where it is going to come from. How many anti-poverty programmes have failed for this reason? Similarly, the failure of summits, conferences and workshops to follow through on the resolutions passed at the end of the proceedings is often attributable to transgressing one simple rule: people have to go back to their jobs; they have other fish to fry. They don't have the time – especially the bigwigs. When something doesn't work or doesn't happen, the likelihood is that you're breaking some fundamental rule of human nature. Most revolutionary changes in a business organisation are like that – dreamed up in haste by consultants, only to peter out when human nature reasserts itself.

In science, of course, the laws are such that – at the macro-level – the cone of uncertainty vanishes into a straight line. Scientific equations are hard predictions that if the left-hand side is fulfilled, the right-hand side will follow. Unfortunately, as we have repeatedly stated, this clarity does not extend to the world of human affairs in general and business in particular, where an irreducible element of uncertainty will always be found. After all, we all have free will which allows us occasionally to flout the rules!

The good, the bad and the media

Depending on the outcome of your particular game, you may describe the rules as good, bad or just plain ugly. However, even the legendary Wild West – epitomised by the many "spaghetti" Westerns starring an avenging Clint Eastwood – had rules. They may have been unwritten, but they were *understood*. They were not drawn up on gleaming mahogany desks by distinguished fellows in an ancient Scottish golf club. The rules were informal and silently agreed upon, enforced by the so-called "code of the cowboy". For example, you didn't take another man's horse. But if a man cheated at poker, you were quite entitled to shoot him because you just *didn't* cheat at poker! Nor did you count your money at the table while the cards were being dealt. However, once the cards were in your hand, you had to know when to hold 'em and when to fold 'em – the golden rule of poker.

Most commentators will agree that we have come a long way since the rootin' tootin' tumbleweed-strewn saloons of the Wild West. Yet the unwritten rules still apply in another game with an equally lawless frontier: business. The first thing any new recruit should do in a company is suss out its invisible rules – if he or she wants to get on, that is. But witness the showdown between the marshall of satellite TV, Rupert Murdoch, and the football-crazy citizens of Manchester in the late 1990s. In September 1998, news broke that the world's most famous soccer club, Manchester United, had accepted a bid of £625 million from Murdoch's BSkyB to acquire the company that controlled the club. To ordinary folk, Murdoch's power and influence is almost beyond comprehension. His business game is motivated not by money, but by a desire continually to expand his formidable empire. His purchase of the rights to broadcast NFL football in the US has elevated him to the number four position among American broadcasters. It has also given him the leverage and financial clout to own superteams that play football, basketball and ice hockey in the two media capitals of the US – Los Angeles and New York. He also holds the rights to broadcast the Premier League matches in the UK. He now controls the most profitable satellite-TV operator in the world. He is also very well connected politically, numbering among his friends the British Prime Minister, Tony Blair.

You would therefore feel it legitimate to draw the conclusion that if anyone had the means to influence the rules of the game, it was the media mogul Rupert Murdoch. Moreover, he would have the support of the Labour-leaning Manchester United fans. Yet, he was stopped in his bid to add the ultimate jewel to his crown not by the BBC or the British Office of Fair Trade, but by the football supporters themselves. Under the co-ordination of SUAM (Supporters Against Murdoch) – founded within hours of the announcement of the bid – and the Football Supporters Association, a popular revolt was instigated. Fuelled by a growing concern about higher ticket prices and a fear that the transaction would endanger the "soul" of the game, the revolt spread and ultimately led to the deal falling through. In retrospect, Murdoch was obviously unaware of the unstated rule that English soccer clubs are not like American baseball teams which go automatically to the highest bidder. In Chris and Tara Brady's book *Rules of the Game*, the authors refer to the "too-fat-cat" rule: while it is permissible to be a fat cat in Britain, you can't be too fat cat. Likewise, in Murdoch's Australia, the poppies can't be too tall. In other words, don't take too many liberties with the British public: success is okay but excess isn't. Having said all that, class remains a highly influential unwritten rule governing British society; and Eton still gives you a good start in life. Murdoch didn't go to Eton.

It's all about values, stupid

Foxes have a nose for the intangible, informal, unwritten rules of the game and instinctively try to avoid overstepping the mark. In golf, foxes give short putts on the green that might have made their opponents sweat. On the cricket field, foxes will immediately walk if they know they've nicked the ball straight off their bat into the hands of a fielder. It is an informal rule of cricket that you don't wait for the umpire to give you out. Changing the occasional thud of willow against leather for the continuous shout of traders on the floor, the London Stock Exchange operated on the informal rule of "my word is my bond" for centuries. And you won't get anybody more foxy than a stockbroker. In companies, foxes never break the unwritten rule of merit, which is to choose the best person for the job irrespective of gender or colour.

Hedgehogs are not so sensitive; they have their own agendas. The classic example of a hedgehog-type blunder occurred on 1 February 1981 in a limited-overs cricket match between Australia and New Zealand. The latter required six runs to tie the game with one ball of the game remaining. The batsman facing the delivery was the Kiwi No. 11, Neil McKechnie. He had never hit a six in an international game. Even so, the Australian captain, Greg Chappell, ordered his younger brother, Trevor, to bowl a "sneak" (an underarm ball along the ground) to deprive the opposition of even the slightest chance of a tie. This he did and it was within the written rules. However, it went clean against the spirit of the game and outraged New Zealanders to the extent that they talked of scrapping diplomatic ties. In retrospect, the Chappell brothers mightily regretted the incident, going to show that the unwritten rule rules, OK!

It is for this reason that big business is regulated by statutory anti-trust and anti-monopoly bodies in places like the US and UK. Whilst there is a thicket of explicit regulations governing mergers and acquisitions, the overriding and unwritten rule is whether or not a transaction is in the "public interest" or not. The objective is that no individual or institution should come out a winner at the expense of everybody else.

The latest company to fall foul of this unwritten rule is Microsoft, which undoubtedly was *the* company of the 1990s. They were asked by the courts in America to break themselves up into two pieces, a ruling which they have managed to overturn. Yet, in the minds of many of the American public, Microsoft has got too big for its own boots and, more importantly, for the good of America. However brilliant their legal defence, they could be digging an even bigger hole for themselves in the perceptions of ordinary middle-class Americans. Bill Gates, the foxy nerd who struck it rich, could become Gates the mighty hedge-hog.com. Even the second richest man in the world can have problems with his image.

This would seem an appropriate time for us to introduce the ultimate, invisible system that ought to be controlling human behaviour – the moral rules of the game. These rules can be compared to what surfers describe as "full stop rock" at the famous surfers' resort of Jeffrey's Bay in the Eastern Cape of South Africa. The rock is concealed under shallow water and, to all intents and purposes, is invisible until you hit it. Then you know all about it! The trend today is that big business – whether it likes it or not – has to sub-scribe to these rules, because there are activist NGO watch-dogs following their every move and ready to bite if needs be. The public anyway have formed a cynical attitude to-wards the motivations of big business. Whenever the media break a new story, such as the Ford/Bridgestone saga where fatal accidents have been attributed to the covers of Fire-stone tyres fitted to Ford Explorers peeling off at speed, the damage to the company's image can be enormous and no amount of public relations spin can undo it. Unless you are seen to act quickly to remedy the problem and recompense the victims, you are in for a torrid time.

The best lesson in damage control in the recent past by a major corporate player is Coca-Cola's recall of 2,5 million bottles in Belgium in June 1999. This followed reports that children were being treated at a hospital after drinking Coke at their school. It appeared that production problems at two plants – one in Belgium and the other in France – may have been linked to this incident. Bans on the sale of Coke were imposed in several European countries while consumers in others steered away from drinking the stuff. Not only was Coca-Cola swift in implementing the recall; it also made a public apology for the incident and pledged to reimburse the medical expenses of those affected. After a fortnight, business was back to normal, proving that foxes sometimes come in the shape of a Coke bottle! Besides which, they have the fizz of the liquid inside.

Quite unfairly, foxes are perceived as creatures with plenty of guile but little moral sense. The truth is that foxes have a sensitivity to moral issues seldom demonstrated by hedgehogs who feel they are above the law. Foxes have good manners because they respect the little things in life. In this respect, what a splendid example of a fox was Fritz Schumacher, the German economist, who wrote the classic treatise *Small is Beautiful, A Study of Economics as if People Mattered*, first published in 1973. That went right against the trend in those days. Foxes are sometimes labelled as eccentrics, but they follow the old motto "manners makyth man". Similarly, foxy companies have their idiosyncrasies, but they understand that a clean, decent image is a competitive advantage these days. Moreover, they believe in human interaction. It does a lot more for improving employee morale and changing behaviour for the better than new-fangled management techniques that come and go ever will.

One of the most famous articulations of the moral rules of the game is found in the Old Testament. The Ten Commandments are not only fundamental moral laws – otherwise they'd have been called the "ten guidelines" – they also form a good practical basis for running a modern society. It is interesting to note that of the ten commandments, eight prohibit certain behaviour and only two place positive demands on you. Falling into the former category are commands *not* to have other gods; worship golden idols; blaspheme; murder; commit adultery; steal; lie about your neighbour; or covet his wife, servants and possessions. In the positive category, the commands are to respect the Sabbath and honour your father and mother. In today's world where lack of spiritual values, greed, bad language, violent crime, promiscuity and rape, theft, deceit, envy, workaholism and unruly children are a sad reflection of how little we have progressed, the commandments would appear to be a solid ethical framework for hedgehogs and foxes alike. They are not sentimental or soppy. On the contrary, the commandments are as hard as "full-stop rock". For example, they are needed to stop modern evils like paedophilic rings on the Internet. Yet, they do not rule out the principal driving force of free enterprise, which is to pursue one's own interests. They merely prohibit certain shady ways of doing so. Being foxy is fine: being a wolf is not!

Islam also offers absolutely hard and fast rules of morality. Indeed, it is the unchanging nature of those rules that give Muslims a fundamentally secure basis for life and the confidence to become entrepreneurs and run foxy family businesses.

However, for those who would prefer something with less of a religious connotation, the "four-way test" read out at the beginning of Rotary Club functions concerning the things we think, say or do is a good start: (1) Is it the truth? (2) Is it fair to all concerned? (3) Will it build goodwill and better friendships? and (4) Will it be beneficial to all concerned? There's nothing amazingly original about any of these questions, but how many people – let alone companies – can answer them in the affirmative when making a decision? To the criticism that all this stuff sounds old-fashioned and prudish, our retort is that economic growth is only sustainable in the long run if there is a fair degree of trust between the governing classes and the governed; the country is peaceful and free of corruption and crime; citizens are generally healthy and free of stress; and a sense of justice prevails at large. We all talk now of working towards a civil society. Well, civility goes with the kind of values implied in the four-way test.

The old order changeth

Picture the moral rules of the game as an invisible spider web hanging in the ether, waiting to catch unsuspecting celebrities. Nothing can move a prominent individual faster from hero to zero than being caught in the web. Occasionally, a celebrity can wriggle his way out like Bill Clinton with his ingenious definition of sex. According to this definition, dimpled chads would not have counted as votes in the last presidential election. Work that one out! But the vast majority of the spider web's famous victims end up being cocooned and forgotten.

Over time, the spider web changes shape and position. What was acceptable yesterday is no longer acceptable today. For many years in Italy, company directors oiled the wheels of the state's bureaucracy with lavish bribes. It was the done thing. Suddenly the tide turned after the intervention of an aggressive magistrate; and many a financial director of an illustrious company was left high and dry, gasping for air on the beach as his colleagues abandoned him. On a wider scale, think back to the Romans. They offered nations around them a simple choice: either volunteer to be part of the Roman Empire or be annihilated by our legions. This brutal principle of empire-building stood until the middle of the last century. But then the rule changed and invasions were no longer allowed. Iraq's Hussein and

Serbia's Milosevic were caught in the web. Now the web is closing in on dictators suspected of torturing and slaughtering their own citizens in large numbers, as well as those who siphon the nation's wealth into their foreign bank accounts. In Roman times, CNN wasn't around to film what the legions did to subjugate other nations. Now, the victims of a Western bombing raid on Baghdad are interviewed in their hospital beds. To television viewers, strong-arm tactics are unacceptable if innocent victims are a visible consequence.

In the world of commerce and industry, "corporate governance" is not just a buzz word. It is a new piece of the spider web, changing the rules of the game about how a company should be run. The positions of chairperson and CEO should no longer be vested in the same individual, as this concentrates too much power in a single pair of hands. For the sake of checks and balances, the chairperson should be nonexecutive. The major subcommittees of the board of directors should also be chaired by nonexecutive directors. Companies should issue reports on their performance in areas such as safety, health and the environment, as well as ones describing their social responsibility programmes. The traditional annual report is not comprehensive enough.

Hence, it is not the rules of the game that applied in the past that you should be considering in the first quadrant of our matrix, it is the ones that will apply in the future. Rules change. Just think of smoking! Next, it may be carbon emissions that have to be reduced in light of global warming and more frequent conditions of extreme weather. But, for a real flip-flop, you need look no further than the area of corporate strategy. Diversification was all the rage in the 1960s to reduce the risk associated with any one particular business. Now, the fund managers and market analysts want companies to focus. Stick to your knitting, go back to your core business, they say. Indeed, they want you, the company, to be the pure play, while *they* decide on the portfolio mix and diversity. Some would call it poetic justice, but of course the rules of the stock market have changed for the fund managers as well. In these days of instant information, frictionless trading and emphasis on short-term performance, selective crashes of individual shares – as opposed to the market as a whole – are becoming increasingly common. Unexpected profit warnings are a kiss of death and down goes the share by up to 50 per cent in a day. Markets generally can go up or down three to five per cent in a single session! The rules for a volatile market are very different to the ones that apply when the market is operating smoothly. Woe betide the fund manager who doesn't adjust his strategies accordingly. All this suggests that a decision which is correct today may be wrong tomorrow, should the rules change. And you have to be prepared to do things differently when the rules *do* alter. How many businesses have been turned into non-businesses by a change in the rules without the owner even being aware of it? By contrast, how many entrepreneurs have made fortunes because they were the first to spot that the rules had changed?

The general public now have a record proportion of their assets invested in the stock market, either directly in shares or through unit trusts and mutual/retirement funds. In view of this, they are going to have to become accustomed to the uncertainties associated with the left-hand side of our matrix as their wealth waxes and wanes in line with movements in the market. Equally, broader share ownership has interesting implications for the economy, because there is now a much stronger linkage between the stock market and the real economy via the so called "wealth effect": when people feel richer they spend more, and when they feel poorer they spend less. Back in the last century, shares could rise and fall and it would only affect the spending habits of the rich. Now, market volatility could influence the way the middle and lower income groups dispose of their income as well.

In preparing business scenarios, an important rule of the game to examine is the changing demography of the world as a whole, of the country in which you are based and of the market that you serve. You need a feel for this rule over the next twenty years; and, sadly nowadays, you have to include the likely impact of the HIV/AIDS epidemic and other diseases on your customer base. Probable advances in technology also feature as a prime rule of the game. They may enable your business to expand into new areas or they may threaten some of your products. Illustrating the last point is the famous story about Western Union being handed the telephone on a plate by Alexander Graham Bell. They turned him down because they thought the future still rested on telegrams and the morse code. An up-to-date example is the way CDs wiped out LPs. It would not have been smart to open an LP factory in the late 1980s! Now, despite Napster's legal woes, the Internet combined with MP3s is transforming the music industry once again. If nothing else, we are going to have virtual jukeboxes where you can listen to your favourite songs and jive the night away – using your personal computer as a record player.

A company's future competitive position vis-à-vis its rivals in the same market is very much a rule of the game. Here we can quote South African Breweries and how they saw things before the new millennium started. SAB visualised the beer market of the 21st century evolving into three leagues. The first was the premier league in which world-class companies like Anheuser Busch and Heineken were currently located with worldwide premium brands. The second league was that of national champions in which SAB, sundry British brewers and Carlsberg were represented. The third league was the niche/boutique one where specialist beers produced by European monasteries resided. Given this rule, SAB foresaw a danger for themselves in remaining in the middle league. For another rule of the game was that the middle league is vulnerable to intrusion from world-class players in the top one. The latter could – through economies of scale and selecting best practice from around the world – gradually eat up the markets of the national champions. SAB therefore had the choice to ascend into the world-class category or descend into niche businesses. They opted for ascension: this entailed a move of their head office from Johannesburg to London as the most appropriate base from which to launch their campaign for premier league status.

The "G" word

However, nothing illustrates the point of looking forwards rather than backwards better than globalisation. Before it arrived, many businesses were comfortably protected from the chilly winds of international competition by tariffs and quotas imposed on imports. Now it's open sesame: you either set standards equivalent to best practice in the rest of the world or your business dies. Globalisation is like playing golf without handicaps. The scratch player will always win. So unless you start emulating Tiger, you don't stand a chance. Thus, the globalisation rule has necessitated extremely painful adjustments to companies and societies alike – protagonists would say for the better; antagonists, who include the demonstrators that have thronged the offices of the World Bank and International Monetary Fund, would say for the worse. One thing is for sure: the nature of work and jobs is undergoing a metamorphosis which is not going to reverse itself. The two great engines of job creation for most of the last century – the public sector and big business – have shut down. In fact, globalisation has converted both of them into net job destroyers as they seek to be leaner and meaner than their next-door neighbours. That leaves medium-sized, small and micro enterprise as the area of most potential for future employment. It suggests another rule of the game for parents: their kids are going to have to be taught to be entrepreneurs during their school years if they want to find work. The accent will need to be on creativity and problem-solving rather than learning by rote. If parents really want to turn their offspring into foxes, there is no better way to do it than divide their pocket money in half and put one half into a savings account that can only be used to set up a business. The other half constitutes normal disposable income. One foxy child said to his parents that this arrangement was fine, provided they doubled the pocket money first!

Globalisation is also transforming the agricultural industry in the world today. If you're a commodity farmer in maize, wheat, cotton, cattle or sheep, the new rule of the game is that you have to achieve economies of scale on a par with world-class agri-businesses in Western countries. In order to do this, size becomes critical. Farms are therefore merging or are being bought out, with the consequence that land ownership is becoming more concentrated. Now is this a good thing, when another rule of the game is that land is a very emotive issue? We seem to have conflicting rules. On the other hand, dividing up large farms into smaller ones to satisfy land hunger isn't going to work either. Anybody banking on commodity prices in real terms rising to assist such a process is in for disappointment, because the world has a permanent surplus of commodities – that is another rule of the game. The alternative is to focus on speciality products or move out of conventional farming altogether by going into bed-and-breakfasts, game farming and trophy hunting, breeding disease-free animals, etc. One farmer near Mafikeng is now the largest parrot exporter in Africa! However, there is an answer to the thorny issue of world-class efficiency versus wider land ownership. It involves lateral thinking, which lies at the heart of our matrix. We'll explain it after we have covered "win-win" outcomes in the next section.

For now, though, a final word on globalisation, having just dealt with the moral rules of the game. It is in the nature of competition that the gap between the winners and the losers widens. Remember the maxim: "To the victor go the spoils." Globalisation at the moment could be renamed Americanisation because America sucks in the brains from the rest of the world. Indeed, America can cherry-pick talented Third World doctors, teachers, engineers and computer programmers at will, unintentionally doing more harm to the countries exporting these precious skills than by declaring war on them. The end result is that everybody regards America as the winner. This belief feeds on itself and makes America even more powerful in the global economic game and the rest less powerful. As an aside, the same "halo effect" applies to Murdoch's former acquisition target – Manchester United. As the richest and most successful soccer club in England's Premier League, it automatically attracts the best and the brightest football stars. So guess what – it is the odds-on favourite to win the league yet again. How boring for the fans who support other clubs!

However, if the gap between the haves and the have-nots widens to a totally unreasonable extent, then another rule of the game kicks in, which is injustice. Nothing could be more expressive of this rule than the words of a young Brazilian woman at a recent conference held in Porto Alegre in Brazil: "Can we not imagine a better world than this? Where the air will be free from the poison of fear of insecurity? Where the TV set is not the most important member of the family? Where food and communication will not be commodities because the right to eat and talk to each other are human rights? Where justice and liberty, Siamese twins condemned to live apart, shall again be conjoined back-to-back?" When the majority of people in any situation feel that injustice has gone too far like this young woman, they start a rebellion. This would not be in America's interest. So America has to optimise between two rules of the game – the globalisation one and the injustice one. But this is precisely what foxes are about. They don't pursue any one rule of the game as an ideology to the utter exclusion of all the others. Hedgehogs do!

In the business world, rules constantly clash. For example, one rule says that you ought to maximise profits for shareholders, while another says you should make a permanent contribution towards the communities where you operate. No clearer example of this tussle exists than the drug companies and their quandary over the prices they should charge for HIV/AIDS drugs in developing countries. But banks are next in line. They are coming under increasing pressure to behave like they did in the good old days when the bank manager was a pillar of the community and made credit available to people who would not normally get it. Against this, shareholders are demanding that banks concentrate on their highest value-adding activities such as servicing large corporate clients and high net worth individuals. Somehow a compromise solution has to be found.

Curves of pleasure and pain

In every competitive sport, you have a result involving winners and losers – in other words a "win-lose" outcome. Where the gains exactly match the losses, science calls this a "zero-sum" game. Physical laws like the one relating to the conservation of mass and energy are zero-sum: if mass or energy disappears from one part of the universe, an equivalent amount will reappear, maybe in a different form, somewhere else. Thus mass and energy can be transferred but the total amount in the universe will remain the same.

Life can also have win-lose, zero-sum outcomes. We have already mentioned sport but gambling falls into the same category. Take a poker game between two players: if one player wins a million dollars, the other must have lost it. CEOs often regard business as a zero-sum game. They only feel they've won if somebody else is licking his wounds because he's lost. In some circumstances – like tendering for a large project – they are right. But there are other outcomes, life being more subtle than sport or science.

Imagine an all-out nuclear war between two nations where mutual destruction is not only assured but actually materialises. With devastated cities on both sides of the border, that is definitely a "lose-lose" outcome. You can also have " win-win" situations in human relationships created by love, friendship, parenthood or the pursuit of knowledge. When two people fall in love, you don't normally call one a winner and the other a loser unless you have a deep disregard for one of them. Good teachers can have synergistic relationships with their classes so that everybody at the conclusion of the term is happy and inspired. Stephen Covey in his book *The 7 Habits of Highly Effective People* maintains that the only viable outcome in the long run to a negotiation is win-win or else the parties should walk away. The reason is that a win-lose outcome will fester in the mind of the losing party and gradually erode his enthusiasm for the deal. Since the winning party may well be relying on the continued co-operation of the losing party, he will ultimately lose in the end as well.

This reasoning leads to the enunciation of three of the

most important unwritten rules of the game: (1) virtually all decisions about the future involve a judgement of risk versus reward, because life is a risky business, (2) in most situations decision makers must take into account the reasoning and state of mind of other decision makers, and (3) even where there is conflict of interest, the outcome must be beneficial to both parties for the decision to stick. These three rules apply as much to companies as they do to individuals. Game theory, which was originally developed in a book entitled *The Theory of Games and Economic Behaviour* by John von Neumann and Oskar Morgenstern and published in 1944, expands on these rules. Let us begin with a diagram that we have christened "curves of pleasure and pain":

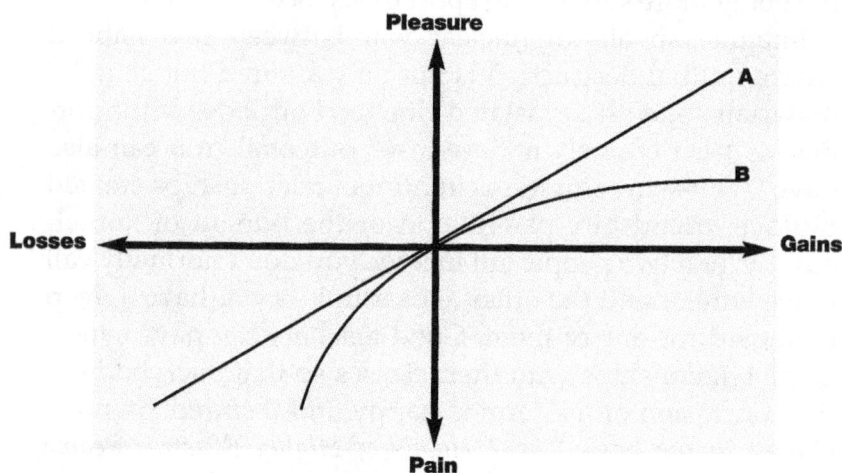

The horizontal axis denotes gains and losses. These could take various forms, but for the purposes of this book we'll denominate them as monetary gains and losses. The vertical axis measures the pleasure or pain of an individual as he makes gains or suffers losses. It is clear that Person A is either very rich or has an inveterate gambling streak. If he wins or loses the same amount, the graph tells you that however much that amount is, the pleasure and the pain are equally balanced against one another. Bunker Hunt, the American billionaire, was once asked how he felt about losing a billion dollars on the silver market. His response: "You win some. You lose some."

Person B is more like most of us – of modest means and risk-averse. On the one hand, the pain associated with a loss rises exponentially beyond a certain amount of money. On the other hand, the pleasure linked to a monetary gain starts levelling out when the sum becomes ridiculous and individual B doesn't know what to do with it other than leaving it to the kids who will promptly be spoilt by it. If you can't conceive of ever having too much money for any addition to become irrelevant, then your curve on the right-hand side of the diagram rises in a straight line!

The left-hand side of the curve is, however, completely different if you're a person of B's temperament. Beyond a certain amount, it doesn't matter what your attitude is: the pain of a loss will eventually outweigh the pleasure of a gain. To illustrate this point, think of a coloured disc where 70 per cent of the area is coloured blue and 30 per cent red. Would you be prepared to spin the disc on the basis that if the pointer was on blue when the disc came to rest, you would win a million dollars? But if it was on red, you'd lose it, in which case your house, your spouse and your car go up in smoke. Supposing 99 per cent of the disc was blue and one per cent red, would you review the situation and risk it? And what if we said you could only lose a hundred thousand dollars on red but still make a million dollars on blue? Mathematics says you're an idiot if you don't take any of these bets; but then the rules of mathematics do not incorporate human psychology – the rules of real life do. Curve B also explains why most people get more conservative as they get older. They don't want to lose the assets or reputation they've accumulated. Meanwhile, the young have nothing to lose: they can be radical.

Curve B has relevance in quite different contexts. Earlier we referred to the capacity of the human intellect to play tug-of-war with opposing ideas. On the emotional side, we have mixed feelings about people and things. For example, when we help ourselves to a particularly generous portion of chocolate cake, we experience the direct pleasure of consuming something wonderfully rich; but we also feel pangs of guilt about our lack of self-restraint. Hence, we yo-yo up and down the curve with dietary schizophrenia.

Curve B also highlights the danger of narcotics. The addict will seek bigger highs (gains) from harder drugs as he runs into the law of diminishing pleasure on the right of the chart. Sadly too, his increasing dependency on drugs means that he loses control over his life – options and decisions become irrelevant. In addition, the curve explains why relief from physical pain like toothache and psychological pain like anxiety over health can cause such intense pleasure: you're moving very quickly up the steep side of the curve on the left. It also supports the theory that the most effective way to increase the general happiness of a nation is to target the ultra-poor and improve their quality of life. In essence, you are giving them a leg up the left-hand side of the curve by reducing their daily misery. Jeremy Bentham, the philosopher and social reformer who founded the philosophy of "utilitarianism", would nod his head in approval. In his major work, *Principles of Morals and Legislation* published in 1789, he stated that the object of all legislation should be "the greatest happiness for the greatest number". He was also a fox because he maintained that his principle of "utility" was best served by allowing every man to pursue his own interests unhindered by restrictive legislation.

Given that Curve B represents the psychology of the average person, Covey's proposition that outcomes to negotiations should be win-win to have any chance of lasting a long time appears valid. For if you negotiate something that is very advantageous to yourself but equally disadvantageous to the other party, he or she is going to feel far sicker about it than you are going to have reason to rejoice. Their motivation to undermine the deal is therefore going to be stronger than your wish to make it stand. You might have good lawyers on your side to draft an unbreakable agreement which can hold up in any court, but what you don't control is the attitude of the other party during the period that the agreement is implemented. You have to accept that the rules of the game in the mind of the other person may be different to your own and worthy of consideration. Rules can clash and then you have to compromise. This brings us back to the land issue raised earlier. Perhaps the way you satisfy all parties is to have bigger, more competitive farms, but then convert them into companies with a wide range of shareholders including the farmer and the employees on the farm. That way, land ownership becomes diffused. Maybe you then float the farm on the stock exchange. Who knows? The sky's the limit!

Implicit in Curve B is another unwritten rule of human behaviour: a reluctance to tinker with the status quo. Nobody is going to jump from the known and certain to the unknown and uncertain unless the known and certain is already extremely unpleasant and painful. Again the logic is simple. The unknown and uncertain offers mixed chances of gain as well as loss for the prospective jumper, and the potential pleasure associated with a gain is outweighed by the risk of major pain associated with a loss. In normal circumstances, therefore, the inclination is do nothing but stay put in familiar territory: it is the preferable option over potential oblivion, no matter what the upside. To use that overworked expression, to shift a person's paradigm or a nation's mind-set requires the affected party to have a shock to the system (not smart) or develop an understanding of what may lie on the other side before the shock happens (smarter). That's why scenarios are so useful: by offering a glimpse of the possible, they act as a catalyst to achieve the leap of understanding necessary for movement. The people of Northern Ireland and Israel need positive scenarios of what their countries could be like if they laid aside centuries of religious animosity. Then they might find one another and move to higher ground. Incidentally, inspirational tales of the past can often achieve the same result. The film *Erin Brockovich* tells the story of how a sassy, young miniskirted mother took up the cause of an American community, and won a legal case involving contaminated water against a gigantic power utility. It sent a powerful message: when ordinary people put their minds to it, they can do extraordinary things and make a difference. It also helped that the movie starred the Oscar-winning actress with the radiant smile, Julia Roberts!

Sometimes, however, the choice is between the lesser of two evils and showing people that if they don't do something which prima facie looks against their interest, there is a worse scenario waiting in the wings. For instance, you don't normally hand money over to a stranger for nothing in return. But if that stranger happens to say "your money or your life" and presses a cocked pistol against your temple, you *do* hand the money over. The alternative is worse! Dick Turpin, the famous eighteenth-century English highwayman, used this technique very effectively till he was hanged in York in 1739.

Finally, Curve B has an intriguing feature. If the time frame on the left or the right is a date sometime in the future, we discount the losses or gains because they mean less to us. For example, if the adverse effects of smoking or HIV/AIDS were felt immediately, people would be more averse to risking their lives on the immediate gratification involved in smoking a cigarette or having unsafe sex. Equally, monetary gains in the future aren't worth as much as cash in the bank now. But the area where our natural habit of discounting the future creates a real blind spot is the environment. For the beneficial impact of making sacrifices in our current lifestyle may only be felt in a few generations' time. And as some wag put it: "Why should we bother about the next generation? They have never done anything for us." Alas, the short-sightedness highlighted by this observation is becoming more relevant by the day.

It takes two to tango

This brings us to the celebrated example of the "prisoner's dilemma", as formulated by the mathematician Albert Tucker. Two men – let's call them Bill and Ben – are arrested for robbery. They are refused bail and isolated from one another in separate cells. However, the evidence is circumstantial as there are no hard witnesses. It requires one or other of them to confess for the charge of robbery to stick. Otherwise, they will be charged with carrying concealed weapons at the time of their arrest – an offence which carries a considerably lighter sentence. Both know the consequences of their decision to confess or remain silent. If they both confess, they will both get a five-year sentence; if neither confesses, they will both get one year for carrying a concealed weapon; and if one confesses while the other does not, the confessor will go free and the one who remains silent will get twenty years.

What is the best option for each prisoner? If Bill cannot trust Ben, it is arguably best for him to confess in order to limit his downside to five years at worst and zero at best.

Ben's reasoning must be the same. So, as untrusting individuals, they should both confess and get five years. If, however, they are members of the Mafia and have taken the oath of *omerta* (silence), then it pays for each of them to remain silent and go to jail for one year for the lesser offence.

The dilemma comes in when Bill and Ben are just friends. They are taken to separate interrogation cells without having any chance to compare stories or plan a strategy. The police tell Bill that Ben has already confessed. Bill has to decide whether the police are telling the truth or lying. Is Ben a friend or a double-crosser? The horns of the dilemma are very pointed and sharp for Bill.

There is no logical and satisfactory answer to this conundrum. Depending upon his personal risk profile and regard for Ben, Bill will either play safe and confess to the robbery; or take the plunge and remain silent. The intriguing thing is that this type of dilemma is repeated again and again in real life. Politicians make this judgement call whenever they have something to cover up. Should they rely on their colleagues to keep silent during the probe, in which case the cover-up option offers the best way out. Or should they tell the truth at the outset and take the rap? The problem in the cover-up option is that if they are wrong about their colleagues and the truth surfaces, they are in for the high jump. The cover-up becomes the issue as opposed to the original misdemeanour.

Here's another illustration from the real world. If I'm a grocer pondering on cutting the prices of my fruit and vegetables, the big question is whether other grocers in the neighbourhood will follow suit. If they do, every grocer will be worse off; and if they don't, I will grab their customers so I'll be better off and they will suffer. Perhaps we should instead form a cartel and fix the price of fruit and vegetables for the entire neighbourhood, with the added benefit that it is extremely unlikely that any individual grocer will break ranks and do to me what I'm thinking of doing to him. But that's precisely why cartels in most countries are illegal, because they are established for the benefit of the producers and at the expense of the consumers. It's only if you are an international cartel like OPEC that you'll get away with it. So, generally speaking, open competition is enshrined in law and the pricing dilemma that we've just alluded to persists in every player's mind.

The arms race, which seems to have somewhat abated, once posed the same dilemma to the two superpowers – America and Russia. If I developed a nuclear weapon superior to yours, I was at an advantage. If, however, you responded by creating a new generation of weapon which equated with mine, then neither of us were better off militarily – but we were sure worse off financially. Sense now seems to prevail on both sides; but don't rule out America exploiting Russia's precarious financial position to have another go at achieving military superiority. "Son of Star Wars" is reported to be on the drawing board.

We've already mentioned the three rules of the game that flow from these examples in the first paragraph on page 70. Nonetheless, it is worth re-emphasising that no company is an island, as is assumed in many a strategic plan. You have to play scenarios on the responses of the competition to any action you intend to take – before taking it. For example, if you decide to merge with another company to become a larger entity, then two of your competitors may decide to combine into an even larger one. Vicious and virtuous circles also display the same feedback principle, this time with your customers. Hike your prices too much and your customers disappear so that you have to hike them even more to maintain your revenue. Lower your prices and you may attract more customers than you anticipated, in which case you can lower them even more. As Isaac Newton said, for every action there is a reaction. Hence, there is no point in waltzing into a boardroom with a proposal, entering into negotiations on a contract or presenting a sales pitch to potential customers unless you've worked through the range of reactions which are outside your control. The penalty, should you not do this homework, may be an undignified exit with arms flailing and a bruised ego. Not worthy of a fox.

Key uncertainties

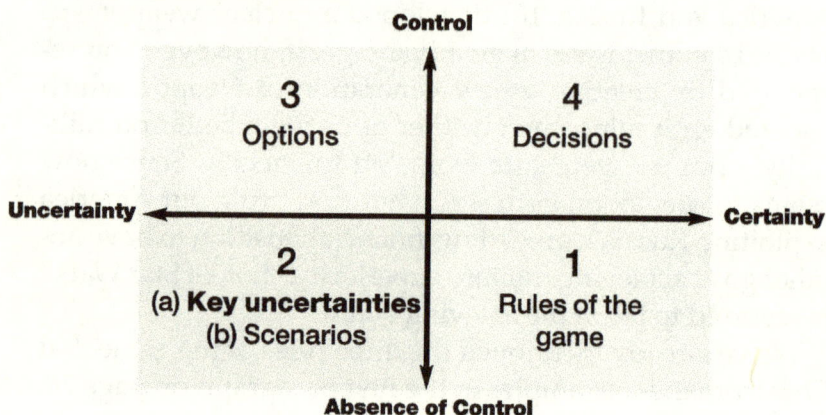

Control

3 Options	**4** Decisions
2 (a) **Key uncertainties** (b) Scenarios	**1** Rules of the game

Uncertainty ← → Certainty

Absence of Control

"Houston, we have a problem"

There's a saying among science-fiction buffs: "The meek shall inherit the Earth; the rest of us are going to the stars." One or two celebrity oddballs, like *Star Trek* creator Gene Rodenberry, decided to take the latter half of the statement literally. Before they died, they organised to have their ashes launched into the inky blackness of space. And there they are, orbiting forever. However, for the vast majority of us, the reality is that – in life and in death – we physically remain part of this Earth. Well, that's not entirely true. Among us are the lucky ones blessed with the right stuff, who blast off into space on quests which help us learn more about what is out there beyond the gravitational confines of this "pale blue dot" (Carl Sagan's phrase).

We travel into space because the conquest of mountains and seas has made it one of the last frontiers full of enticing unknowns. We go there because we don't know what's out there. For this reason any space journey is fraught with uncertainty and danger. The astronauts and their thousands of support personnel have to rely on what they do know, which is miniscule compared to what they don't know. Add to this their faith in the computers and other technical equipment involved in their flight, and you realise they're taking one heck of a gamble.

Back in the days of the Apollo missions, NASA enthusiastically hurled human beings at the moon at the speed of a bullet. They were exceptionally proud of their technologies – almost as proud as the builders of the *Titanic*. This ended abruptly soon after the Apollo 13 space vehicle leapt from the Kennedy Space Centre in Florida on April 11, 1970. John Swigert, Fred Haise and Jim Lovell were at the controls of what was essentially a tall tin can boasting the same computing power as a modern-day scientific calculator!

Fifty-six hours into the Apollo 13 mission an explosion on board sent the power readings haywire. At that instant, all the certainties of the mission disappeared as the crew were confronted with an emergency situation for which they hadn't been trained. The reaction of the mission commander on board, Jim Lovell, was the now famous quote "Houston, we have a problem". Upon investigation, the problem was far bigger than they anticipated. One of the oxygen tanks had exploded, resulting in an almost complete loss of capability to generate power and to provide water or oxygen to the crew. The NASA officials immediately accepted that the mission to the moon had to be scrapped and everything had to be done to bring the crew home. What was uncertain was – how?

Let's break for a minute and look at possible reactions to the discomfort of suddenly being thrust into a sea of uncertainty. The typical hedgehog reaction would be to rush back to its hole in the ground, curl itself into a ball and hope the problem would sort itself out. The reaction of a fox would be to look for the main influencing factors, see how they could be used to advantage and, in so doing, begin to cope with the new situation. With necessary apologies to Neil Armstrong, this crossing-over from the right-hand side of the matrix (certainty) to the left-hand side (uncertainty) requires one small step for a fox but one giant leap for hedgehog-kind.

At NASA ground control, the next step was decidedly foxy – to look for the main driving forces of the situation by drawing on the multiple perspectives of some of the finest brains in the space business. Unlike the rugged gung-ho frontiersmen of the Wild West, the heroes of this frontier were teams of scientists with pocket calculators and slide rules; there were no laptops in those days! Very little was known about the effects of an explosion like this on the craft and crew, so you can imagine the list of uncertainties this situation offered: How was the craft damaged? How long would the power last? How long would the oxygen last? Could the power be restored? Would the craft start falling apart? Would the explosion affect the craft's trajectory, sending it into outer space? If the astronauts managed to head the craft back towards Earth, would the command and lunar modules be able to detach from one another? Would the damage prevent the craft from re-entering the Earth's atmosphere? What were the dangers of another explosion?

What was the quickest route to get home? And what were the realistic odds of getting the astronauts back home? Because no-one was prepared for a situation like this, the chasm between the old certainties and the new uncertainties might have seemed unbridgeable.

However, there is a continuum between certainty and uncertainty, just as there is between factors inside and outside of our control. By studying the uncertain, we may be able to break it down into elements of greater and lesser risk, of greater and lesser predictability. In the same way, between absolute control and absence of control lies the middle ground of influence and persuasion. Hence, we can travel inwards and outwards along the two principal axes of our matrix. Which is why studying the Apollo 13 mission is so fascinating. It offers us a perfect example of how people in a situation of extreme stress are still able to establish and analyse the key uncertainties, so that a sensible range of options can be mounted against what the future throws at us.

As the name suggests, key uncertainties are those variables most relevant to a particular situation and with the highest impact potential, either as an opportunity or a threat. They therefore drive the design of possible scenarios. In this regard, where a scenario planning forum raises many uncertainties, it is important that the number is whittled down to a few pivotal ones: namely the ones on which the scenarios pivot like a see-saw. For example, both of us have recently been facilitating workshops to produce scenarios which are relevant in the war against poverty in South Africa. Quite independently, both workshops chose the process through which national development strategies are implemented – will they be driven in a top-down fashion from the centre or be shaped by community demands from the bottom up? – as a pivotal uncertainty. This led to the fashioning of a third alternative: grassroots-driven development with co-ordination from on high in those areas where real value can be added.

In the 1980s, most global scenario teams selected the relationship between America and Russia as a pivotal uncertainty – would the arms race continue or would there be détente? Times change and, with the collapse of the Soviet Union, the nineties were dominated more by uncertainties in the world financial and economic systems. The "noughties", as the present decade is known, continues to be dominated by these uncertainties, which now include the tremors in the American economy. Interestingly, as far as single-business scenarios are concerned, a recent exercise selected the attitude of central banks to their gold holdings as the pivotal uncertainty for the gold market in the foreseeable future. The banks still hold over 30 000 tons of the precious metal in their vaults, which is around a quarter of the gold ever extracted from the Earth's crust. With current demand for gold approximately matched by mine supply and jewellery and investment bars which have been melted down and recycled, the banks only have to dribble a small amount of their stock onto the market every year to ruin it. On the other hand, if they ever lose confidence in holding paper currencies like the dollar, sterling, euro and yen as their reserves and add to their gold holdings, the bulls would have a field day. As one gold expert wryly observed: "The gold price can go up or down but not necessarily in that order!" Moving to the world of black gold or petroleum, the pivotal uncertainty must be not whether but when and in what form new rules will come into force to reduce carbon emissions. The second Earth Summit in Johannesburg in 2002 may be the moment of truth.

In the case of Apollo 13, ground control and crew concluded that the two key uncertainties were oxygen supply to the crew and power supply to the craft. Without oxygen the crew would die, and without power the craft wouldn't get back home.

Wild cards

Key uncertainties are factors which we have positively identified, but we don't know which way they're going to go. However, there are also other factors that we are only dimly aware of. They may represent opportunities or threats but they can't be part of any official analysis because they're too vague or too far away on the horizon. We call them "wild cards", and the best way to capture them is to exercise the right-hand side of the brain, associated with creativity and spatial awareness, as opposed to the left-hand side associated with analysis. It is accepted by most psychologists that men are left-hemisphere dominant, whereas women lean towards the right. This suggests that women are always in their right minds! Therefore, when analysing situations that are fraught with uncertainties and have no established patterns on which to base solutions, it is often the fairer sex who contribute the more dynamic scenarios. They have a knack for picking the really surprising outcomes or UUs – unknown unknowns – as opposed to the KUs or known unknowns.

To get a better feel for the way-out nature of wild cards, let's return to the cosmos and ask "what happened before the Big Bang?" For, given the expansion of the universe, it is a fair assumption that *something happened* and that there was some form of starting point from which the universe originated. Modern science has arrived, through our knowledge of the nature of space, time and gravitation, at the same conclusion as the fifth-century Christian saint, Augustine of Hippo (don't ask), who claimed that the world was made "not *in* time, but simultaneously *with* time". In plain

95

speaking: nothing happened before the Big Bang because there was no "before". Time only started *with* the Big Bang. Thus speculation on the causes of the Big Bang and what happened preceding it can only produce the wildest of wild cards. We have to accept the unanswerability of some questions, even though our imagination impels us to explore for an answer.

A mid-1980s global scenario study incorporated the following wild card: "Surprisingly, the one thing that terrifies Japan is the possibility of a devastating earthquake during the scenario period." The earthquake happened at Kobe in early 1995 and proved that natural disasters are an ever-present danger. However, you can have wild cards on a more personal basis. Think of the strain of planning your young son's birthday party. He wants to invite twenty of his friends to play a series of games in a public park. What are the key uncertainties in determining the success of the party – those factors you know you don't know? Will it rain? How many of his friends will arrive on the day? Will you have enough food and drink when you have in fact bought enough provisions for an army? But the wild card you don't know you don't know is that the public park has been selected by a visiting chapter of the Hell's Angels as a stopover for their breakfast run. And that's really wild.

Wow, that was close!

We move from screaming unruly children in a public park to the screams of men on the fields of battle. Key uncertainties are an integral part of warfare. In his thoughtful treatise on military science, *Strategy and Compromise*, the distinguished naval historian Admiral Samuel Elliot Morrison makes the point that in the quest to know as much as possible about the enemy, military advisers and strategists employ intelligence gathering that is never complete and is of-

96

ten misleading. For example, the information of an enemy's strength and intentions may well be incorrect. The generals who play scenarios of the battle that lies ahead and make the final decisions know that the information at hand has tremendous gaps, but anything is better than nothing. Military decisions are therefore based on what is known and what is known to be unknown. If a wild card then emerges out of the blue – like the enemy having a new and vastly superior weapon – then the general who has a sixth sense, or a fox's instinct, might still snatch victory from the jaws of defeat. In warfare, admits Admiral Morrison, mistakes which the top brass like to call "strategic errors" are inevitable. He says: "Other things being equal, the side that makes the fewer strategic errors wins the war."

Historians only now tell us how close we came to an all-out nuclear war in October 1962 because America and Russia at times completely misread the other's position. Earlier that year Cuba, convinced that the Americans were about to attack them, had asked for extra military aid from the Russians. The latter responded by sending missiles and building missile bases on the island capable of launching nuclear strikes on American cities. In October, President John Kennedy learnt about this and ordered a naval blockade to stop further shipment of Russian arms. He then demanded that all missiles and missile bases be removed from the island. The world held its breath for a week before Russian Premier Nikita Krushchev agreed to the demand in return for an American pledge that they wouldn't attack Cuba. The blockade was then lifted. What recent analysis of the archival material has shown is that, despite both sides having formidable intelligence networks, each leader was being given woefully incorrect information on how his counterpart was thinking. So we nearly blundered into a nuclear war. But ask yourself: how often do you make decisions based on a perfect knowledge of all the facts? Admit it – the answer is seldom, if ever. Uncertainties are woven into life and weighing them up should be second nature to anybody who wants to make the best of a situation. The second quadrant of the matrix cannot be sidestepped.

We have now come full circle back to the question of the fate of the crew of the Apollo 13. Did the combined problem-solving talents of the team on the ground and in space steer the astronauts through the stormy seas of uncertainty back to dry land? Were the craft and the crew destroyed by the crushing deceleration forces and searing heat during re-entry? Or would they skip off the atmosphere and out into space to become, in Commander Jim Lovell's words, "a monument to the US space programme"? The answer to these questions depends on whether or not the key uncertainties that they identified helped them paint useful scenarios which ultimately led them to consider the most likely options and make the most effective decisions. No offence: you'll have to read on to see if there was a happy ending.

Scenarios

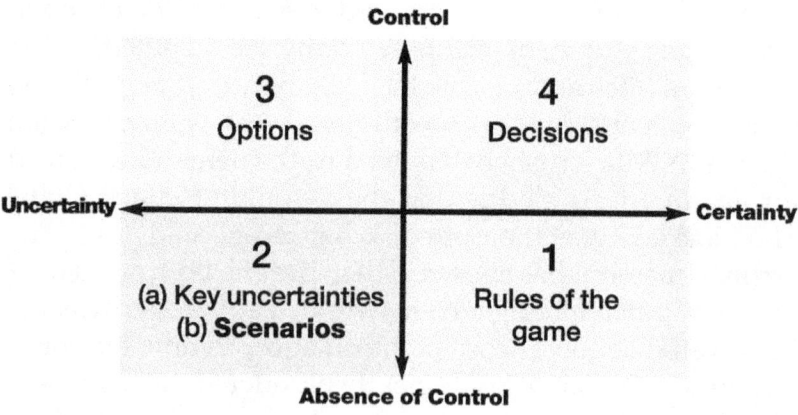

If they were still alive today, Jacob and Wilhelm Grimm would have been brilliant at writing scenarios. You may recall from your childhood that these two German brothers produced a collection of some of the most colourful and enduring fairy tales of all time – notably Snow White, Cinderella, Sleeping Beauty and Little Red Riding Hood. In the early part of the nineteenth century when they wrote these tales, multinational companies did not exist and scenario planning was not a paid occupation. Now they would be wined and dined by some of the most powerful foxes in business, looking for stories to enthral the young and old alike in their organisations; or maybe J.K.Rowling would be author of choice because of Harry Potter's rise to fame. It is not a coincidence that the book that has recently topped the New York nonfiction bestsellers' list for a long time employs the Grimm technique. It is entitled *Who Moved My Cheese?* by Dr Spencer Johnson. The story is about mice and little people and their different behaviour when their current stockpile of cheese in a maze is exhausted and they have to go in search of new cheese. It is just as enchanting as Cinderella but delivers a powerful message of how to view change as an opportunity rather than a threat.

Scenarios are stories about possible futures. Many hedgehogs in business confuse the term "scenario" with a forecast or prediction of a single future. Nothing could be further from the truth. Scenarios are, in fact, multiple pathways into a future that is unknown. While constrained by the rules of the game and driven by the key uncertainties, they should evoke the same feelings as a really good novel. Each scenario must have a simple, vivid theme which is logically consistent in itself, but differs materially from the other scenarios in the set. It must have a compelling title which enters the common vocabulary of the audience being ad-

99

dressed. The title should conjure up the image of the scenario without the need for the text to be read. There must not be too many scenarios, as the human mind is only capable of thinking in three dimensions. For this reason and because a prime objective of scenario work is to reduce the complex to the easily understandable, we advocate two or three scenarios (four at the very outside) for any particular situation. Only pure mathematicians can think in four or more dimensions!

However, let's go back to first principles and the Oxford English Dictionary. It defines a scenario as "a sketch or outline of the plot of a play, giving particulars of the scenes, situations, etc.". An alternative meaning taken from a dictionary of music is "an Italian term, meaning a sketch of the scenes and main points of an opera libretto, drawn up and settled preliminary to filling in the detail". Obviously, Italian composers used to peddle scenarios around well-heeled, music-loving bankers in the hope of raising money for a full production before they wasted too much effort on the score. The first known use of scenarios in a connection outside the creative arts and inside the more clinical world of science came from the sociologist, novelist and screenwriter Leo Roysten. He suggested to a group of physicists, who were searching for a name for alternative descriptions of how satellites might behave, that they call them "scenarios". He explained that this was the term used in the film industry to describe the outlines of future films. It seems fitting, therefore, to examine the scenarios that must have been playing in the minds of the crew of Apollo 13 and their helpers to get them back home.

When the proverbial hits the fan

Ever had the feeling that you're always in it and it's just the level that changes? After the on-board explosion, the crew of Apollo 13 were so far in it they needed chin-high waders! Their situation called to mind Murphy's law: "Everything that can go wrong will go wrong" and O'Brien's variation: "Murphy was an optimist". As one problem was solved, another one arose. To summarise their predicament: an explosion had destroyed a vital oxygen supply virtually robbing the command and lunar modules of power and the crew of water and limiting the supply of oxygen. In order to conserve power, the three-man crew had to move from the main navigational command module to the two-man lunar module designed only to travel to the moon's surface and back to the command module. They could only return to the command module just before splashdown.

Moreover, the explosion came after the craft had made its mid-course correction out of an immediate-return-to-Earth trajectory. So it was committed to travelling into an orbit of the moon and couldn't simply hitch a ride in the form of a direct trajectory back to Earth. The two craft, although attached, were incompatible in certain ways – the lunar module navigational system was not designed for getting back to Earth and the square canisters used to remove carbon dioxide from the command module did not fit into the round openings of the lunar module environmental system.

Without the ability to navigate, they had no hope of getting home. If carbon dioxide wasn't removed, the crew would asphyxiate. Power was needed to steer the craft: yet power was all but nonexistent. The power that remained needed to be conserved and so all but the essential requirements were cut. When the power was cut, the temperature dropped. When the temperature dropped, condensation formed on all the electrical circuitry, posing the danger of arcing and complete failure when it came time to power-up. All in all, the crew were up to their necks in it.

To follow up on our fan analogy: prima facie it would

seem that, when the proverbial hits the fan, it will not be distributed evenly and therefore no predictable pattern can be discerned. You can bet, however, that all concerned on the craft and in Houston went through the type of thinking process embedded in our matrix to narrow down the range of possible dispersion patterns. They examined the rules of the game, which mainly comprised the laws of physics; they selected two key uncertainties, namely the availability of power and oxygen; and they formulated various scenarios of the likely outcomes. Seeing that they didn't know how much power was available and they didn't know how long they could survive in the face of carbon dioxide build-up and lack of water, this all might sound airy-fairy and contrived. Which is why the Brothers Grimm would be pretty handy here! But it gave them a better clue to the options open to them and the best course of action. You will notice below that the first two scenarios on offer were utterly negative. Yet, they had good education value by informing the team as to what they should do to *minimise* the chance of either of these scenarios materialising.

The first scenario was "Close but No Cigar". Assuming they didn't have enough power to get back to Earth, they could still effectively control the carbon dioxide and conserve water and food. They wouldn't die immediately. They would hover agonisingly close to Earth until gradually and slowly they would starve to death or die of thirst. The second scenario was "Tin Tomb". Assuming they had enough power to get back to Earth, their survival mechanisms could fail them before they got there. They would be DOA (dead on arrival) with the command module being converted into a very expensive body bag. The third and positive scenario was "Sweet as Apple Pie". Assuming they had enough power to get back to Earth and their survival mechanisms remained intact, they would arrive to a hero's welcome and have apple pie with the president on the White House lawn.

We know what you're thinking: even if the astronauts were allergic to apples, they would focus on the last scenario to help them formulate their options. But that misses the whole point of scenario planning. It is only by studying all three scenarios simultaneously and looking at what you want to achieve as well as what you want to avoid that you get a feel for *all* the options. In the extreme case of life and death, we have a natural tendency anyway to do all this in the blink of an eye. It is when our lives are not at stake, and there is no emergency, that the error of concentrating on only the desired future creeps in. Take the hockey-stick projection so beloved in many companies. Like the *Nike* swoosh, it accepts a trough in the short term, but a market soaring to infinity thereafter. To adapt Keynes's famous quote, in the long term we are all optimistic! But Pollyanna would not have survived at the controls of Apollo 13.

Negotiating the rapids with the wisdom of Wack

The point we want to make from the previous narrative is that the uncertainties of a situation can be built on to give you a chance of success. There is a logic to identifying the two key uncertainties that would have the greatest impact on your business, life or situation at hand; but these uncertainties need to be translated into scenarios to give you a vision of your options. In other words, the bridging mechanism to get you from the key uncertainties to the options available is the set of scenarios or stories – the more vivid, the more contrasting but underpinned by logic, the better. This will encourage you to think the unthinkable and identify opportunities you didn't even think were there.

Problem: just when you need the Brothers Grimm for your next scenario planning session, you realise that they lived in the early nineteenth century. So where do you find the talent for story-telling? An answer: multiple perspectives from inside your own backyard. The diversity of knowledge and insight of different people within a company can provide the richness of material to develop scenarios. And it needn't just be your intellectual top guns. Encouraging ordinary people to engage in more creative and divergent thinking has the added advantage for a company of promoting expression and helping people to converse. It is this very harnessing of diversity and encouraging of creativity within groups and individual frames of mind that equip people to dream up scenarios of an unusual nature and then expand on the range of options necessary for decision-making. As Peter Schwartz said: "Scenario-making is intensely participatory, or it fails."

Imagine you and your staff are on a corporate outward bound course. You arrive at the bank of a wide river, and there's a rowing boat in front of you with which to cross the river. After a quick bout of team-building and strategic planning, you as the leader set the objective: to get to *that* specific tree on the other side. After examining your options, you work out the specific strengths of each member of your team to deal with the task at hand. Roles are delegated and, with a blood-curdling war cry, you and your team launch yourselves into the river and paddle like mad to get to that tree. Moments later you are swept downstream by the river's powerful current that you didn't know about and factor into the equation. According to Paul Valéry, a twentieth-century French poet and philosopher, "a fact poorly observed is more treacherous than faulty reasoning". Ian Mitroff in *Smart Thinking For Crazy Times* put it another way: many serious errors of management can be traced to solving the wrong problems precisely. If the team had undertaken some scenario planning in advance of plunging in, the unknown magnitude of the river's current would have been one of the key drivers in designing the scenarios. The other driver would have been the unknown combined physical stamina and co-ordination of the team under such circumstances. Using these two uncertainties as drivers, the unexpected outcome might have been captured in a scenario with a catchy name like "Deliverance". As Pierre Wack said: "It is better to be vaguely right than precisely wrong". Then you can make contingency plans – like walking back up the river to *that* tree, totally drenched to the bone!

It's all in the name

As we said earlier, graphic names for scenarios do help enormously in spreading the word. They become part of the in-house vernacular whenever the future is being discussed in a company. "Imperial Twilight" was one such name. It was applied to a scenario developed in the 1980s to show that the arms race between America and the Soviet Union was unsustainable because the Soviet Union was running out of money. The upshot would be the end of the Soviet Union, which is exactly what transpired. An environmental scenario sketched during the same decade was entitled "Rich Heritage". It drew attention to the fact that the present generation inhabiting the planet had to pass on to the next generation the same level of biodiversity as it had inherited. What one advertising executive said about brand names applies equally to scenario names. He commented: "A good name keeps the pie in the sky because pies on the ground are pretty boring objects." There's magic in a name!

At a recent workshop addressing job creation, a diverse body of interested parties identified the key uncertainties of job creation in the area as the commitment and involvement of the communities within the area, and the level of investment from outside into the area. From this, four music-themed scenarios were developed:

"PHILHARMONIC ORCHESTRA"

Potential investors, excited by the display of enthusiasm and entrepreneurship of the community in the region, agree to build a series of holiday resorts and develop factories and commercial properties that will draw on the experience and facilities in the region. This attracts more investment and attention, resulting in a boost to tourism and the local economy, providing jobs and opportunities for the community. The orchestra, made up of different clusters of skilled instrumentalists, work together in harmony to produce a world-class symphonic sound.

"CREATIVE DISCORD"

Excited by the arrival of potential investors, the local community put on a display of spontaneous enthusiasm and entrepreneurship in the form of establishing a network of separate markets. The investors, for whatever reason, decline to invest; but the community, now aware of their own potential, maintain the momentum and the region becomes a hotbed of entrepreneurial enterprises. The result: the communities play different tunes at different tempos. Although the overall sound is discordant, each group of players is bowled along by their own enthusiasm as they toot their particular horns.

"LONELY BUSKER"

Investors, for whatever reason, decline to invest. The enthusiasm of the communities is low to nonexistent. Land issues are a major problem and no parties are willing to address the issues actively. Like the lonely busker on the street pavement, playing his harmonica with his cap in his hand and hoping for the odd cent from a passer-by, each community survives by eking out a living.

Potential investors are excited about the area, see opportunities and plunge in. But there has been no prior consultation with the communities to examine what is best for the area. Each party has different expectations, with the consequence that investors stand over their subsequently abandoned factories and resorts like a conductor facing an empty orchestra pit.

Through the looking glass

When Alice protested through the looking glass that you can't believe impossible things, the Queen set the issue straight: "I daresay you haven't had much practice. When I was your age, I always did it for half an hour a day. Why, sometimes I've believed as many as six impossible things before breakfast." Lewis Carroll lit up the lives of many Victorian children by taking them into his world of make-believe. Coincidentally, in *Alice's Adventures in Wonderland*, hedgehogs feature as the balls in royal games of croquet with flamingoes as the mallets and soldiers – bent double – as the hoops. Since all three prefer to move of their own volition rather than behave as inert objects, the games usually end in chaos with the Queen calling for the heads of all those who misbehaved, and the king subsequently pardoning them.

The secret of successful scenario planning is not just the richness of the story line or the striking nature of the title. The content of the scenarios must also be relevant for them to come alive, not only in outer space, but also in inner space. Each person within a group has his or her own model of the real world and what is relevant based on his or her experiences. This is referred to as the person's "microcosm". The real world and its relevant parts are then the "macrocosm". Scenarios link the world of perception with the world of fact. In order to gain new insight from scenarios, one has to identify which information is of strategic importance and then transform it into material which penetrates the consciousness of the people for whom the information has potential consequences. It may not be new information but something that is already known and is right in front of the nose of the observers. It is just being misperceived. That is why Pierre Wack called scenario planning "the gentle art of reperceiving".

To put it in business terms: a company's *perception* of its business environment (microcosm) is as important as the actual state of the market (macrocosm) because its strategy comes from this perception. To be effective, then, the real target of scenario planning should be the microcosm of the decision makers. Unless their mental images of reality are influenced, the impact of scenarios will be negligible. In short: unless their minds are opened, their options will be closed. Pierre Wack cited the example of the oil scenarios he produced for Shell before the first oil price shock in the early 1970s. Although they were suitably prophetic in highlighting the instability of the market, they didn't connect with the senior executives of Shell. Pierre realised that unless he uncovered the managerial mind-set, his writing of further scenarios would be useless. He therefore did a whole series of interviews with managers to unearth what really made them tick and what language should be used to communicate new ideas to them. Consequently, Pierre's next set of scenarios on the second oil price shock, as we mentioned earlier on, really struck home.

It would be remiss of us as authors if we didn't end the scenario section with a golf story. After all, a round of golf has eighteen stories – one for each hole – and if you include the drink in the pub afterwards, nineteen. We have stressed on several occasions how scenario planning should embrace the unthinkable. Well, a photograph hanging in the corridor of the Durban Country Club reveals four golfers who played together and achieved just that. On the same par-four hole, the eighteenth, one player got an albatross, which is three under par and therefore a one; he drove the green. The second player got an eagle, which is two under par and therefore a two. The third and fourth players only managed a birdie and a par, in other words a three and a four. Now, would anyone in the entire golfing world ever write a scenario for that? It happened on 21 April 1994.

Options

	Control	
3 Options		**4** Decisions
Uncertainty ←	→ Certainty	
2 (a) Key uncertainties (b) Scenarios		**1** Rules of the game
	Absence of Control	

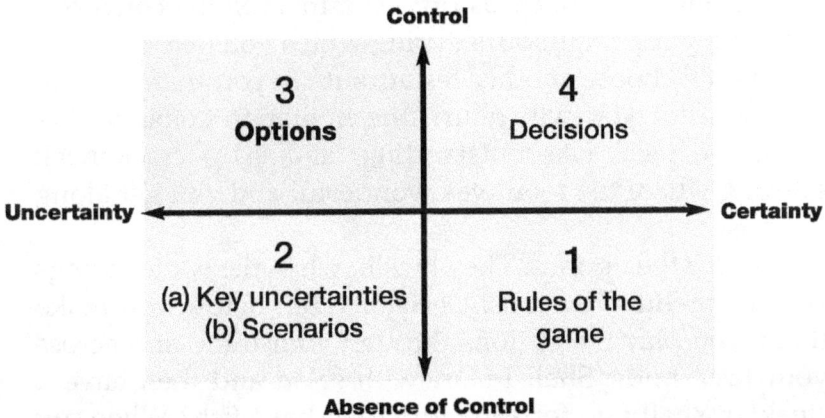

Food for thought

When Maggie Thatcher was British Prime Minister, she had a favourite phrase to overcome opposition in the Cabinet to any of her views – TINA, or there is no alternative. Hopefully, this section will demonstrate that TEMBA is a far better principle than TINA: there exist many better alternatives, all of which should be taken into consideration before you make the actual decision.

If you're the type of person who thinks we should cut to the chase and just make decisions, here's an example to prove that even you are susceptible to our type of matrix thinking. You have new neighbours who, to get acquainted, ask you out to a restaurant you've never been to before. The rules of the game for the evening are that you can only choose to eat what's on the menu of the selected restaurant and you have to be finished by closing time. The key uncertainties are whether the food and the service are good or bad at this unfamiliar restaurant, and whether your new neighbours are stimulating or dull. The scenarios flowing from these uncertainties are: (1) an evening where you doze off from tedium while wondering whether you have eaten something that was off; (2) a marvellous conversation with your neighbours during which you joke that next time you'll choose another restaurant; (3) you share little in common but you will return the invitation someday because the meal was outstanding; and (4) a crackerjack evening where the food was wonderful and you get along famously.

Now for the options. They kick in when the waiter brings you the menu. Decisions! Decisions! But before you make them, you play the options through your mind and across your taste buds. Shall I start with salad and then have a steak; or shall I go for soup and then have fish? When my neighbour asks me whether I like white or red wine, which shall I say? Am I going to finish with a sticky tart or cheese? Etc., etc. Yet, menus have many more applications today. Companies offer employees menus where for a certain monetary sum they will give you the chance of having a nice car but you then have to scrimp on the medical aid; or, vice versa, you can take lots of health insurance but then you drive around in a tin can. For hedgehogs who are used to being told exactly what their employment conditions are, the introduction of choice is bewildering. They are uncomfortable with options!

But it goes beyond restaurants and companies. Menus on what you can do on your computer; menus on aircraft offering a wide range of movies on your pop-up video screen; menus of occupations offered in career-guidance sessions; and, broader still, the astonishingly vast menus of consumer goods and services that well-off people nowadays face when they are choosing how to spend their disposable income – these all involve options. Indeed, technological progress is providing an infinite array of options. So you see, even if you're an action-oriented person, this section is for you.

Holidays in Chevrolets; jewellery and rugby

"Are we there yet?" We have all asked the question as youngsters on a long car journey to a holiday destination. The only oases of relief were the stops to refuel along the way. Imagine a child who has seemingly endured this lifetime on the back seat persistently nagging his family that at the next stop he be allowed into the refreshment area to buy *one* item for the next leg of the journey. The family acquiesces to shut him up. As he excitedly enters the store, he is confronted by a veritable cornucopia of sweets, popcorn, potato chips and cold drinks. Shelves upon shelves of wonderful mouth-watering goodies and he is allowed to pick anything – as long as it's one thing and he doesn't make a mess in the car! Does he have a seemingly unlimited range of options? No. He has a tremendous range of *opportunities* but his *options* are limited. The difference? Opportunities only become options when they *fall within your control.*

One of the beauties of scenario planning is that it provides real choices for action. These choices are not random possibilities but are specifically relevant to our situation because they have been developed out of the earlier processes identified in our matrix. The richer the scenarios, the more varied the options. What makes options particularly important is that although they are derived from uncertainties outside our control, they are restricted to actions within our control. As such, the third quadrant is enthusiastically explored by foxes but is somewhat of a no-go area for hedgehogs. Whereas hedgehogs are dead-set on following a chosen path, foxes are guided by instinct. Consequently, whenever the path ahead forks and involves a choice, foxes are quite ready to venture off the straight and narrow to explore alternatives that are "beyond reason". In that sense, the left-hand side of our matrix represents the (more intuitive) right-hand side of our brain.

Control is power. But the true nature of power is having control in times of uncertainty. That control comes in the form of options; so the person who can exercise more options in the face of uncertainty has more power. Pierre Wack once wrote two scenarios for the world of gold – "Plan" or "Be Planned". His point was simple. Either gold-mining companies roll up their sleeves and get involved in the downstream retail market of jewellery and thereby influence demand; or they should expect to bob up and down in the ripples to the gold price caused by central bank sales. He maintained that the power of oil companies lay in the fact that they have so many options to play around with between the well in the ground and the filling station in the village. Vertical integration has its advantages – it turns you into a price-maker as opposed to a price-taker. This wasn't bad advice, since a feature of mining is how long it takes to sink a shaft and come into production. All that money flowing out and the only relevant price is the one you get when you're up and running! It makes sense to influence it, particularly with gold being the oldest brand around – signifying sun, sex, power, money and winning the race. What more do you want?

Now it's time for us to give you our own tip. Keep your eyes on the rules of the game: if they change, then the options can change too. For example, until recently, the rules of rugby stated that if a side was awarded a penalty and they decided to kick the ball into touch, the throw-in was then awarded to the opposing team. This meant transferring control of the game to the opposition. When this rule was changed so that the team awarded the penalty could kick the ball into touch and still have the throw-in, it provided an exciting new option. If a team is now given a penalty close to the opposing try line, they can kick for the posts for three points; or go for touch *closer* to the tryline in the knowledge that if they score a try and convert it, they will obtain an extra seven points. The implication of this rule amendment is that rugby becomes a much more interesting game to watch when the score is close in the dying minutes of a match. Business has the same fascination for a different reason: the rules are changing all the time, creating new windows of opportunity and new options.

Stars and dogs and Apollo 13 continued

A way of getting managers to discuss strategic options is illustrated in the diagram overleaf. If a company wants to assess the value of its underlying businesses, ask the board to post each business into the appropriate square. Is it a core star, a noncore star, a core dog or a noncore dog? We all know what to do with core stars – keep them. Equally, we

```
                          Core
                           ▲
                           │
            ?              │        Keep
                           │
Dogs ◄─────────────────────┼─────────────────────► Stars
                           │
         Sell or           │
          Close            │         ?
                           │
                           ▼
                        Noncore
```

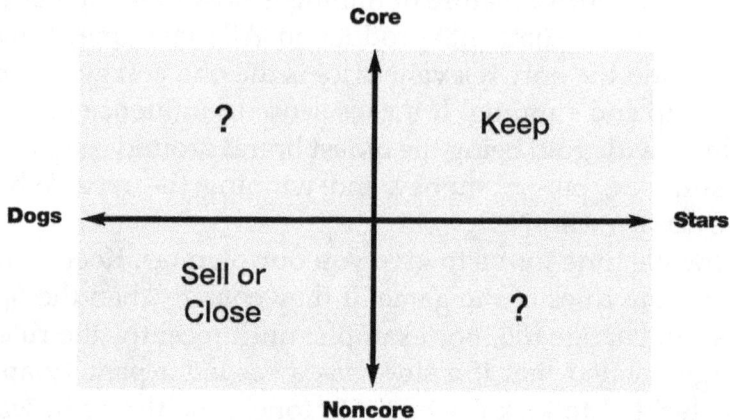

know what to do with noncore dogs – get rid of them or, as they say in the veterinary profession, put them down. But what do you do with noncore stars and core dogs? You might wish to hang on to the former because they consistently contribute to your financial results. On the other hand, with focus being in fashion, you might decide to sell them for a decent sum and use the money to invest more into your core businesses.

Core dogs are different. So much management time is spent trying to turn a core dog around that, after the 51st restructuring, everybody is sick to death of it. Basically, you can re-engineer a dog as much as you like and it still barks! So as Jack Welch, Chairman of General Electric, puts it: the options are fix, sell or close. Then, just to make matters complicated, the rules of the game can change, turning a dog into a star (a dog-star!) or a star into a dog.

Speaking of stars, let's not forget about the three astronauts still hanging in on board Apollo 13. The three scenarios of possible outcomes described earlier – "Close but No Cigar", "Tin Tomb" and "Sweet as Apple Pie" – would have provided the astronauts and the support team in Mission Control with the most realistic options available. The objective was obviously to bring the astronauts home alive. However there was no instruction manual for what should be done under such circumstances. In this unique life-threatening situation, therefore, the range and detail of the scenarios were essential in order to develop as many options as possible to help them make the most effective ongoing decisions. So what options within their control would they have had? Among them were to:

– conserve power by shutting down all but the critical systems;

– conserve water by rationing;

– reduce carbon dioxide levels by attempting to adapt the filtering system in the lunar module;

– use the sun as a navigational point of reference, debris around the lunar module having made it virtually impossible to see the stars;

– try and increase speed around the moon to give them enough momentum to sling them onto a path back to Earth;

– try and redirect power to critical systems; and

– exercise a "burn", which would use power, to correct their path at the right moment.

Although, in retrospect, the options for the crew of the Apollo 13 may have seemed logical and orderly, the crew's method of implementation certainly wasn't. This is an essential point to bear in mind: options are only effective if they can be implemented; otherwise they're just "good ideas". Time was not on the side of the crew and Mission Control, so the implementation depended on close teamwork. For example, a whole new flight plan was needed to put the astronauts on a fresh course for home. This would normally have required three months. Mission Control managed it in three days. The exact time and duration of a "burn" to change their alignment so that the orbit around the moon would slingshot the spacecraft back towards the Earth had to be calculated. This was one of those rare moments that maths teachers will forever boast about, as it showed the importance of a healthy knowledge of vector calculus! The problem of connecting the square lithium hydroxide canisters of the command module to the round openings of the lunar module environmental system to remove carbon dioxide build-up required creative thought on the part of engineers on Earth. They had to do a dummy run with materials similar to those that were available on board the craft. This was achieved using piping, plastic bags and cardboard, all connected and sealed with tape.

Interestingly, the same tape that was used to save the lives of the crew may well have been the product of a truly foxy company, which presents a good example of flexibility and adaptability. It is forever developing new options in the face of a changing market environment. 3M, whose name is synonymous with Scotch Tape, started as Minnesota Mining and Manufacturing. As times and circumstances changed, they evolved into a sandpaper manufacturer; then into adhesive tape invented by a banjo-playing engineer; Post-it notes; and more recently high-tech optics. Here is a company that is in control of its destiny and has exploited uncertainty to its advantage. It has thrived by retaining its greatest strength through thick and thin – innovation.

To summarise, realistic and action-oriented strategic planning requires options. Formulate as many options as possible and then look realistically at those that are achievable and can most effectively be implemented by you. Remember that options aren't recommendations, just as scenarios aren't forecasts. So be as "blue sky" as you like in a discussion on options. If people think your option is too wild, you can always say it was just an option. Whereas one option, or

even part of one, is used in the end, you can only confident-
ly proceed if all the alternatives have been identified and rejected. In this way, options give you more control and allow
you the comfort and certainty that you made the best decision you could under the circumstances – even if you are
subsequently proved wrong.

Returning to golf, the options are the clubs in your bag.
Each club is there to strike the ball a different distance. It is
only when you're out there on the course that you'll decide
which club to use, depending on your distance from the
hole, your lie and the wind. Making decisions without considering the options is rather like playing a golf course with
only one club in your bag – difficult.

Decisions

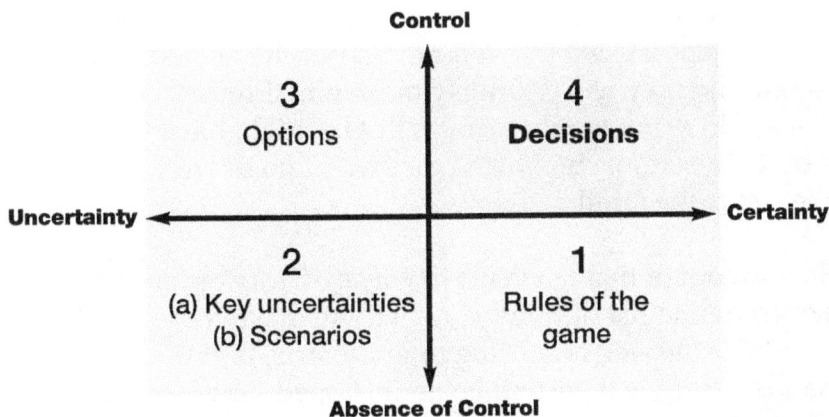

Chocolates, white water rafting and a world cup final

Remember our young friend at the beginning of the last section who is about to step into a child's dream and a dentist's
nightmare? He is allowed any item in the shop providing
it's one thing and won't make a mess. Those are the rules!
So he has opportunities. However, if he is clever, he will re-

alise that there are several uncertainties influencing his choice. He is aware that there is still quite a journey ahead but he is uncertain how long it will be before the next stop. Moreover, he is uncertain whether or not he will be allowed a similar treat at the next stop. So, does he look for something that will last, or go for quick gratification, assuming he can get something at the next stop? You can imagine the options that will plague his young mind:

– a packet of sweets. They will last, but then he runs the risk of the rest of the family piling into the packet;

– a chocolate bar. It will have to be eaten quickly if it's hot in the car. But the chances are that if he grudgingly thrusts a gooey piece towards his family, they'll hastily refuse his offer. So he'll eat the whole thing himself with the downside that it could make him thirsty;

– potato chips or popcorn. They are a good idea if it's a long way because they won't melt. But they could still get messy and they will definitely make him thirsty.

– a cold drink would be nice. But he might have to ask to stop for a comfort break and that won't go down well with the rest of the family.

So now, out of that heavenly expanse of tasty opportunities which define his options, how will he make the best decision? The answer, according to our matrix, is entirely in his hands; but at least it will be an informed decision. Forrest Gump had a perceptive mother whose simple and somewhat idealistic philosophy was that life is like a box of chocolates – a tempting array of options ready for the picking and any decision is rewarded with anything but a bitter taste in the mouth. That's Hollywood for you! The reality, of course, is that in business and in life, the challenges and opportunities offered are seldom like those neatly displayed before the kid in the candy store. They are more like those encountered by our intrepid team of rafters out for a bit of bonding on the river and who, after *not* working through our matrix, are now huddled together and hurtling down a raging torrent. It matters not that they are down the creek with paddles as opposed to up the creek without them. They still have to make an effective decision.

The present trend in global markets is like a swelling current. Panic is starting to set in down corporate corridors as it becomes obvious that ahead lies a more volatile global economy with the possibility of a very bumpy ride. We are now white water rafting! Anyone who has wilfully engaged in this struggle with Mother Nature will bear testimony to how thrilling it can be. But it invariably claims some victims. This is where teamwork and decisions will either thrill you or kill you. Abandoning control and jumping off the raft is dangerous, and so is losing control, hitting a rock and falling off. The best decisions in this particular situation will come from working through the matrix – identifying the rules of the game, establishing the key uncertainties, constructing scenarios and drawing up the options available. That way you make decisions which mean that you squeeze between the rocks and make it to the calmer waters further downstream.

If you don't mind, we'd like to put you in a very uncomfortable situation. Imagine the scene: it's the Soccer World Cup Final. At the final whistle both teams are tied 1-1, and extra time yields no further goals. The match goes to a penalty shoot-out, five penalties each. Team A have scored five penalties and Team B have scored four with one penalty left. Congratulations – you are the goalkeeper for Team A facing the last penalty. If you save it, your team wins 5-4 on penalties; and the most coveted trophy in the world of sport is yours, together with instant fame and millions of dollars in endorsements. If the ball gets past you, it's a sudden-death penalty play-off, and the game continues. Pressure. Lots of it. Do you dive to the left or to the right? No self-respecting goalie would walk on the field at this level without having played this scenario over and over in his mind. He would have factored into his matrix the likely line-up of penalty-takers on the other side; whether they are left- or right-footed; whether they favour kicking the ball to the left or right; and whether they favour kicking it high or low. By running through this information on the last player who is about to shoot, you, as the goalie, will be as prepared as you can be. Whether or not you eventually make the right decision is not the issue. You did your best – and this is how the true stars of sport are born.

A successful failure

Let's return to the story that we've made a focal point of this book – the crew of the Apollo 13. It's decision time, and the decisions of our three foxes in space are now emblazoned in the history books. Firstly, the crew moved into the lunar module and shut down the power to all but the non-critical systems. This decision took into account the drop in temperature that would be caused by a loss in power. They had played the scenario that the resultant build-up of moisture through condensation could pose the danger of arcing when the power-up to jettison the lunar module was required for splashdown. They decided to take this risk on the grounds that any arcing would be controlled by safeguards built into the command module after the disastrous fire aboard Apollo 1 in January 1967.

The second decision was to conserve water, as it was no longer being produced after the oxygen tank explosion. This decision was made when it was realised that, at the ordinary rate of consumption, their water supply would be exhausted five hours before the essential water-cooling required for Earth re-entry. However, the data from the Apollo 11 flight showed that the craft's mechanisms could survive seven to eight hours in space without water-cooling. Again this decision was based on a previous experience and therefore was backed by a degree of certainty. The third decision related to the use of whatever materials were available to connect the square lithium hydroxide canisters, used for removing carbon dioxide from the command module, to the round openings in the lunar module. This was a classic case of implementing a decision based on the resources available.

The fourth decision was to remain on a moon trajectory instead of using valuable power to turn the craft around and head back to Earth. They would then use the gravitational pull of the moon to slingshot the craft back on a course for home. This decision was made with the knowledge that to stop the craft, turn it around and power it back would use up all its power. Given the orbital dynamics of the moon, a small burn would do. They had worked through the options!

The final two decisions were the really tricky ones. They had to utilise two burns at exactly the right time and angle in order to speed up the craft on the route home and effect the survival of the crew. This decision could only be made with precise measurements of speed, trajectory and direction. The first of the two burns on the route back from the moon's orbit was the most critical in that it required absolute certainty of the position of the craft in relation to the Earth. It also involved a rotation of the craft that would enable the astronauts to use the sun as the most accurate point of alignment for the rest of the trip. When the craft was rotated to the attitude Houston had requested, the sun was where it was expected to be – in fact it proved to be less than half a degree off. The decision to rotate at that moment was instrumental in bringing the crew home. In the book *Apollo Expeditions to the Moon*, the words of the Flight Director Gerald Griffin convey the tension and excitement leading up to the final burn which shortened the time home: "Some years later when I went back to the log and looked up that mission, my writing was almost illegible I was so damned nervous. And I remember the exhilaration running through me. My God, that's kind of the last hurdle. If we can do that I know we can make it. It was funny because only the people involved knew how important it was to have that platform properly aligned."

What is noteworthy is that no decision was made in and of itself. The success of the adjusted mission to bring the astronauts safely back to Earth was the result of many decisions shaped by incremental actions and the information they produced. Overall the experiences gathered throughout the whole mission contributed to a better understanding of a variety of factors, including the dynamics and dangers of space flight; possible rescue procedures; decisions that might be made in preparation for future missions; and the benefits of good teamwork under extraordinary circumstances. This, and the fact that the crew managed to return safely, prompted Commander Jim Lovell to call the mission a "successful failure".

Let's put this experience into a business context. It can be argued that the most successful companies are those that are best at learning, having discovered that effective decision-making is essentially a learning process involving experimentation and teamwork. This is in line with the "personal construct" theory as put forward by its main proponent, George Kelley. He believed that we make decisions based on our own constructs, which in turn are derived from our experiences, our previous decisions and what we have learnt from them. This theory therefore highlights the fact that our decisions are limited if we cut ourselves off from the experiences and opinions of others. To varying degrees, such decisions turn out to be self-centred and narrow in scope – typical of the reclusive hedgehog. What scenario planning encourages is the expanding of our constructs through dialogue with others around a broader range of possibilities – the typical pattern of sociable foxes. This opens the way for decisions which are unthinkable when considered in isolation. Symbiosis was an essential ingredient in the production of this book. Neither of us could have done it on our own. You build on each other's ideas.

A question that is often asked when we present the matrix at workshops is: "It sounds like a lengthy process; do you have to work through the entire matrix before making every decision?" The answer is that first time round you should. Subsequently, the matrix need only be updated when circumstances change. The important thing to remember is that, because the matrix represents a natural thought process, reference to it is ongoing. Whether we are making the decision to go for the fish or the beef offered by a stewardess on board a domestic flight; or whether we are about to agree to a multi-billion dollar merger with another company, we may return to the matrix more than once. We've all had second thoughts!

Unless something arrives like a bolt out of the blue and requires a split second decision – even then the matrix is implicitly used – the lead-up to a decision should involve the continual feeding of information into the matrix and upgrading or changing that information as the situation develops. For example, had our involuntary white water rafters prepared for being swept downstream, they might have worked out whether to go left or right of the first rock they encountered. Once committed to a decision, they would wait for the outcome before adjusting their options for the next challenge. At least, by returning to the matrix again and again, they would give themselves the opportunity to refine their decisions as they progressed down the rapids. Moreover, even if the outcome of a decision were not the intended or expected one, experience and information would *still* be gained and fed into the matrix for the next decision. As we've already said on several occasions, decisions and actual outcomes may be far apart. Tracking the convergence or divergence between result and intention is as important as going through the matrix in the first place. It tells you how much you have to adjust your original plan. Napoleon once remarked that "the problem is always in the execution, not the idea".

Go, fly a kite

Feedback loops like the one we've just described are central to the process of scientific thought. They have been the intellectual driving force behind some of the most important discoveries in the history of mankind. Hypotheses are established which result in experiments being done. The outcomes modify the hypothesis, leading to the conduct of further experiments and so on. Armed with an ever-increasing body of data and an ever-decreasing gap between hypothesis and fact, scientists eventually put forward their hypotheses as scientific propositions subject to peer review. If they pass muster, over time they become law. But that is not the end of it. Later generations may modify the law if it breaks down under certain circumstances. The law is obsolete rather than untrue. We still use classical physics in our everyday world of objects because it is perfectly satisfactory. However, in the realm of the quantum and the quark, the laws have changed. Science should be seen as a body of knowledge which is grown incrementally by each generation of scientists. Aristotle, Newton, Einstein – they inherited the genius of all who came before and left behind their own indelible footprints.

Sometimes you're lucky. Benjamin Franklin, the eighteenth-century printer, author, philosopher, diplomat, scientist and one of the founding fathers of American "foxology", proved his hypothesis that lightning was an electrical charge without requiring a feedback loop. He flew a kite during an electrical storm in 1752. Attached, as the popular story goes, to the wet string was a key. Before he made the decision to fly the kite, he had worked through the matrix and in particular the scientific rules of the game. He estimated that, given the electrical nature of lightning, a charge should manifest itself in the key if the kite was struck. At the same time, he had an almost fatal ignorance of the intensity of the charge released by a bolt of lightning. Lightning did strike the kite, the key was charged and the rest, as they say, is history. Fortunately, he survived the experiment and went on to invent, amongst many other things, the lightning rod, bifocal spectacles and the Franklin stove. He also offered the "one-fluid" theory which distinguished between positive and negative electricity. In recognition of all his scientific accomplishments he received honorary degrees from the University of St Andrews and Oxford University.

For most people entry to such eminent universities is through hard work, dedication, lots of studying and more hard work. But is the enthusiastic embracing of this kind of academia the best decision for young people leaving school? In his "biography" of the world's most famous equation, $E=mc^2$, David Bodanis recounts Albert Einstein's sister, Maja, telling of the now infamous event in her brother's schooling when his Greek teacher complained to her that nothing would ever come of Albert Einstein. She adds: "And in fact Albert Einstein never did attain a professorship of Greek grammar." Indeed, it was as a humble inspector of patents in Bern that he broke upon the world scene with his special theory of relativity. Presumably, he was rebuilding the universe in his head while he was sorting through the patent documents.

The new generation of nineteen-year-old entrepreneurs in the information technology field are not your average school-leavers. They are uninhibited enough to think nothing of breaking new ground. They are quite at ease on the left-hand side of the matrix, handling the uncertainties of new start-ups and dreaming up amazing options to push technology to its limits. Diplomas and degrees are not their measure of success. For them, success comes from taking the foxier route associated with true entrepreneurial spirit. Many have made their millions that way. The secret is a "can do" outlook. This comes from an awareness of what they can control and what they can't; and then from experimenting with different options in mapping out their future until they find the right one. This is why we should encourage our children to be familiar with and work through the matrix. It will give them the ability to make genuine assessments of the manifold pathways opening up before them rather than relying on guesswork. A wonderful piece of Irish wisdom goes like this: "If you don't know where you're going, any road will take you there." At the very least, we should give our kids a guidance system!

One of the problems of the normal school curriculum is that it is firmly planted on the right-hand side of our matrix. As a pupil, you learn to respect the rules of the game – be it the rules of the school, the rules of English grammar or the rules of arithmetic; but you don't learn to identify key uncertainties, sketch scenarios and choose between options. You don't learn how to handle the world of grey where decisions are anything but clear-cut. Parents think that it's supportive to say to a child "'be what you want to be". In reality, we should be saying to our children the more assertive "be what you can be and don't miss out". Fly the kite! By developing self-confidence and the faculty of curiosity in our children, we are equipping them with the most powerful tool for shaping their future and to give them the edge – the Mind of a Fox. When people ask you what do you do in future, remember the foxy answer is: "I do what I can."

The matrix in action

Having gone through the four quadrants of the matrix in some detail, we now want to demonstrate how it works in practice as a whole. What better way to kick off this process than a letter from the authors to the White House offering some friendly advice on the future to the new incumbent.

Dear Mr President,

Congratulations on attaining the most powerful position in the world. However, like all other jobs, there are constraints on what you can do. We're not talking of the checks and balances written into the US Constitution limiting your power vis-à-vis Congress and the Supreme Court. We want to list some rules of the game for the world – rules which are pretty certain to operate during your presidency and which are beyond your control.

Let's start with the demographics. Basically, the world is divided into two camps. There are the "rich old millions" – some 900 million to be more precise – who live in the developed world. We call them old because their birth rate has been declining, longevity has been increasing and a geriatric boom is underway. Immigrants, though, from the developing world provide a significant infusion of youth. This latter world consists of just over five billion people of whom nearly half reside in China and India. We classify them as the "poor young billions". Obviously, the split is not quite as simple as this as there are poor people in rich countries and rich people in poor countries. Nevertheless, for our purposes, this picture accurately serves as the first rule of the game. While you won't be able to change this picture much even if you serve two presidential terms, you can set in motion a process that begins to eradicate poverty quite significantly – probably the number one objective in the minds of most people with a conscience in the world today.

This, however, leads to the second rule of the game – globalisation. We now have more open markets than probably at any previous time in our history, but equally we have greater economic competition between nations. Competition implies winners and losers. The world economy is not exactly a zero-sum game, because among the poor young billions have been some winners, notably Asian Tigers like South Korea and Taiwan and parts of China, India and South America. And among the losers are some countries which are there, not because they've been driven to the wall by competition, but because they're miserably governed. Even so, it is not unsurprising that the main result of globalisation so far has been to confer the most benefits upon those who were the favourites in the first place. As they say, to the victors go the spoils and you were already a victor before anybody else had time to get out of the starting blocks. In fact, America has done so well out of globalisation that it is fast becoming a one-horse race – Europe and Japan having dropped behind in the economic race and Russia in the arms race.

We don't want to be party-poopers and spoil your celebrations, particularly with talk now of a "hard landing" in your economy; but we have an untenable state of affairs in light of the third rule of the game. We are one world and too many losers will ultimately bring you down along with everybody else. For good or ill, we are becoming more interdependent, which means each of us has less control over our own destiny. Think of what would happen if the oil stopped flowing from the Middle East!

Unlike the 100-metre dash where nobody's performance is affected by anybody else's on the track, the world economy has to grow for America to continue growing. Your multinational companies and exports like Hollywood movies both increasingly rely on prosperous markets outside America. For America's foreign customers to be prosperous, they also have to produce and sell their goods and services at a profit to you and each other. While some (the rich) are doing this, the majority (the poor) aren't, and now labour under the load of an international debt that they cannot repay. While you have a full-employment economy and can boast about it, most developing economies have a serious unemployment problem. They have no means of getting out of the quagmire as long as a significant amount of their budget goes towards repaying debt, and your world-class companies can outsmart and outmanoeuvre any fledgling industries they try to nurture. In short, we are a seriously dysfunctional global family with you at the head and the younger children in hock.

But being one family in one world, we have a new rule of the game that has crept up upon us over the last fifty years – global climate change. We have selected this phrase rather than global warming because there remains some uncertainty among the scientists as to the degree of warming that is taking place. The one thing that cannot be denied, however, is a rise in the frequency and scale of extreme events like droughts, floods, hailstorms and hurricanes as the global climate moves through a series of temporary states to a new equilibrium. These events also affect more people, given that the world population has doubled since 1962. If the evidence grows that the world is indeed warming up significantly and this can be linked to carbon emissions, guess who has to make the biggest sacrifice in bringing down fossil fuel consumption? – America! You have to lead the way instead of shifting the burden of change elsewhere. In this regard, your evident hostility to the Kyoto protocol on global warming was not exactly helpful. Perhaps, in a few hundred years, people will look back at our energy profligacy with the same sense of disbelief that we entertain for our ancestors' attitude to slavery.

Yet another consequence of being one family multiplying on one Earth is the growing possibility of worldwide epidemics. We already have the phenomenon of HIV/AIDS. Although it appears to be no longer a threat to the rich old millions, it is still spreading among the poor young billions. You cannot have healthy economies with sick people: thus HIV/AIDS may stymie efforts to help the poor nations to catch up the rich. But don't relax. With urbanisation, migration and the mutation of bacteria and viruses into drug-resistant forms, an old-fashioned plague of some kind which will affect everyone is looming large; and the doctors' arsenal of antibiotics is looking desperately thin. It may be the animals the rich eat which do them in. Or it may be something as simple as a new strain of the good old staphylococcus aureus microbe which up till now has been held in check by penicillin.

We would like to complete the rules to which you are subject on a positive note. The rapid spread of products spawned by the latest technological wave – cellphones, personal computers, the Internet and genetically engineered

```
                              Control
                                ▲
        3                       │    4
        Options                 │    Decisions
        Constructive engagement │    ?
        Isolation               │
                                │
Uncertainty ◄───────────────────┼───────────────────► Certainty
                                │
        2                       │    1
        (a) Key uncertainties   │    Rules of the game
        Nuclear terrorism       │    Demographics
        Disintegration of world │    Globalisation
           order                │    Global climate change
        (b) Scenarios           │    Potential for epidemics
        Friendly Planet         │    New technological wave
        Gilded Cage             │    Favourable values for
                                │       economic growth
                                ▼
                        Absence of Control
```

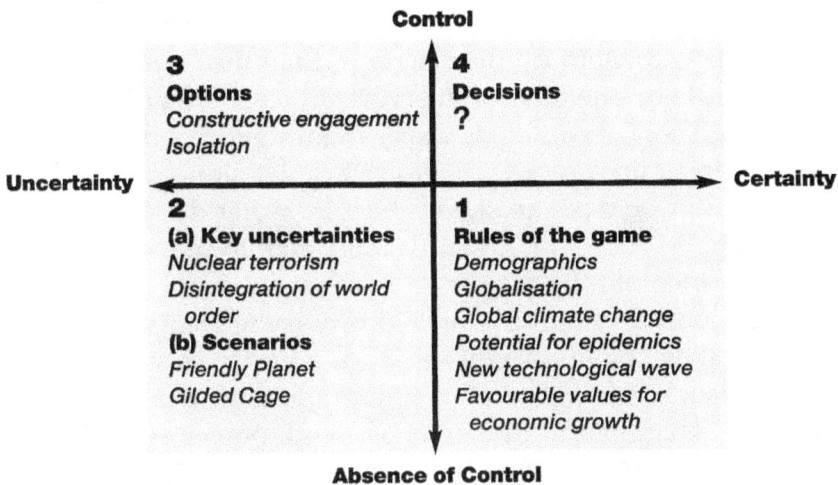

crops and medicines – has produced an unprecedented period of economic growth for some. Talk is of the "new economy" and the "long boom" if we can get through the current downturn. The challenge is to make these advances
even more pervasive in the developing world and allow
them to leapfrog over previous generations of technology.
Adding further momentum to the process is the fact that
values supportive of business and free enterprise have become more widespread. Governments are moving towards
a pragmatic blend of ideologies: they are taking a pinch of
this-ism and a pinch of that-ism, putting them into a pot
and concocting a brew that works for them.

But what of possible surprises beyond your control? We
call them key uncertainties. From your point of view, nuclear weapons landing up in the wrong hands must be at
the top of the agenda. Proliferation means aggravation, and
the knowledge of how to construct a nuclear device is now
freely available on the Internet. So it's just a matter of time
before somebody really nasty gathers the money, the materials and the engineering skills necessary to manufacture it.

You only need one terrorist organisation to hold the rich old millions to ransom by planting a hidden nuclear bomb in the middle of one city for everyone to realise that conventional military capability is useless against such a threat. An army can't find a needle in a haystack, let alone destroy it. Or it could be a rogue state which in secret develops nuclear-tipped rockets with sufficient range to reach a Western city. Incidentally, we haven't even mentioned the threat of the poor man's "nuke" – biological and chemical weapons.

The other key uncertainty that we'd worry about – if we were you – is a general disintegration of world order caused by age-old motivations of greed, power and ethnic and religious hatred. The interventions that you've recently made to keep the peace in trouble spots around the world like Somalia and the Gulf have been costly; and, increasingly, parents don't want their sons to risk their lives and health on problems which have nothing to do with the United States. The hazards associated with exposure to depleted uranium have made the Europeans equally unenthusiastic. And the United Nations has neither the money nor the clout to take on the role of global cop.

So what are the scenarios that arise from these rules of the game and key uncertainties? We'll sketch two mainframe scenarios which for convenience are named "Friendly Planet" and "Gilded Cage". In Friendly Planet the rich old millions resolve to find common ground with the poor young billions to eradicate poverty and disease, to tackle problems of the environment, to bring international criminal syndicates to justice and to root out dangerous terrorist organisations. All nations jointly agree to solve any problems which are a threat to world peace. It sounds terribly utopian, but the alternative for the rich old millions is to hole themselves up in a Gilded Cage. That cage could be blown to smithereens at any moment by nuclear-armed terrorists or be gradually overwhelmed by millions of illegal immigrants slipping through the bars to escape anarchy elsewhere. The law of entropy will prevail as nations descend to a common low.

Now we come to the options inside your control as leader of the most powerful nation in the free world. You can either turn outwards and engage in a process of constructive dialogue with a representative sample of leaders from the developing world. This leads to a set of concrete action programmes by the rich old millions which do not involve hand-outs but the empowerment of poor people to help themselves. The emphasis is on small community initiatives which induce self-sufficiency and create small circles of responsibility and accountability, rather than grand, majestic projects which increase dependency and line a few pockets. The rich also level the playing field by getting rid of their tariffs and quotas on foodstuffs and other goods imported from the developing world. Even though the US has the power to do as it pleases – remember the story of the big gorilla sleeping where he wants to – enlightened self-interest dictates that the gorilla can't have it both ways on globalisation. We don't know whether you play golf but it's like the richest members of the club giving themselves a handicap but denying everyone else in the club the right to do so. Not only is it unfair, it is counterproductive to the health and spirit of the club.

The alternative and less favourable option is that you turn inwards and try to isolate yourself from the poor young billions by making the cage you live in impenetrable to outsiders unless they are highly skilled, in which case you allow them through the bars. We know that you belong to a party which has a tendency to go this route. But human ingenuity being what it is and necessity being the mother of invention, desperately poor people will always find ways of breaching your barricades. Furthermore, the reciprocal of an isolationist strategy is that Americans will become less and less welcome in the developing world as widespread resentment over the negative impacts of globalisation turns into fury. There are plenty of social activists already fanning the flames. American tourists are notoriously twitchy about security and will therefore increasingly confine themselves to home base. There's no fun in being taken hostage while on holiday.

If you want to make a big footprint on this Earth and go down as one of the great presidents of the first century of the new millennium, think about the first option. Like the great social reformers of the late nineteenth century re-shaped industrialisation to give it a more human face, you have the chance of reshaping globalisation so that it brings more benefits to the poor young billions. It's your call, Mr President.

Yours sincerely,

Two South African Foxes.

High Road or Low Road?

We now turn to an actual scenario exercise that dates back to the mid-1980s. It concerned the possible political and economic paths that South Africa might take into the 1990s. The principal architects of the study were Michael O'Dowd and Bobby Godsell, two Anglo American employees, who in turn based their model on some original work done by a French political risk analyst, Edouard Parker.

The foremost rule of the game governing South Africa's future at the time was a simple one. Because the whites had the guns and the blacks had the numbers, no "winner-takes-all" scenario existed. If the whites hung on to power, there'd be a rising tide of violence which would be unstoppable. If the blacks tried to take the country by force, they'd fail or,

3
Options
Political – winner-takes-all
versus compromise
Economic – status quo
versus transformation

4
Decisions
Political – the High Road
Economic – ?

Uncer-tainty ← → Cer-tainty

2
(a) Key uncertainties
Strategies of power
Economic strategies
World/SA dynamic
(b) Scenarios
High Road
Low Road

1
Rules of the game
No winner-takes-all outcome
Interim need for power-sharing
Economic realities eroding
apartheid
Negotiation transforms individuals
Conditions for a winning nation
equally apply to South Africa

Absence of Control

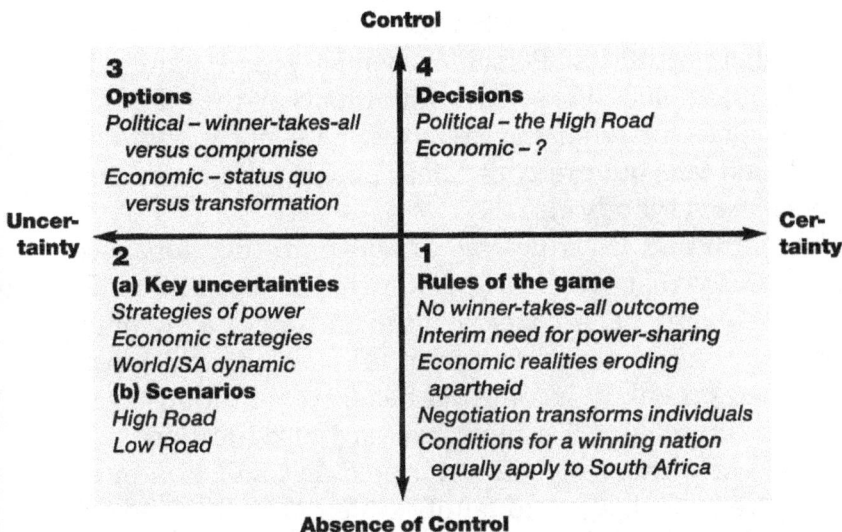

after a long struggle, inherit a wasteland. A second rule therefore followed from the first: a positive scenario could only materialise for the country if there was compromise on both sides and some interim formula for sharing power was agreed. Thereafter South Africa could, and should, evolve into a genuine, representative democracy.

The third rule related to South Africa being a modern industrialised society with comparative advantages like abundant mineral resources, cheapish power, an important trade route around its coast, beautiful tourist spots and proximity to African markets. These economic realities had already nudged companies and trade unions into power-sharing arrangements, and were undermining the last remnants of statutory apartheid. Moreover, the daily contact at work between people of all backgrounds, and the imperative of getting on with the job, pre-empted a French or Russian-type revolution. So the signs were good.

The fourth rule was an interesting psychological one. If only one could get all the parties around the negotiating table and throw away the key to the room, it would transform their attitudes. Personal chemistry and familiarity would make each side see the individuals on the other side of the table for what they really were – not devils with horns and tails but pretty ordinary people with virtues and vices like everybody else.

The fifth and last rule was drawn from the global scenario study that was being conducted in parallel to the South African one. It concerned the portrait of a "winning nation". For any nation to win in the sense of achieving a sustained growth in income per head, six conditions needed to be fulfilled: (1) a high standard of education; (2) a strong work ethic which in turn rested on small, non-intrusive government, a sound family system, low taxation and minimal corruption; (3) mobilisation of capital to satisfy the needs of the new generation of entrepreneurs; (4) a dual-logic economy in which there were positive synergies between large world-class mining, manufacturing and service industries on one hand and the small business and informal sector on the other; (5) social harmony in which minorities co-existed happily with the majority; and (6) an ambition to look outwards and be a global player. These six attributes were as applicable to South Africa as to any other nation on Earth if it wanted to succeed economically.

Against this background, three key uncertainties were identified. The first revolved around the strategies of power that might be adopted by the contending parties at the time. Would they go for winner-takes-all or would they negotiate in a spirit of give-and-take? If either side went for winner-takes-all, the other side would be compelled to follow suit. The second uncertainty related to economic strategies. Would whoever ruled in the future adopt the kind of pragmatic policies necessary to turn South Africa into a winning nation or would they go for a heavy-handed, ideological approach? The third uncertainty was the future dynamic between the world and South Africa. Would sanctions remain or would they be dropped and South Africa be welcomed back into the fold?

This produced two principal scenarios. The first was the "High Road" of negotiation leading to political settlement. This had to be followed shortly thereafter by the implementation of economic strategies which would propel South Africa to winning nation status. The "Low Road" was a story of confrontation leading to conflict and eventually a civil war which would reduce South Africa to rubble. Simple choice. Most experts at the time expected South Africa to take the Low Road because no government had ever negotiated itself out of power. In retrospect and against all odds, South Africa took the political High Road because there were outstanding individuals on all sides who put the country ahead of their personal and their party's interests. A government of national unity acted as a precursor to a fully fledged democracy. The events were amazing and unthinkable, but they illustrated the power of scenario planning, because nobody was brave enough at the time to *forecast* what actually happened. Instead, a possibility became a probability and a probability became a reality.

However, the second crossroads – the economic one – is still ahead for South Africa. Political transformation has yet to be followed by economic transformation and the common vision to give a better life to all has yet to be implemented. The foxes, namely all those young entrepreneurs who dream of starting their own businesses, are still out in the cold. This leads us to the two rules of the economic game which have to be obeyed in order to create a winning economy. The first is money times velocity (the number of hands it passes through in a year) equals price times transactions. This equation tells you two things: (1) if you just pump money into the economy without increasing economic activity (transactions), all that happens is that prices rise and inflation takes off; but (2) if you really want to light the candle of economic growth, you have to increase the velocity of circulation of money, which means pushing up the number of transactions. How do you achieve the latter? The answer is to promote the dual-logic economy referred to earlier as the fourth characteristic of a winning nation. This will involve a dynamic link between small, entrepreneurially run businesses and the existing world-class multinationals in South Africa: they buy and sell from each other as well as export overseas. The second economic rule is savings equals investment: if people don't save, you won't have capital to invest and therefore satisfy the third condition of a winning nation – mobilisation of capital. To get the public to save, you can't just *tell* them to do so. Rather you have to *induce* them through tax concessions on interest received or by offering higher interest rates on small deposits. In short, the finance minister has to be foxy too and realise that money is like manure: it's better when it's spread around a bit! And if it isn't, Karl's rule comes into play – as in Marx: when the mass of the population feel they have zero prospects, expect a revolution.

As a footnote, HIV / AIDS was picked up on the Anglo scenario team's radar screen in the mid-1980s. In those days it was described as a wild card – something that might affect South Africa's future, but nobody knew how and to what extent. Now the epidemic has been elevated to a rule of the game because it is impossible to eradicate under any scenario in the short term. The next section deals with it in more detail.

The sexual rules of the game have changed since 1965 when unsafe sex was defined as "not remembering to put the Mini's handbrake on" or "two drive-ins in a weekend". Now it is a matter of life and death. With the fall of apartheid, South Africa faces a second struggle against an enemy more formidable than any human foe because of its stealth and invisibility – HIV / AIDS.

The first two rules of the game are simple: HIV causes AIDS and, unlike other diseases, kills mainly young people who are in the prime of their life. The third rule is the lethal one in the long run. The virus has a delayed action. If it killed people immediately like the Ebola virus, preventive actions to halt its spread would be taken by society and individuals

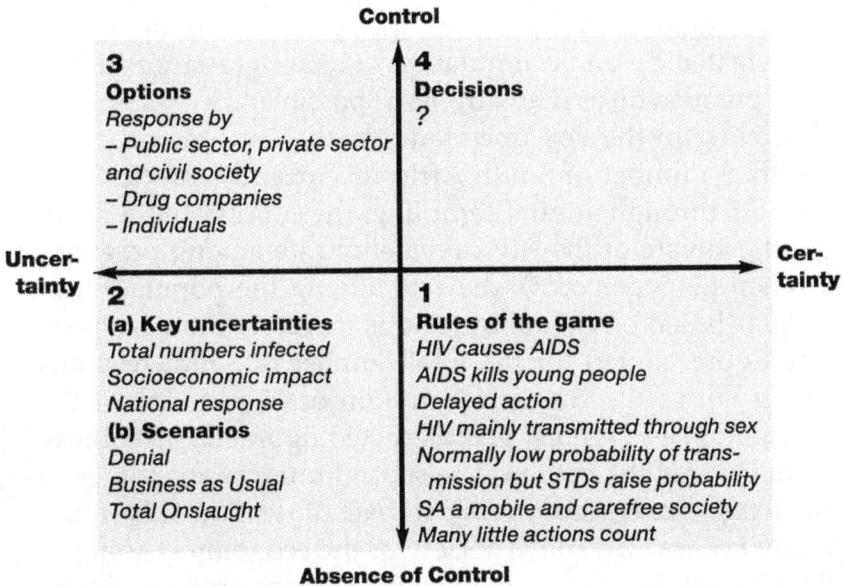

Control

3	4
Options	**Decisions**
Response by	?
– Public sector, private sector	
and civil society	
– Drug companies	
– Individuals	

Uncertainty ←→ **Certainty**

2	1
(a) Key uncertainties	**Rules of the game**
Total numbers infected	*HIV causes AIDS*
Socioeconomic impact	*AIDS kills young people*
National response	*Delayed action*
(b) Scenarios	*HIV mainly transmitted through sex*
Denial	*Normally low probability of trans-*
Business as Usual	*mission but STDs raise probability*
Total Onslaught	*SA a mobile and carefree society*
	Many little actions count

Absence of Control

alike. As it is, denial is possible until it is too late. The fourth rule is that in South Africa the virus is mainly transmitted through unsafe sex: in other countries the chief culprit is drug injection. The fifth rule is that, under normal conditions, HIV has quite a low probability of transmission. However, the sixth rule is that South Africa has a high frequency of untreated sexually transmitted diseases (STDs) like syphilis and gonorrhea; and if either sexual partner or both have an STD, the chances of transmission rise dramatically. The seventh rule is that South Africa is a mobile society with a fairly carefree attitude towards activities like drinking, driving and sex. The combination of people having multiple sexual partners dispersed over a wide geographic area with low or no use of condoms offers an ideal environment for the virus to spread. The eighth and last rule is that there is no magic bullet to turn the epidemic around. It will be defeated by an accumulation of small grassroots initiatives pursued on as many fronts as possible.

Moving to the key uncertainties, the first one concerns the total number of South Africans currently infected. Although, through annual sampling, the country has a fairly good estimate of the HIV prevalence rate among pregnant women (24,5 per cent), the rate among the population at large is based on modelling and is therefore more suspect. The figure quoted for the total number of South Africans living with HIV / AIDS is 4,7 million or 11 per cent of the population as a whole. The predicted figure in 2010 ranges from six to eight million. The second uncertainty relates to the long-term socioeconomic impact of HIV / AIDS. Nobody really knows how much society or the economy is going to be affected; but the change could be substantial and surprising. The third uncertainty – and most critical of all – is how the nation in the short term is going to respond to the challenge posed by the epidemic.

Basically, there are three scenarios. The first one is "Denial" where the nation continues to behave as though the epidemic does not exist. Eventually, the AIDS deaths rise to a level where the scenario can no longer be sustained; but meanwhile valuable time for combating HIV is lost. The second scenario is "Business as Usual". The HIV/AIDS epidemic is acknowledged as a threat, but it is not considered an important priority. Public attention is drawn to the disease whenever there is a special day or conference. Otherwise life goes on pretty much as usual, except that the number of young, gifted and dead rise remorselessly. The third scenario is "Total Onslaught" where the government, captains of industry and other influential leaders jointly declare war on the virus. It receives the highest priority in terms of money, manpower and other resources. The nation rises to the occasion with the same resolve as it would if it were invaded by a human enemy to be repelled at all costs. Victory is the only thought on everybody's mind.

The options comprise the range of actions available to government, the private sector and civil society generally. Quite simply, it boils down to where the disease stands in the national list of priorities. Will it be elevated to the No. 1 issue or will it remain a middle-order item? The kind of actions which will signify an increase in national emphasis on the epidemic are the implementation of proper HIV/AIDS prevention programmes in every primary and secondary school, university and technikon as well as on the shop floor; the availability of a voluntary counselling and testing facility to all citizens, accompanied by a wellness programme for those that test positive, and counselling for those that test negative to stay that way; the free issue of drugs to stop mother-to-child transmission; the establishment of a network of STD clinics so that people can get themselves regularly checked out and, if necessary, treated;

a support system to care for the orphans; and the intensification of the search for a vaccine. Indeed, vaccines and cures at this stage are very much wild cards. If they come about, fantastic! But don't count on them for planning purposes.

You might say that this list breaks a fundamental rule of the game, which is affordability. The answer is that each community does as much as it can on each of these fronts within the realms of affordability. Obviously, therefore, the response of drug companies is crucial. Will they cut the prices of HIV/AIDS therapies to a level where they can reach the masses? And will they assist in setting up the infrastructure necessary to administer the therapies? The other serious option is the one that can be exercised by the individual in terms of protecting his or her own body. HIV is not an airborne disease like flu: in the majority of cases of HIV transmission, it requires a conscious decision on the part of the individual to indulge in risky behaviour. The exceptions are rape, child abuse, mother-to-child transmission, blood transfusions and accidental contact involving blood. Nevertheless, as the first "A" of AIDS spells out, it is almost always *acquired*. Hence, the degree to which individuals are prepared to change their sexual habits becomes a crucial variable in how the epidemic finally pans out. And the best way to change behaviour in youngsters is to offer them options to minimise the risk of infection, rather than issue them with a specific set of instructions to do so. They need to feel that they are in control and free to choose.

So let's get up close and personal. Suppose you're lecturing your young daughter about the birds and the bees. The matrix comes in very handy. The rule of the game is simple: unprotected sex runs the risk of HIV. She can't change that – it's a biological rule, *not* a parental rule. Like crossing a rifle range when shooting is in progress, there are inherent dangers. The key uncertainty is not whether but when, where and by whom she is first going to be propositioned to have sex. The scenarios are "no"; "yes" with no consequences and "yes" with consequences. Her options are to abstain with no risk of transmission; have protected sex which reduces the chances of transmission; or just do it which carries a big health warning. You love her and in no way wish to diminish her joys of discovering love and sex for herself. Moreover, no-one else has the same interest in protecting her body as she does. She is in control, and thus has every right to choose from amongst the three options. Eventually, when she settles down with a partner she trusts, she can choose differently. Nevertheless, in the meantime if you were her, your decision would be to abstain, abstain, abstain, but in a *sexual emergency* insist on a condom. And if any sugar daddy should approach her with predatory intentions, here's a whistle for her to blow. You'll come running to rescue her from his clutches!

Now we must revert to the national situation and examine the fourth quadrant of the matrix on page 127. It is one big question mark. Who knows what decisions will be taken and which scenarios will materialise? We don't. But the future is not, as they say in the classics, "in the lap of the gods". It will be determined by individual South Africans.

Cinderella Rockefeller

Imagine you are Cinderella – the poor sister. But there is no grand ball to dress up for, no glass slipper to be lost, no prince to discover it and seek whom it fits. Yet you are struck with this burning ambition to overtake your ugly sisters and leave them breathing in your dust. What do you do? The answer for today's confident modern maiden is: open up your own business. What advice can the matrix give you so that one day you're as rich as Rockefeller?

The first rule of the game surrounds the eight characteristics of being world class. Given globalisation, no matter how small you are, you will probably be facing world-class competition – if not in the form of a company like Coca-Cola, then in the form of a franchise like McDonald's. So you have to shape up or ship out. Therefore the No. 1 characteristic is passion. You must choose something you're passionate about because you're probably better at pursuing your passion than doing other things. The question is how you turn that passion into a commercial opportunity. Once you've settled on a line of business, focus is the second characteristic and being different or unique in some way is the third. Collecting a team of like-minded talented young people, usually old school chums, around you is the fourth characteristic and studying global practice is the fifth. The sixth is never to give up on innovation of your product or service, while the seventh is to have an in-built

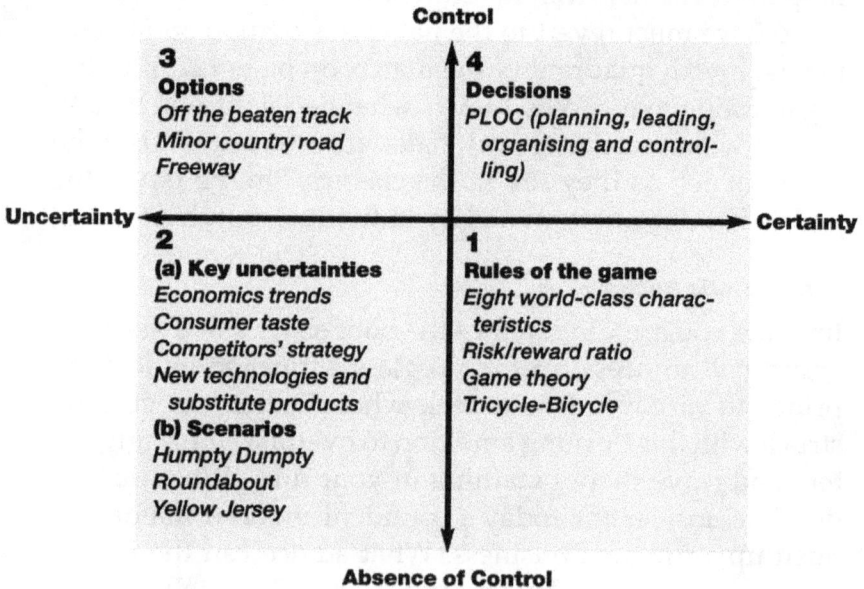

Control

3
Options
Off the beaten track
Minor country road
Freeway

4
Decisions
PLOC (planning, leading,
*   organising and control-*
*   ling)*

Uncertainty ←——————————————→ **Certainty**

2
(a) Key uncertainties
Economics trends
Consumer taste
Competitors' strategy
New technologies and
*   substitute products*
(b) Scenarios
Humpty Dumpty
Roundabout
Yellow Jersey

1
Rules of the game
Eight world-class charac-
*   teristics*
Risk/reward ratio
Game theory
Tricycle-Bicycle

Absence of Control

radar system picking up on opportunities and threats. Last but by no means least – and remembering all we said earlier – you have to be ethical in all senses of the word and to all stakeholders.

The second rule of the game concerns the potential risks and rewards associated with the business you've selected. If you recall our pleasure and pain curve, you have to ask yourself what kind of loss you can stomach should things go wrong. Then you have to tailor-make your start-up cost so that it does not exceed your limit, or find others to share the risk with you before you go ahead. In the latter case, it's better to go for venture capital in the form of equity rather than debt. A wonderful initiative in America is the Tuesday Forum where, on the first Tuesday of every month, venture capital seekers and providers meet at a suitable venue to matchmake. While you're raising capital you need to re-member that statistically the first few businesses are usual-ly failures before you hit the right button; thus the need to keep some funds in reserve to try again.

The third rule of the game relates to game theory which we've already explained. What are other competitors likely to do when you enter the market and how can you counter their response?

For the fourth rule, remember the old adage "don't run before you can walk" and transfer it to the world of cycling. It becomes "don't graduate to two wheels before you've learnt to ride on three". A tricycle has three wheels posi-tioned in a triangular configuration designed for maximum stability in order to supply balance for a beginner. In the case of a first-time entrepreneur, the front wheel represents the strategy which gives direction to a business. The two back wheels are the operating efficiencies and financial con-trols which provide stability to ensure that the business is sustainable. However, as the business grows, so the need becomes apparent for the original founder to back off from personally doing everything on the ground and become a manager of other people doing these tasks. This involves a different set of skills and the acceptance of a hierarchy, which causes the organisation to shift from a horizontal to a vertical structure. The equivalent is graduating from a tricycle to a bicycle where the front wheel is still strategy and the back wheel is a combination of operational and financial systems required to manage the business. The entrepreneur is now the manager perched on the elevated seat striving to keep the bicycle balanced as it rounds bends and jumps on bumps in the road. The cycling analogy explains why so many start-ups fail. Either one of the wheels of the tricycle is missing to start with, causing it to overturn; or the entrepreneur is like the kid who graduates too fast to the bicycle stage, then takes his hands off the handlebars and says "look, Ma, no hands" as he heads into the bush!

The key uncertainties awaiting your new-born business are daunting. The first is the immediate future of the economy, and specifically your market, after you've opened your doors. We're afraid to say that good timing is more a matter of luck than anything else, because market turning-points are usually unpredictable. Then there's the question of customer taste. They say there's no accounting for taste and it's fickle at the best of times: one moment you're in fashion, the next you're not. So you continuously need something new up your sleeve. If that's not enough, competitors can pull surprising moves out of the hat just when you've settled down; and new technologies can come along which make your product obsolete by offering cheaper or better substitutes. All these uncertainties demonstrate the need for a radar system to detect incoming missiles!

What are the scenarios for your business? Basically three. The first is "Humpty Dumpty". Your business falls off the wall fairly early on and neither you, nor your friends, nor your bankers can put it back together again. The second scenario is "Roundabout". Your business survives but it never gets beyond the survivalist stage either because you are not steering your tricycle properly on account of having no strategy; or because your back wheels aren't balanced and you lack the combination of operational efficiency and financial control. The third scenario is "Yellow Jersey" which implies long-term success, seeing that this is the jersey that the ultimate winner of the Tour de France cycling race wears as he collects his prize. You don't have to win individual stages but the race overall. The same applies in business: rather than focusing on short-term increases in market share or the quarterly financial results, the entrepreneur with the yellow jersey aims to grow shareholder value in the long term. Endurance – rather than the ability to make short sprints – is what really counts.

Bearing in mind these scenarios, we now move on to the top half of the matrix to examine the options that you can choose between. The first is to go off the beaten track and open up an entirely original business. However, you need an organisation behind you as sturdy as a mountain bike to withstand all the ridges, rocks and ditches presenting themselves en route. The second option is to take a minor country road and start a more conventional business which basically caters for the local market. There will still be the odd pothole and corrugation in the road to give you an occasional shock. But now you have to be wary of other traffic and in particular other entrepreneurial cyclists who may try to overtake you as you reach your business destination. The third option is to cycle up on to the freeway, advertise yourself on the Internet and carve out a global niche. The caution you have to exercise here is to stay away from freeways which can only be used by vehicles of the four-wheel kind, namely bigger businesses that can achieve greater economies of scale than you can. Moreover, the bicycles which are likely to pass you now are the ultra-light racing ones ridden by ultra-fit guys in lycra bodysuits and streamlined helmets. Standards are much higher in the international arena!

At this point, you make your selection; and we can't make it for you. But as we've said all along, it's one thing to make a decision and quite another to get the result. Here, the PLOC principle comes into play – planning, leading, organising and controlling. The plan is the chain of decisions and the resources required to turn the idea into a commercial reality. Leadership is what you have to display to get all your troops facing in the right direction and to persuade those not under your command but nevertheless vital for the success of the project, like financiers and suppliers, to give you their whole-hearted support. Organisation and control are the two back wheels of the tricycle. When you get more experienced, they are combined in the back wheel of your bicycle. They ensure that your business remains balanced even when you hit a rough patch or the wind blows straight into your face.

So, good luck, Cinderella! Maybe you'll lure a prince into matrimony one day because you're worth a fortune. Then you'll live happily ever after in a castle you purchased off the Internet.

Crouching Tiger, Winning Fox

Time flies like the wind: fruit flies like bananas! We hope time has flown for you; and you have had as much fun reading this book as we have had in writing it. We have touched many bases; unashamedly mixed our metaphors such as Tiger crouching over his putt as a winning fox; and produced our own miniseries of Apollo 13. With all the means at our disposal, we have tried to convince you to become a resourceful fox. We want you to be as bold and quick-witted as the fox which, when captured the other day by a hound at a hunt, dragged the hound into a nearby lake in the hope of getting him to let go. A huntsman came to the rescue of both animals, and they lived to fight another day. The huntsman bowed to the fox in respect as it disappeared through the hedge.

Even as you set yourself BHAGs (big, hairy, audacious goals), you often need the nimbleness and flexibility of mind to switch to Plan B to make them happen. Our matrix hopefully prepares you for the unexpected as well as those parts of your life which resemble a roller-coaster ride – when you feel there are powerful forces that are outside your control taking you up to the crest, keeping you hovering in suspense for a few heart-stopping moments before sending you careering down the other side. There are always things you *can* do – like holding on tightly in this case and screaming if you must!

Charles Kingsley made the following remark in his enchanting tale about a young chimney sweep called Tom who joined the Water Babies in the stream: "The most wonderful and the strongest things in the world, you know, are just the things which no one can see." He furnished "life" as an example in that it makes you grow, move and think – and yet you can't see it. Kingsley's quote is as true today as it was in 1863 when he wrote it. Accordingly, you will have noticed how much emphasis we have laid on obeying the invisible, unwritten rules of the game if you want to succeed. Breaking the rules sounds exciting when you're young and naturally rebellious. But it doesn't lead to progress except when the rules are somehow flawed in the first place.

Hence, it is worth following in the footsteps of Mrs Doasyouwouldbedoneby who personified the rules of being a good fairy and gently taught Tom to obey them. Otherwise, you may suffer the dismal fate of the nation of Doasyoulikes who broke every rule in the book and ended up with extinction.

There's a Jewish expression which embodies a similar outlook on life as Kingsley's: you can divide the people in this world into those who would hide you in their loft and those who wouldn't. The selfless and the rest.

On a different note, the film *American Beauty* demonstrated that dysfunctional families are *the* invisible rule of the game in Suburbia; and we should be thankful for the odd moment of peace and tranquillity. So much for progress in the real world. But then foxes do accept that we live in a state of imperfection, and we must make the best out of it.

We also want you to be curious like a fox. It's okay: curiosity only killed the cat. Foxes go through open doors to see what's on the other side; but their nose is twitching and they are ready to turn tail if the adventure becomes too exciting. Opportunistic on the one hand, they are survivalists at heart on the other: remember what we said about keeping opposites in mind. An immensely rich and eminent fox was once asked whether he preferred diamonds or gold. His response was diamonds because woman's vanity would outlast man's greed: diamonds *are* forever! Foxes are neither too vain nor too greedy. They know that vanity dulls the keenness of their senses; and greed distorts their power of reasoning. The same fox commented once that real wealth was acquired through owning, not working. With this in mind, we put in the piece on owning and running a small business because, you never know, you might hit the jackpot and become supersonically rich yourself. The terms "foxy" and "entrepreneurial" are pretty much interchangeable. Yet, you will recall that we talked a lot about values. Social foxes who make a difference in other people's lives are needed just as much as business foxes in this world. Our matrix is as applicable to an NGO striving to do its charitable thing as it is to a company trying to deliver value to its shareholders.

Foxes are trusting creatures, especially of their own kith and kin. However, they have a healthy scepticism of hedgehogs and statistics. In the latter regard, a foxy environmentalist recently quipped that 87 per cent of all statistics are made up on the spur of the moment! This leads us to two themes we have consistently pursued throughout the book: (1) you only get at the truth by discarding all the falsehoods along the way and (2) you only know what you do control when you have learnt about the things that you don't control. We could have called the book *The Heresies of Hedgehogs* and then gone on to prove that the mind of a fox is superior to that of a hedgehog. It would have borne out the first principle! Rather, though, we have followed the injunction of Brother William of Baskerville, who said in Umberto Eco's *The Name of the Rose*: "Perhaps the mission of those who love mankind is to make people laugh at the truth, *to make truth laugh*, because the only truth lies in learning to free ourselves from insane passion for the truth." Anyway, history reveals that a fraction of "heretics" like Copernicus and Galileo are proved right in the long run.

Thus, we readily admit that our matrix is not a perfect, all-inclusive answer to how you should handle the future. But it is a sufficiently close reflection of the way we *naturally* think for us to believe that it serves a useful purpose. In other words, we have tried to make explicit the internal thought processes we instinctively go through when facing a challenging situation. We've also tried to give the technique of scenario planning a shot in the arm by putting it in its proper context in the chain of reasoning that leads to a good decision. We are sure that one day scenario planning will take its rightful place alongside strategic planning as an essential management tool. Common sense dictates it in a world of accelerating change and increasing discontinuity. Moreover, although we've been pretty negative about hedgehogs throughout this book, they have every right to exist and a society without them would be the poorer for their absence. So we are not asking the whole world to become foxes. After all, hedgehogs with a penchant for stability and order offset the slightly anarchical tendencies of foxes.

However, we would suggest that it is better by far to think like a fox, particularly in these uncertain times. It is not that Peter Drucker's concept of management by objectives – the very foundation of American management thinking for the last half of the previous century – is wrong. It is incomplete. When the future resembled the past as it did in the 1950s and 1960s and less so in the 1970s and 1980s, you could set objectives and measure your performance against those objectives. But now we live in a world where millions, or maybe billions, of people have instantaneous access to information and, more importantly, breaking news. When changes happen, particularly in markets, they can be of such a magnitude that they turn all the assumptions on which you have based your objectives upside down – just like that. Management by objectives does not allow for this, as it is firmly located in our fourth quadrant: get experts in to analyse the uncertainty out of the future and assume that you have total control to achieve the objectives specified. Alas, things aren't so neat now and you simply cannot operate like that anymore. In the current environment, strategic thinking must be seen less as a process of gazing into a crystal ball to determine your long-term future and more as a way of preparing yourself for any eventuality that may come your way. Flexibility in thinking is the important outcome. However, a sensitivity to what should remain the same and you should be steadfast about is also crucial. Foxes strive to find the right balance. Regular visits to all four quadrants of our matrix are therefore essential to ensure that you have set the most appropriate objectives in the first place and that you review them in a logical manner as the fog enveloping the future clears.

And you can be wrong! Then at least you have the means to analyse why you went wrong. It could be that you misidentified a rule of the game; or you didn't capture a key uncertainty or surprise; or you bet on the wrong scenario. Or even that you implemented the decision wrong. The matrix should never be put in the bottom drawer of the desk like a strategic plan. It is a compass to negotiate your way through the fog and make course corrections as necessary.

Do you recall Winnie-the-Pooh, A. A. Milne's Bear of Very Little Brain? He felt that "a Thing which seemed very Thingish inside you is quite different when it gets out into the open and has other people looking at it". Scenario planners want to bring our unconscious prejudices to the surface so that we can acknowledge them and look at the forces driving the world in an unvarnished way. The masters of the scenario game – Herman Kahn, Pierre Wack, Ted Newland, Peter Schwartz and Edouard Parker – all leave you with a feeling that, by removing the filters, they have opened up a brand new world of possibilities. You'll get the same feeling from reading *The Tipping Point* by Malcolm Gladwell in which he explains how little things can make a big difference. A fox after our own hearts! Once you delve into his book, you'll never view epidemics in the same light again. Well, we want our matrix to be contagious too so that it assists people to reperceive the future in a way that works better for them.

The proof is in the pudding. We've tried the matrix out in seminars that we have facilitated and it has worked like a charm. It brings fresh angles to the debate around the table. More importantly, it brings people from disparate backgrounds together – managers, union representatives, public servants, local community leaders, etc. – and binds them more closely to one another because they are all involved in formulating the content of the matrix. The spontaneity and interaction of the group as each person builds on the ideas of others means that the final picture cannot be predicted in advance. Indeed, we recommend minimal preparation in advance of a scenario planning session. Moreover, at the end of it all, no-one is under any illusion about the real rules of the game governing the activity in which he or she is a participant. This makes subsequent negotiations easier because they will take place within a common framework of understanding.

Laird Hamilton is still alive today because he is familiar with the matrix. He is the king of big wave surfing and knows just how many factors are completely beyond his control in heavy seas. Yet he has revolutionised surfing with two modifications within his control: putting straps on the board to bind the feet and being towed by a jet ski instead of paddling to catch the waves initially. In the extremest of extreme sports where waves can reach the monstrous height of ten metres, he survives because he is smart.

But try the matrix for yourself. Try it in your personal life when you next have to make a difficult decision about people, money or a job. Try it when considering the opening up of your own business. Try it in your company at your next annual strategic get-together.

And may the fox be with you!

Postscript

Whatever path the future takes, the "rich old millions" are going to spend more time in Quadrant 2 of our matrix (where things are uncertain and beyond their control) and less time in Quadrant 4 (where things are certain and under their thumb). Hence the relevance of our book: making people think more like foxes and less like hedgehogs.

The signs of looming trouble have been there, now that our ability to destroy ourselves far outstrips our ability to preserve ourselves. Moreover, the idea that mutually assured destruction acts as a deterrent is as obsolete as the two-superpower model for which it was devised. Something more constructive has to replace it.

In a book published in 1992 with the title *The New Century**, one of us wrote the following: "Against that [the containment of any future war through joint action by America and Russia] the odds of a nuclear exchange are increasing as the knowledge of producing ballistic missiles and nuclear warheads disseminates through the Third World (the nuclear risk also applies to any conflict between Pakistan and India over disputed territory on their borders).

"The growth of fundamentalist Islam poses a serious challenge to Western lifestyles and values. This in itself is not a geopolitical problem. It only becomes one if attempts are made by zealots to impose Islam on countries wishing to pursue other paths of development. The attractions to the 'poor young billions' of a religion based on the strict code of the Koran are obvious. It anchors their existence in spiritual certainties when all is flux around them; it gives a clear sense of purpose in a world that for many has no meaning

*Clem Sunter, *The New Century* (p. 129 and p. 145), published by Human & Rousseau/Tafelberg, Cape Town, 1992.

whatsoever; and it abhors materialism, a quality the poor do not possess anyway through force of circumstance. The Middle East, Pakistan, the southern republics of the former Soviet Union and northern Africa are all falling under the spell of fundamentalist Islam. That is a formidable area of influence. How much further it will spread and at what rate is unknown. Equally unknown is whether the spreading of an idea will degenerate into a war of beliefs. A nuclear *jihad* is not out of the question. Fundamentalist Islam is a wild card with the ability to alter the balance of power in important parts of the world."

Later on in the book, the author added: "The arms trade, especially the movement of ballistic missiles, chemical weapons, biological weapons and nuclear devices must be very strictly controlled. Where possible, the weapons should be destroyed."

Chilling stuff – considering the lack of control we have now. If there is a nuclear exchange, where does the radioactive fall-out caused by the detonation of the bombs end up? For example, the fall-out from the accident at the Chernobyl nuclear power plant reached as far up as Scandinavia. In times like these, you have to play scenarios to capture all the possible consequences. We cannot choose when we are born and – for most of us – when we die. Nevertheless, we can choose *how* we live in the epoch allotted to us. Let us choose, each in our own way, to work towards a Friendly Planet and avert such desperate consequences.

Games
FOXES
Play

Planning for
***Extraordinary* Times**

I Can't . . . or Can I?

Four things I'd been better without
Love, curiosity, freckles and doubt.
DOROTHY PARKER

How often do you change your mind? What causes you to change it? Perhaps a newspaper article, except we tend to read newspapers which accord with our views. Maybe an office memorandum, except they are usually as dull as ditchwater and are ignored unless they contain an implied threat. Actually, it is not easy to change somebody's mind with the written word. Occasionally, a book comes along, like *Animal Farm* by George Orwell, that can do the job. But think about conversation. *That* can change your mind, especially if it is with people you trust and respect. Their gestures, intonations and emotions add strength to the content of what they are saying. You respond. There is an interplay in which you are an active participant. As a consequence, your opinions of people and the future can change. Your views on politics and the economy might also be amended, though less frequently and perhaps to a lesser degree. On the other hand, your moral and religious beliefs may never be swayed either by the written or spoken word.

This book is about conversation. Indeed, we introduce a model later on which serves as an agenda for a strategic conversation. Any organisation can use it to change its mindset. 'Change management' is what some people call it, but to get people to manage differently, you have to change their minds

159

first. Attitudinal shift precedes behavioural change. You will also be introduced to some people who never change their mind. They have an idea and that's it. We call them 'hedgehogs'. The majority of Americans love leaders like that – look at the result of the presidential election in 2004. *Time* named the successful candidate as its person of the year. In fact, the 'hedgehog model' underpins much of the management theory taught at Ivy League business schools in the US. There's even a smash hit in business literature suggesting that only hedgehogs convert from good to great leaders.

But don't you smell a rat here? On the one hand, we are deluged with books on change, change, change, and on the other hand, we are told that real champions don't change their minds. So our favourite animal is not a hedgehog, not a rat, but a fox. The rest of the book is about them. 'Foxes' do change their minds – when they realise they are wrong about something or something better exists out there. Against devout hedgehogs like Thatcher, Reagan and George W. Bush stand foxes like Nelson Mandela and F. W. de Klerk. If they hadn't changed their minds, South Africa would never have experienced the miracle that it did. They compromised. By compromising, they won the game.

Thirdly, this book is about games, the games foxes play. Playing games is second nature to all of us. We learn from early childhood how to play games. In fact, life is a game. You're born, you play the game once, then you die. Unless you believe in reincarnation. In which case, depending on how you performed, you come back as an eagle, a rat . . . or a lawyer!

There's been a methodology around for years, at the heart of which lies game playing. It's called scenario planning. Each scenario is a possible outcome to the game. You weigh up the consequences, then you make a move. The military uses this technique. A few businesses do too. But the best example is a country that used scenario planning to improve the quality of its conversation about the future – South Africa. Back to those foxes! They were the transition generation. You can say that South Africans are natural foxes. So are scenario planners. They all have the ability to change their minds; and change other people's minds as well. Where else than in South Africa would you find ex-Marxists and trade unionists becoming chairmen of some of the foremost companies in the land?

I can't . . . or can I? Thank heavens, Dorothy Parker admitted to curiosity and doubt. She was a fox, even though she wanted to be a freckle-less hedgehog.

Anyone for a game?

"'Tis all a Chequer-board of Nights and Days
Where Destiny with Men for Pieces plays:
Hither and thither moves, and mates and slays,
And one by one back in the Closet lays."
RUBÁIYÁT OF OMAR KHAYYÁM

There is a royal and ancient game that for centuries was the enviable pursuit of princes and noblemen, but which has, over the past hundred years, found a home in the heart of the common man (and woman). It demands of the player a passion and precision of movement that can become all-encompassing. The game is, in essence, played as an individual pursuit. However, there is a regular occasion when a team from America finds itself up against the might of Europe, when old hands play shoulder to shoulder with future stars in a genial, yet ruthless, display of mastery of this seemingly genteel game. Each time these teams compete against each other, the battlefield is littered with the stripped confidence of icons and the shattered aspirations of Young Turks; and it is virtually guaranteed that the Americans will lose.

No, it's not the Ryder Cup and golf. It's that other courteous blood sport – chess. Not in the same league you might say when it comes to capturing public attention; but the event we are about to describe made it to the front page of the *Wall Street Journal*. Every year since 1978, member countries of the North Atlantic Treaty Organisation have converged on a venue to compete in the ultimate game of strategy and tactics. Soldiers and civilians, representing some of the finest minds of the Western military establishment, battle it out in what is the only international military chess competition in the world. To some people this may sound a little quaint; but the fact remains that the current world economic, social and political landscape has been shaped by centuries of conflict, often driven by leaders who honed their strategic and tactical abilities playing chess. Napoleon, for example, was a strong player of the game, and Prince Grigori Potemkin, whose conquests expanded the borders of the Russian empire in the eighteenth century, was so addicted to the game that he often commanded junior officers to engage in games of chess in front of him so that he could study the strategies that unfolded.

What is interesting about this annual NATO military chess tournament is that America, which dominates the alliance in most other ways, never seems to do all that well, and Germany invariably emerges the victor. The success of Germany is normally attributed to that country's universal conscription of eighteen-year-old males into its armed forces. Their diverse background provides a wide range of playing strategies. The failure of the American military chess team to win has generally been explained by the relative unpopularity of chess in that country, and the fact that most of its leading players are involved in real combat around the world. However, Germany's dominance in the tournament is about to be challenged by the inclusion of former Warsaw Pact countries into NATO. This move will introduce exciting new teams of players who promise to raise the level of the game, because they grew up under the shadow of the Russian chess super-power next door. Against that, America and Britain's performance will probably improve over time. Why's that? Madonna and Harry Potter have taken up the game and increased its popularity among children.

The Ancient Greek term *strategos* originally denoted a commander-in-chief (or chief magistrate) in Athens. Its meaning then mutated into the art that person was supposed to possess, namely the art of projecting and directing the larger military movements and operations of a campaign. Strategy, as the word is known in English today, is very much part of the vocabulary of military leaders. On one occasion, George W. Bush described his job of Commander-in-Chief of the US Armed Forces as setting the strategic direction in Iraq and ensuring that the generals were given the resources *they* estimated were required for the job. Strategy has also developed into a corporate buzzword used by CEOs.

Strangely though, the chess analogy has not crossed from the war room to the boardroom. Nor has the concept of games generally.

For example, we talk of war games but seldom if ever mention business games – and certainly not business chess. Perhaps the reason for this is that generals know before they go into battle that there are a whole set of conditions over which they have no control and about which they have little knowledge other than what military intelligence has gathered (and we know how reliable that can be!) So they play games and simulate the different paths the battle can take. If the enemy does this, we'll respond in this way, and if the enemy does that, we'll respond with a different tactic. Alternatively, if we initiate a particular battle plan, how will the enemy respond and what are the consequences of each response and how will we counter-respond?

Maybe the cause of the lack of this kind of reasoning (or rather imagination) in the boardroom is that businesses are out to make money, and prefer to do their own thing in meeting this goal. They see themselves as an island in the sea of the market. They aren't overly adversarial to other players unless they have to be, and it is not a matter of life and death. Yes, they may have to take out a few competitors on the way; but it is not the prime purpose of business to defeat the enemy. So, unlike the military, they feel no need to play games to figure out the nature of the competitors' response. CEOs, moreover, feel much more in control in the business world than generals in a war situation because they are not subject to the extremely rude awakenings that war sometimes has to offer. They don't have thousands of unnecessary casualties to contend with if their strategy proves incorrect. They lead relatively pampered lives away from the field of operations. In fact, the nearest they get to a declaration of war is a hostile takeover bid.

The control paradigm in business is further intensified by the linear strategic planning techniques offered by many of the great business schools in America and Europe. The common thread running through these techniques is: select a single set of assumptions; base your plan on those assumptions; then mobilise your troops in support of the plan. Such an approach is actually far removed from the methods now taught at West Point and Sandhurst to cope with today's security threats. On top of that, management consultancies tend to make control and certainty a centrepiece of the particular formula they want to peddle, on the basis that clients pay for precise answers to their problems. They know, like doctors, that their clients don't want 'iffy' advice. Then, overlaying the business schools and consultancies are the 'Billy

Grahams' of business – the immaculately frightful televangelists who twice a year conduct global seminars by satellite and whose stock in trade is oozing confidence about their particular message.

Gurus can't appear doubtful about the future – at least not in public!

The ironic result of all this is that military personnel are much better trained to handle surprises and uncertainty than their business executive counterparts. They are humbler in their expectations but nimbler in their responses. Business whiz kids often think of themselves as smarter than the stuffy breed of person who joins the army, particularly as the former are paid so much more. In reality, many of those kids – particularly the ones who have MBAs – simply don't possess the degree of flexibility (or mental agility) required in war games. The more confident they are, the more linear their approach tends to be in assessing the future. They don't change their minds. Instead, they focus on the short term because that's where their bonuses direct them to look. They forget the old acronym: one battle does not win the war (though it's a heck of a lot better than losing the battle).

Hence the reason for this book – to introduce military-type thinking to business people. Not of the command / control kind, which is the stuff of the thousands of motivational epics which land on the bookshelves each year. No, we're more interested in the games, the scenarios, the risks, the show-stopping discontinuities that are now part and parcel of the world at war as well as the world at peace. Think of the American Marines and the British Special Air Services or the SAS. When they're called in for an assault on an enemy position, they have scale models, they have an understanding of the modus operandi and probable behaviour of the enemy, they visit every scenario over and over again in their game plan. Nevertheless, they know the limits to their knowledge and are ready to adapt spontaneously to any completely unexpected development.

We are qualified to give this alternative picture. In our last book, *The Mind of a Fox*, published in June 2001, we offered a very specific world-view to George W. Bush in the first months of his first term as US president. In an open letter to him, we painted a picture of a world increasingly divided, a world in which the nature of war had changed completely, where terrorist groups could basically build a nuke off the internet; where his prime risk was a massive terrorist strike on a Western city, and where the strategies and tactics to win a war on terror were totally different to those employed in conventional warfare.

We received an interesting comment from an American woman who bought our book at the airport to read on an overnight flight to New York on September 10, 2001. She finished it before she went to sleep, and subsequently recalled that the only thing she thought was ridiculously over the top was our suggestion that terrorism could redefine George Bush's presidency (the word was only mentioned once in the lead-up to the 2000 election). Then she woke up to the announcement that the plane was being diverted because of the terrorist strike. The rest, as they say, is history.

The 9/11 Commission in Washington recently reported that the principal reason for the intelligence agencies failing to detect the plot beforehand was a 'failure of imagination'. We imagined it – albeit using a scenario of nukes being planted in the middle of a city as opposed to planes being flown into tall buildings. We were vaguely right because we never underestimated the sophistication and patience of modern terrorist organisations, combined with a deep resentment and religious hatred of the West. And it's much better being vaguely right than precisely wrong. That's where games are central to envisioning the future. Interestingly,

Rudy Giuliani – the mayor of New York at the time of 9/11 – confirms this approach with his phrase 'relentless preparation'. All the emergency service departments in New York had gone through the drills for a plane crash in the city (one had even been simulated). So even though no one imagined planes being used as missiles to hit buildings, the evacuation and fire drills were similar to a plane crash and saved thousands of lives on the day. In other words, the exact scenario does not have to materialise for the process to pay off.

At this juncture, we feel obliged to point out some significant differences between games and the real world. In a game of chess, for example, the rules never change. Bishops move diagonally, rooks horizontally and vertically, and victory is achieved when the king is checkmated. In life, only the moral rules don't change. All the other rules can and do change and have to be examined before moves can be contemplated. And the meaning of victory in a field like business can differ from person to person. In chess, the gameboard never changes shape and will always have 64 squares, half white, half black. In business, you can change the shape of the gameboard yourself and so can your opponent. The number of squares can grow or shrink; and irrationality, emotion, greed, fear, envy and anger can turn the colours of the squares into every shade of the rainbow. The whole gameboard can even be tipped over temporarily by external events like the bombing in Bali. In chess, the players move the pieces. In the real world, the pieces can take on a life of their own and resist being pushed around if they feel it is not in their best interest – like nonaligned nations and employees.

All in all, business is much more complicated than chess, and demands greater imagination. Business strategy is therefore more of an art than a science (just like war). It is not a game to be played by planners who are solely analysts and believe that the future is a projection of the past. The future is never like the past, because there is always something new, something different. The gift of intuition, the gift of capturing the extraordinary, are therefore vital ingredients in playing successfully on life's gameboard. These are talents that foxes possess – but more of that anon.

Straight talk about strategy

In politics, the path from A to B is never straight.
It almost always goes through C, D or F.
L. PAUL BREMER

During Victorian times, travelling abroad was a real mission. It was not simply a case of weighing anchor and setting sail, it was about planning for a major adventure. So it was a strategic decision to go overseas and choose a foreign destination. Subsequently a series of disciplined tactical manoeuvres had to be executed in order to implement the strategy: what coach to take you from home to the harbour; where to stay before embarkation; which ship to be a passenger on; when best to sail; what provisions to take in addition to the ship's own fare; what medications to pack, etc. (the choice in those days was fairly limited and certainly did not include seasick pills). For the captain of the ship, the operational decisions that needed to be made in order to arrive at the destination were somewhat grander: what provisions to take for the entire complement of crew and passengers, what to do if extreme weather conditions prevailed, at which ports to replenish stocks, what spares to have on board during the voyage, etc.

The sailing metaphor is a useful one to explain the difference between *strategy* and *tactics*. Strategy is about where you are going. Tactics is about how to get there (including logistics). Once you've set off on the voyage, there are only two strategic decisions you can make: change the ultimate destination or cancel the journey altogether and go home. Everything else is tactics. If you stray off course on account of difficult weather, getting back on course is a tactic. If you are becalmed, how to ration the food is a tactic. If you are in danger of being attacked by pirates, steering clear of them is a tactic. Make no mistake, being an expert tactician is as important as being an expert strategist. If you're a bad tactician, you can sail the boat into the rocks and lose all life and goods on board. But they are different functions.

An old nineteenth-century saying sums it up quite well: "Strategy differs materially from tactic; the latter belonging only to the mechanical movement of bodies, set in motion by the former." In other words, a handful of strategic decisions determine all future operational decisions. Yet so many businesses confuse strategy with tactics. They spend three days having a strategic workshop of which a couple of hours are spent on strategy and the rest of the time on operational matters which are totally subsidiary to strategy. We have found that in the largest of companies a genuine strategic conversation covering *all* the bases and unearthing the deepest issues need take no longer than four to five hours, on average a day or, comfortably stretching it, two days. The topic is after all about the commanding heights of the business and there the landscape is relatively simple, with only a few issues needing resolution.

Understandably, it makes sense to have this type of strategic conversation before the start of the normal annual planning cycle, the purpose of which is to put together next year's production targets and budget. The latter constitute the steps on the road to the company's long-term destiny, so it is prudent to have a discussion about where the road

169

leads beforehand. Nevertheless, as you will see later on, we do make accommodation in our strategic conversation model for some discourse on tactics. This acts as a warm-up for the operational planning meetings and sets some broad parameters for them. In addition, we want to ensure that the strategy session doesn't end up in a haze of hot air where nobody is going to pick up on anything afterwards. So many strategy workshops are instantly forgotten as soon as people return to the office. They remember the parties in the evening and the chat in the pub, but nothing more.

In conversations around strategy, one could say that the best strategists are the marksmen of the boardroom – the archers who put their fingers to the wind before drawing back their bow (absorbing the context before letting the arrow fly). They understand the meaning of the catch phrase 'ready . . . aim . . . fire'. 'Aim' is strategy and 'fire' the tactics. It sounds logical, but it is often implemented the other way around. Many businesses, especially those run by brash young entrepreneurs, indulge in 'ready . . . fire . . . aim'. That is, they rush into action and then dream up the rationalisation afterwards. It's okay if by some fluke you hit the target, but wild misses are the normal result. A case of hubris, then nemesis. Apologies all round. Reload. And the worst thing is implementing a winning tactic in the short run, only to find that it triggers a response which is totally unanticipated and ruins your strategy in the long run. It's called the law of unintended consequences.

On the opposite side of the fence, other businesses, especially those with a penchant for an excessively bureaucratic or participative style of management, end up in an everlasting cycle of "ready . . . aim . . . have a workshop . . . aim . . . have a conference . . . aim . . . have a summit . . . aim . . . and if all else fails, bring in the consultants and establish a subcommittee of the board . . . aim . . ." They never fire because they never establish a target to aim at. They don't change their minds. They never make their minds up!

These last two approaches to strategy are obviously wrong. The right approach can be summed up in the following diagram, which hopefully hits home:

Chart 1 *The Shooting Range*

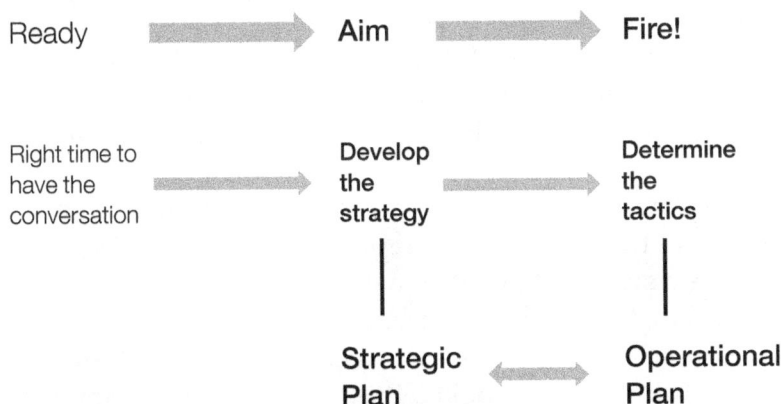

Ready $\Longrightarrow$ Aim $\Longrightarrow$ Fire!

| Right time to have the conversation | $\Longrightarrow$ | Develop the strategy | $\Longrightarrow$ | Determine the tactics |

Strategic Plan $\longleftrightarrow$ Operational Plan

However, there is one thing that's incorrect about this diagram, which is very difficult to represent on paper. When looking at the future, you're always shooting at a moving target. The dynamics can change just like that. So ahead of pulling the trigger or releasing the bowstring, it is essential to play the game of *what if*. Not to be paralysed into inaction, we stress, but to adapt if necessary and maybe take one or two of the *what ifs* out of play with a pre-emptive strategy. Seasoned sea captains – or sea dogs as they were called in Elizabethan times – recognised the bene t of this method by considering the following kinds of questions before embarking on an ocean voyage:

- What if one of our ports of call falls into the hands of our enemies?

171

- What if key members of the crew fall ill or die?
- What if unfavourable weather conditions play havoc with our schedule?
- What if conditions at our final destination are too hostile?

Notice that the *what ifs* were all relevant. They weren't vague anxieties inviting the retort 'so what?' The captains didn't necessarily have the answers before they set sail. But they were mentally prepared for surprises. It was part of the 'ready' phase to consider possibilities of having to readjust the 'aim' (strategy) or 'fire' (tactics) in the event of unfortunate scenarios.

Alas, many forms of strategic thinking popular today assume that the future can be represented by a fixed straight line. It's a sign of the control we think we have over the environment. One such model can be depicted like this:

Context → ends → means → resources → implementation and control. No crooked thoughts in here! No options.

Now just play the scenario of going into a restaurant and asking for a menu. The waiter brings it over but it only has one item on it. You complain there's no choice. He retorts: "Ah, but the chef guarantees that the dish is better cooked this year than last year." You would not be satisfied. Yet this is precisely how companies using a linear model discuss the future. How can we do the *same thing* better?

We prefer to think of the future as a cone of uncertainty that opens up over time – the further away from the present moment you are, the greater the degree of uncertainty.

In terms of planning, therefore, a short-term strategy of say six months to a year is quite easy to develop with a budget and a set of measurable outcomes in place to monitor progress. The decisions are in fact more tactical than strategic, more about the practical means of getting there than the end in itself.

Chart 2 *The Cone of Uncertainty I*

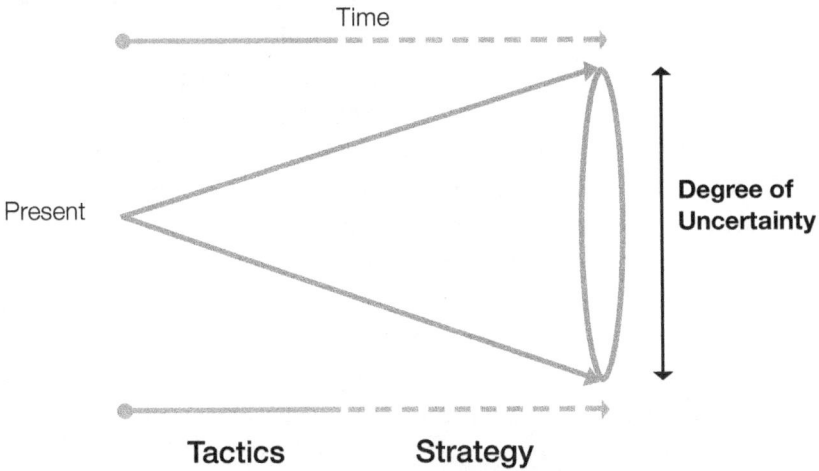

Time

Present

Degree of
Uncertainty

Tactics   Strategy

By contrast, as the cone of uncertainty expands over time, long-term strategy demands more flexibility and imagination. You may even have to question the purpose of the mission, as well as the means of accomplishing it. This is clear for two reasons: the further away the future is from the present, the greater the degree of uncertainty it entails; and the more numerous are the factors beyond your control. This explains why many CEOs would rather be measured on the success of their short-term tactics than their long-term strategies. They want to make sure of next year's bonus in case they have to bow out. Such a corporate planning environment does not encourage the long-term viability of companies. As each CEO goes through the revolving door and the new one is ushered in, the strategy changes. This has spawned a whole new eld of 'change management' techniques served up as instant remedies to organisations perpetually in a crisis mode. Yet the crisis originated in short-term strategies wholly at odds with each other, and wholly at odds with creating sustainable growth in the long run.

Generally, businesses operating within more developed markets should find it easier to change strategic direction because they employ more sophisticated planning techniques and have the resources to do so. Furthermore, it could be argued that in these more developed markets there is less uncertainty, because the conditions are more established than those in developing countries where the challenges are greater and strategic decisions taken by businesses are therefore more courageous. But it actually turns out to be the other way round. CEOs in the West completely misread the tea leaves in the arrogant belief that they can shape the future their way, whereas their Third World colleagues interpret the patterns before drinking the tea. The cup is their 'cone of uncertainty'.

Amazing, too, are the number of Western books on leadership which focus solely on charisma and inspiration. Leadership is also about picking the right strategy. There's no point in marching your troops over the hill, however inspired they may be, if it's the wrong hill. So if as a leader you don't have a strong sense of direction, choose a strategist (or scout) who has. On the one hand, he may save you from abominable decisions which lead you down the precipitate path to failure. On the other hand, he may discover the best way to the top in the most unlikely of circumstances.

It may be true that improved technological know-how and access to information make it easier for modern businesses to temper external forces and to ride out inclement economic conditions. Yet, the move from an industrial to a knowledge economy, together with globalisation, has seen a huge increase in complexity. Markets are more restless, businesses are more decentralised, decision-making is more diffuse. As businesses widen their influence on the environment, so they are able to influence the environment of the other players in their vicinity. Hence the perception that a company is a self-sufficient island cut off from its competitors is erroneous. Actually, a new form of uncertainty brought about by the interconnected nature of business is emerging, where remote causes way outside of our control and springing from an unknown place on the other side of the world can have major consequences for strategy. Damage control means including those two words: *what if?* They are essential to get a feel for the interconnected complexities that impact on strategy and its execution – in other words, the curved balls the enemy or the environment can throw at you to really mess things up. Imagination, uncertainty, painting relevant scenarios and juggling with options should therefore become second nature to us. We need to understand the full measure of choice, as it underpins our decision-making process.

So, we're asking you to break out of your traditional planning habits. And, if you *are* willing to be a bit of a rebel, the secret to dealing with the future and planning for extraordinary times lies in conversation.

The power of the spoken word

Speak to me pretty, speak to me nice;
Quote me those wonderful phrases, once or twice.
BRENDA LEE

The true nature of communication lies not in the grammatical structure and content of the text but in its intended (sender) and interpreted (receiver) meaning. In conversations, it is sometimes something that is not said that says it all. Emotions and opinions can just as easily be transmitted through bodily behaviour: a shrug of the shoulders, a nod of the head, a smile or a frown. Nonetheless, an emotionally laden conversation that is not properly managed can leave unresolved issues that will threaten the stability of any agreement and the sustainability of any relationship. In a strategic conversation, such unresolved issues could undermine the integrity of the entire process and derail it. Hence, the secret to managing such a conversation lies in the careful examination of its context and the social dynamics between the people having it. This can only be achieved once each participant in the conversation has an idea of the possible sources of ignorance and misunderstanding that could filter out the true meaning of elements in the conversation. In business, particularly, any conversation around strategy runs the risk of not achieving its desired outcome if a clear picture of the interests of the participants and the business model they're using is not achieved. Not only does this hinder alignment, but it also leaves strategic value on the table.

So, how is it possible to interpret the course of a conversation correctly and harness its collective value? The secret is to look beyond what is said and examine what drives it. To understand a conversation's peculiarity – its uniqueness of interplay – it is necessary to be aware of the possible sum of the exchanges in the minds of each person around a table. Recording and minuting are not enough. You have to regard conversation not as a series of simple expression of thoughts, but as an intricate series of games. This not only recognises the 'human-ness' of conversation and places what is expressed in the correct context, but also facilitates the management of the conversation.

There are two byways into the mind: through conversation (involving active listening) and through reading. In any organisation, communication is via both. Whether it is face-to-face, via teleconference, fax, phone or e-mail, we conduct business through the exchanging of information in written, verbal or nonverbal form. The outcome of such communication is determined through the absorption of the content and interpretation of meaning. Because of the very nature of speaking with people as opposed to reading, say, what they have written, conversation provides better insight. The mind is in a more intuitive state, there's minimal emphasis on paper, and the views presented are more spontaneous and based on honest experience. Consequently, for an organisation to cope with choice and to achieve more effective decision-making, strategy must be dealt with through conversation. This is a whole lot better than the circulation of long, monotonous documents with appendices containing computer projections lending dubious authenticity to the exercise.

Depending on the spoken word is nothing new. Before formal currencies were established, business transactions took the form of bartering – two goats were worth one sheep, three sheep were worth one cow, and three cows could be exchanged for one wife plus, if you were good at bartering, a keg of ale. Although today currency puts a price on commodities, people still put a value on price. For this reason most business transactions, except those that take place in countries ruled by ruthless dictators, still involve an open exchange of conversation between buyer and seller.

In the third millennium, things haven't changed all that much. Every day, in our social life and in business, we conduct conversations that fill the 'space' between us. The purpose of conversations is essentially twofold – to establish, maintain and develop social bonds; and to communicate ideas with the intention of attaining an outcome. Whereas the first form of conversation is *social*, the latter is *strategic*. Of course there are occasions when the two forms of conversation overlap, such as in the mind of a young man chatting up a girl on a first dinner date! Because there is an intended outcome in a strategic conversation, whether it is to secure the last slice of apple pie at a hungry family reunion, or to finalise the merger of two multinationals, the success of the outcome is determined by how the conversation is managed.

Continuing the example of the young man on a first date, the outcome of the carefully managed conversation will be measured afterwards in distance from each other on the couch.

Surely a desired outcome that is achieved without a properly managed conversation is still the desired outcome? Maybe so, in the short term. But the long term is about relationships and trust based on handshakes, not lawyers. It makes sense that only a strategic conversation that is properly mastered will lay a secure foundation for such bonds to be forged. How many negotiations have failed because badly managed conversations left value on the table? How many managers have been toppled because they left in their path a wake of conversational debt?

So is such a strategic conversation possible? Yes, if the very factors that challenge strategy over time – increased uncertainty and reduced control – are an integral part of the conversation. This was the essence of the prototype model which we introduced in *The Mind of the Fox*. We wanted executives to confront the unknown, to accept that we haven't scraped the surface of the top molecule on the very tip of the iceberg in understanding the world around us. We wanted them to begin the conversation blessed with that essential quality possessed by all true explorers – humility. Not for one minute were we suggesting that they should dive hell for leather into the void offered up by the future. Leaping off a proverbial bridge will only reward a business executive with a new perspective in life if he has a bungee cord tied to his ankles first. Otherwise, he is dead meat.

So what is this bungee cord made of? We venture wisdom. The use of this term is often accompanied by images of a skinny old man in a loincloth with a long silvery-grey beard. He is perched on the steps of a monastery clinging to the slopes of a mountain. Actually, you don't have to be old or know a lot to be wise. The essence of wisdom lies not so much in knowledge per se, but rather in the manner in which knowledge is put to use. More importantly, wisdom demands a certain scepticism about all claims of knowledge, because more is unknown and uncertain than known and certain. The result is a ceaseless ow of movement between con dence and doubt; and it is this fine line between them that a wise person walks, using logic when he is con dent and imagination when he is in the dark.

Chart 3 *The Prototype Matrix*

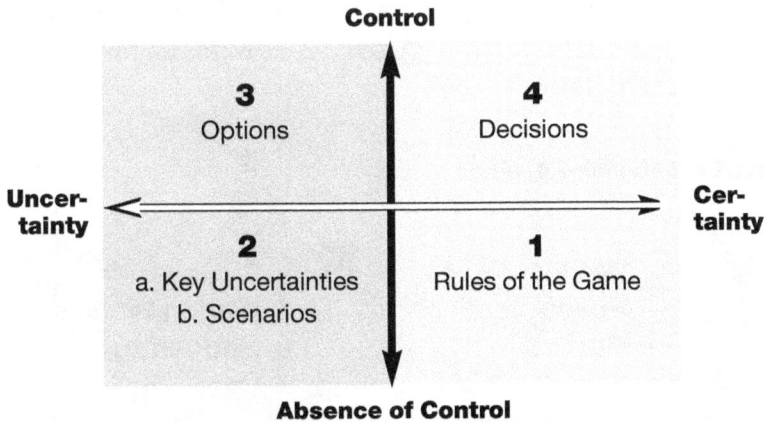

Control

3 Options	**4** Decisions

Uncertainty ⟵⟶ **Certainty**

2 a. Key Uncertainties b. Scenarios	**1** Rules of the Game

Absence of Control

So we came up with a simple matrix that compelled top management to ask two questions in discussing the future of their business and designing their strategies:

1 What do you and do you not control?
2 What is certain and uncertain about the future?

We started in the bottom right-hand quadrant by asking them to consider the factors beyond their control but certain to govern their lives. We then tested their imagination on key uncertainties which might affect the progress of the company and what scenarios might ensue. We then moved to the control side and stimulated a wide-ranging discussion of options to meet the challenges posed by the scenarios, before asking them to put a stake in the ground on decisions. It worked. Sales of *The Mind of a Fox* exceeded 50 000 and many companies from leading multinationals to small and medium-sized businesses in South Africa are now using our technique. Like all models, though, we've been updating the matrix ever since we introduced it. The purpose of *Games Foxes Play* is to set the model out in its present form (it is no longer a matrix, as you will see). Before proceeding to describe the latest version, however, we would like to list three likes and dislikes which have driven us to make the adaptations that we have.

Chart 4 *Likes and Dislikes*

✓
- Circles
- Foxes
- Games

✗
- Rimless
  Wagon Wheels
- Hedgehogs
- Dots

Rimless wagon wheels versus circles

Conversation is a game of circles.
RALPH WALDO EMERSON

Strategic workshops can be frustrating, especially if they are run according to the rimless wagon-wheel approach. At the centre of the accompanying gure is a hub representing the CEO plus his or her close confidantes. They represent the cabal. Emanating out of the hub are the spokes, at the ends

Chart 5 *Rimless Wagon Wheels*

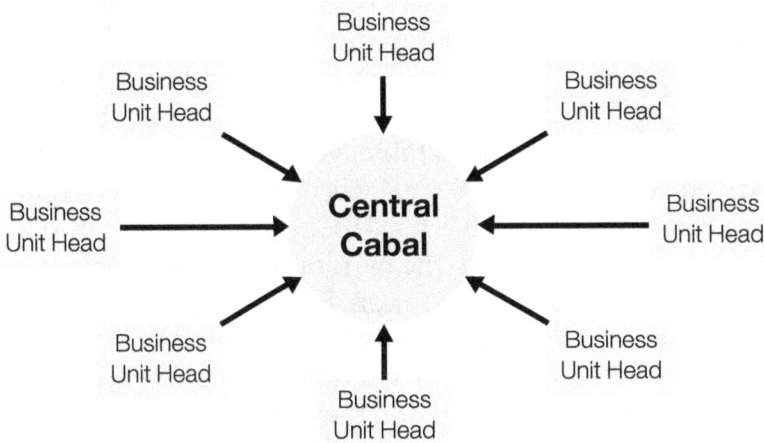

of which are the business units. The sole purpose of the work-shop is for the business unit heads to feed their ve-year plans and projections into the central cabal, which acts like a gigantic sponge absorbing this information. The cabal then decides on overall company strategy in a completely separate forum. The business unit heads never get to participate in such a discussion. They merely talk about their own unit's future. No rim joins them around the periphery because no general conversation takes place on the overall business. They are effectively 'siloed'.

How far west do you think the pioneers of American frontier life would have got if their wagon wheels had been without rims? They would have got bogged down just outside of Boston. But how many companies adopt this approach because of an autocratic CEO who wants to keep strategy all to himself, or maybe include one or two of his close chums? Plenty!

In contrast, we believe in circles when it comes to effective strategic sessions: conversation circles. For the whole business. We believe that the forward movement of a company into extraordinary times can only be ensured if the direction of the conversation is circular. Each part of the conversation tips into the next part in a fairly seamless manner. So in sessions we facilitate we prefer to have the executive team sitting literally at a round table, with everybody in sight of each other and having an equal voice. Sometimes this requires a cultural change which is hard to imagine. In one company, the CEO was nicknamed 'the handbrake' for the dampening effect he had on the conversation. But if it happens the way it should, the results can be truly remarkable. We've had directors privately coming up to us afterwards and saying that it was the best strategy session they had ever attended.

There are reasons. As business organisations grow, they need to draw more and more on the expertise of those within the organisation. Where better to find it than in your top executive team? In the so-called knowledge economy, 'flatter' structures are the embodiment of the modern organisation. They encourage the free flow of ideas and energy between all the elements of the organisation, thereby promoting buy-in and innovation across the board. While some, mainly larger, organisations still cling on to the old hierarchical ladders, most organisations that value creativity encourage ideas to bubble up from below. Approachability is a key characteristic of managers in these new structures. Gone are the days when decisions either 'trickled down' or were 'thrust down', depending on the personality of the heavyweight at the top.

The direction of conversation in a 'flat' structure is more circular. Ideas are passed on for continual assessment, review and adaptation, and subsequently these ideas build momentum and direction. Unlike the spokes of a rimless wagon wheel, the flow of conversation around a circle is, by its very nature, inclusive, and the points are contextualised.

Contributors to the conversation see the value of their input being recognised by peers and more senior and junior staff. More importantly, they are given an opportunity to gain insight and perspective into the reason for the organisation's existence. As scenario strategists, we see the value in extending scenario sage Peter Schwartz's belief that "scenario planning must be intensely participative or it fails". We believe that all planning must be intensely participative or it fails. Hence every level of an organisation should have conversation circles in which strategy is discussed.

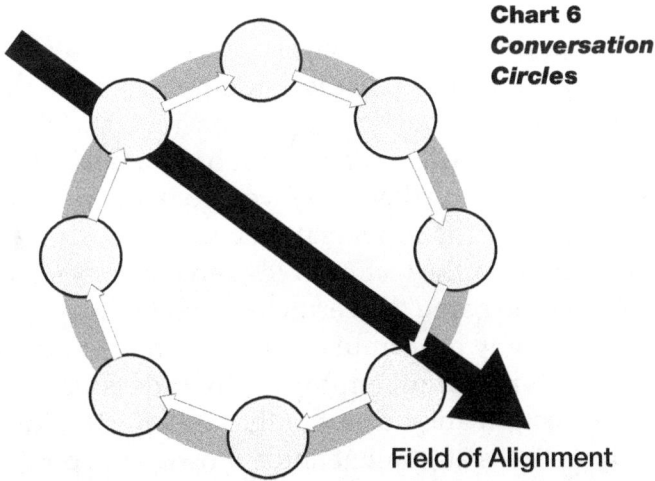

**Chart 6
Conversation
Circles**

Field of Alignment

When the strategic conversation is circular, it ows like a current through the heads of all the people sitting around the table, creating its own 'field of alignment'. This method of conversation allows those involved to escape (at least temporarily) from the silos of their business units to capture the bigger picture. They consequently have a better idea of their role in ensuring the company's overall success. A conversation circle has other associated advantages: it encourages a richness that can only come out of diversity, enabling greater insight into the views of people from disparate backgrounds;

it sends a clear message of an organisation's commitment to participative management; and the inclusivity of the process recognises individual input, thereby developing an environment that respects and retains talent. Above all, it's meant to be fun. Not like those sombre affairs where pearls of wisdom are passed down by important people speaking in slow and measured tones to a gathering of staff in the canteen. This is cut and thrust, a chance in a lifetime to air your views. And guess what? People are more creative when they are having fun and feeling relaxed. Think of the atmosphere in the local pub!

For all the reasons given so far, any strategic conversation within an organisation ought to cascade through the entire organisation. Conversation circles should start at the top and work their way down over a period of months. Obviously, the further down you go in the organisation, the more specific the conversation becomes and the more it revolves around the tactical roles departments should play in winning the game. Nevertheless, while the direction of the company may be formulated at the senior executive level, it is important for all employees to understand the company's direction and be part of the strategic thinking process, as this creates alignment and a sense of purpose within the company. Hence, some of the material discussed at CEO level should find its way down, and original comments on it from employees should find their way up. Wisdom is not the preserve of the senior management team alone.

Our recommendation is, in a way, a top-down democratic approach. Not in the narrow sense of democracy which means giving everyone the vote. But in the wider sense of granting people the right to have their say and deliberate on the issues of the moment – business by discussion if you please. If it doesn't happen (and we're afraid that in most companies it doesn't), the employees just come to work to collect their cheques. They're not involved. They don't understand the objectives. Think of two professional soccer teams being requested to play a soccer game for ninety minutes where there are no goalposts. They run around, dribbling here, dribbling there, passing the ball back and forth all over the pitch, then change ends and do exactly the same. There's no score at the end because there are no goals to shoot at. Imagine what that does for the motivation of the two teams and their performance. A variation is to demand that the two teams play the game where there are goalposts but they are being continually shifted. This doesn't do much good for morale either. Yet some CEOs just can't make up their mind on strategy. They chop and change, depending upon which management consultant they have in tow.

As facilitators we don't like prepared papers on strategy. They straitjacket people, put them in a groove. Instead we encourage those involved in our conversation circle just to bring their accumulated knowledge and experience to the table so that they contribute spontaneously to the discussion. We are more concerned with the depth and breadth of the conversation than its length (although as we've mentioned our conversations tend to be much shorter than the average workshop). Primarily we want people to think out of the box.

But let's be frank – inclusive conversation can be a beast to manage and it invariably requires a certain level of harmony and a special kind of leader. Opponents of 'flat' organisational structures, for example, will talk about the dangers of completely open, unstructured conversations that may dilute the decision-making responsibilities of management and slow down the implementation of strategy. This argument is more frequently advanced as a company grows and an established decision structure is essential. The desire for management to control operations in order to ensure the maintenance of focus is understandable; but images of a babbling free-for-all put forward by the more power-retentive management types misconstrue the idea of an 'inclusive conversation'. It is quite possible for strategic conversations to be open and inclusive, but at the same time businesslike and intense – as long as they are carefully structured. Moreover, conversation circles need not interfere with standard lines of authority and decision-making chains, if – like any other function – they are given a specific remit, and are properly scheduled. However, if these words don't alleviate your anxieties, just use our conversation model at the most senior executive level. It will definitely shorten the annual strategy session and make it productive.

Returning to our concept that conversation circles can create a 'field of alignment', they are an ideal tool for resolving conflict between contending parties, each with their own interests and perception of the game. Before negotiations begin in earnest, a strategic conversation along the lines suggested lays the groundwork for a common understanding of the game in which the parties are represented (as well as a mutual understanding of each other's roles). Negotiations have a better chance of success, particularly if the consequences of failure are mapped out in a credible scenario. In this vein, an interesting use of our technique was to structure a discussion on the future of the game bird population in South Africa. Present were the shooters, the environmentalists, the farmers and the safari operators. By the end of the session, everyone was aware of the rules of the game for conserving the unparalleled number of species of game birds that exist in South Africa. Probably the industry in South Africa in most need of such a discussion is the health care industry. What is the role of the public and private sectors in winning the health care game for the country as a whole? What is the downside of losing the game?

Foxes versus hedgehogs

You spotted snakes with double tongue,
Thorny hedgehogs, be not seen.
WILLIAM SHAKESPEARE

We don't want to repeat all that we said in *The Mind of a Fox* about hedgehogs and foxes. Suffice it to say that we like foxes and dislike hedgehogs (the *human* version that is). The comparison was first introduced by an Ancient Greek poet called Archilochus around 650 B.C. In a fragment of his verse, which has survived to the present day, he said: "The fox knows many things – the hedgehog one big one." Why he chose those two animals to illustrate this difference in thinking we shall never know, because he's been dead for over two and a half millennia. However, his analogy was taken up in the middle of the last century by an eminent British philosopher, Isaiah Berlin, in his famous essay, *The Hedgehog and the Fox*. He wanted primarily to draw a distinction between those philosophers who based their theory on a single idea and, if that idea proved false, the whole theory crumbled; and those philosophers who built up their theory on a variety of observations, and even if several of those observations proved incorrect, the theory could still stand.

Widening Berlin's interpretation to mankind in general, the image of what hedgehogs see ahead of them is narrowed to a central vision. They simplify life around one great idea, more or less disregarding everything else, and bet on that idea. The rewards, if their single idea or theory is correct, are substantial, but then again so is the degree of damage if they are wrong – arguably risky stuff in today's complex, interconnected, uncertain and volatile world. Foxes, on the other hand, know many things, and regard life as a balancing act between competing claims. Foxes think of life as a system composed of many parts and interdependencies, and it is only through the knowledge of the system as a whole that one can optimise decisions about the future. A critical difference between human hedgehogs and foxes is that the former like to think they are in control whereas the latter know they are never fully in control. The success of foxes therefore lies in their adaptability to their external environment and the resourcefulness of their responses. Followers of foxes and hedgehogs will notice the difference in trails they leave behind. Fox prints weave to and fro through forests, avoiding dangerous spots and approaching possible sources of nutritional value. Hedgehog steps never deviate from the chosen path. This is why members of the Hedgehog Preservation Society in the UK build small tunnels underneath the motorways, so that they can cross unhurt.

Nonetheless, there are plenty of admirers of hedgehogs around. Jim Collins, in his bestseller *Good to Great*, argues that companies that embrace a hedgehog philosophy and are focused on a single path are more likely to succeed in what they set out to do. He goes on: "For a hedgehog, anything that does not somehow relate to the hedgehog idea holds no relevance." We contend that employing such a high-risk strategy is increasingly incongruent with the interdependent world we live in, and can steer dangerously close to fanaticism. Fundamentalists are by definition hedgehogs. Nevertheless, we don't have any problem with focus, particularly when it means the opposite of scatterbrained. Foxes *are* focused, but also possess whiskers to pick up the sensitivities and interests of the players around them. And they are just as prepared to stand on *moral* principles as hedgehogs, but not on ideas and dogma.

In the business world hedgehogs seek an *optimal* strategy (for everlasting growth), whereas foxes are after a robust strategy which will see them through the bad times in order to prosper in the good times. Nothing more, nothing less. We prefer the fox's humbler but less brittle approach, because it gives you a better chance of being around in the longer run. As Albert Einstein is reputed to have said: "You can simplify things as much as possible, but don't make them simpler than they should be."

Dots in space versus games

The military makes a great hammer,
but not every problem is a nail.
GENERAL HUGH SHELTON
Former Chairman of the US Joint Chiefs of Staff

You may be forgiven for thinking that strategic planning sometimes drives you dotty. Dots are what companies come out with at the end of strategy sessions. Dot: "We are going to double our production in five years." Dot: "We are going to grow our bottom line at 10 per cent per annum in real terms." So what's the problem? Organisations have used this method for decades. You set a goal and head off; after all, organisations need direction.

The problem comes when the dot is set in space. The CEO issues a strategic directive and everybody falls into line without knowing or questioning the context of the dot. It becomes mesmerising. Anything said about it is without nuance or qualification. It hypnotises people into doing imprudent, irresponsible and sometimes downright dishonest things to achieve the dot. Moreover, when the environment changes, everybody still clings to the dot. Even when the dot has gone spectacularly beyond its sell-by date, the troops still march on (particularly if someone was stupid enough to publish the dot in the first place). We've all had these dots on our horizons at some time in our lives and been fixated by them. Some are harmless, some dangerous. Some are even terminal, such as when you continue to watch the dot as you fall off the cliff. By now you will have guessed: dots in space are the single ideas beloved by hedgehogs. They convert uncertainties into facts to keep the dot alive and, worse still, twist the facts altogether when pressure really mounts. For a big enough dot, hedgehogs are not above 'sexing up' intelligence dossiers by hardening the language here and there.

Nonetheless, we don't dislike dots as long as they are put in context. Indeed, you will see in our model that dots are the equivalent of the measurable outcomes we insist are part of the conversation before it is wrapped up. But before agreeing on dots, you must understand the context in which they are made, so that, should the context change, the dots can be revised.

In the last section, we asserted that foxes were systems thinkers. But we don't like the word 'system' for two reasons. It is too abstract a word to describe business, which after all is a flesh-and-blood affair run by human beings for human beings. It implies that if you have enough information about the system, the outcome may be predicted, whereas business is inherently unpredictable, precisely because human beings are unpredictable. We prefer the word 'game', because games *are* played by human beings and can have unpredictable results. Hence the rest of this book is about games.

Edward Arlington Robinson once said: "Life is a game that must be played." The reality is that life is a series of *sub-games*. A sub-game in this context is any form of interaction between two or more people – let's call them *players* – where the intention of each player is to achieve some measure of gain for themselves. The word 'gain' should be interpreted here in the widest possible sense of being spiritual or material, short term or long term. Every sub-game has its own set of rules, scoring system, rewards and punishments; and features people who are on your side in the game, against you, or are ambivalent – in other words neutral.

A sub-game can also involve any interaction between a person and his or her environment. So, whether we like it or not, from the moment we scream our first breath to when we sigh our last we are locked in a series of adventures with people and the environment around us, with the aim of securing that certain degree of gain. Like players on a field, whether we are crying for a feed, trying to cheat death or simply surviving a trying day, we strategise to win over our adversaries and adversities, physical and otherwise. In short – we *play* games all our lives, either as individuals or in teams.

Some people might dismiss the concept of life being a game – or more realistically a series of sub-games – as flippant. Nothing could be further from the truth. Sub-games can be highly complex and are both sequential and concurrent in their timing and location. An example of sequential sub-games would be the emotional, intellectual and social games employed during the educational path from preprimary school to employment. Primary schooling is normally spent in sub-games, where the dynamics are underpinned by the developing of the child's curiosity and the entrenching of the school's authority. Secondary schooling and the growth of individual self-confidence support an environment that encourages sub-games of negotiation. College or university sparks sub-games of rebellion that are then reined in when the reality of a pay cheque requires playing in the more structured sub-games of business.

More challenging is the balancing of concurrent sub-games, like those between business and family. Working harder may bring in more money but it may be at the expense of valuable family time. Concurrent games call for decisions around trade-offs that in turn may have long-term consequences. An example would be a busy parent's cancelling of an important business trip to attend a school sports day or school play. The parent may not remember but the child certainly will (even more so if you don't pitch up).

Because humans are social animals, most of the games we play are naturally with other humans and are conducted through the medium of *conversation* and *behaviour*. Conversation in this sense is the exchanging of verbal and written information, whereas behaviour is nonverbal and non-written and often differs in intent and content. These two functions apply as much on a school playground as they do in the boardrooms of giant multinationals.

The secret to the difference between merely having a conversation, or acting out a role in any game, and securing genuine and permanent gains, is the employment of effective strategies which rely on *knowing how to play the game*. This presumes among other things: understanding the game; respecting the fact that there are interdependencies between all the players with each having expectations about the other's behaviour; and a flexible attitude which acknowledges that games are risky and sometimes demand radical shifts in strategy. The best course of action therefore necessitates the successful consolidation of the information at your disposal at any one time into a level of knowledge and wisdom which allows you a fair chance of winning the game. This book is designed to give you the tools to do just that.

Effective strategy not only involves knowing *how* to play the game, but also knowing *what* game to play. Put yourself in the position of a student about to select a career. Now picture careers as games, each with its own rules. Now match your strengths and weaknesses to each game and ask which game suits you best. How many students go through that process? How many career officers understand the rules of each career game when advising their young clients? This is the time in your life when you are at your most free to choose, because once the career is chosen, you are subject to its rules. Moreover, entry into any game comes with a cost. There is the direct cost of obtaining the qualifications to enter that game. Think how much it costs to become a doctor or engineer. Then there is the opportunity cost of all the other careers you are passing up in order to pursue your selected option. If you choose, you refuse. Fast forward to being an adult and try the negotiation game. It is clearly one of give and take. If you are going to play, you have to be prepared to *give*. Marriages that last are all about that.

Equally, effective strategy means knowing when a game has *changed* to the point that you either have to adapt to the new rules, or plan an exit. As we've already mentioned, the difference between real life and chess is that in real life the rules can change, whereas in chess the rules define the game and are therefore set in concrete. For example, the rules of a particular business sector can be changed so much by advances in technology that it is no longer recognisable as the sub-game it was. Winners become losers and new winners emerge. Look at how much radio has been changed by TV!

Some of our readers might say at this stage that theories on games and how to play them already exist. We will touch on all of them. However, what sets this book apart is its presentation of a new approach – which we have dubbed *The Conversation Model* – that combines elements of Game Theory, Chaos Theory and Systems Thinking. Crucially, we have ensured that our model is understandable by ordinary people making everyday decisions. It is plain common sense. One of the problems of the aforementioned theories is that they are mathematically so advanced that only a fraction of decision-makers use them, even though they contain valid and extremely relevant material for today's competitive and uncertain world. They also ignore the passions, emotions and arbitrariness of real-life human beings playing real-life games. David Hume, the eighteenth-century Scottish philosopher, was spot on with his take on human nature: reason is the slave of passion, he said, not the other way around. Even in the age of electronics and information technology, we are still messy, unpredictable entities. Thus, we have taken the best ingredients of each of the above theories and, with the addition of Scenario Planning, come up with a method as close to real life as possible. And it is very popular because everybody understands the concept of a game from early infancy.

How can we be so sure? Simply, the overwhelming response we have had from the diverse array of individuals and businesses who have used our material to improve their handling of the future and the way they implement decisions. Whether the group comprises bankers, miners, bishops, broadcasters, doctors, scientists, teachers or lawyers (not recycled) – they love playing games. They are seduced into lowering their guard because games are, well, something to enjoy. They take the sting out of reality.

As you will soon see, we have also developed over the last three years a set of visual aids to assist the conversation about every aspect of the game. Specifically in business, we have discovered that the visual medium is the best way to surface the instincts and intuition of the top executive team and get them to air their views in a creative, but structured manner. Practical people don't like dealing in purely abstract concepts. They like visual stimuli, since the eye is directly wired to the imagination. Moreover, numbers, though vital in the end for budgets and operational plans, bog down discussions on subjects like risks, uncertainties and scenarios because so much of what is important about the future cannot be quantified with any precision. The issues have to be handled in a more open forum. Hence, we prefer to play a series of mind games with our clients, which may lead them in directions they never expected to go. But the result is a comprehensive picture of the gameboard they're playing on as well as the tactics available in different positions on the board.

We see our job in this book as encouraging decision-makers to re-perceive the future in such a way that they are not often caught off guard (never say never!). They know the game they are in and how to play the game, whatever surprises are thrown at them. We want to persuade people to put on the equivalent of night-vision goggles so that threats (as well as opportunities) are more clearly visible than the naked eye will allow. We want to train the mind to penetrate the opaqueness that inevitably envelops the future – to see emerging shapes as it were – in a real and practical manner. We want people to recognise the fact that games are filled with controllables and non-controllables, certainties and non-certainties, and that true competitive advantage lies in accepting the paradox.

The opinion that life is a series of games has, by obvious association, the assumption that as players we strive to win over others. It is, whether we like it or not, in our nature. The respected evolutionary biologist, Professor Richard Dawkins, suggests in *The Selfish Gene* that our need to win against others and protect our self-interest is in our genes. We are all simply survival machines built by a short-lived confederation of long-lived genes that have replicated and adapted over time to changing conditions, threats and opportunities. Genes are the primary policy-maker; brains are the executive. However, as our brains have become more highly developed, they have taken over more and more of the actual policy decisions, using tricks like learning and simulation to do so. Thus games – and the enjoyment of winning them – are central to our development of strategies for survival.

Anyone who follows sport has experienced the agony and ecstasy of losing and winning. That's the essence of the game.

195

If games were predictable they wouldn't be fraught with the emotion surrounding the uncertainty of their outcome. We would be prepared for every eventuality; the fun would go out of sport; and there would be no such thing as bookies, ups, downs, celebrations and commiserations – which sound more like our lot in life.

Given our definition of the word 'game', and in terms of the number of players, it could be argued that, other than staying alive, the most *popular* game played in the world is the game of *business*. Think about it: every single day of the year billions of people all over the world strategise in social, economic, emotional and intellectual games with each other in the hope of achieving some measure of gain such as a momentary nod of approval from a superior; influencing a departmental discussion; closing a deal; securing cash in the bank; robbing competitors of market share; or getting the upper hand in some corporate power struggle. Every day some people win and some people lose. We are going to help you to win.

The Conversation Model

Being President is like running a cemetery. You've got
a lot of people under you, but nobody's listening.
BILL CLINTON

Some people get things wrong, some famously so. For all his faults, Bill Clinton was a great listener, even if he felt his subordinates weren't listening to him. He got people to participate. The secret to successful strategy for an uncertain future out of our control is *not* to leave it in the hands of a single person. Not even a small group for that matter. It is rather, on a broad basis, to involve those who are expected to implement that strategy. By approaching strategic thinking with the mind of a fox; incorporating a diversity of experience and opinions through conversation circles; and recognising that other players will influence your line of attack, because business is a game, it is possible to design a far more robust strategy for the extraordinary times that face modern business than conventional techniques allow. Furthermore, it is easier to execute the strategy on account of the buy-in already obtained from the executives involved.

We wouldn't have continued the fox analogy in this book if we were not able to enhance it considerably. Over a period of three years since the publishing of our last book, we have had feedback both encouraging and critical. We have listened and taken note. At first we thought that our matrix would need a little fine-tuning. However the opposite was true. We realised that it needed a fundamental reassessment. The prototype was designed to put scenario planning on the map by integrating it into the normal decision-making process. We wanted to convert scenario planning from a fairly esoteric, intellectual discipline into a methodology that was practical, down to earth and considered relevant by the average line manager. We succeeded. But in the process we discovered that the 'game' metaphor was even more powerful than scenario planning in unleashing people's imagination.

So we adapted like foxes to this new insight. The result: a model for a strategic conversation, and how to plan for extraordinary times. It is logically divided into two phases:

A Defining the game; and
B Playing the game.

Defining the game (and the changes taking place in it) lays the foundation for playing the game and deciding on tactics. Despite this being eminently logical, it remains a fact that many businesses still rush into the game without first doing their homework on what the game is about. Imagine the Arsenal and Chelsea soccer managers laying down the strategy for a Premier League clash if the two teams were still hazy about the rules. Similarly, any company that employs a strategy without properly understanding the nature of the game it is in cannot operate effectively. As such, part of the competitive advantage for any company lies in its ability to understand the game better than its competitors.

The first phase – defining the game – comprises five steps:

1 Scope of the game
2 The players
3 Rules of the game
4 Key uncertainties
5 Scenarios.

The second phase – playing the game – also has five steps. They combine the strategic insights gained in the first phase with a more focused view of the possibilities ahead:

6 SWOT
7 Options
8 Decisions
9 Measurable outcomes
10 The meaning of winning.

This ten-step model for a strategic conversation can be illustrated as in *Chart 7*.

The conversation model is anything but a conventional linear model. For one thing, every step is interconnected; and secondly, given the advantages of conversation circles presented earlier, the direction of the process is circular, i.e. a con-

Chart 7 *The Conversation Model*

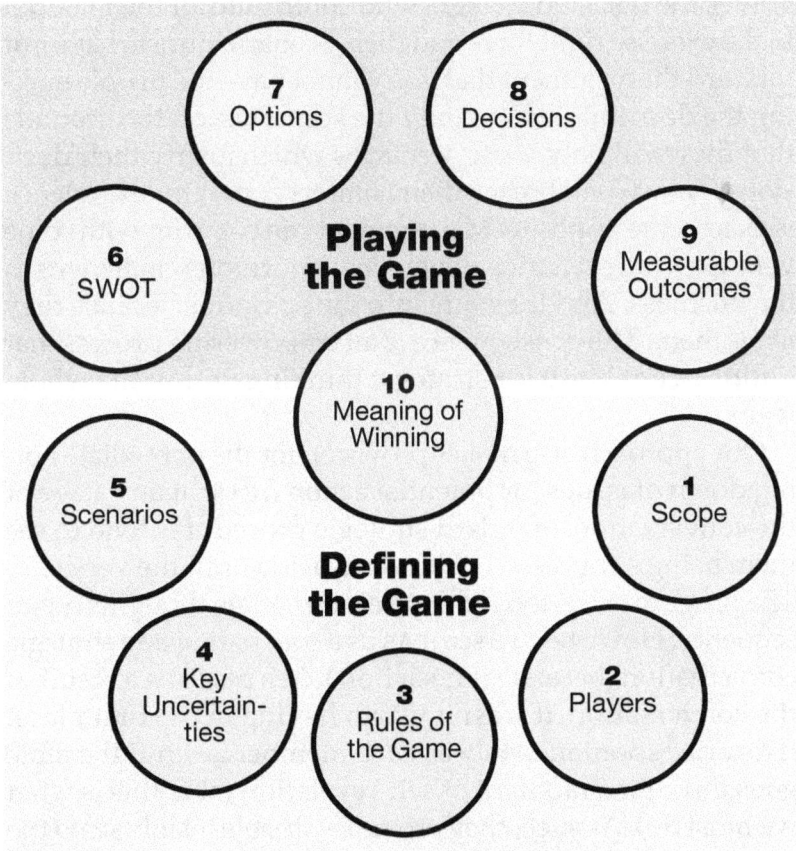

clusion reached later on in the conversation can lead to a re-view of earlier material. A critical point to note is that our model differs markedly from standard scenario planning methodologies that turn on the insights of a group of scenario specialists from outside an organisation. They interview the executives, hold meetings with them, but then quite independently put together the scenarios. These are fed back into the corporate team who review them and, if they are happy, formulate strategies around them. By contrast, implementation of the conversation model from start to finish involves the decision-makers who contribute all the material to the exercise right there and then. Scenario purists have put forward the argument that you cannot have the people making the decisions also writing the scenarios, on the grounds that they will only write scenarios which justify their decisions. They won't breach their comfort zone. Our experience is exactly the opposite. Management can come up with some very extreme scenarios which pose enormous challenges to the business. And they buy into the scenarios because they *wrote* them. The consequence is an empowering process that builds a capability for strategic thinking within the whole team.

Our approach also makes provision for the immediate noting down of issues for potential action (IPAs) at any stage of the conversation. Standard strategic procedures tend to see them being suppressed or brushed aside until the very end. The programme is too rigid to accommodate thoughts out of sequence. However, we see IPAs as a core part of any strategic conversation, because if no action takes place as a result of the conversation, it wasn't worth having in the first place. IPAs arise spontaneously as each member around the table goes through a moment of self-revelation (aha, this is what we must do). As such, they provide valuable insights into the challenges facing the company and avenues for innovation. In fact, it has often been the case in sessions that we have facilitated that some of the best ideas come out of the blue. We encourage this randomness of thought, as it is very much in step with the words of the philosopher Isaiah Berlin on foxes: "[they] pursue many ends, often unrelated and even contradictory. Their thought is often scattered or diffused, moving on many levels, seizing upon the vast variety of experiences". The logistics for capturing IPAs are dead simple. We keep a separate flip chart or board to capture them in order that they may be reintroduced into the conversation at the appropriate moment, i.e. when discussing options and decisions. The following diagram, that looks like a robot from a Star Wars movie, shows how IPAs can be treated.

Chart 8 *Strategy to Action*

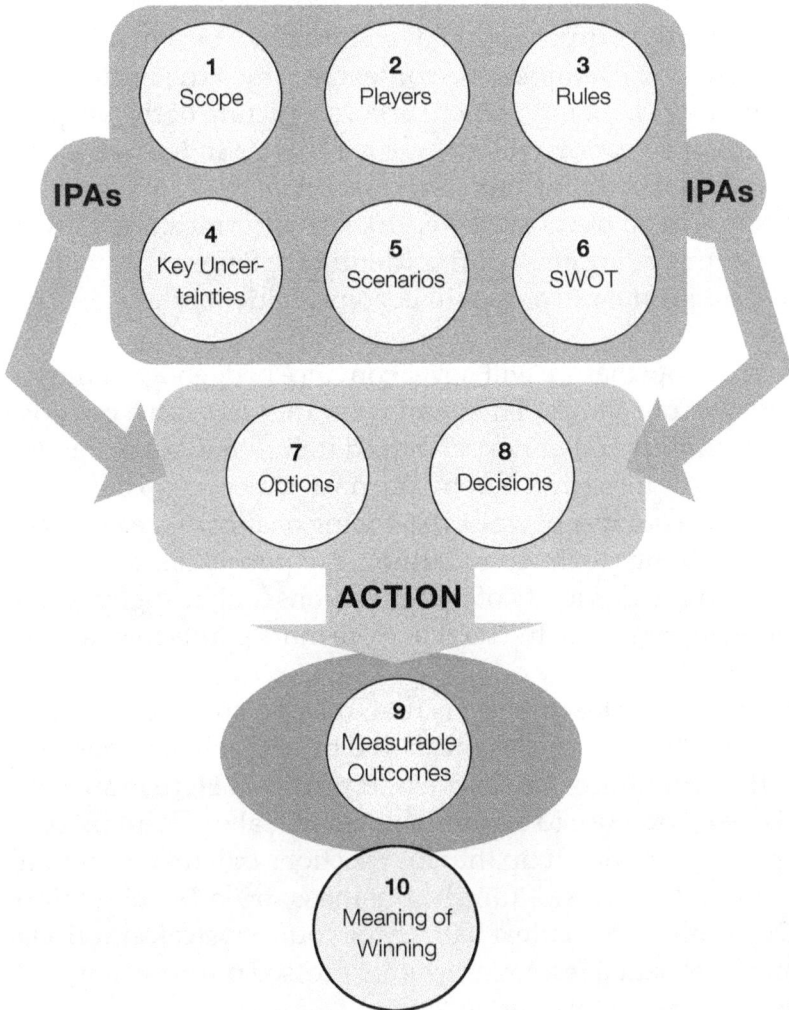

| 1 Scope | 2 Players | 3 Rules |

IPAs

| 4 Key Uncertainties | 5 Scenarios | 6 SWOT |

IPAs

| 7 Options | 8 Decisions |

ACTION

9 Measurable Outcomes

10 Meaning of Winning

When we undertake facilitation work, we are inevitably asked whether, before any strategic conversation can take place, it is necessary to define the purpose of the organisation. This is a common misperception. Any attempt to define an organisation's purpose at the front end will have the effect of restricting the parameters of the conversation to an area within the purpose as it now is perceived. But how can one tell whether the purpose should or should not be amended until you have examined the context in which the company is operating? In reality, a more accurate picture of the purpose of an organisation will emerge *towards the end* of a strategic conversation. Using our conversation model, it makes sense to close in on purpose in step 10, when the meaning of winning for the organisation is identified. Before that, a 'feel' at best for the purpose will become evident after steps 1, 2 and 3.

We know that we will never convince hedgehogs of the validity of our views. They will want to start with a purpose and simplify the universe around it. But then we believe in the foxy approach whereby purpose may end up being defined in a number of ways, depending on the perspective each person brings to the conversation. For purpose in business is open to a wide variety of interpretations (unlike rugby where the team runs onto the field to score more points than the opponents).

Even more fascinating is that, on a personal level, an individual's 'purpose' as measured by actual behaviour may differ from his or her expressed purpose. Here is an exercise we often use to explain this point. Take a plain piece of paper and divide it up into four sections that represent your personal purpose – family, business, friends, recreation. Depending on an ideal balance of your physical, emotional and intellectual resources, your expressed purpose may look something like in *Chart 9*:

Chart 9
Balanced Personal Frame

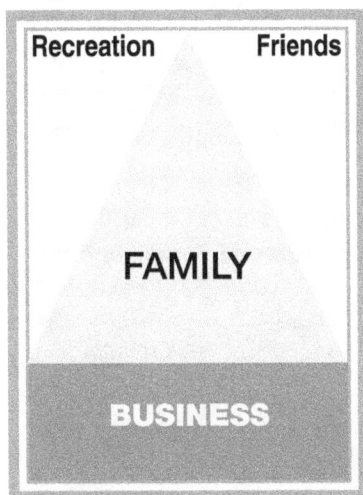

Chart 10
Unbalanced Personal Frame

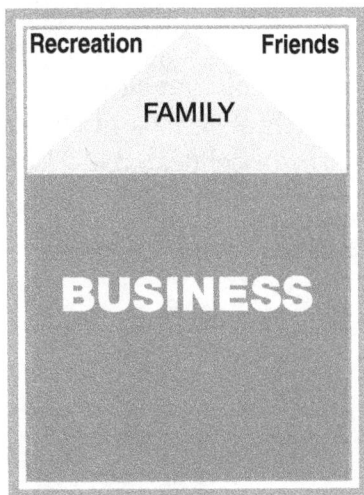

Business as the source of income for the family is represented as the stable foundation. Meanwhile, the family lies at the centre of the frame, with recreation and friends also being given plenty of space. Now, hand on heart, be honest with yourself. Given the everyday pressures of earning a living and trying to balance family concerns with business demands, your picture of personal purpose may actually look more like *Chart 10*.

Indisputably, this is a horribly unbalanced personal frame. After all, we are called human *beings* and not human *doings*. Nevertheless, as a re ection of the way more and more people live, it is uncomfortably close to the truth. In his book *The Seven Spiritual Laws of Success*, Deepak Chopra talks of one-pointed intention that is "unbending in its xity of purpose". He goes on: "There is total and complete exclusion of all obstacles from your consciousness." Alas, if the obstacles include putting a reasonable amount of time aside for family and friends, you can end up a spiritual disaster. Thus, one-pointed intention gives us a really prickly feeling!

Similarly, today's modern business has to balance its central interest of generating pro ts with other concerns such as sustainable development and social responsibility. Ideally, these three items could be expressed in a company's purpose in the form delineated in *Chart 11*:

Chart 11
Balanced Business Frame

Chart 12
Unbalanced Business Frame

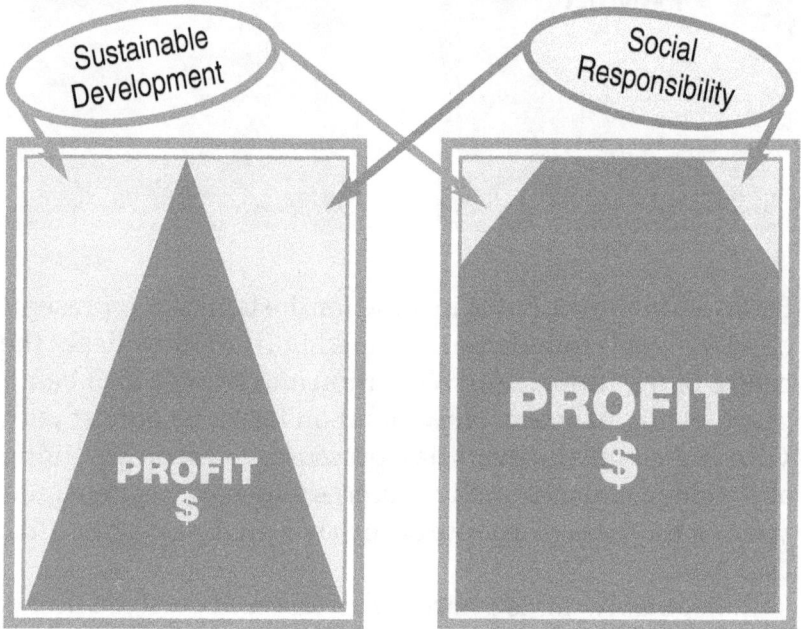

Sustainable development and social responsibility can be seen as curtains being pulled back to display the profit on centre stage. We like to call this work of art: *Impressions from the Annual Report.*

However, given the unwavering demand of shareholders for a superior nancial return, and given that the CEO together with other members of the top executive team usually have sizeable share options themselves, the in-house business purpose can realistically be drawn as in *Chart 12*.

This work is titled: *By Actual Resource Allocation*. It describes the amount of energy, time and money that, if measured, is in truth spent by the executive team on the individual elements of the 'triple bottom line'. As you can see, sustainable development and social responsibility are little more than hooks upon which the profit is hung. It is no coincidence that people who work for companies with an unbalanced business frame tend to be in the unbalanced personal frame themselves, working ungodly hours for the almighty buck. The employees of one institution guilty of this practice referred to it as the 'empty wheels' syndrome. The hamsters get so exhausted that they eventually quit their wheels.

Does this strike you as wrong; or do you reluctantly accept that it is part of winning the game? In a different vein, are you going to comply in a grudging way with the wider role expected of business in society today i.e. do the minimum to pass muster; or are you going to work towards the balanced business frame in *actual fact*? The only way to decide is to have a strategic conversation which concludes with a debate over the meaning of 'winning'. It won't necessarily lead to consensus, but it might result in the company living less of a lie.

The appalling loss of life from the Asian tsunami of 2004 should put everything in perspective. We live on this isolated ball in space which occasionally becomes a very dangerous place to be. When calamities happen, it is desperately important that we exhibit exactly the kind of qualities which are normally crowded out by our desire to advance our careers or make the company grow. If we join hands, we can survive even the most dreadful experiences. If we don't, we shall lose the game now and forever.

The scope of the game

The fascination of shooting as a sport
depends almost wholly on whether you are
at the right or wrong end of the gun.
P. G. WODEHOUSE

In Africa, much is made of the so-called 'big five', comprising the lion, the elephant, the rhino, the leopard and the buffalo. It is assumed that they are the animals most people want to see when game viewing, and this is why they are singled out and grouped together. The assumption is not entirely true. The last one – the buffalo – doesn't really capture the imagination of most game viewers; it's the other four that people want to see. So why is it in the 'big five'? The name is in fact a hunting term given to the most prized game trophies. A buffalo is right up there with the others because of its bellicose and unpredictable nature – a real challenge to any hunter. Even the lion, the so-called 'king of the beasts', will give a wide berth to a grown buffalo. The two enjoy a simmering degree of respect for the other's power and position within the pecking order. A lion is no match for a fully grown buffalo, but a buffalo calf would be fair game for a hungry lion. Yet, if you were to score animals on a game-viewing outing according to their appeal and accessibility, a buffalo, as a member of the 'big five', would score more than an impala but not nearly as much as a lion. So it all depends on context as to how you rank a buffalo. Context is where the whole game begins.

The same is true for business. It is crucial for any organisation to contextualise its position and performance by examining how it sees the game it is in. Questions should be asked about the type of game that is being played; the nature of the game and its boundaries; and where the organisation

Chart 13 *The Conversation Model – Scope*

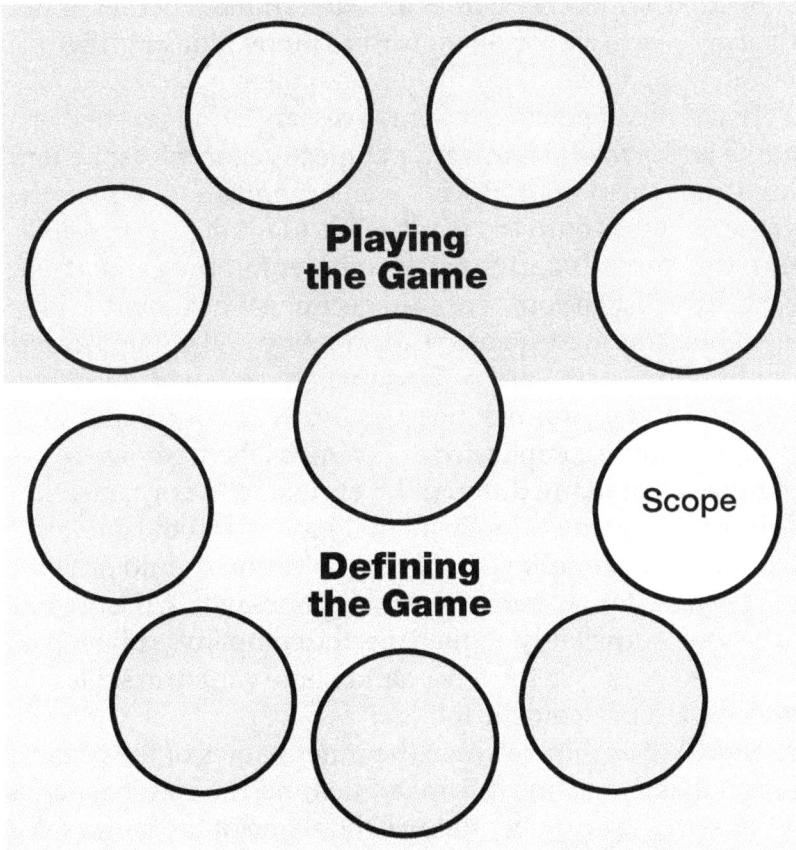

Playing
the Game

Scope

Defining
the Game

ts into the game as a player. Interestingly, unlike sport which is played on a eld or court of a predetermined size, the game of business has no boundaries outside of the constructs of its players, and can therefore be as broad or narrow as they wish to make it. Equally, within business, there will always be links between the games being played by the different sectors. Think of any major project and the number of different companies involved in its feasibility study and commissioning. They play separate games but come together for the project.

A player's talent therefore includes the ability to identify possible links with other games and determine whether or not they are worth exploring for further innovation or growth of one's own game.

Two types of perspective are necessary to judge whether a game is worthwhile. Inward perspective (or introspection) identifies the potential within an organisation to play the game, whereas outward perspective identifies the possibilities, the rewards and the risks inherent in the game itself. Remember when you were a kid deciding which sport to play at school. You chose games you thought you'd be good at and might find fun (inward perspective), having watched a few matches and examined the rules (outward perspective). It is slightly more complicated in business where games are being played at many different levels inside the organisation – divisional games, departmental games and the games of the individual employees. No organisation should attempt to play an external game unless the games within the organisation are sufficiently aligned, i.e. the company is playing as a cohesive team. On the other hand, some variety in skills and outlook is a prerequisite too.

The relationship between the inner games of the organisation that determine its capabilities and the external game it plays in the economy defines the scope of the game – the balance between potential and possibilities. The scope changes according to circumstances outside and direction within. The merger between two companies, for example, may increase their combined potential and therefore extend their range of possibilities and scope. Or the synergies may be outweighed by a clash of cultures which diminish possibilities and scope. Associations or partnerships with players in other games may expand scope. On the other hand, a bad management decision may damage a company's reputation, devalue its stock price and hinder its future scope.

To repeat what we said at the beginning, the gameboard upon which a company plays is defined by the company itself. Identifying scope as a starter in a conversation is designed to encourage participants to confront what they think is obvious – "We make widgets for watchamacallits and damn fine widgets they are too. Just read the mission statement in our Annual Report. What else do you want?" This is what they like to believe, but is it true? In examining the scope of the game in which the company operates, it's similar to evaluating the *fish:pond* quotient – is the company a big fish in a small pond; a small fish in a big pond; a growing fish that is feeding on the smaller fish in the pond; a complacent fish in an increasingly polluted pond; an ageing fish in a changing pond; or a floating guppy in a fishbowl about to be flushed?

It also makes sense to kick off with scope because it is familiar territory that people can move into straightaway – it encourages a participatory environment. It is seemingly innocent. If we were to represent the scope of the so-called 'big five', we could simply take a photo of them, together or separately. But how can we 'capture' the scope of an organisation in a conversation? Imagine that you had an empty frame in front of you and you had to fill it with a picture of your organisation – not of the buildings and the staff, but a representation of its operations. What would it look like? Within the framework of the industry it is in, how does it feature? Does it have a national presence or even a global presence? These are some of the questions that need to be asked in identifying the scope of a business.

The elements of scope – the balance between potential and possibility – can be represented in three diagrams: the Picture Frame, the Seven Frames and the Looking Glass. Before we continue, it is important to remember that none of these frames has a rigid content. The latter may be refined or revised as a result of any strategic conversation in any year. One in a million may be like the enigmatic smile of the Mona Lisa, which will remain forever the same! Moreover, we do not mean you to use *all* the visual aids we have inserted in the rest of the book literally. Many of them should act as 'prompts' to conversations. In the end, it is up to you to decide in what way you want to employ our diagrams.

An organisation is de ned by the type of business area it is in, the activities it performs in that area and the nature in which it plays the game. The Picture Frame represents a picture or a snapshot, the frame being the operational boundary of the organisation, and the space inside being the current scope of its business and activities. Expressed in one way, the picture could contain all your core businesses with the more important at the centre and the others radiating outwards in order of signi cance to the organisation. Non-core businesses you want to sell would lie outside the frame altogether. Likewise, activities undertaken by the organisation to produce its goods and services can be split into core activities at the centre with the more peripheral ones towards the outside. Activities you are likely to outsource, because they are either a drain on the company or no longer form part of the core competence, would similarly lie outside the frame. We promise that just this analysis alone excites an animated discussion.

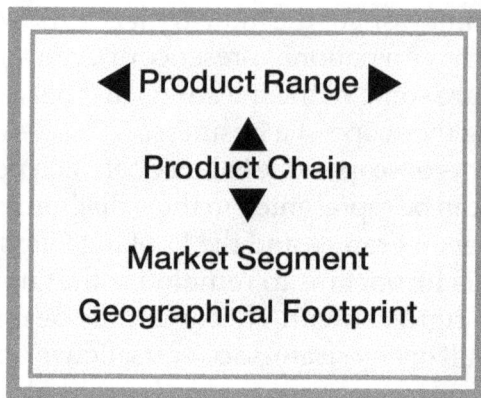

◀ **Product Range** ▶

▲

Product Chain

▼

Market Segment

Geographical Footprint

**Chart 14
The
Picture
Frame**

However, the strategic conversation only really takes off when you start asking what you want the picture to look like in five to ten years' time. How different do you want it to be, if at all? To assist with this part of the debate, we have divided the picture into four components: product range (which covers both physical products and services), product chain, market segment and geographical footprint. As can be seen from the diagram, we regard product range as equivalent to horizontal diversification and product chain as equivalent to vertical integration. Examples of questions that should be asked include the following:

Product Range

What is your product and service range? (For those starting out, what is it to be?) Do you want to widen the range to achieve more diversification? Do you want to narrow it to achieve more focus? Do you want to keep it the same? Is the attention of top management too widely dispersed or appropriately concentrated? Is the mix of your products/businesses right? Do you want to change the mix in light of market trends or greater intensity of competition? Are there any businesses in your portfolio that are not core to your product range? Do you want to sell them? Are there any new products that can be organically developed from existing core competencies? Have you any products in the pipeline that constitute a step change because of innovation? Can you add services such as maintenance to any of your physical products and thereby increase your range that way?

You may also wish to recycle some of your products for environmental or commercial reasons. Obviously, if you want to change your product range radically, you may have to take over another company with the core competencies in the area into which you want to move. Growing those competencies from scratch may take you a long time.

Product Chain

In your industry, what are the processes that make up the production (or value) chain from the ground to the customer? In which ones are you represented? Do you want to go further upstream to control your inputs or go further downstream to capture value closer to the customer? Are there missing links in the chain where you might wish to develop core competencies? In which part of the production and marketing chain do you think you are strongest and in which are you the weakest? In the latter case, are you forming alliances or joint ventures with other companies more specialised in the relevant fields? Should the range of functions currently performed in-house stay the same, or should more of them be outsourced?

Some companies, such as oil companies, like to be represented in the entire chain (in the case of oil from the well to the petrol pump). Others like to stick to a link in the chain and dominate it nationwide (retail chains) or worldwide (fast-food chains).

Market Segment

Is your current market growing or diminishing as a result of changing demographics? Where are the best opportunities to expand? Do you want to broaden your customer base with new products aimed at different income and age groups? Should your marketing campaigns be suitably modified? Or might there be a downside to the exclusiveness or timelessness of your brand? Are you too dependent on a specific industry or company for your sales, and should you be looking for other clients?

Geographical Footprint

For each step in the process defined so far, are you adequately represented in terms of geographical footprint? Are there other cities, states or countries of interest to explore in terms of marketing to them, establishing businesses in them, or both? Are you sufficiently diversified in a geographical sense so that no city, state or country can impact on your results too seriously if that city, state or country goes through harsh times, or is global reach a bridge too far?

So, how's your *fish:pond* quotient now? Fancy other ponds?

Manchester United Football Club is an example of a company – now listed on the stock exchange – that has grown way beyond its traditional scope – the game of football. From this core it has moved into the merchandising and retail game. It sells many products which are dependent on the brand being successful. Thus, the irony now is that should the football side suffer a losing streak, the merchandising and retail game will pay the penalty. The real game (of soccer that is) impinges on the business game. Moreover, with the worldwide explosion of broadband technology, Manchester United is on the verge of entering the broadcasting business. It is expected to be amongst the first football clubs to broadcast all its matches on the internet in real time in an effort to reach a subscriber base of 'displaced supporters' around the globe that number in the millions. So what conclusion do you draw? The club has to keep on winning!

The concept of using pictures as part of the strategic process is, we agree, somewhat unusual. Nevertheless, we would argue that evaluation through graphic representation is a powerful and enlightening tool. Child psychologists will often turn to the artwork of young children to get an idea of their issues. These pictures are not assessed on the artistic accuracy of their components but rather on their proportion and relationship. Questions would be asked about how and where the child represents herself in the picture. Is she standing next to other people in the picture or is she on the outside? Who in the picture is larger than the others? Where are lines of contact and where is there representation of emotional disengagement? And, more importantly, is she smiling?

So, even though we don't want you to take our diagrams too literally, it is worthwhile to ask how the yardsticks used by child psychologists can be transferred to the corporate world. Well, it can be done by giving executives a plain piece of paper, and asking them to draw a picture frame like the one we showed earlier; then fill in the picture with their representation of the organisation and the game it is in. Not every manager is a Monet, so the product may consist of simple line drawings, a sequence of shapes or sketches, or even a written picture, depending on their level of artistic skill. For example, an accountant may find it very difficult to draw anything that does not involve numbers – and we've all seen how creative some accountants can be with these! On the other hand, some groups will draw the company's annual report – creative indeed! It's a revealing exercise, as it gives a first indication of how the organisation thinks. The most important strategic insight gained from this exercise is whether the organisation has the imagination to grow in conditions which it least suspects. The more impressionistic the drawings, the more likely it is that it can.

The next diagram – The Seven Frames – places a company in the context of other games played outside and within it. There are always games within games or, as our diagram shows, a bigger picture behind a smaller one. Moving inwards, one should evaluate the role of the company in the internal sub-games being played inside it. The question here is: how much should a company interfere in its internal games? Similarly, how much should a government interfere in industry or corporate games? Where should a line be drawn in terms of interference, because not all interference can be considered negative? In soccer, a manager is expected to interfere when the team goes off at half-time to the dressing room. He will give them a piece of his mind if they're losing and encouragement if they're winning. However, if he continually shouts orders from the sideline during a match, he may confuse them at best and demoralise them at worst. So there's good interference that encourages innovation and team spirit, and can help win the game; and bad interference which creates animosity and frustration instead of alignment. Balance is sometimes hard to achieve if a team has a hot-blooded manager, a company has a hands-on CEO or a country a dictatorial leader.

Chart 15 *The Seven Frames*

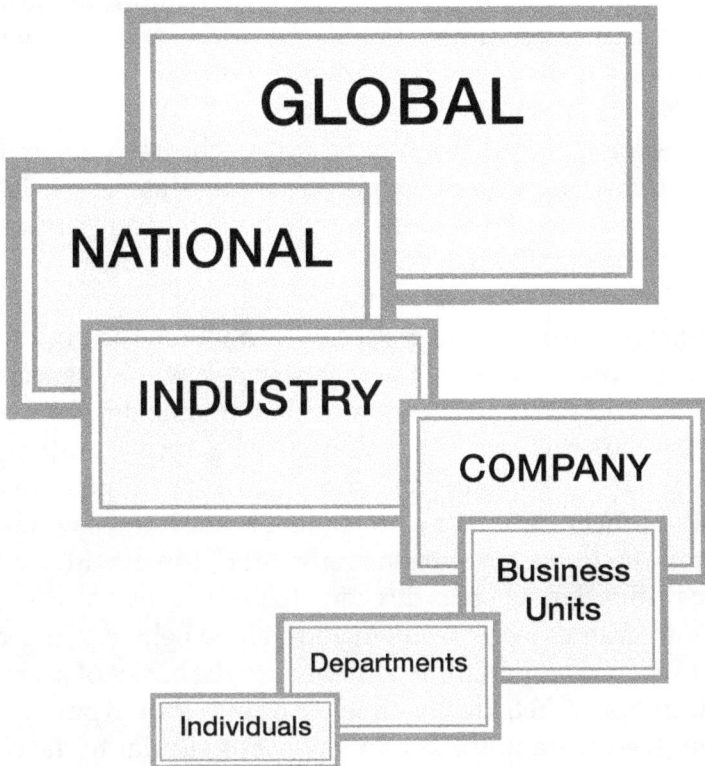

GLOBAL

NATIONAL

INDUSTRY

COMPANY

Business Units

Departments

Individuals

You will recognise the middle frame as the one we drew for the company in *Chart 14*. In relation to this, the inner frames represent the games that go on inside the organisation, i.e. the games played by each business unit and department, as well as those played by individual employees (remember the balanced and unbalanced personal frames unveiled earlier). Clearly, you need some alignment between all these games in order for the group as a whole to function as an effective entity. But where do you draw the line between centralisation and decentralisation so that you get everybody 'singing from the same hymn sheet' (a phrase beloved by CEOs) without killing entrepreneurial spirit?

Another implication of the diagram is that the CEO should receive a summary of the strategic conversations undertaken by the business units, because he or she will simply not have the same level of knowledge of the game as the people who play it every day. This applies particularly where the game is being played in another country which has unfamiliar rules. The perception of the players living there is crucial to future investment decisions by the holding company resident in a foreign land.

The outer frames represent the increasingly larger and more complex environmental games within which the organisation must play – those of the industry as a whole, as well as national and international games. Sustainable development can only be achieved through a correct balance or alignment between the organisation's inner and outer frames. An excessive concentration of focus on the inner frames will lead a company to become increasingly out of touch with the realities around it; whereas directing too much energy towards the outer frames might result in your falling behind your leaner and meaner competitors who keep to the basics of a strong game in-house. Yet, ideally, all seven frames should be aligned through a common thread. In a way, it's similar to the concept behind the popular *Where's Wally?* books. In the latter, a cartoon character called Wally is hidden amongst a myriad of other similarly coloured characters, with the object being to find him. Each page represents a different time or place in history, but the common thread is a hidden Wally. In business the concept goes beyond the simple game of finding a character. It is to do with building an understanding of context and continuity – both essential for ensuring sustainable growth. A successful organisation is one that directs its energies along a path that weaves between the internal (organisational) and external (environmental) frames, revisiting them continually to achieve a competitive edge in the wider and narrower game. This interface between the frames is the true scope of the organisation – the balance between its internal potential and external possibilities.

An example of the importance of this balance can be found in the scope of the banking sector in a developing economy like South Africa. The inner frames of the banks naturally concentrate on solving the paradox between creating a customer-centric model and streamlining their organisational and operating structures to bring down costs. However, performing this egg dance on its own misses out on the bigger picture. For, in order to play the game properly in a developing economy, the external frames of the banks should be sending them signals on the need to assist job creation and encourage entrepreneurial start-ups. Besides expanding their client base, initiatives in this direction will help create an inclusive economy with a viable middle class bent on preserving stability. The result: a more sustainable national game and greater value for the banks in the longer run.

For similar reasons, it makes sense for a multinational company to have a conversation around the Seven Frames for each of the countries within which it operates. The national frame in each case qualifies as the context of the company's operations there. If the rules of the game for the company are not aligned with those of the national frame, then the company has two options: change its own game to suit the local game better or get out (obviously, where corruption is the name of the game, it's preferable to get out). Each national game is different. Cultures and social customs – the unwritten norms that help define the rules for each national game – are varied and complicated. One man's burp is another man's compliment.

Equally, multinationals need to understand the international game in order to play effectively across borders. All those GATT and World Trade Organisation rules, all the potential stuff to come out of the Kyoto Protocol on global warming, all the regional rules like those imposed by the European Union on anti-competitive behaviour, need to be examined as part of the outermost frame. The conditions set for these games are way beyond the control of any multinational to influence. Their only choice is to comply (though some mount hugely expensive legal challenges which are normally fruitless). Consequently, it goes without saying that alignment needs to be secured if all the picture frames are to fit. And this is as true of the frames pointing inwards to the employee as it is of those which point outwards to the world at large. But alignment can be derailed through glaring mismanagement or through the most noble of intentions. Take individual performance bonuses. Managers driven by such incentives may well abandon any ideas of teamwork that might dilute their reward. In the same vein, business units or departments that are driven by performance-based incentives may form silos that exclude the involvement of other units or departments. These actions can cut across alignment to the extent that the company loses the overall game. So beware!

During the part of the conversation when an organisa-

tion is considering scope, a critical self-analysis has to take place at the same time (to match internal potential with external possibilities). Hence, the inclusion of the Looking Glass, so that you can take a long, hard look at yourself in the mirror. Later on, it will help you identify strengths and weaknesses; in the latter case any gaps between your current potential and the new opportunities afforded by expanding the scope of the game. Your options will then include actions to
ll the gaps. To help you get a feel for your re ection, we have inserted six elements in the Looking Glass.

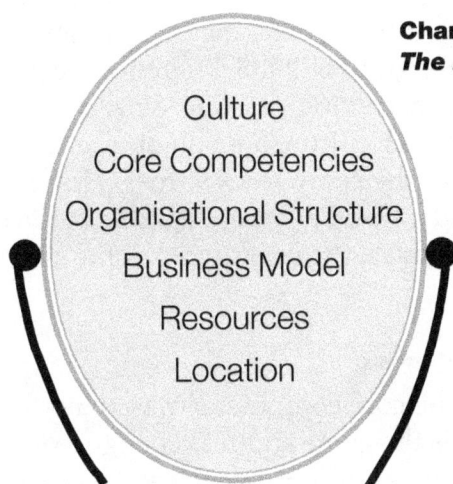

Chart 16
The Looking Glass

Culture
Core Competencies
Organisational Structure
Business Model
Resources
Location

The kind of introspective questions you should be asking yourself are:

Culture

In describing the scope of my game, is the culture existing in my company at the moment the best one to win it with? If I'm a multinational, how do I cope with the cultural differences between my workforces in different countries, and how do I superimpose some form of corporate identity that welds them together as a cohesive team? Where I am expanding the scope either to include other products or other steps in the product chain, is the culture materially different in these new areas? For example, in the mining industry, exploration demands a far more entrepreneurial culture than managing mines to exploit the deposit. Elsewhere, retailing demands a completely different culture to manufacturing and wholesaling. Does my remuneration structure encourage the kind of culture which I believe is suitable for the industries that I'm in? Where I'm selling into a new market segment, e.g. younger consumers, how will I change my culture to appeal to them? If I'm thinking of taking over another company, will our cultures merge, or will the differences be perpetual stumbling blocks to achieving genuine synergies?

Interlinked with culture are values and similar questions can be asked of the company's values. However, ethical issues are already raised at various points in the conversation which tend to reveal the underlying value system inside the company.

Core Competencies

Do I possess the core competencies to play the game as it is played now? Is the game about to change to the extent that a completely new set of competencies will be required? Is my training and development programme geared to produce the requisite core competencies in each of the countries I'm operating in, and do those countries have adequate feedstock coming out of their education system? If not, where in the world am I going to obtain suitable recruits? If I am extending the scope of my game, can I do it organically by building on my core competencies so that I can spread them into the new areas? Or will I have to acquire them by forming some form of commercial partnership/relationship with another company? If I'm stepping out of the frame into a completely new product or business, do I grow the skills from scratch myself inside my own company? Or do I approach candidates holding senior executive positions in other companies who I know already possess those skills, and – should I secure their services – let them build new teams around them? Do I look around for a suitable takeover target and do all these things at once?

Organisational Structure

Is my organisational structure correct for the game I'm in? If the game is evolving, is my structure evolving along with it? As with a soccer team, should I be changing the arrangement of the players on the field to get better results? Is my structure too flat so that I lack sufficient control? Is it too hierarchical so that it makes for clumsy and slow decisions? Where I am entering new games, what is the structure of my competitors and should I emulate it? If I am about to widen my geographical footprint, will I need to move from a centralised to a more decentralised structure?

Business Model

Is my business model robust enough to cope with all the scenarios that my existing game can produce? How will I have to amend my business model if I am entering new games or new countries? How much flexibility should I build into my business model to cope with the variations of doing business on different continents? What are the differences between my business model and those of my competitors? Do the differences give me a better chance of winning the game? If not, how am I going to change my model?

Resources

In terms of the relative importance I attach to the games I have identified under my scope, does my allocation of human, financial and other resources reflect my priorities? Should I be concentrating my resources on a narrower front to defeat my competition (normal war strategy), or should I be acquiring more resources in order to achieve a better standard of performance in the various games I am playing? Should I be cutting back on overheads in order to release money so that I can have more troops on the ground? Or should I be making total cuts just to be a lighter, tighter fighting force overall? What could these retrenchments do to staff morale? Where I am contemplating other games, do I really have the resources to enter them, especially if they are much bigger games? If not, where in the market will I obtain those resources?

Location

Where is the present centre of gravity of my operations and where will it be in ten years' time? Should I be moving my head office now so that it will tie in with my future geographical footprint? In order to play the game most effectively in each of my host countries, in which city is it best to have a local office and principal representative?

In ending this section, we would just like to point out that any general worth his salt asks all these questions before he commits his troops to battle. The Looking Glass is very much part of developing military strategy after the scope of the battle (terrain, enemy numbers and disposition, weapons) has been estimated. However, given how much the nature of the war game has changed in the last twenty years, one must ask whether governments have gone through the same process of logic in equipping their defence forces for current rather than obsolete threats.

Players

All the world's a stage,
And all the men and women merely players.

WILLIAM SHAKESPEARE

Unlike chess, which has two players, business has to contend
with many players (frequently referred to as stakeholders).
We are most interested in those who can have a significant

Chart 17 *The Conversation Model – Players*

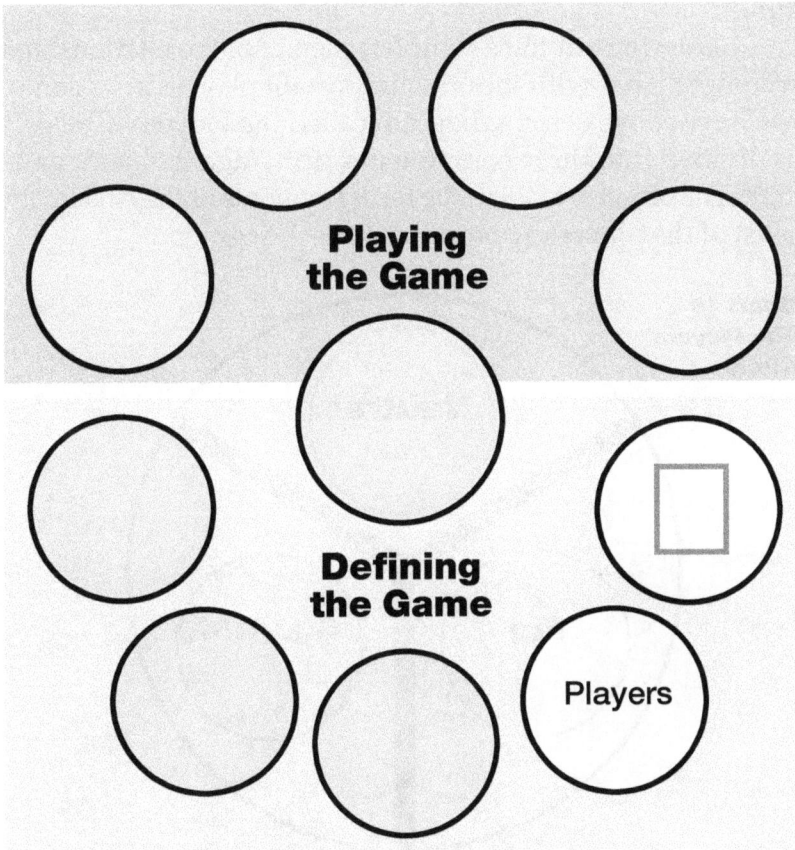

impact on the bottom line. To keep to the sporting analogy, if you are to win, you need to know as much as possible about the people playing in the same game. Understandably this includes both those players on your side as well as those in the opposing teams. In terms of business strategy, however, we have included a third category: players who are neutral. It is best to think of neutral players as 'poised' between the two camps. In other words, under certain circumstances, they could be 'for' you. In other circumstances, they could just as easily be 'against' you. Sometimes, they are genuinely 'neutral'. It depends where their interests lie at any moment in time.

To assist in painting a complete picture of the relationships a company has with the other important players in its game, we have constructed a diagram called the Players' Circle. It is divided into three components: 'for', 'against' and 'neutral'. The object is to ll in the three segments of the circle with a list of the players appropriate to each segment.

Chart 18
The Players'
Circle

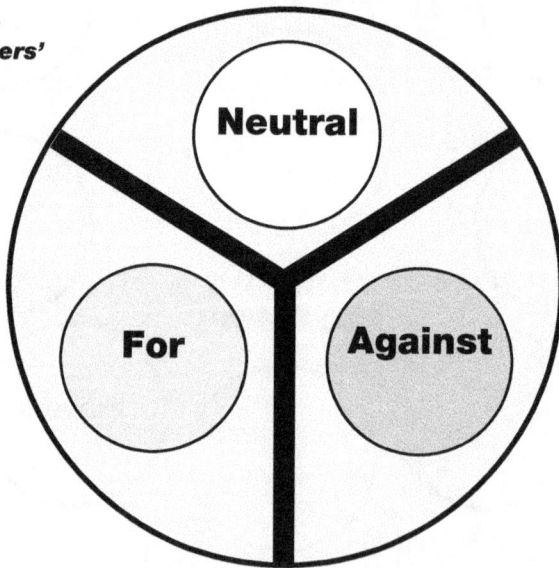

224

In conversations we facilitate, we are frequently asked to clarify exactly what we mean by the three categories. Do we mean by 'for' that the player has a positive/supportive relationship with the company, or that the player actively assists in increasing the bottom line? Likewise, does 'against' mean a negative/destructive relationship, or that the player actively seeks to diminish the company's bottom line? Does 'neutral' mean independent like a referee or, as we have already suggested, sometimes for and sometimes against? The answer is that life is never simple and it depends on the player under consideration. For example, competitors are always against you in our terminology because, while they may respect you, they want to win the game as much as you do. You're battling over the same turf. Suppliers can be 'for' you when you have established a positive relationship with them over time – even though they are going to pursue their own interests up to a point in the annual price negotiations. It depends how reasonable they are and how much they value your relationship. Obviously, if they try to use a dominant position in the supply chain to gouge the maximum price out of you, you would put them in the 'against' column. The same will apply if they offer your competitors discounts which they don't offer you; or if they don't deliver on time; or if they regularly break other conditions of the contract because of wilfulness or inefficiency. It's all a matter of judgment where you put each company or institution with which you have an interaction (even your competitors are sometimes 'for' you when you collaborate with them in a trade association which promotes the industry as a whole). And then there is your family. Where would you put your parents, spouse, children? For example, children are usually 'neutral' as infants, 'for' between three and twelve and shift to 'against' as teenagers!

Let us now go through the major players in business and provide some pertinent questions and comments on each.

Who are your real competitors, the ones you go head to head with? You should identify them by name. What are their strengths and weaknesses compared to yours? So many companies do a SWOT analysis on themselves, but never swot up on their competitors. Maybe it's vanity! You would have thought such an exercise would be an elementary first step in plotting strategy. After all, the first thing a tennis player at Wimbledon does before facing his opponent on court is to watch videos of his opponent's previous matches to see if he has a weak forehand or backhand or can't volley at net. He adjusts his strategy accordingly.

Then there's the relative size of your competitors compared to you. Do they qualify as 450-pound gorillas while you weigh in as a mid-sized orang-utan? Can they threaten you with economies of scale which you will never hope to achieve? The red lights should be flashing if you are starting to become a troublesome itch in their side. They can swat you to death. Maybe it's time to quit the game or else tie the knot with one of the gorillas. Jack Welch once said that you have to be No. 1 or No. 2 or fix, sell or close your business. He's not absolutely correct, because you can be highly differentiated and survive in your own niche. BMW is neither the No. 1 or No. 2 global car manufacturer, but it makes a tidy profit.

Perhaps it's the other way round and you're a Goliath surrounded by nimble Davids with greater agility and lower overheads than you. Remember, a swarm of bees can kill you! Sometimes in an industry there's a whole bunch of small guys out there operating in the informal zone who can outmanoeuvre you with special deals and sell at half your price. They (and their hives) must be taken into account.

Then what about all your indirect competitors who may not be in exactly the same sector as you but who are competing for the same buck? If you're in jewellery, what about

all the other luxury goods manufacturers? If you're in air travel, what about all the other forms of transport? You don't have
to make a list of all the companies in the category 'indirect
competitors', but you must bear them in mind because any
change in their status for better or for worse may have a profound impact on your game.

Suppliers

Suppliers can fill any of the three segments depending on
your relationship with them. It's tragic how many suppliers have no understanding of their customer's game and vice
versa. The relationship is basically adversarial and founded
on ignorance – neutral to negative. IT companies in the 1980s
and 90s were in the habit of selling systems to customers,
which were far too exotic for their needs. They were doing
nobody a favour. They were only thinking of their own game.
On the contrary, suppliers should be helping you to win *your*
game, not theirs. Today, supply chain management is the new
slogan. To make it real, you should be sitting down with your
suppliers not just to hassle over prices on an annual basis
but to gain an understanding of each other's games (and
maybe adjust the contract to suit both sides). Then you can
move to the 'for' column in each other's circle. Again a SWOT
analysis of your key suppliers is no bad thing, because you
inherit all their strengths and weaknesses, opportunities and
threats as a lower member on the food chain.

Customers

When did you last do a customer survey to ascertain what
customers think of you? If you're in the middle of the product chain, what do the end-consumers think of you and your
product? Come to think of it, what do the public feel generally about you? Many world-class companies take it for granted that brand excellence is a perpetual thing and their cus-

tomers can automatically be placed in the 'for' column. Not so fast – if it's an assumption you should check it out. Independent surveys give you the brutal, honest facts. Don't rely on hearsay. It's worth recalling that your customers may be 'poised' to use one of your competitor's products – in which case they are in 'neutral'.

Employees

Would you believe it, but we've had the executive teams of companies put senior management in the 'for' column and employees in 'neutral'. That's a strategic issue, if ever there was one! Greece won the second most coveted soccer trophy in the world in 2004 – the European Championships – not because they had the most talented individual players, but because they had the *best team*. Your employees are your team and if they are in 'neutral', you are hardly likely to win your industry's premier trophy in any category. In today's networked business environment, you often hear the phrase "your people are your assets". Though the expression is becoming hackneyed, it is nevertheless true. The public want to know that you are a decent employer and put your money where your mouth is.

Trade Unions

Where labour forces are unionised, trade unions are important players in the corporate game. When labour relations are good, trade unions are usually put in the 'neutral' column; but when they're bad they go in the 'against' column. Obviously, the latter is a drag on the business and is at the very least a strategic issue for the human resources director.

Shareholders

Like soccer fans, shareholders are usually 'for' you if you are doing well and 'neutral' to 'against' you if you are doing badly (depending on whether they perceive the cause to be a tough external environment or bad management). Shareholder support can be crucial during crisis periods. It therefore confounds common sense how many board remuneration committees go out of their way to anger the shareholders by granting the CEO plus his top sidekicks unreasonable pay hikes in bad times. The financial community, including pension fund managers, stockbrokers and financial analysts, are not amused either.

Where a company has a major shareholder, the relationship can have a huge influence on the destiny of the company. It's always interesting asking subsidiaries what their opinion is of the holding company (having promised it will never get back!). In one case, the subsidiary put its holding company firmly in the 'against' column on the grounds that the latter consistently vetoed all capital project proposals in order to maximise dividends out of the company.

Sometimes it's not nice being a cash cow. You can be milked to death.

Government

Most companies put government in 'neutral', which is where it should be as a neutral referee. Occasionally, it is put in the 'against' column if it has just levied a burdensome tax increase on a particular sector or made life more difficult in another way. Multinationals must of course consider the governments of all the countries in which they have operations as players. The relationships with these various host governments may differ dramatically, calling for changes in the geographical footprint if problems in a particular country can't be overcome. On the other hand, where governments are consistently put in the 'for' column by big business, they can be accused by their opponents of 'crony capitalism'. Nevertheless, building a strong relationship with government and demonstrating a long-term commitment to the country are, in many cases, the passport to successful investment by foreigners.

Communities and NGOs

With consumers becoming more discerning in their choice, having communities and NGOs in the 'for' or at least the 'neutral' column is becoming increasingly a factor in winning the game. Have you ensured with all your projects that local communities have participated throughout the feasibility phase? Have you set up corporate social responsibility programmes around your operations which make a sustainable difference to the quality of life of impoverished people in the vicinity? Are environmental impact assessments on your projects conducted by neutral, independent bodies? Otherwise, NGOs can really bite you if they are effective watchdogs. And so can quangos and gongos. No, they are not mythical beasts like griffins. They are quasi-nongovernmental organisations and government-organised nongovernmental organisations. Essentially hedgehogs in disguise!

Media

We've left the fourth estate to last, but don't underestimate what a powerful player it can be. The relationship, if good, is usually 'neutral', because it is built upon a healthy tension. They want sensational stories and you need to be in a position to negotiate that sensation to your benefit and not at your expense. The most critical question to ask yourself is this: if something really nasty happens, have you got a contingency plan in place which not only corrects the problem but handles it honestly and openly? The first 24 hours after an incident can make or break a company's reputation for a very long time. Cover-ups lose you the game.

So when do relationships with any of these players become

elevated to the extent that they qualify as strategic issues? The answer is when your ability to play the game is severely impaired because the relationship is not in the right part of the circle. Moreover, you may have to abandon the game if something is not done to improve the situation. Relationships with competitors will always be adversarial, and therefore their strategies count as much as yours in the final outcome of the game. You can out-strategise them; you can take them over to convert them from 'against' to 'for' (except that cultural differences often undo the good of any merger); or you can just slug it out together in the local market and look for fresh opportunities overseas (preferably in territories where your competitors are absent).

Conversation around players is also important when there is the need to negotiate a major contract. This type of analysis will give you the chance to identify the players with the greatest value in the negotiation process. It will also allow you to assess whether they are likely to start in the 'for', 'against' or 'neutral' column. As the negotiation proceeds, you can plot their change of position. Your final objective may not be to win the game per se, but to ratify an agreement in which all parties consider they are winners. These agreements tend to last longer than the win-lose variety.

To add to the challenge, one of the effects of globalisation is player complexity – there are more players than ever before and their influence over the game has become increasingly diffused. We ultimately live in one world where the value of meaningful relationships is the true measure of competitive advantage. The secret to winning the game lies in the ability to build relationships and then use them as leverage to enhance your position in the game. But let's not get sentimental. There are no friends in business, only those with shared interests who are momentarily willing to play your game because it is also theirs.

We'd like to end up this section with a bit of wisdom and humour. When one of us was facilitating a session for a church recently, we had almost completed the list of players when someone asked: "Where would you put God?" "In neutral," replied one of the priests. "Really," said someone else, "I thought God was on our side." "That's the problem," responded the priest, "Everybody thinks God is on their side, whereas God is on everyone's side." Game, set and match to the priest.

Rules of the Game

How would you like it if you were a business executive
and when you made a mistake, a red light
went on and 18,000 people started screaming?
JACQUES PLANTE
Canadian ice hockey goal tender and the first player to wear a mask in a game

Every game has its rules, but they are not always set rules like those given on the inside of a *Scrabble* box. The rules of life are more subjective – more like parameters as perceived by each player. Even moral rules are subject to different interpretations, particularly when it comes to exceptions. Rules may be influenced by the players, such as in a game of 'tag' being played by children, or they may be determined by forces or factors outside of the control or influence of the players. Laws of government and corporate codes of conduct fall into the first category, the forces of nature and principles of science into the second. T. H. Huxley, a nineteenth-century English scientist, put it thus: "The chess-board is the world; the pieces are the phenomena of the universe; the rules of the game are what we call the laws of Nature. The player on the other side is hidden from us."

Some rules don't change, such as those in chess, where the

rules have remained unchanged since the game originated in India in medieval times. However, in business there is only one rule that doesn't change, and that is that the rules of business vary in different locations and are always changing (wherever you are). They change from culture to culture; from country to country; they change through developments in technology; and they also change as a result of social and political events. They can also literally change overnight.

Broadly speaking, the rules of any game include both writ-

Chart 19 *The Conversation Model – Rules of the Game*

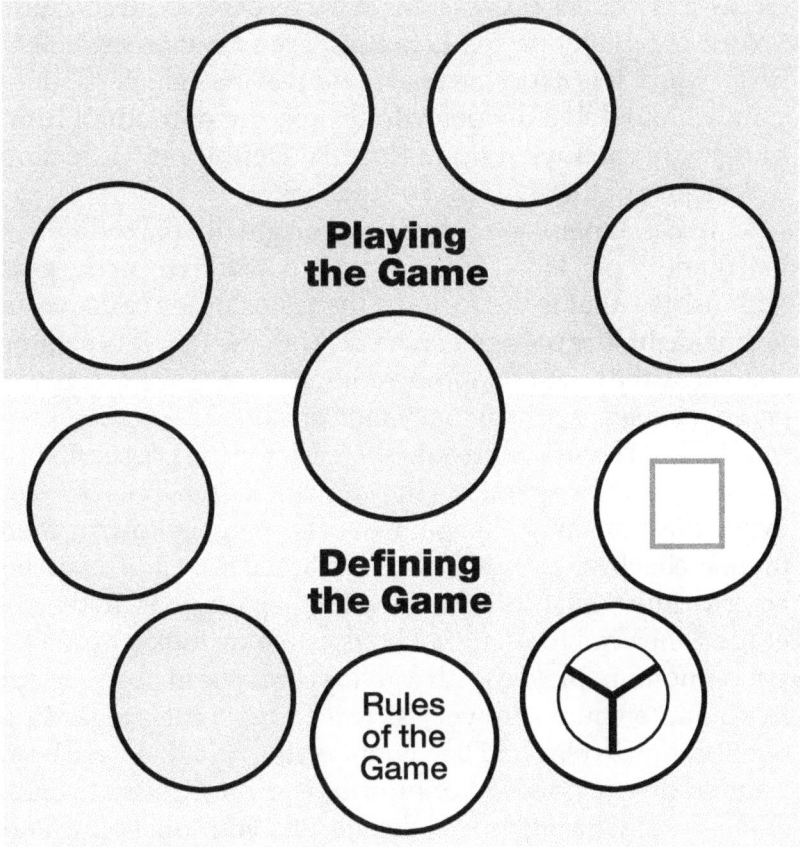

**Playing
the Game**

**Defining
the Game**

Rules
of the
Game

ten and unwritten rules, and the difference between them is very important. As an example, let's compare two national sports – one in America and the other in Afghanistan. When it comes to sport (and their constitution), Americans, it is well known, are very particular that rules should be written down. They should also be specific and preferably complex. Apparently, paradoxically, this makes them easier to apply. Take for example the game of American football, as governed by the National Football League, that rules a 'fumble' as the following: " . . . any act, other than a pass or legal kick, which results in loss of player possession. The term *fumble* always implies possession". There's even an addendum: "Note: If a player pretends to fumble and causes the ball to go forward, it is a forward pass and may be illegal." Should you wish to delve deeper into the exposé of football fumblings you can look it up in Rule 3 ("Definitions"), Section 2, Article 4, of the NFL official rulebook.

Whereas American football was originally played with a ball made of pigskin, it is a goatskin – with the rest of the goat still inside – that is the focus of the testosterone test known as buzkashi, the national sport of Afghanistan. It is a game shaped by the time-honoured tradition of recognising courage and horsemanship. Essentially men on horseback (called 'chavandozlar') compete on a dusty track for the possession of a dead goat. The winner is the chavandoz who manages to evade the crunching engagement of scores of bellowing men on horseback, to gallop around a marked spot and to speed across a line whilst still clutching the hapless goat. To the average American football fan buzkashi may look a little like pandemonium played with a goat's carcass and no rules; but it is in fact a game with very strict *unwritten* rules regarding qualification to play and behaviour on the field that have been handed down via word of mouth over hundreds of years, and enforced through social debate, physical squabbling and the occasional beheading. Some may argue that it sounds rather uncivilised, and yet fail to see the similarities with one of its derivatives – polo.

So, whether written or unwritten, all games have rules. This is essentially and unequivocally a determining factor in the nature of any interaction between people, and between people and their environment. Remember those videos that were played backwards on the TV programme *America's Funniest Home Videos*? They were funny because in real life you don't see riders who have fallen off their horses into a puddle, and are covered in mud, immediately jump back on their horses all nice and clean. It breaks the rules. Even heavy metal music has rules because it is music of sorts. But to return to our sporting analogy, if you are aware of the rules of a particular sport and as long as you do not break them, everything else is fair game; and that is the area in which you can freely exercise your interpretation of the game and operate to your advantage. These rules may be comprehensive and explicit as in the game of American football, but the game of business is more buzkashi than Superbowl. Some of the rules are predictable (like tax and company law), everything else is not; and it is this unknown area that represents an exciting array of untapped possibilities.

The rules of any game in life are therefore an amalgam of written and unwritten rules that have been put in place by a host of governing bodies including schools, governments and sports administrators. Then there are rules that have been introduced by the players themselves, and finally there are rules that have just come about through changes in the market or the environment with no human intervention whatsoever. All these rules may or may not change over time.

Just as there are rules that determine the relationship between animals – such as where you stand in the food chain, e.g. lions trump the rest – the rules of business, as viewed by the business community, will determine whether a company survives in the corporate jungle. Recognition of these rules is paramount, because they shape the genetic blueprint of the game – its DNA. We therefore call them the *descriptive, normative and aspirational* rules of the game. Woe betide anybody who doesn't examine them before deciding on strategy.

Descriptive rules, as the name suggests, describe the basic rules of your market, i.e. what in your estimation is predictable about it. For example, you may be in a declining market, a growing market, a market becoming increasingly competitive, a market that is going to be more/less regulated, or one where the opposition is consolidating into larger business enterprises. They embrace any contractual arrangements limiting your sphere of action including agreements with parent companies, licensing conditions, treaties and informal deals with third parties. Descriptive rules also determine a company's basic *licence to operate* in the countries (or regions like the European Union) where it does business. These include legislation and tax codes, but more importantly the 'unwritten rules' that govern business relationships. It is these rules that often differ from country to country. Here is a selection of unwritten rules from one Far Eastern country: sign the contract and then the negotiation begins; if you cause someone else to lose face, you lose face yourself; and when driving, anything behind you is of no consequence i.e. *what ifs* you spot in your rear-view mirror are too late, so don't torture yourself.

Two critical questions that should be asked around descriptive rules are: have there recently been any changes in the descriptive rules which could affect any part of your business and are there likely to be further changes?

A good example of a recent change in these rules is black economic empowerment in South Africa. You need a BEE in your bonnet to operate here. No question. The top executive team can also *make* rules which give a company its corporate identity. These rules are then handed down to each department as descriptive rules of the game. They cannot easily be challenged.

Normative rules are the *moral rules of the game* to which any world-class company has to subscribe to keep its world-class badge. You don't have to be a rocket scientist to list them. Honourable people know them off by heart. They are your conscience. They are the rules that, if adhered to by a company, demonstrate a noble sense of purpose that the public respects. Break them and you lose the badge of honour in a nanosecond. Normative rules include those on corporate governance and SHEC (safety, health, the environment and the community). In the military lexicon, they are normally called the 'rules of engagement'. Such rules are universal in the sense that they are valid across the world (unlike descriptive rules). Where a company applies different standards in this sphere, the fact is immediately picked up by the media, with the offender being publicly castigated.

Yet, for many companies driven solely by the quest for increased profits, normative rules of the game are at best tolerated. But this is a risky game because minimal compliance can so often lead to individual employees flouting the rules with fatal consequences.

Important questions that should be addressed at this point of the conversation include: Are there any new normative rules in the pipeline in host countries? Which countries in the world can be ruled out of bounds because the company cannot operate there according to the normative rules it has laid down for itself? Company values are the backbone for the normative rules of the game and should therefore be made explicit at this stage. No gifts, no thick brown envelopes, no commissions via intermediaries, no lowering of standards in Third World countries, no disparities in working conditions, no creative accounting, etc. People will soon get the drift: foxes can become quite hedgehog-like over values.

Aspirational rules are the *rules to win the game*. What are the aspirational rules for each step of the process and for the business as a whole? Answers might include management focus; branding; other forms of differentiation to make your product/service unique; cost leadership; maintaining an entrepreneurial flair; attracting, developing and retaining talented young people; a perpetual spirit of innovation (both incremental innovation to achieve operational excellence and radical innovation leading to a change in the game you play); and understanding the rules of your customers by forging long-term relationships with them. Without being biased in any way, we can give you a great example. Fox News, a cable TV news network in America, differentiates itself from the other networks by being quintessentially American, openly supportive of the Administration and covering major domestic stories (such as high-profile murder trials) in considerable detail. It has made large inroads into the market as a result. Aspirational rules of the game can be equated to the value drivers of the business. They should create commercial value in the game and enhance the ability for survival and growth. A company's 'vision' can often be developed from the aspirational rules, as they constitute an understanding of the meaning of winning the game.

The importance of knowing and understanding the rules of the game cannot be stressed enough. But here's the twist: there is no complete set of rules for any game at any one time. Because each game is influenced by the actions of the entire roster of its players, every game is continually changing. If it didn't change, all the rules would become known and the game would cease to evolve. Therefore the most effective player in any game is that player whose understanding of the rules of the game is closest to the 'real' permutation at that moment. In other words, they may not 'know' the game, but they have a better 'feel' for the game; and are in a better position for 'intuitive' decision-making.

In a way a game and its combination of rules is like a lottery with a permutation of, say, ten numbers, and where part of the combination of numbers, say six of them, remain pretty constant. Furthermore, some companies know more of this set combination of six numbers than others. The payouts are incremental and shared equally amongst those with the same correct numbers. The company that wins is the one which knows all six of the set numbers and then gets, say, a seventh and an eighth one right. But then the rst and maybe the second of the set of six numbers may change because of the change in strategy of that one company. Everyone then has to re-evaluate the game plan. And so it goes on.

Some markets are so tight and business is so competitive that a detailed conversation about the rules is a prerequisite for any degree of competitive advantage. Moreover, some changes in the rules are so deceptive that they could be missed unless there has been an upfront conversation about them. Yet so many companies play the game in wondrous oblivion of the rules, let alone any changes in them.

Through their continual evolution, the descriptive, normative and aspirational rules of a game exist in a continually shifting yet balanced relationship that can best be expressed in the form of a triangle:

Aspirational

A

Chart 20
The DNA Triangle

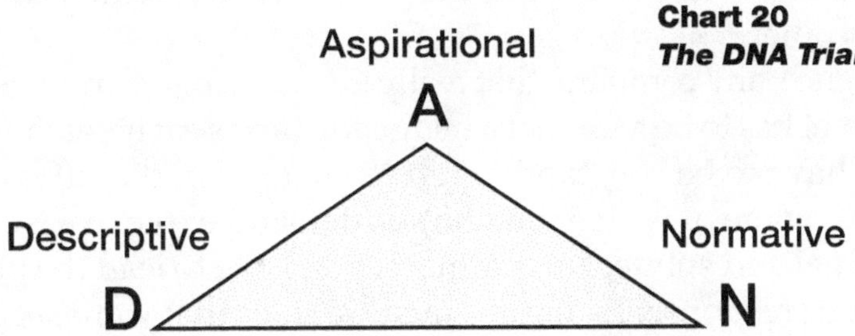

Descriptive

Normative

D

N

The descriptive and normative rules for a game are located at the base of the triangle and the aspirational rules at the apex, because the aspirational rules can't be achieved unless the descriptive and normative rules are fully complied with. Any company that wishes to be sustainable acknowledges this. Moreover, companies that fail to achieve the aspirational rules are encouraged to 'get back to basics': to revisit the descriptive and normative rules and examine whether or not they are being followed.

Similarly, just as some animals thrive under certain circumstances and not under others, depending on the fit of their genetic make-up with the environmental conditions around them, so too are some companies better aligned with the DNA of a game by virtue of its being compatible with their own inherent character and temperament. Sometimes just the very conversation in a company around a game's DNA is enough to throw up anomalies in the company's compatibility with its environment, which may explain why the company is struggling vis-à-vis its competitors. Like a polar bear is better suited to arctic conditions than a brown bear, a company with its roots firmly planted in a particular industry and steeped in its culture is better equipped to handle the future than a relative newcomer. On the other hand, if the newcomer is a fox, it may have spotted a change in the rules which turns the industry's DNA upside down and makes all past experience irrelevant. Indeed, a revolutionary fox often induces the changes in the DNA of the game in order to favour the newcomer.

Hence, any company that really wishes to move from good to great has to be a fox, *not* a hedgehog (foxes eat hedgehogs). You have to be constantly alert to changes in the rules of a game, some of which may be sudden and explosive, some gradual and subtle. Furthermore, you have to lead the pack in your response. Examples include rules that were aspirational (such as those governing social responsibility and environmental concerns) that become normative or even descriptive rules. Any company that doesn't comply with these rules is now out of the game. Similarly, unwritten rules sometimes become written rules. Many world-class companies understand this and respect and adhere to unwritten rules before they are written down in the statute book. In other words, resourcefulness covers pre-emptive action as well as creative response. This doesn't mean that in order to be successful one must concentrate on adhering solely to the descriptive and normative rules of the game at the expense of the aspirational rules. It is a temptation, particularly when faced by a highly regulated business environment. However, any attempt by a company to regulate its own game by constructing too many written descriptive and normative rules runs the risk of distorting the game and limiting its entrepreneurial spirit and capability for innovation.

Of course, no company can exist on its own. It is part of a chain which stretches from the raw materials supplier to the end consumer. Each part of the chain has its own DNA rules. This relationship can be illustrated as in *Chart 21*.

Chart 21
The DNA Chain

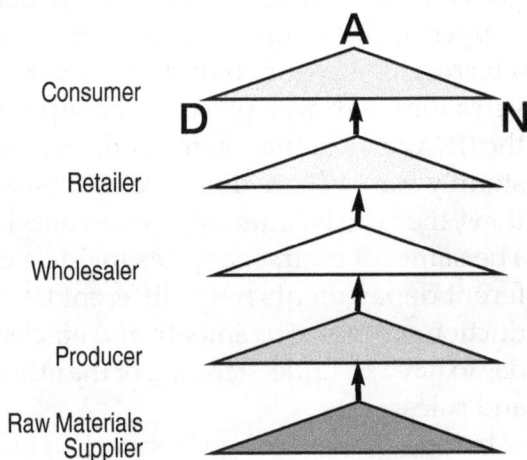

241

Nevertheless, for a chain to be effective there needs to be some DNA alignment between its constituent parts – some common themes pervading the chain as a whole. If any part of the chain ignores, say, the normative rules of the game, it can threaten the stability of the entire chain. For example, if it was found that a subcontractor to a leading brand of sportswear was using child labour in the manufacture of its element in the chain, human rights lobbying groups would be quick to call for consumers to boycott the final product. The damage to the brand and its raw material suppliers and retailers could be substantial. This relationship becomes crucially important when parts of the supply chain are in different countries. Each of the latter may have different descriptive rules, but double standards – as we've already remarked – are a killer.

If the supply chain is not aligned, it can destroy real value. Antagonism between the links weakens them. There has to be value on the table for everybody in the chain. Unfortunately, where huge imbalances in negotiating clout exist between players in the chain, this principle is thrown out. One joke doing the rounds in the farming community in Wales goes like this: "What is the difference between a terrorist and a supermarket? Answer: You can occasionally negotiate with a terrorist!" If your company is smart, it will conduct conversations with each player in the supply chain to understand the DNA rules of their game and, vice versa, they can understand yours. Where there are inconsistencies or contradictions, they can be mutually ironed out. The chain stays intact. The same, of course, applies inside a company where different departments have different DNA rules. For the production process to be smooth and efficient, every department has to have an understanding of the other departments' needs and rules.

In today's increasingly networked business environment,

we ought to shift away from viewing a supply chain as a long line of sequential service providers to one of interconnected partnerships through a widespread building of relationships. This building of relationships can only take place if, in the process, it creates value for each player in the network. In turn, the player adapts his or her role to optimise the output for the network as a whole. Because players have the best knowledge of that part of the game they are contributing to, and the associated rules, an effective network will entail regular conversations amongst all players to generate a working knowledge of the network rules coexisting alongside their own rules. This builds a common understanding among the players, so that if rules pertaining to the overall supply chain change, a team solution can easily be provided.

Furthermore, the concept of networking recognises that in the same way as different players make up a single supply chain, so every player is connected to *other* supply chains, each with its own DNA rules of the game. This increases the complexity of any game for your average networker, but that's how it is in today's interdependent world. You have to be all things to all people. The result looks a little like *Chart 22.*

Chart 22
The DNA Network

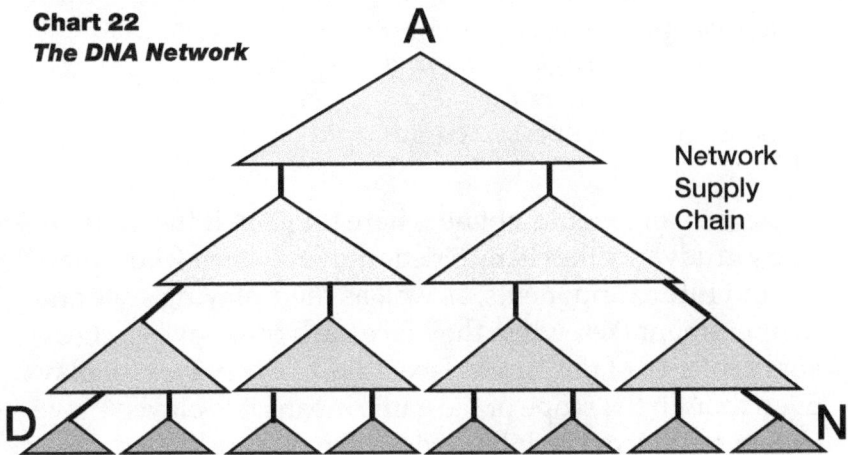

A

Network
Supply
Chain

D

N

The network supply chain demands a wider degree of alignment within its various components than a single supply chain. Equally, each individual chain within the network has its own unique DNA rules, demanding flexibility from players at the intersection of the chains. Any misalignment results in the loss of value, any misidentification of which chain you're in does the same. So, it's a lot more complicated than the business model of only fifty years ago.

With all these written, unwritten, descriptive, normative and aspirational rules of the game that emerge through conversation, as well as the demands for compatibility in interpretation of these rules amongst all the players within the greater supply chain network, you could be forgiven for thinking there's more out there that is unknown and out of your control than you first realised. You still want to be a hedgehog? You're kidding! If you were playing this game like a fox you'd factor these complexities into your strategy as best you can. You'd play business chess.

Key Uncertainties

I wouldn't give a fig for the simplicity this side of complexity, but I'd give my life for the simplicity on the far side of complexity.
JUSTICE OLIVER WENDELL HOLMES

Chess masters would not be where they are if they did not study in advance the characteristic moves of their fellow players and future opponents, as well as their playing style and temperament. Yet, when they face each other over a chessboard, plenty of uncertainty exists as to the pattern of play. Even though the scope of the game means it is played move by move and the possibilities for each move are limited, there

Chart 23 *The Conversation Model – Key Uncertainties*

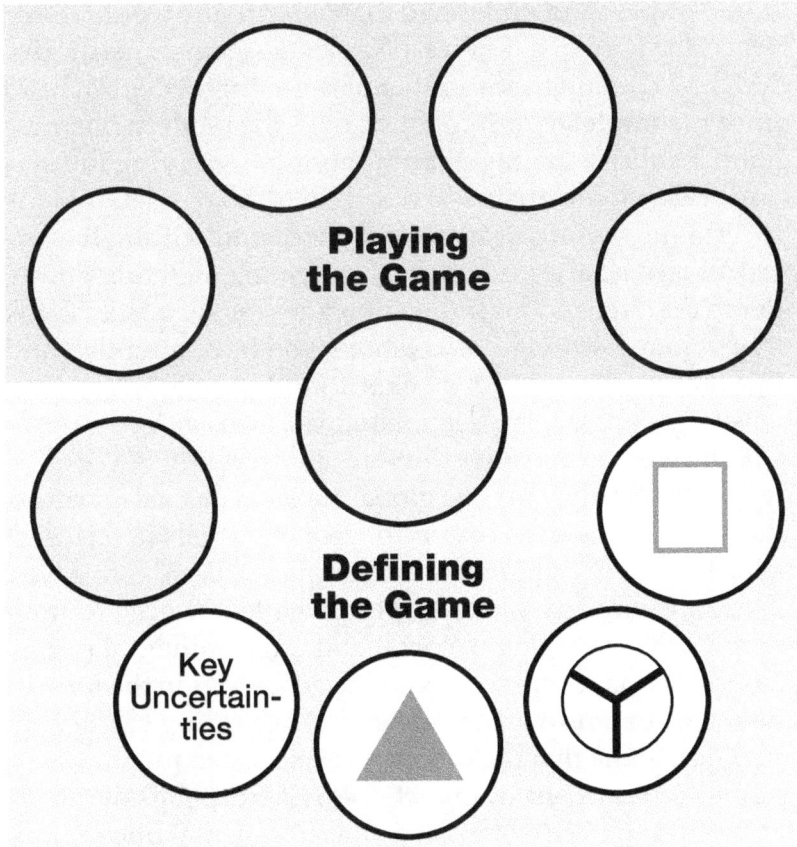

Playing the Game

Defining the Game

Key Uncertainties

are still degrees of uncertainty surrounding an opponent's overall strategy. One miscalculation on his intended move (which means you make the wrong one) and you can end up being mated. This is what makes the game of chess so exciting – for those who nd chess exciting, anyway.

In the game of business, however, uncertainties for any company are not limited to the strategy of other players in the game, but also include events and conditions that exist within the company and the industry, as well as national and

245

global uncertainties. The game of business is therefore far more complex and undefined than what many would think. Hence, the normal definition of 'risk management' as the discipline of counting the number of fire extinguishers in head office is completely out of touch with the modern business game. Real risk management is about identifying the systemic risks of the business, which in turn are related to the uncertainties a business faces without and within. It is extraordinary how classic strategic planning methods simply ignore this fact and make no allowance for surprises. Think of how many strategic workshops you have attended and how many times risks of a generic kind have been comprehensively debated. We bet not many, if ever.

If one were to consider the sort of uncertainties a company encounters, they may be global, national or local in nature. They radiate inwards in ever-decreasing shells (the closest being local as in right inside the company). Besides this type of classification, they can be grouped into political, technological, economic, legal, social and environmental uncertainties. We have represented these groupings in the form of the petals of a flower, colour-coded according to the geographical arena that the uncertainty is located in.

Chart 24 shows how, in fact, the various petals of uncertainty overlap. For example, an environmental uncertainty can lead to change in technology, which may have an unknown impact on society. The closer the uncertainty is to the central area of the flower, the more sense a company can usually make of it. But it also depends on the size of the company. The local arena is particularly important for small companies, whereas multinationals would place more emphasis on the national as well as global arenas of uncertainty within each petal. Political rulers of countries or regional blocs (such as the European Union or NATO) may need to focus equally on all three.

This is not to say that uncertainties that are global or national in nature will not have an impact on a small company. Remember the seven frames in the scope of the game. The most important consideration in key uncertainties is the word 'key'. Key uncertainties are those uncertainties that can have a major in uence on a company's bottom line. They are key in that even though they may seem inconsequential to the untrained eye, in reality they can smack you hard or provide a great opportunity. A single person having a heart attack, for example, may seem insigni cant to all but the victim and his or her family, but it could just be that the late, lamented person is a head of state. Imagine if, say, the leader of Pakistan or India meets with an untimely demise, to what extent tensions in the region could escalate and change the nature of political risk. Imagine an assassination like that of Archduke

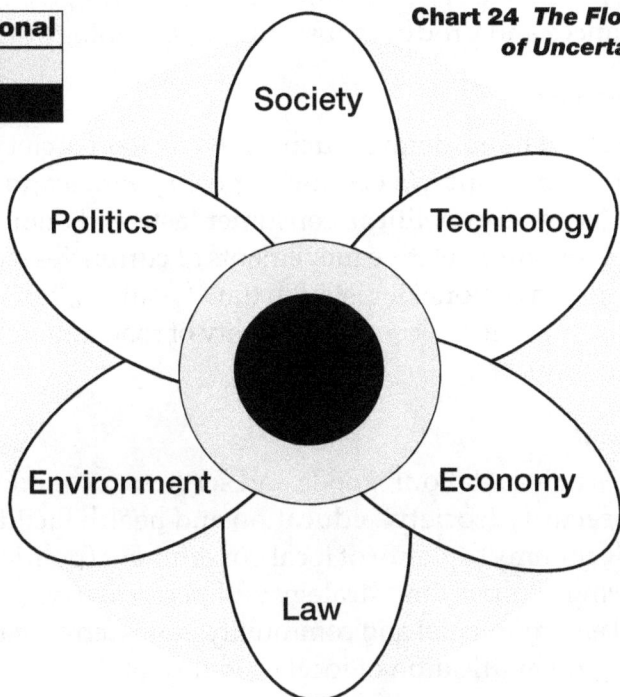

International
National
Local

Society

Politics

Technology

Environment

Economy

Law

Chart 24 *The Flower of Uncertainty*

247

Ferdinand in Sarajevo in 1914 and what that could trigger. On the other hand, man-made or natural catastrophes like 9/11 and the Asian tsunami tend to have a selective impact on business: obviously affecting those companies in the direct path of the tragedy the most; indirectly affecting associated industries like airlines, tourism and insurance; and leaving the rest relatively unscathed.

Examples of key uncertainties within each arena include:

Global

The global economic cycle (economy), international terrorism (society/politics), natural disasters and climate change (environment), shifts in international regulations (law), the price of oil and other forms of energy (economy/technology), base metal, food and other commodity prices (economy), security of supply of raw materials (politics), technological advances and product substitution (technology), etc.

National

The effect of epidemics such as HIV/AIDS (society/economy), each country's economic performance and political risk (economy/politics), consumer taste and demand (society/economy), relative movements of currencies (economy), changes in national legislation (law/politics), trade liberalisation or barriers (economy), quality of road and rail network (economy), etc.

Local

Prices of local labour, goods and services (economy), safety and security (society), education and health facilities (society/economy), quality of local government (politics), neighbouring competitors' strategy and performance (economy), local environmental and community issues (environment/society), diversification of local economy, etc.

Uncertainties can cross over borders. An epidemic can start off locally and then become a national or international phenomenon. A technological shift likewise. Competitor strategy can hit you at any level, depending upon whether the competition consists of small local players, foreign firms or multinationals with local franchises (e.g. McDonald's, Starbucks). Civil war can spill over national boundaries and infect entire regions. Normally the uncertainties an industry faces (as opposed to the company as an individual entity) fall into all three categories. It may well be of value to pigeonhole industry uncertainties in a separate box.

Local uncertainties may also include uncertainties within the company such as the risks associated with declining efficiencies; too little control (theft, corruption, fraud); or too much control (bureaucracy). Added to these are the possibility of accidents causing death, injury or downtime; computer viruses; loss of reputation through unacceptable work practices; and a talent exodus through poaching by competitors. Or there may be an unhealthy level of internal politics or succession issues at the top. It could be argued that the level of these uncertainties can be influenced by decisions within the control of the company (unlike say a global economic downturn or recovery). However, accidents happen within the most sophisticated and carefully prepared endeavours – the space shuttles Challenger and Columbia are perfect examples.

The strategic conversation around key uncertainties needs to be facilitated very carefully. If it is handled properly, it can unlock insights into the kind of circumstances which might change your strategic direction. It can also help you envisage emergency tactics to keep you on course in the event of winds approaching hurricane level. There are no rights or wrongs other than, whatever approach is adopted, it should give people the wings of imagination. The conversation is about stimulating insight into all relevant possibilities and developing a framework in which the implication for the company of each possibility can be teased out. This is no place for being prescriptive about the order of proceedings, as intuition and creativity of thought play a crucial role in the conversation. The outcome may be a random list of key uncertainties on a flip chart. For some companies, that's good enough to move on to the next step of preparing scenarios.

However, we have something more detailed in mind for the purpose of processing the information that emerges from the discussions. We recommend this alternative purely because the experience is so unique and the information generated is like a treasure house. Thus, like gems need sorting, the uncertainties captured should be codified as far as possible according to petal (society, technology, etc.) and arena (global, national or local). They should then be numbered so that they can be plotted on the corporate equivalent of a radar screen, which we will come to shortly. One of the most important reasons for having a radar screen is so that you can continually ask yourself whether or not an uncertainty is turning into a reality and if so whether appropriate contingency plans have been put in place to handle it. In a general sense this concern can be articulated in the following question: Does our company have a sufficient degree of flexibility in its decision-making processes to adapt quickly enough to significant changes in its circumstances?

So how can a company capture these changes on a radar screen and have an idea of the consequences should they materialise? Given that uncertainties are by their nature unpredictable, and that the focus of attention is on their impact on the company, a 'radar screen' will reflect these two key features. We have therefore developed a graph with varying degrees of predictability on the vertical axis and expected impact on the horizontal axis. We call this a Predictability Impact

(PI) Chart. Before going into the chart in detail, we must explain why we chose 'predictability' as the measure on one axis, as opposed to 'probability' or 'certainty'. The reason is that it covers the two sorts of things which we have in mind as key uncertainties for our chart. The one kind consists of ever-present factors like commodity prices, exchange rates or, perhaps, the future of the Chinese economy. You can say that these items are 'unpredictable' because of the dispersion of possible outcomes, but you would never use the word 'improbable'. The second type of uncertainty comprises shock events such as disruption of oil supplies through terrorist attacks, the outbreak of a new epidemic or your company becoming the object of an unwelcome takeover bid. You can state that these events have become more 'predictable' or maybe 'probable', but it would be awkward to remark that they have increased in 'certainty'. It just doesn't sound right and could even convey the wrong impression.

Besides, we must draw another distinction between predictability and probability. The first tends to be subjective in that it incorporates the level of confidence you have in your judgement, as well as the odds of something happening. Probability tends to be impersonal and objective, a mathematical term. The logic goes like this. In a laboratory experiment that is repeated a sufficient number of times, the different outcomes are counted and a probability is attached to them (like spinning a coin gives you a 50/50 split on heads and tails). In real life, you can't repeat things that often so you can't attach probabilities. You can merely take a stab at how predictable something is – not in the sense of giving a specific percentage but rather saying that it is more or less likely or totally unlikely or reasonably likely.

Moreover, although predictability and probability normally go hand in hand, i.e. something that is highly probable is highly predictable, occasionally they part company. Human frailty being what it is, our powers of prediction let us down and something happens which in hindsight was highly probable but we didn't predict it (because we did not have enough information at our disposal). That's how accidents unfortunately happen. The scenario was never played out in the minds of the people responsible. A sound business judgement obviously rests on identifying a threat or opportunity and getting the level of predictability and impact about right. It's as bad to conjure up an obscure risk as a reason not to go ahead as it is to ignore a clear and present danger when proceeding. But the long and the short of it is: don't attach specific probabilities to key uncertainties or scenarios. Otherwise, you may make a fool of yourself by being accused of bogus accuracy. One scenario planner who gave a 65 per cent probability to an event happening was asked by the CEO: why not 66 per cent, why not 64 per cent? What's so special about 65?

In order to start constructing our PI Chart, we begin with a basic truth about uncertainty. One can divide the future into known unknowns and unknown unknowns – things we know we don't know and things we don't know we don't know. We made this distinction in *The Mind of a Fox*. Donald Rumsfeld subsequently made exactly the same point in a memorable quote and was laughed out of court by his opponents and media hedgehogs alike. Too bad for them. Unless a person has supernatural powers of foresight, the list of uncertainties relevant in his or her life will never capture them all. So you have to keep a general level of flexibility in your outlook to handle the unknown unknowns that come at you from 'left field' or, as you can see in our chart opposite, from below the line.

A good example was that Saddam Hussein acted as though he had weapons of mass destruction, when he didn't. He was an imposter who illogically brought about his own destruction (unless he truly believed the Americans wouldn't attack).

Chart 25 *The PI Chart I*

Predictability

High

Known Unknowns

▲

Low

Impact

Low   High

▼

Unknown Unknowns

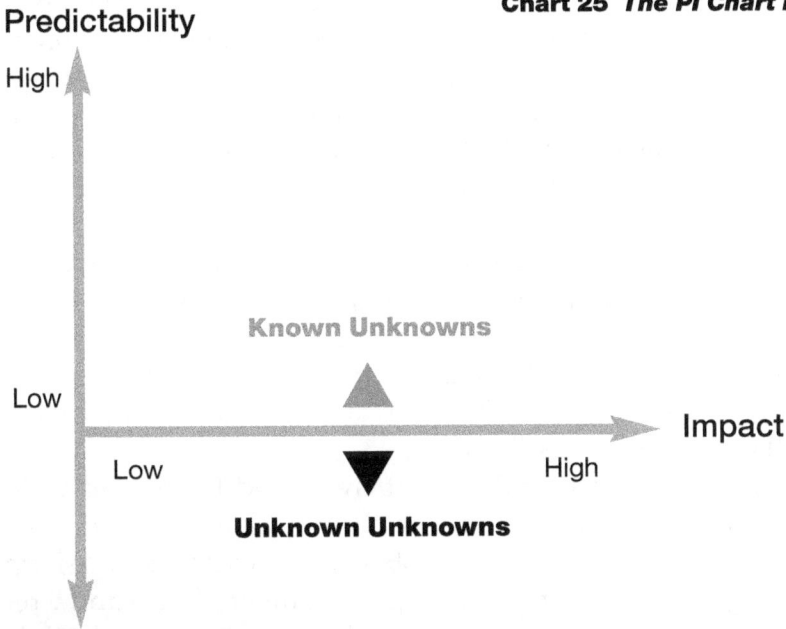

To the British and American intelligence agencies as well as Donald Rumsfeld, his behaviour was an 'unknown unknown'. Equally, to these same people, 9/11 itself probably quali ed as an unknown unknown, because they didn't think an Arab terrorist group was capable of organising such a massive attack on Western soil. To many South Africans – particularly those who invested offshore – the recent strengthening of the rand was an unknown unknown. They couldn't believe that an African currency could strengthen against the US dollar. They were wrong! Whenever a paradigm is strong, watch out for the opposite.

By contrast, a known unknown is one we know exists, such as the next earthquake on the San Andreas Fault in California, but whose timing and magnitude are unknown. As you can see in *Chart 26* on page 103, the 'known unknown' uncertainties can be graded on the PI Chart according to their level of predictability. The ones with a very low degree of predictability, due to the absence of hard facts or very low probability of occurrence, we call *wild cards*. Similarly, those which surpass a given and very high degree of predictability qualify as *rules of the game*. By the laws of elimination, the ones left with a low to medium degree of predictability are the ones we define as the *key uncertainties*.

Now the parameters have been set, it's a case of 'plotting' the key uncertainties on the radar screen according to their predictability and potential impact. Let's say, after all the uncertainties were discussed, grouped and numbered, the ten most important were identified and plotted. The completed PI Chart could look like *Chart 27*.

The two uncertainties numbered 3 and 10 are *wild cards*. It is worth keeping an eye on them because, if conditions change, they can turn from blobs on the lower deck into sharp images at the centre or top right. Numbers 1, 2, 8 and 9 require close monitoring right now because of the impact they can have. Perhaps the company can reduce its dependence on the outcome of these factors through some judicious diversification or hedging programme.

Itemising the uncertainties this way deepens the discussion and allows people to debate their significance in more precise terms, and make more sense of the overall risk profile of the business. It also prioritises the company's intelligence-gathering needs. More importantly, it helps to focus and fine-tune the company's strategic thinking in that, once the uncertainties have been tagged, the objective of the company may be to improve its take on the predictability of the event under consideration, reduce the potential impact of the event, or a combination of both. Obviously, some things have an inherent level of unpredictability surrounding them that no amount of analysis can reduce. World GDP growth, the strength of the US dollar, the gold price and the oil price come

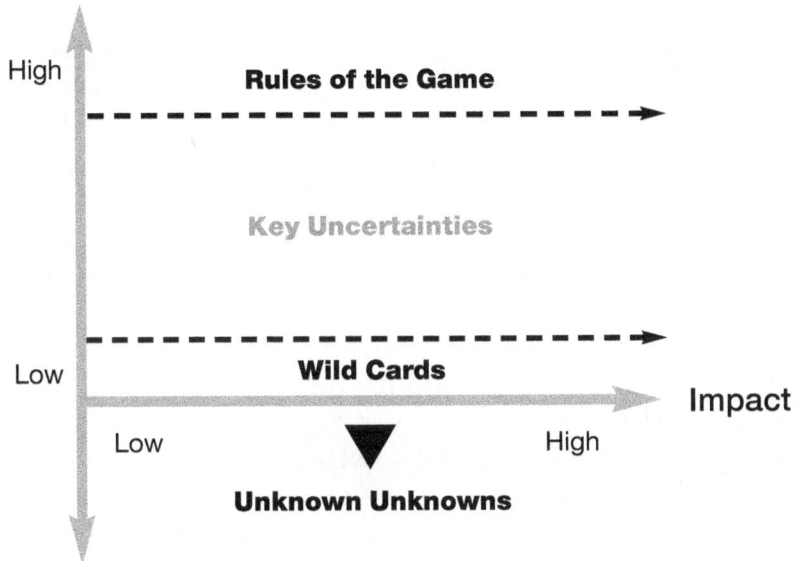

Chart 26 *The PI Chart II*

Predictability

High

Rules of the Game

Key Uncertainties

Low   **Wild Cards**

Impact

Low   High

Unknown Unknowns

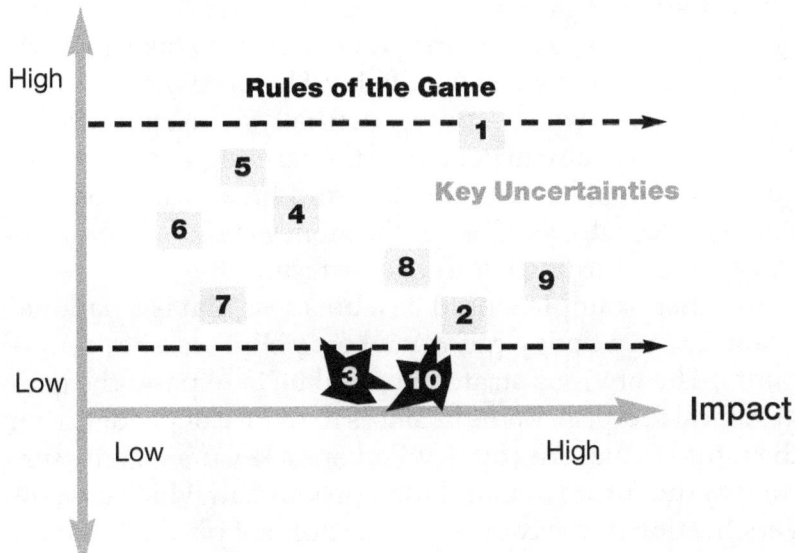

Chart 27 *The PI Chart III*

Predictability

High   **Rules of the Game**   1

5
                Key Uncertainties
6   4
              8   9
    7   2
              3   10
Low

Impact

Low   High

255

to mind. All you can do is work out what the sensitivity of your profit and loss account is to each of these factors and what you will do if they change direction. Some guru was once asked how he knew when a trend was no longer a trend. His response: when it becomes a turning point! Foxes shrug their shoulders and get on with life.

We'd like to back up this chart with some practical examples. Let's start with a farmer. Weather is a key uncertainty. It's completely out of his control so what can he do about it? He could shoot rain-making rockets into the sky, which is what some governments do, but he probably hasn't got the resources to do that. Apart from which, if he is successful, he runs the risk of incurring the ire of other farmers in the neighbourhood who will think he's swiped their rain. Seriously, though, his options appear to be as follows. He can consult meteorologists as the year progresses to improve his intelligence on whether the season is going to be a good one weather-wise or not. He can watch TV weather forecasts. He can make a strategic decision to sell his farm and buy one on the other side of the mountain where it's known to rain more frequently. He can put in an irrigation system to take the variability of rainfall almost out of play. He can switch crops or animals to ones which are more naturally accustomed to dry conditions. Or he can get out of the farming business altogether and turn his farm into bed-and-breakfast accommodation. Alternatively, if he has the money and the acreage, he can consider turning it into a game farm.

Another example would be a business that is a national champion in a dodgy country where politics is a key uncertainty. The obvious strategy would be to expand the geographical footprint of the business to reduce dependence on the future of that one country. Perhaps a key uncertainty surrounds the future demand for a product, in which case diversification of the company's portfolio of products would be wise. In both cases, the scope of the company would be revisited. On the other hand, maybe a competitor has a strategy or technology up its sleeve, which is a key uncertainty. In this event, should the company form an alliance with the competitor or take it over? If your operations are energy-intensive and the oil price is a key uncertainty, how will you reconfigure the design of your plant to cut back on energy consumption in the production process?

All these examples have a common theme. Identify the uncertainty and do some form of risk assessment in terms of severity of impact and probability of occurrence. You then have different options in terms of managing the risk. Reduce it by reducing its probability (the frequency of road accidents is diminished by driving slower). Reduce it by mitigating its impact (the impact is mitigated by buying a car with airbags as well as by wearing a seatbelt and driving slower). Eliminate it (by stopping driving altogether and moving into an old-age home). Transfer the risk with insurance. Or retain the risk and live with it. You can flaunt your two-carat flawless white diamond and insure it; or put it in a safe and wear a zircon replica (like some Hollywood movie stars do, knowing they have the original back home); or if you're really conservative do both (insure it and wear the replica). It's up to you, and collectively it's up to the company, once the risk has been identified.

Our PI Chart can also be adjusted to identify trends that have developed over time, or how a key uncertainty's degree of predictability and impact has changed. An excellent example is how HIV / AIDS has evolved through different stages of predictability and impact in sub-Saharan Africa compared to most Western countries (see diagram overleaf).

From its beginnings as an unknown unknown in 1980, through its status as a wild card and key uncertainty in the 1980s and 1990s, HIV / AIDS is now a rule of the game with an

257

Predictability

Chart 28 *The HIV PI Chart*

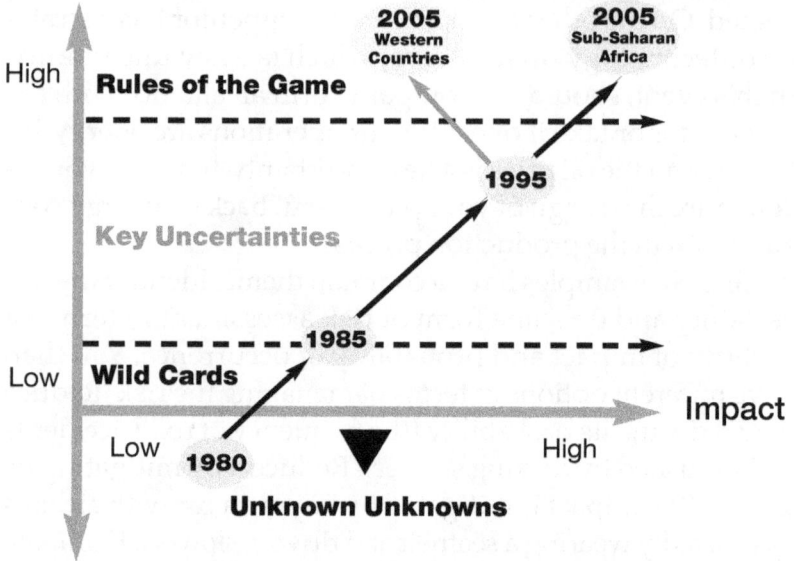

impact which is anticipated to be lower in Western countries than in sub-Saharan Africa. However, it remains a key uncertainty in China and India.

We'll end off this section with a quote from a well-known children's song: "If you go down to the woods today, you're in for a big surprise." Traditionally, woods were not places to venture. Danger in the guise of a big bad wolf lurked therein, ready to pounce on an unwary traveller. Of course, in the case of the song, the surprise was nothing worse than a teddy bear's picnic. Companies sometimes end up in the woods and then two proverbs spring to mind: "Can't see the wood for the trees" (can't see the big picture) and "You're not out of the woods yet" (you're still in a tricky situation).

In both proverbs, 'woods' are places of confusion and difficulty, a somewhat intimidating and irregular clump of trees. We have found that this part of the conversation more than any other turns executives into foxes. They see the big picture and therefore know how to plot grand strategies. They see the small picture and let no fine detail escape them. In short, they see the woods *and* the trees and are well prepared for surprises. With these capabilities, they can be out of the woods in a flash – with only fox prints to show they were ever there.

Scenarios

I skate to where the puck is going to be, not to where it has been.
WAYNE GRETZKY

We all love a good story. Whether it's in a book we are reading or movie we are watching, we are drawn in by the richness of the characters, the excitement of the plot, the beauty of the locations, and we have a fascination with how the story will pan out. We continually work through possible outcomes and test these against the events as they unfold, taking pleasure when we get things right and enjoying the surprise when we don't. Our love of stories is generally initiated when we are young. Stories told with relish by parents and teachers have the effect of not only entertaining young minds, but also of exercising them. They are also used to convey messages and lessons in life's morals and virtues, the most common being that good always wins over evil – ugly stepsisters don't get handsome princes!

Storytelling is an important part of all cultures. Africa, especially, is blessed with stories passed down over hundreds of years that are as applicable now as they were when they were first told. At an early age, children in Botswana are taught the story of the wolf and the fox that found a small hole in a fence surrounding a farmer's chicken coop. The two squeezed through and celebrated their find by feasting on the hapless chickens. Whereas the fox made a point of interrupting his feeding, returning periodically to the hole in the fence, the wolf took advantage of the windfall to gorge himself. When they heard the farmer coming with his gun the two rushed back to the hole to escape. The fox, who had kept checking to see that he could still fit, slipped through the hole effortlessly. The wolf however, now full and fat, got stuck and paid the ultimate price.

But the value of stories doesn't end when we leave childhood behind us. They are found wherever there is creative thought. Purely analytical thought, on the other hand, demands the comforting discipline of parameters – hence the popularity of accounting among those who don't want to become actuaries! Analytical thinking therefore runs the risk of ignoring factors outside of its parameters; and this is the main reason why, in an environment of growing uncertainty, traditional forms of analytical strategising are inappropriate. What is needed is open-ended thought and imagination that spirals around possibilities and scenarios – the type of mental process used by Detectives Sturgis, Rebus and Banks in solving the murder mysteries created by their originators, Jonathan Kellerman, Ian Rankin and Peter Robinson. Even Agatha Christie's Hercule Poirot – the doyen of detectives – played scenarios which at first seemed outrageous and implausible until all was revealed.

Scenarios are particularly useful in modern strategy for a number of reasons. Firstly, they have the capacity to change minds in a non-prescriptive manner. If people are encouraged to imagine a possible scenario that is better than the one they're in at the moment, they are able to imagine the positive consequences of operating in such a scenario. This allows them to develop an enthusiasm for the task at hand and helps them change of their own volition. Much better than order-

Chart 29 *The Conversation Model – Scenarios*

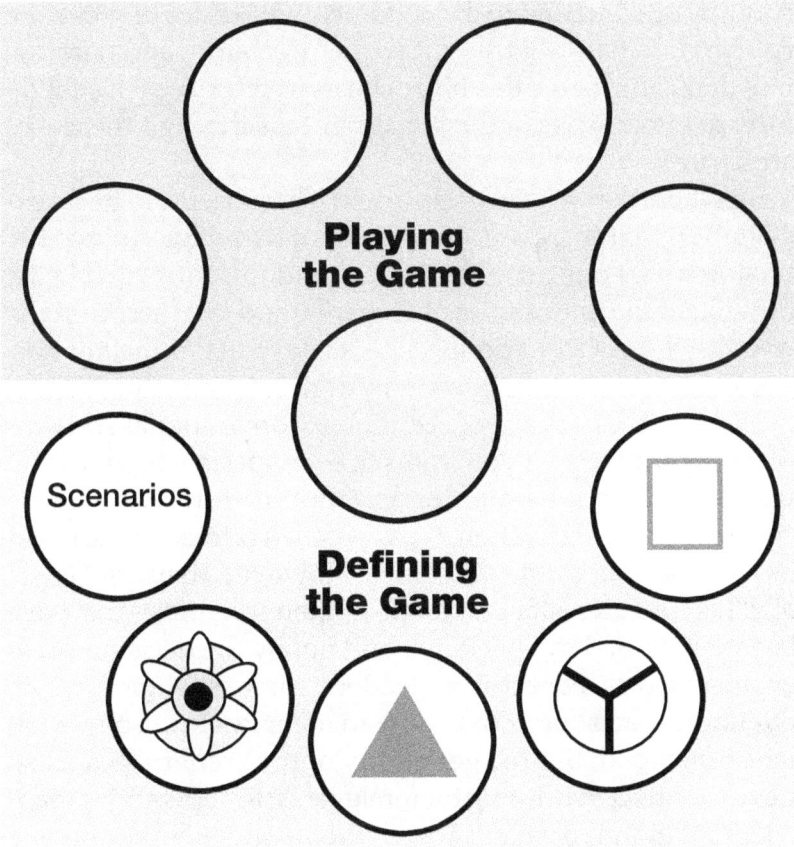

Playing
the Game

Scenarios

Defining
the Game

ing them around or forcing them to change. Similarly, the use of scenarios in strategy builds a collective alignment amongst the teams using them, thereby enhancing efficiencies and creating a renewed sense of purpose to ful l whatever strategic or tactical decisions are made. People often find it easier to comprehend information if it is in the form of a scenario rather than a list of facts and gures. For this reason, scenarios provide a clearer understanding of the complexities of any game. Trying to understand, say, a referee's rulebook is easier if you can imagine a situation unfolding in the game to which the rule applies. But unlike the certainty of the rules of sport, the rules of business are fraught with uncertainty and parameters that can change in a blur. The most effective way, therefore, to make sense of this uncertainty is through the use of scenarios.

So where can you buy scenarios? There seems to be an expectation that there are scenarios 'out there' for any type of business and one only has to, say, find the correct website, download the relevant set of scenarios and plan accordingly; or call in a set of scenario specialists who will flex their minds, ask some challenging questions, digest the data and feed it back in a neat package of scenarios. Conventional scenario planning indeed relies on teams of such specialists who draw up elegant and intricate stories about the future. After due consultation and iteration, these are then offered to the client as a range of possible outcomes. However, they are generally 'big' pictures – long but well-written scenarios – that have been developed by specialists and not by the decision-makers themselves. For business leaders, some of whom have an attention span shorter than a TV ad, it makes for a somewhat laborious read; but the generality of the scenarios can also have the effect of diluting their relevance for operations management in the company, thereby reducing their buy-in.

No self-respecting businessman is willing to risk spending money on something over which he has no influence. Influence is leverage; influence is power. It is the difference between success through strategy and success through luck. If business is a game, players win because they are *active* participants, not *passive* receptors; and this is the point of differentiation between our model and traditional forms of scenario planning methodology.

If scenarios are to be relevant and effective, it would seem logical that they should be prepared by the people who feature in them, and they should incorporate an element over which those same people have a degree of in uence. In other words, based on our terms of reference, the most relevant scenarios in the game of business are those prepared *by* the players, *for* the players and *featuring* the players themselves as stars *in* the game. This inclusive philosophy is the essence of our book. We believe in a form of strategic thinking which recognises the complexity of the games we are in and yet provides us with the most effective way to *play* the game. The purpose of scenarios is therefore to create a better future, to win the game. We're talking proactive stuff, not just responding to futures completely outside our control.

This is one of the reasons we avoid using the phrase 'driving forces', which is much in vogue among scenario planners. It implies that you're not the driver. As John Connor said in *The Terminator*: "The future isn't set. The only fate is what we make for ourselves." Bearing this in mind, the core of our approach can be represented in the following diagram:

Chart 30 *The Scenario Gameboard I*

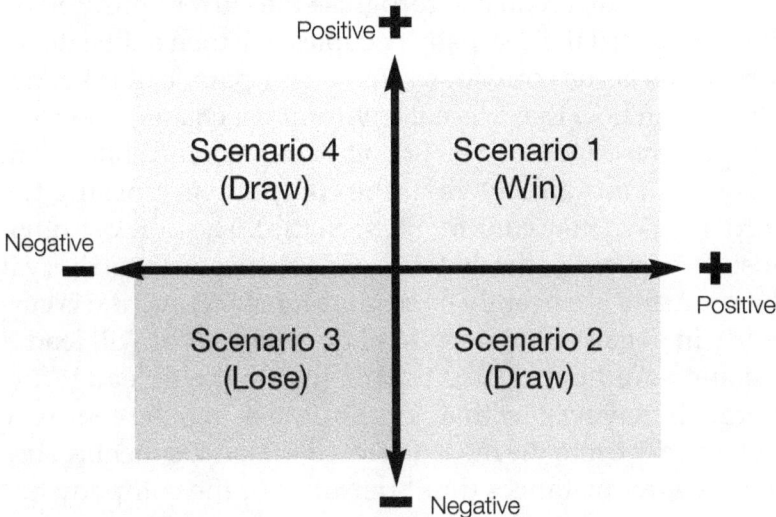

263

We have called it the Scenario Gameboard. Like any other gameboard, it represents an interactive game with more than one player. That's what business essentially is, unless you're a monopoly. The movement of a particular player, or several players, can be 'plotted' on the board. There is an ugly corner of the gameboard that should be avoided (scenario 3 in our diagram) and there is a sunny corner that offers all sorts of benefits should you land there (scenario 1). There are also parts of the gameboard with mixed fortunes (scenario 2 and scenario 4).

Consequently, your success can be judged by your movement and position on the gameboard. As with most other games, there are events out of the control of the players, like the outcome of the throw of the dice, and yet there are definite advantages to knowing how to play the game better than the other players. You have a better chance of winning, and that is the intent of business.

We often like to imagine the scenarios represented on a gameboard as if they were neighbouring countries on a map. In the description of the scenarios, we include some markers or flags by which you can recognise the current position on the gameboard the company occupies. We then delineate future paths across the board that a company can take, depending on how the external environment changes, how the company responds, or a bit of both. The flags and shift in language will announce when the company is crossing the borders into a new country (or scenario). The purpose obviously is to avoid paths that descend into negative territory if the company is currently in positive territory; and if it is currently in negative territory, to choose paths that will lead it out and avoid paths (like the plague) that will lead it further in. It may well be that, for the time being, the company will not move into the most desirable scenario, either because current circumstances don't permit it or the company has to pass through another scenario on the journey there (direct access being barred).

There are ways though in which the concept of our scenario gameboard differs from the common idea of a gameboard. The most significant is that there is no set gameboard. It is not designed by any third party and bought across the counter in a toyshop. The very people playing the game design it. The players therefore don't have to try and read through the rules, because they know the rules of the game. They are therefore best qualified to play the game. Wouldn't it be great if we could design a game so that we would always win? We would write the rules to our advantage and skew the conditions so that we commanded the most leverage.

But the game of business is not like that. As we know, most events that shape the game are outside of our control and many of them are uncertain; and we also don't make all the rules ourselves. A new rule, for instance, creeping into Formula One racing and Premier League soccer is that money determines the winners. This makes the winner more predictable and the sport more boring to watch. Loss of audience is a distinct possibility so the resultant gameboard has to reflect that – a mixture of good and bad scenarios. If we are to achieve any form of control over our future by playing the game better than others, then the identification of the pivotal uncertainties shaping these scenarios is critical.

So, how is this possible? The answer lies in the midst of the PI Chart (*Chart 27*) we presented in the last section. It is amongst the key uncertainties listed there as conceivably having the most impact on the company that the ones most relevant to the development of the scenarios will be found. Their selection is a cause for conversation, intuition and prudent facilitation.

If a company has been open and honest in its strategic conversation, the PI Chart should consist of a small collection of the most important key uncertainties. If the PI Chart is congested, it is for one of two reasons: either the uncertainties haven't been winnowed down properly, or the company is in a minefield of uncertainties and should call in a helicopter to be airlifted! Invariably though, closer examination of, and conversation around, these key uncertainties will identify similarities between two or more of them. This will make it easier to cluster them, because scenarios should never be too narrowly defined. If the key uncertainties are too specific, the scenarios they produce can quickly become redundant and so does the gameboard. Similarly, using key uncertainties that are too broad produces vast and fuzzy scenarios in which it is difficult to position yourself. Examples of effective clustering would put commodity prices, exchange rates and physical demand for your product under the label 'market'; while unit costs of production, output per man hour and other productivity parameters would be merged under the heading 'efficiency'. The breadth of the scenarios will also depend on their required time frame – the longer the time frame the broader the scenarios ought to be. It is also quite possible to sweep up some of the remaining uncertainties into the text of the scenarios, even if they are not used in determining the axes of the gameboard. Obviously the logic of the scenarios must be able to accommodate the additions made.

We have found that sometimes when a company is able to see the most relevant key uncertainties plotted on its PI Chart, there will be little disagreement as to which uncertainties will act as axes for the scenario matrix, because they will be quite obvious. Generally, though, further conversation should take place around possible candidates, with intuition being the deciding factor; after all, those playing the game every day tend to have a sixth sense about the twists and turns that should be part and parcel of the gameboard.

To nudge consensus along on the identification of the

scenario drivers, sensible facilitation is required. We don't like to be prescriptive, but here are some guidelines:

1 Using two key uncertainties that are outside of a company's control will produce four scenarios in which, at best, the company can adapt its strategy or be more resourceful. Traditional scenarios are generally composed of uncertainties of this type. There is nothing wrong with this if two variables in the external environment stand out so sharply that they cannot be ignored. But things can fall a bit flat. As we've already emphasised, a gameboard that confers some control to the players themselves as to where they end up on the board is likely to get a more positive reception.

2 Using two key uncertainties that are within a company's control or influence will produce four scenarios that are applicable if the company is concerned with a more internal focus, such as a change in management style. For example, one company used the presence and absence of people-centred policies on one axis and output-oriented policies on the other.

3 Using one key uncertainty that is outside of the company's control and one that is within the company's control will produce four scenarios where the company has a measure of influence over its destiny. At the very least, it will be prepared for changes in the external environment. We find this combination the most empowering in that it recognises both sides of the equation.

Purists may complain that we're stretching the definition of scenario planning too far by allowing the principal actor (the company) to play such a prominent role in the way the scenarios unfold. Scenarios should only depict external developments, they may argue; and aren't you contradicting the principle that scenarios should be beyond the control of the company to which they apply? However, our experience has shown us that the enthusiasm and imagination displayed by people in formulating scenarios is directly related to how much they participate in the story line. Everyone wants a part! So you have to imagine that a scenario is like a Greek tragedy where free will is a delusion and the Fates decide your destiny. Indeed, Delphi may claim to be the source of scenario planning. The oracle there was so outrageously ambiguous that its utterances covered all eventualities. Purveyors of omens and scenarios have a lot in common!

We are sometimes asked during a facilitation whether more than two pivotal uncertainties can be used to design a scenario gameboard. It may be the case that, say, three key uncertainties seem to be equally important in de ning a company's possible future. In such a situation the scenario gameboard would comprise eight different scenarios, as follows:

Chart 31 *The Scenario Gameboard II*

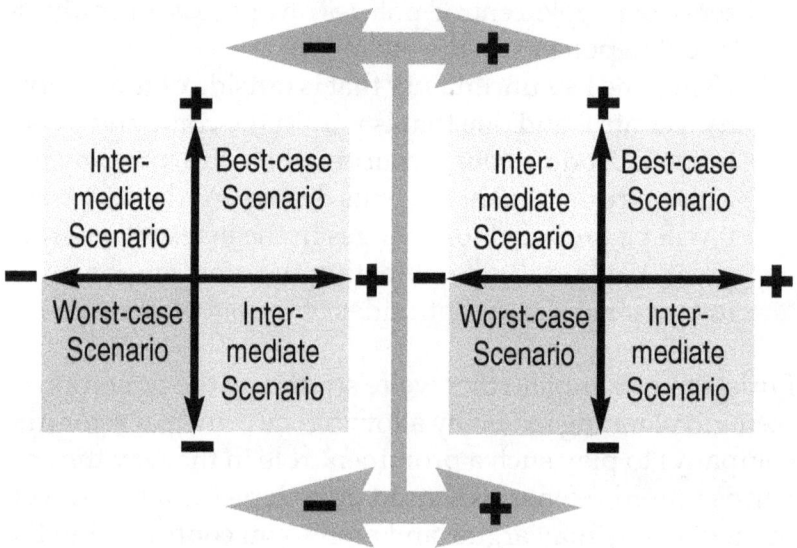

What a nightmare! By the time you get to the seventh scenario, someone is bound to ask what the real difference is between that one and the second one – by which time you'll have forgotten what the second one is!

One company actually wanted a cube made of wire so that the three dimensions could be more obviously expressed. An octet of scenarios would have hung inside the cube. Luckily we dissuaded them from this venture before construction began. The only justification for doing something as complicated as this would be if the variable on each side of the vertical line was within the company's control, while the matrices on each side were determined by a pair of external variables beyond the company's control. You might, say, have four global scenarios against which you want to compare a focused strategy with a diversified one to see which is more robust. Even then, it may be stretching the mind too far to go into eight dimensions.

Returning to earth, the objective of using the scenario gameboard is to make sense of the future, not to increase its complexity beyond our ability to respond. For this reason we recommend a gameboard with a minimum of two and a maximum of four scenarios. Remember that the radar screen has already captured the uncertainties, so they are not lost; and by monitoring the radar screen it is possible to see if a key uncertainty moves up the ranking and needs further analysis in the scenario formulation phase.

But the purpose of our process is not simply to attain a product (the scenarios); and it must be emphasised that there is no right or wrong set of scenarios. The value of the process lies in its power to create an awareness of the game that would normally remain hidden in conventional forms of developing strategy. That is why we have opted for a range of two to four scenarios. It may just be that two scenarios work to transform thinking. It did in South Africa with the *High Road* of negotiation leading to a political settlement; and the *Low Road* of confrontation leading to civil war and a wasteland. If the gameboard had been around in 1986 when these scenarios were launched, it would have been divided into two halves, the left being the *High Road* and the right being the *Low Road*. In business, two scenarios can also do the job, where one is the official future generated by consensus thinking (sometimes called *Conventional Wisdom*) and the other is a surprising future generated by the imagination. Nevertheless, we prefer a 2 x 2 matrix. It's a lens through which people are accustomed to look at the future. Once the scenario drivers have been identified, they are expressed as intersecting variable axes to produce four possible scenarios: one a worst-case scenario (you lose the game), one a best-case scenario (victory) and the other two intermediate scenarios (drawn games). *Chart 32* opposite illustrates this. Where the negative version of one variable overrides the positive version of the other variable, the scenario may be logically impossible. In that event, a cross will appear in that quadrant, ruling it out and bringing the total number of scenarios down to three.

It is important to have both positive and negative scenarios on the gameboard, because often as much strategic insight is gained from avoiding or surviving a negative scenario as is obtained from taking advantage of a positive one. A classic example of the educational value of a negative scenario was provided at a workshop on the future of a church hemmed in by business parks in the centre of Johannesburg. The exodus of residents from the suburb had caused the congregation to decline in numbers and to raise its average age. A young lady was asked to write a negative scenario and she came up with a real beauty. It was called *Geriatric Swansong*. In the scenario, the congregation gradually died off until there was only one member left. He came to church on Sundays to take communion; so did the vicar, the choir, the

Chart 32 *The Scenario Gameboard III*

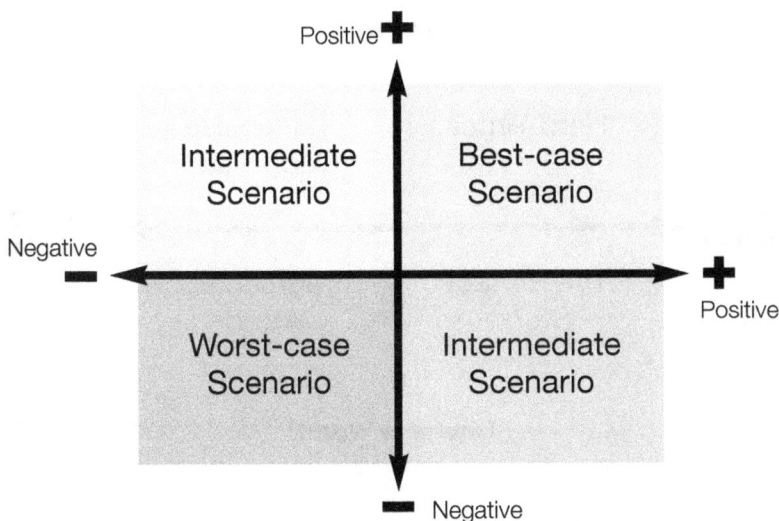

choir mistress and the organist. Then he died and the church was turned into a nightclub called 'The Club of Joy' and it was not ecclesiastical joy that was being dished out in the club. Anyway, this scenario was distributed in the parish newsletter, evoking a strong reaction about how the church should be stopped from being turned into a nightclub. It had far more motivational effect than the positive scenario, which was rather boringly called *Onward Christian Soldiers*.

In a number of our facilitations, we have found that multinational companies like to work with positive and negative global scenarios. One of the key uncertainties surrounds the global market, which is identified in the horizontal 'x' axis as a strong versus a weak market. The other uncertainty concerns the political state of the world, and is expressed on the vertical 'y' axis as a stable versus unstable world. The four possible scenarios that emerge in the matrix (going clockwise from the top right) are shown in *Chart 33* on the following page.

Chart 33 *The Multinational Gameboard*

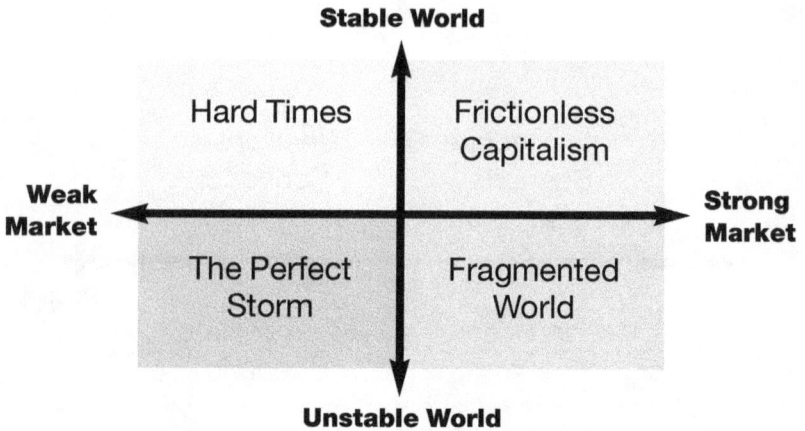

Stable World

Hard Times	Frictionless Capitalism

Weak Market ←——————————→ **Strong Market**

The Perfect Storm	Fragmented World

Unstable World

1 Frictionless Capitalism

This is the best scenario, being a strong market in a stable world where globalisation continues. It's very much business as usual, the only difference being that the global economy becomes more 'multipolar' with the rise of Chindia (China and India). The company's geographical footprint has to be re-examined in this light.

2 Fragmented World

This is a mixed scenario where markets remain strong despite a world of increasing animosity and 'no go' areas for multinationals. The pro t potential in some countries diminishes as a result of new taxes, royalties and regulations being enacted by governments whose outlook is increasingly nationalistic. Consequently, investment strategies have to become more selective.

3 The Perfect Storm

This is the worst scenario where terrorism and regional strife chuck so much sand in the wheels of frictionless capitalism that the world economy dives into full-scale recession. Security of supply lines for key commodities such as oil become paramount. All company hatches have to be battened down to survive the storm.

4 Hard Times

This is a scenario of a normal economic downturn caused by the usual suspects of governments and consumers overextending themselves and building up an inordinate amount of debt, stock markets getting too greedy, companies installing too much extra production capacity, etc. Eventually the cycle reverses when everyone has learnt the lesson (temporarily). Maintaining a positive cash flow during the downturn is vital, so that the company emerges stronger than its competitors when it is over.

The question is: which scenario are we in at the moment and where will we be next year? You choose. Multinational companies can also use this matrix to plot the direction of the individual countries in which they own businesses or to which they sell their products. For instance, a country with a stable sociopolitical structure and a growing free-market economy can be assigned to *Frictionless Capitalism*. On the other hand, a country with a stable sociopolitical structure but a weak economy can be located in *Hard Times*, and so on. The gameboard thereby recognises that there is no overall strategy that can be considered optimal for a multinational. Instead, the company's scenario gameboard should be rolled down to the operating unit in each country with the conversation at that level focusing on how best to move forward in that particular market. Such an approach respects the complexity of a multinational's sphere of operations.

An alternative way of assessing individual countries and

their respective markets in terms of sociopolitical stability and the competitiveness of their markets puts them all on the same gameboard. It goes like this:

Chart 34
The Country Gameboard

Stability **+**

Europe   Australia

US

South
Africa   Japan

Competi-
tiveness ← Russia   China → Competi-
−   tiveness
                                    +

Argentina

Middle
East   Asian
                Tigers

Third World
Dictatorships

Stability **−**

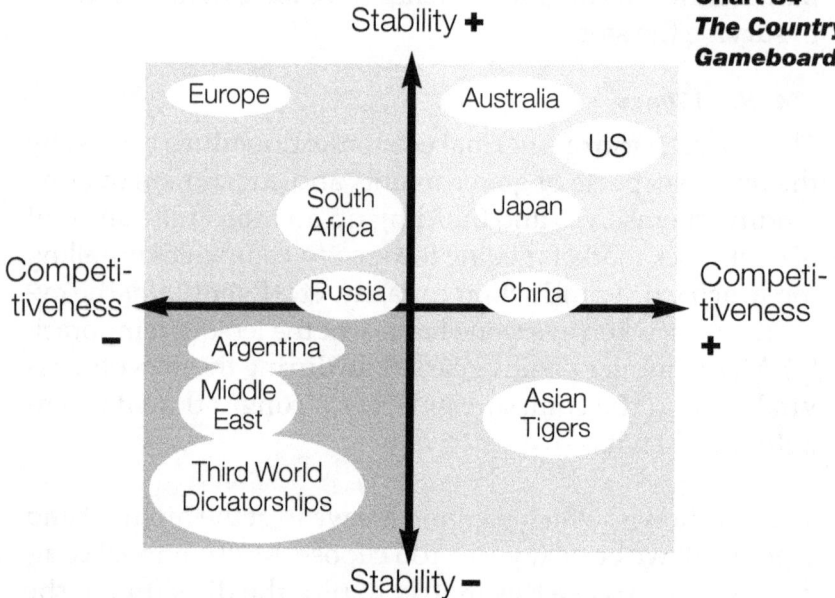

You might disagree with some of the locations we've given to countries. But that's the whole point of the gameboard: to excite debate.

Now let's examine a company typically operating within a *national* market. The 'x' axis of the gameboard signifies the state of the market in which the company is selling its goods and services (beyond its control), and the 'y' axis the efficiency of the company (within its control). As we've already remarked, you have to unpack the yardsticks by which you judge whether the market is positive or negative and your efficiency is rising or falling. Another point you have to decide on is whether you express your change in efficiency in absolute or relative terms, i.e. whether you exclude or include the performance of your chief competitors in making the judgement as to whether your efficiency has improved or declined. That you should take into account the performance of your competitors is unquestionable. But there are two alternatives: you can make the 'y' axis represent relative efficiency or, as you will see shortly, you can plot your competitors' progress on the same gameboard.

Here's the most popular gameboard in our experience of facilitation:

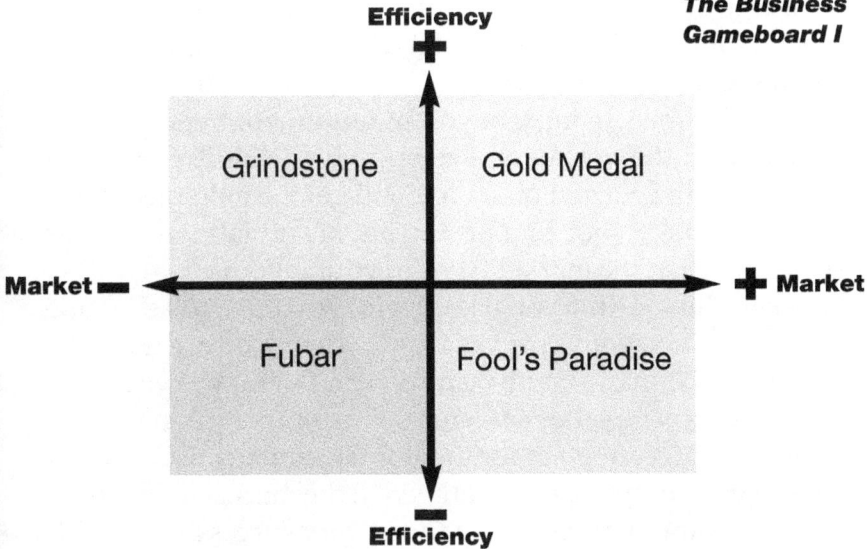

Chart 35
The Business Gameboard I

We are pretty con dent that when examining this diagram, you can immediately project an image of each scenario in your mind without having to stop and analyse it. How's this possible? The names. For those readers who are not veterans of the war in Vietnam, the mystery of *Fubar* will be resolved in the next paragraph.

Obviously, the worst-case scenario is where your competitiveness is declining in a poor market. A strategist with a sense of humour called this scenario *Fubar* during the actual con-

275

versation. Afterwards, she bailed out in the written version and renamed it *Mubar – mucked up beyond any recognition*. But *Fubar* is now well established in the oral tradition of the company. Nobody wants to be in it because it is the last stage before bankruptcy and death. The second scenario of *Fool's Paradise* is where all your faults are covered up by a booming market. Should the market turn and you do nothing you go straight into the *Fubar*.

The third scenario, *Grindstone*, is where you put your nose to the grindstone and grind out better efficiencies than your competitors in a hostile market. We've all been there! And the final scenario is aptly named *Gold Medal* because, like any great Olympic champion, you maintain your competitive streak into the *next* games despite being showered with success in the current ones. You still get the gold medal. It's so easy to take your foot off the pedal and fall into a *Fool's Paradise* when the market turns in your favour.

As in the multinational scenario, you have to ask yourself where you were five years ago, where you are now and where you think you will be next year. But maybe you want to include a competitor as well. You're Company A in the next diagram and your main competitor is Company B. Company B is a large company that has been in the market longer than you have and historically has been very successful in holding on to its client base. You have had issues with efficiency which up till now a blinkered management structure has ignored. Examined against the backdrop of the gameboard, you have been residing in a *Fool's Paradise*. Your competitor, by contrast, has regularly been winning gold medals. However, buoyed by the positive market, Company B is beginning to show complacency, whereas you recognise that you are trailing in the game because of your relative inefficiency and are aware that, if the market worsens, you will be *Fubarred*. You start putting measures in place to address this. Because of factors outside of the control of both companies, the market does indeed worsen. You, having worked through the strategy for change, are prepared, and move into the *Grindstone* scenario. Company B is unprepared for the deterioration in market conditions and overnight sees its dominance in the market disappear. Why? Because you've seized its market share. You are now in a perfect position to make a takeover bid for company B (which you could never have done on the other side of the gameboard because everything is expensive when market conditions are good).

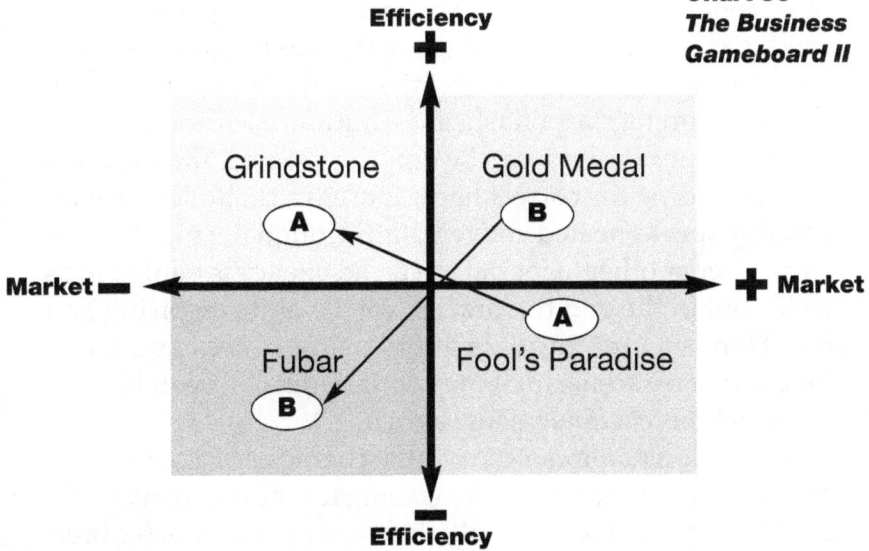

Chart 36
The Business
Gameboard II

The names of the scenarios are a fundamental part of their character as well as their marketability. One of the biggest selling range of toys in the UK is called *Bob the Builder*, based on the TV show which features stories around the character and his team made up of Roley the roller, Scoop the excavator, Dizzy the cement mixer, Lofty the crane and Travis the tractor. Young children crave miniature replicas of earth-moving machinery and tractors as long as they go under these brand names. You hear infants cry out for *Bob the Boodah* and *Bob the Biddah*. In the old days, we had Meccano with iron struts with little holes in them that could be bolted together. Then came *Lego*, which is still popular. Now to satisfy the urge to be in the construction game, we have *Bob the Builder*. It's all in the name! The difference is that Bob teaches children about teamwork, whereas the other games are mainly solo efforts.

But there is value in a scenario name beyond the image it creates in the minds of those involved in the process. The best-case scenario, if summed up in a short, punchy title, can be used to communicate a change in the direction of the company to all employees and get them emotionally involved. Names fit on tags and flashcards, buttonholes and post-its. Even bumper stickers can be employed to get the message across. Finding the correct name is often a challenge, as it invariably sparks heated conversation around the merit of one name over another (especially if an ad agency is hauled in as well). But in the end the process can be quite inspiring and fun. Here's a hint, though: avoid using *Heaven* as a name for a best-case scenario. It may sound ideal but you have to die to get there! *Utopia* is just as bad.

Yet, while a name can convey the character of a scenario, it can't always create the exact meaning for the company in the context of the game. After all, different people attach different meanings to the same word. Take *Chihuahua*. People who have a fear of dogs will immediately feel an aversion to the word because they will picture being 'chowed' in the street by one of them. They're good at scampering back and forth under gates and doing the savaging in between. Yet dog lovers would consider such a dog hanging on to their trouser leg as nothing more than a nuisance (unless it leaves bite marks in the trousers). For this reason, each scenario needs to be clarified and explained further than just giving it a name. Conventional scenario planning demands rich and expansive stories. Our experience is that, however noble their intention, such stories are often impractical, tedious and unread. Whatever form scenarios take, they should be depicted in a concise and logical way – as in an executive summary. Language should be home-brewed, picking up on the everyday 'lingo' used by operating management. Fancy prose bombs out. Information to develop the scenarios should come from those expected to keep an eye on future developments pertaining to their scope of operations. A representative from the human resources department would provide input, say, on impending labour regulations; similarly a representative from the procurement office would contribute his piece on the security of raw material supplies. It is important to include a cross section of perspectives in the scenarios in order to make people think out of their silos.

A great example of getting different parts of a company to cross-fertilise their ideas through scenarios concerns energy. Here is a commodity which everybody uses and which has recently seen a jump in its price, whether you're talking oil, coal or electricity. We've chosen the uncertainty about the validity of global warming and the greenhouse effect as one axis, and the level of the oil price as the other axis. Our gameboard to get the creative juices flowing therefore looks something like *Chart 37* on the next page.

Doing the clockwise routine from top right, we have the following scenarios:

Gasoline Alley

After the recent spike, oil prices resume the low level at which they've been for most of the last 140 years (ever since the Pennsylvanian oil fields were discovered). New oil reserves

Chart 37 *The Energy Gameboard*

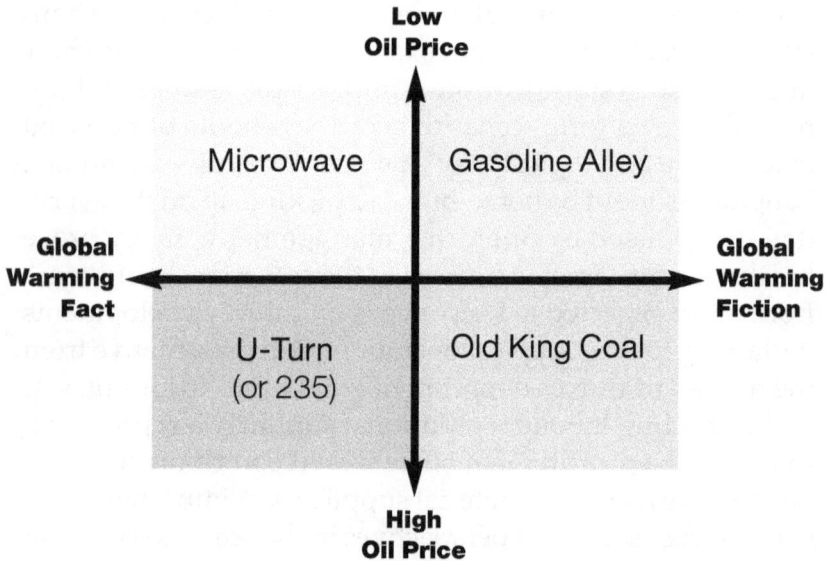

Low
Oil Price

Microwave   Gasoline Alley

Global   Global
Warming   Warming
Fact   Fiction

U-Turn   Old King Coal
(or 235)

High
Oil Price

are found to satisfy the growing appetite of the world's most populous countries like China, India and Brazil. With all the extra carbon dioxide emissions, the world's climate shows no ostensible change. People therefore assume that global warming was a myth.

Old King Coal

Increased instability in the Middle East, a jittery OPEC and lack of new oil discoveries to keep up with demand push the price of oil into the stratosphere at around $100 a barrel. This is particularly worrying for heavy industry, which immediately puts in place enormous energy-saving drives. Solar power, wind power, tidal power and hydropower cannot be made energy-intensive enough to be a viable alternative on a large scale. The best answer seems to be coal, because the world still has vast reserves to be mined. Modern and very efficient coal-burning power stations replace oil-burning stations, and

SASOL's oil-from-coal processing methodology is given a significant boost. People meanwhile turn to hybrid cars (petrol/electric) and fuel-cell cars in greater numbers. They stop driving SUVs to the office or to drop their kids at school. At $100 a barrel you 'invest' in your petrol tank and decide very carefully on the portfolio of activities on which it is to be consumed!

U-Turn or 235 (representing enriched uranium)

Combined with a growing shortage of oil, global warming detection systems reveal a noticeable increase in the planet's average temperature. International limitations on carbon emissions come into immediate effect. A switch to coal is therefore ruled out. As a result, there is a significant injection of new capital into research for alternative energy systems. However, none of these can satisfy the base load of power demand from industry, and so countries around the globe re-examine the merits of nuclear energy. This 'U-Turn' gains momentum as new and safer techniques of handling nuclear energy and disposing of waste are invented. However, with more uranium being transported between mines, enrichment plants and power stations, the threat of terrorists gaining access to fissionable material for nuclear weapons rises.

Microwave

Low oil prices and continuing controversy over global warming mean no change in energy consumption patterns. But the 'doomsayers' are right and the world's temperature inexorably goes up by a few degrees over the next fifty years. The consequences are huge, as sea levels rise and low-lying areas are permanently flooded. Local climate change speaks disaster for farmers.

These descriptions paint a brief picture of the suite of scenarios, and allude to their different characteristics. As the output of a proper scenario session, each description would be, say, about a page and a half to two pages in length; or, alternatively, it could be expressed in a series of bullet points on the gameboard itself.

Identifying the differences between the scenarios is an important part of the process. Just as meteorologists are able to recognise signs of developing thunder activity, contributors to a strategic conversation that define the scenarios should also draw up a list of 'red flags' that might herald the onset of a certain scenario. These may include signs of political instability in a country that provides a company's raw materials; 'chatter' around possible import/export regulations; new technological developments that may shift the balance of power in an industry; and legal precedents that induce consumers to lead a more healthy lifestyle. The 'red flag' process should be highly inclusive and rolled down throughout the company *after* the strategic direction of a company and its preferred scenario have been communicated to staff. In their strategic conversations, staff can be encouraged to put forward their own 'red flags' for evaluation.

On a different note, we'd like to outline a scenario gameboard we recently designed for the City of Cape Town and presented at a banquet there. It contains the following pivotal uncertainties:

1 The inclusivity/exclusivity of the local economy. An inclusive economy would be one that links the mainstream economy in Cape Town itself to all the informal economies that are sprouting up in disadvantaged areas around the city.
2 Sustainable/unsustainable development. This focuses on the relationship between the future development of the city and its natural and physical environment (re-

membering that the Western Cape is one of the richest oral kingdoms in the world).

The gameboard for Cape Town therefore looked like this:

Chart 38 *The City Gameboard*

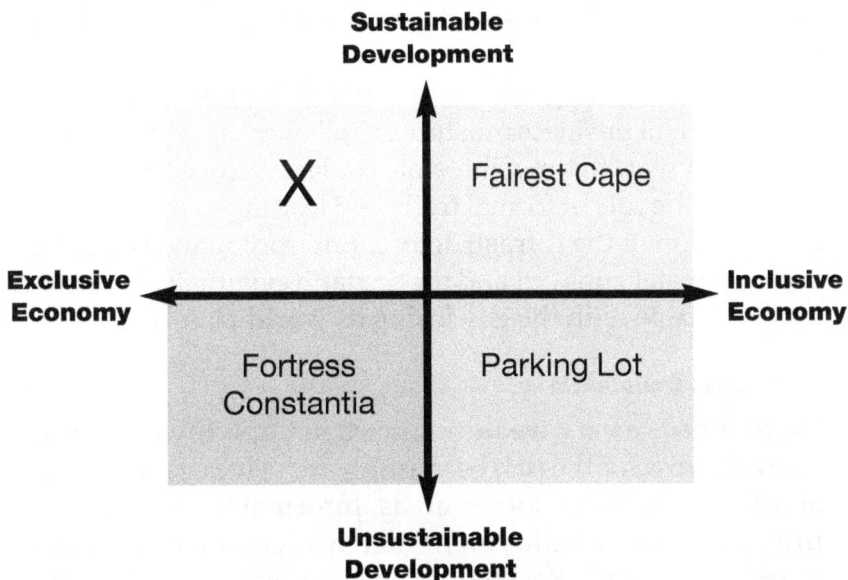

Because it is not possible from a humanitarian point of view to achieve sustainable development in an exclusive economy, there are only three possible scenarios:

Fairest Cape

This is the best-case scenario. Everything clicks together. Big business starts to partner with small business through procurement contracts and other means. An enormous drive to assist entrepreneurs throughout the region to establish businesses and gain access to capital is put in place. Environmental sensitivities are respected, thereby ensuring that the city retains its appeal as a unique tourist destination. The Cape is fairest in beauty and fairest in offering everybody a better life for all.

Parking Lot

This name is derived from a line in the Joni Mitchell song *Big Yellow Taxi:* "They paved paradise and put up a parking lot."

As the name suggests, property developers have a field day and small business mushrooms all over the city in an uncontrolled way. In time, informal trade envelops the streets, usurping the role of formal trade and leading to the physical degradation of the infrastructure. Environmental concerns escalate, water runs out and the scenario eventually becomes unsustainable with the city losing its world-class status.

Fortress Constantia

Constantia is a very wealthy suburb in Cape Town. It turns into a fortress for the rich because an exclusive economy creates few jobs in the poorer areas. Informal trading is suppressed and unemployment increases, contributing to a soaring crime rate. Residential developments take the form of cluster housing projects with high walls and plenty of security guards. However, movement becomes so restricted that getting to and from Cape Town International airport becomes a mission. Tourism fades and there's no money in the coffers to keep the environment in good order.

To summarise, the gameboard should consist of three or four scenarios that have emerged from the pivotal uncertainties; each scenario should have an original name that evokes the character of that scenario in the mind of the reader; and attached to each scenario should be a rich yet concise narrative drawn from the experience of the different actors in the organisation concerned. Is there anything else? Well, you've had a taste of the various gameboards. We think, in addition, it's a good thing to position your organisation on the gameboard according to where you've come from and where you are now, given current realities. Then you have to project where you want to be next year and in, say, five years' time. The path may be hard to follow and events outside of your control may make it impossible. You may also wish to position your competitors and gauge your outlook relative to theirs. Above all, the secret to playing the game lies in the question: *what if?* What if a certain scenario starts to materialise and we want to move towards or away from it? What if a competitor moves towards the best-case scenario ahead of us? What if we could turn the game to our advantage? What if we do nothing? The answers to these questions lie in a judicious appraisal of the company's strengths, weaknesses, opportunities and threats for each of the scenarios. That's right. *Now* it's time to do a SWOT analysis.

SWOT

It is a sublime thing to suffer and be stronger.
HENRY WADSWORTH LONGFELLOW

At this stage, we move from defining the game to playing the game. The conversation should as a result change gears – from one where exploration, debate and pulling things apart and reassembling them are the main theme to one where synthesis, pulling things together and honing them into actions to be taken assume centre stage.

Chess masters know their opponents, not only by name but also by how they play – what their strengths are, where they are weak, the opportunities they offer through their

Chart 39 *The Conversation Model – SWOT*

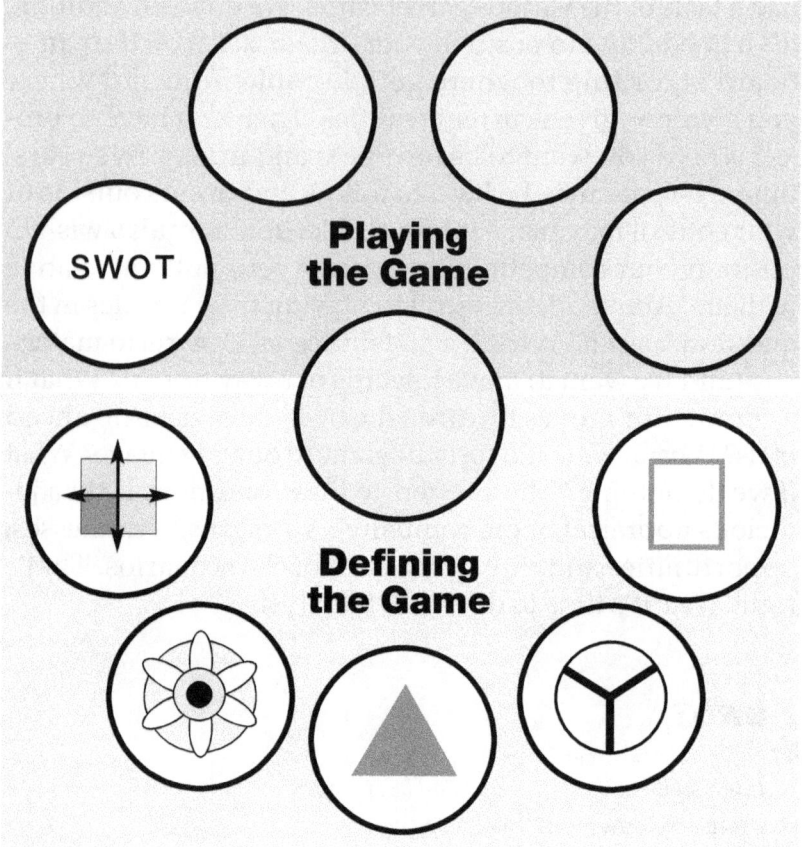

weaknesses and the threats they present because of their strengths. In essence, they do a SWOT analysis of themselves and their opponents before they play a game. In fact, this is a common part of the preparation programme in most sports at professional level and even at college and school.

SWOT is well understood in business, which is why it's a popular procedure for many companies. However, it is generally used in isolation as a strategic tool and is done by the company on itself. It therefore runs the risk of becoming yet another dot in space where its true value and potential can be lost. Used as part of the strategic conversation in the context of the game of business, a SWOT analysis becomes a powerful tool – it helps to bridge *defining* the game and the actual *playing* of the game. As such, it represents a shift in the conversation from elements outside of the company's control to things that the company *can* control. From this moment onwards the company begins to design its implementable strategy with SWOT crystallising a company's understanding of its capabilities. Thus, it prevents wasted time discussing options that are either undo-able or offer very little leverage.

In terms of the game of business, a SWOT analysis can be represented as a cube with inner and outer dimensions as follows:

Chart 40
The SWOT Cube

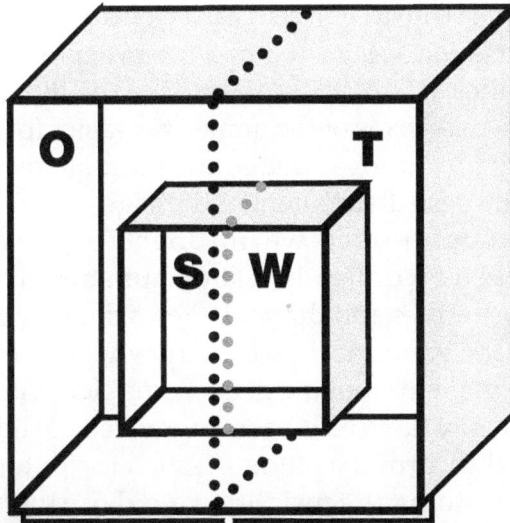

Key:

S Strengths
W Weaknesses
O Opportunities
T Threats

Strengths and weaknesses are inner dimensions because they are internal and relate to the core competencies of the company as well as to its culture, resources and even its business model and organisational structure. Opportunities and threats are external dimensions as they relate more to the key uncertainties within the business environment. Nevertheless, they should be more speci c than the key uncertainties raised earlier in the conversation, since one is now interpreting the *consequences* of changes in the environment on the business in question.

Because of the external nature of opportunities and threats, most companies find them harder to identify in a standard SWOT analysis. They are further from home. However, once scenarios have been developed, the opportunities and threats become much clearer. Within the context of the game, opportunities may lead to a change in the scope of the game for a company, especially if they align with the company's core competencies. Or, vice versa, an expansion in product range or geographical scope may already have been discussed, in which case it represents an opportunity. Further on in the conversation, where a company can exploit an opportunity, it becomes an *option*. Equally, once the threats have been registered in terms of the game, it is easier for a company to identify the options needed to eliminate the threats or, at least, minimise their potential damage.

Astute readers will no doubt comment at this point: "But haven't we already visited our strengths, weaknesses, opportunities and threats?" Yes, when we examined the scope of the game, and especially when we looked at ourselves through the looking glass. Some elements of the SWOT analysis may have also been suggested earlier on in the process and recorded as IPAs – issues for potential action. By re-examining the insights gained during the earlier parts of the conversation, much of the SWOT analysis can be completed without difficulty. A bit of duplication doesn't do any harm. However, what often happens is that, when the company is brutally candid in its SWOT, it will sometimes identify discrepancies between how it initially perceived itself as a player in the game and the reality of its position given the range of scenarios. This means that a SWOT analysis should be conducted with a fresh mind (preferably after the tea interval).

Moreover, to be thorough, it should be conducted for each scenario on the gameboard, because a strength in one scenario can prove to be a fatal weakness in another. For example, a company which is the largest global producer of a particular commodity may bene t most in a strong market scenario: but that same company could be crippled in a weak market scenario if a large element of its production is coming from marginal ore bodies. Alternatively, in a very positive scenario for a country's economy, importers gain and exporters lose as a result of the appreciation of the local currency in international markets. Conversely, in a scenario where prospects are weak, exporters gain and importers lose as a result of the depreciation of the currency. In other words, one man's meat is another man's poison. A gameboard SWOT analysis can be tabulated as follows:

Chart 41 *The SWOT List*

Scenario	Strengths	Weaknesses	Opportunities	Threats
1				
2				
3				
4				

The usefulness of such a table is that, at a glance, it is possible to see in which scenario a company is best placed to operate. It also provides a comparative indication, based on a company's desired scenario as well as the scenario it feels will play out, of what kind of options are out there to remove threats and to capitalise on opportunities.

There are two ways in which you can take the SWOT process

a step further to achieve a better understanding of the risks in the game (and maybe secure a more in uential position in playing it). Firstly, you can conduct a SWOT analysis on your main competitors; and, secondly, you can undertake a SWOT analysis on the principal players in your supply chain, both upstream and downstream. The first exercise emulates the chess master who studies his opponent, as we described at the beginning of this section. A SWOT analysis of your main competitors can prove invaluable in that it may give you a feel for how they would react to a change in scenarios and how you might outplay them in the changed game.

The second exercise reveals possible weak links in your chain. Often a switch in scenarios may be accompanied by changes in the rules of the game. Any player who does not or cannot adjust to the new rules (or the new scenarios) can disrupt the entire chain of supply. For instance, upstream you have to study the countries your suppliers are located in, on the grounds that should conditions turn ugly in any of those countries, there is precious little your supplier can do about it. Hence, an inherited weakness of your business is too much reliance on a supplier based in an unstable country or region. The same can apply to customers downstream. If you are dependent on a market that can disappear overnight for political or economic reasons, watch out.

It must be remembered that a SWOT analysis should never be a one-off, annual affair. Like a game of basketball or football, it should be done after every match (where in business a match is probably the quarterly results). The game of business requires regular conversation around a team's ongoing strengths, weaknesses, opportunities and threats as the season unfolds. That way the team is always re-examining and analysing its most effective options, which might just end up being the difference between winning and being runner-up in the league.

Options

*There are moments in life
when the only possible option is to lose control.*
PAULO COELHO

As players in any game we each play the game differently from each other. How we play the game is determined by our make-up. This means that consistency of play is a trademark

Chart 42 *The Conversation Model – Options*

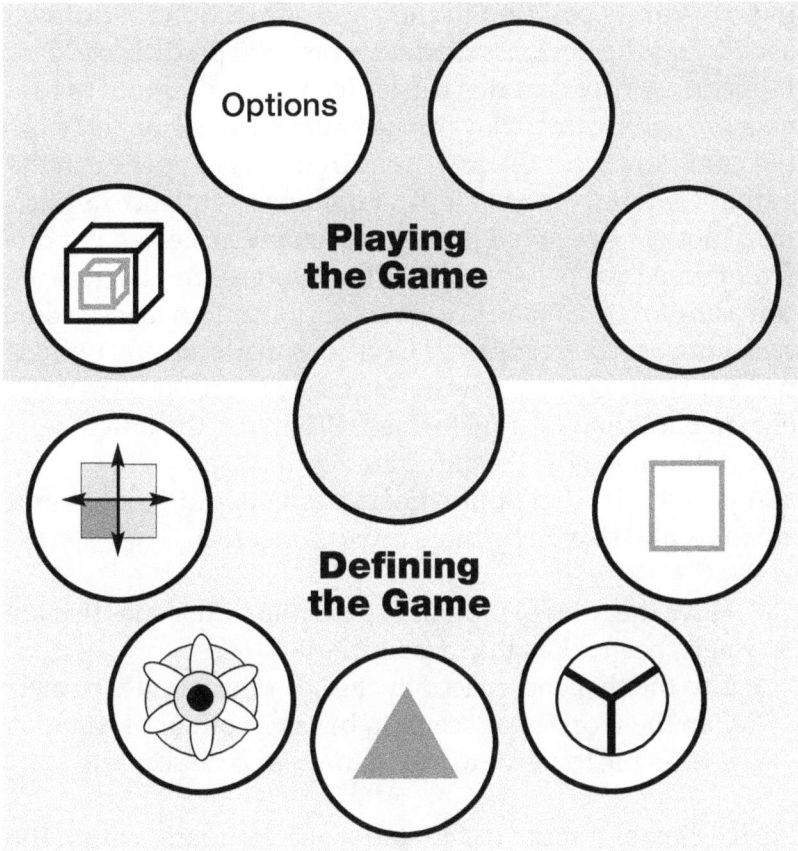

of most players and runs through the options they will choose. However, when the consistency of play becomes predictable, there is a risk that our competitors will anticipate our play, with the result that they gain competitive advantage.

Sometimes there is a need for players to change or adapt their game plan. In business, this means their business model. At this point of our process – after studying the scope of the game, the players, the rules of the game, the key uncertainties, the scenarios facing a company and its current strengths, weaknesses, opportunities and threats – a company is well quali ed to examine carefully its business model in terms of its position in the game. Questions should be asked: Has the business model become too predictable? Has it become so set that it is difficult for the company to manoeuvre in the game? How robust is the business model? Does the company meet the basic requirements to operate in the game? Can the company look at options to enhance its business model? And what if the game changes, i.e. what if different scenarios play out? Does the business model give the company an advantage in each scenario, or does it need some tweaking or radical surgery? Decisions made around options will either support the status quo, or lead to the business model being adapted or transformed. Whatever the outcome, it will determine how the game is eventually played.

It is essential that option generation should be open and creative, and driven by three broad concerns:

1 Have the rules of the game, particularly the ones that are new, been taken into account?
2 Can the challenges faced by the key uncertainties be met?
3 Can the worst-case scenario be taken out of play and is it possible to move towards the best-case scenario?

With a clearer picture of the status of a company within the game and the influence of that company's business model (game plan) on the game, the company is now able to assess its most relevant overall strategy (i.e. the relevant strategic options) as follows:

1 If it is a strong player it should embark on a *growth strategy*, either through organic growth using options that tap into its core competencies; or through a stepping-out strategy that will take the company in a new direction; or,

2 If it is a competent player with a questionable future in the game because of its size or for other reasons, it should examine a *survival strategy*; or,

3 If its weaknesses and threats are overwhelming and it clearly has no future in the game, it should design the most economical *exit strategy*.

Remember those IPAs – the issues for potential action – that were generated throughout the process and 'banked' for further consideration? This is the stage of the process when they are generally discussed. In particular, possible new directions which may have emerged in the earlier debate on the scope of the game are 'stripped down' to a set of more realistic options. It may become clear, for example, that a previously suggested direction is not sensible in light of an uncertainty or scenario. Remember how you used to put together a jigsaw puzzle containing 500 pieces of an English countryside. You would start by removing all of the blue pieces to work on the sky rst. In a similar way, the 'stripping down' process accelerates the building-up of a coherent picture of the options you really have available. This makes option generation easier and gives you a 'feel' for the possible outcomes of options before making any decisions. Obviously, as the construction of the puzzle proceeds, the interaction between the different elements of the overall scene begin to emerge, and will in uence how the options are knitted together and prioritised.

With the 'puzzle' approach in mind, options can be considered from four different perspectives:

1 *Organic options*, where a company's core competencies are already strong and could therefore be used as a foundation for organic growth.

2 *Stepping-out options*, which may arise from the conversation around key uncertainties, with the resultant PI Chart showing that the company is more dependent on a particular product or market than it should be. It may involve a completely new direction for the business, or at least the exploration thereof. Caution should be exercised if this form of strategy is considered, as it possibly requires not only the development of new core competencies, but also a cultural shift within the company. Resource sufficiency and allocation would also need careful scrutiny.

3 *Generic options* are those that have to be pursued for all futures as a result of issues raised with regard to scope, players and changes in the rules of the game. If the company is not adhering to the descriptive and normative rules of the game, the generic options are quite clear: either obey the rules or get out of the game. Furthermore, the aspirational rules of the game (the rules to win) are the value drivers of the organisation. Specific focus should therefore be placed on options around these rules, as they form the basis of future growth strategies.

4 *Scenario-specific options* depend on which scenario is in play, e.g. options for survival in bad times like where to cut costs or close plants as against options in good times to expand the business, pay extra dividends to the

shareholders or both. Options arise out of events beyond our control and, as those events change, so do the options. Option generation that is specific to a particular scenario will equip a company with the necessary strategic and tactical ' ne-tuning' if and when that scenario unfolds. In each case, not only should the challenges posed by some of the key uncertainties with high impact potential be addressed; but the consequences of each option, especially in terms of the responses of other players in the game, also bear examination. If this is not done before any move is made, the end game may produce a result that is the exact opposite of what was desired. The company may then stumble over the unintended outcome and spend a great deal of its nancial and human resources putting out the fire. Considering options for each scenario also gives the company a better 'feel' for which scenario it really would like to move towards in terms of its strategy, culture and purpose.

Let's move on to the subject of narrowing the options. Sometimes options sound great in conversation and, on the surface, seem like good choices; but on further analysis, they might not be the smartest choice. So how do we improve our understanding of the options so that we *can* make the smartest choice? Given that the descriptive rules of a game are the basic licence to operate, and the normative rules of the game are the moral rules of the game to which any world-class company must adhere; it makes sense that for any option to be effective it must not fall foul of either type of rule. We have therefore developed an Ethical Compass to be your guide (*Chart 43* overleaf).

An option that is between NW and NE on the Ethical Compass is both legal and moral and therefore safe to use. An option that hovers somewhere between NW and SW may be

Chart 43
*The Ethical
Compass*

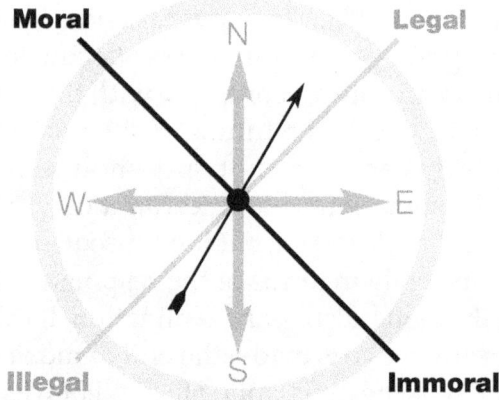

Chart 43 — The Ethical Compass

morally defensible, but it is illegal and therefore should only be taken if a crack legal team is on standby. This is often the game in dictatorship states with a poor record of human rights. It is clearly not a safe option, but one that may have to be taken in order to save one's corporate reputation. An option that is between NE and SE on the ethical compass will quite possibly raise the ire of other players, including consumer associations and other activist groups within the community, but will be easily defendable in court. An example of this is the option of outsourcing the manufacturing of designer label clothing to countries that allow family networks which may include child labour to do it. It may be legal in that country, but is it moral? Options of this nature may yield short-term gains but may prove unsustainable as part of a company's long-term strategy to be seen as a decent employer. Lastly, any option between SW and SE is both immoral and illegal. Any company implementing such an option will sooner or later go south. Do you recall Enron? How options are selected through the Ethical Compass will give you a good indication of what your meaning of 'winning' the game really is.

At this stage, we must raise the 'theory of tragic choices'. It states that not all choices in life are between good and evil; some are between good and lesser good (no problem for anyone) but some are between evil and greater evil. It is this last category that is the really tricky one. Nobody moral wants to do anything evil, but sometimes tragic consequences cannot be avoided. The US and Britain would argue that collateral damage in Iraq, which includes the loss of innocent civilian lives, should not deter the use of force to impose the greater good of freedom and democracy. We're in dangerous territory, because at what point does the level of inevitable (but unintended) evil more than offset the goal of greater good? When does the end no longer justify the means? The theory of tragic choices offers no precise answers, because there are none. But that statement in itself is crucial in differentiating hedgehogs from foxes. A hedgehog will follow his definition of good no matter what. Foxes will consider the consequences and maybe change their minds and follow a middle path. Hedgehogs will argue that this is not principled leadership. Foxes will respond that they believe in principles just as strongly as hedgehogs but *situational* leadership is better, i.e. the situation forms part of the decision. Fox-hunting has been nally banned in England and Wales after more than 300 years of the practice. The question is whether the adverse impact on rural communities will outweigh the obvious relief of foxes. Who's right? Who's wrong? As always, it depends on the situation and only time will tell.

Returning to the money side of the business, options can be subjected to further scrutiny by utilising what we call our Option Dartboard. No, it does not hang on the wall and it hasn't got a bull's-eye. But just as you throw a dart at a dartboard and receive a high or low score depending on where you land, so options can be graded too. The grading system revolves around the amount of resource input the option would demand in terms of money, people, time and the resultant level of output it may produce. The highest grade option would be one that requires little input but would, if successful, deliver an eminently high level of output. Pet names for this option include 'a quick win' and 'low-hanging fruit'. In contrast, any option that demands a high resource input but has little prospect of any signi cant output receives a low score (if it's not off the dartboard altogether). Most options fall somewhere between these two parameters and therefore can be pinned on the dartboard as indicated in *Chart 44*.

Safely assuming that most companies don't have an unlimited budget for the application of their strategy, any option that demands a high level of resource input is *exclusive* in that, by choosing it, the company has to refuse others. In other words, the company would be playing an 'either/or' game and there would be an opportunity cost involved. On the other hand, any option that requires low resource input needn't necessarily foreclose other options. It can therefore be considered *inclusive*, and the company would be in a position to play the 'and' game, i.e. it can pursue this and other options at the same time.

As a means of explanation we have plotted four options. Options 1 and 2 would each demand a high level of resource input to the extent that other options are excluded, with Option 1 offering the least output. Clearly not an attractive option. Options 3 and 4 on the other hand require less resource input each and permit you to do other things as well. Although Option 4 would require more input than Option 3, it does have the potential to generate a higher output. This would possibly make it a better option. The statement that strategy is as much about what you should *not* do as what you should do is only half true. It applies to exclusive, not inclusive options. Life is full of trade-offs, but sometimes it isn't: you can have it all.

Chart 44 *The Option Dartboard I*

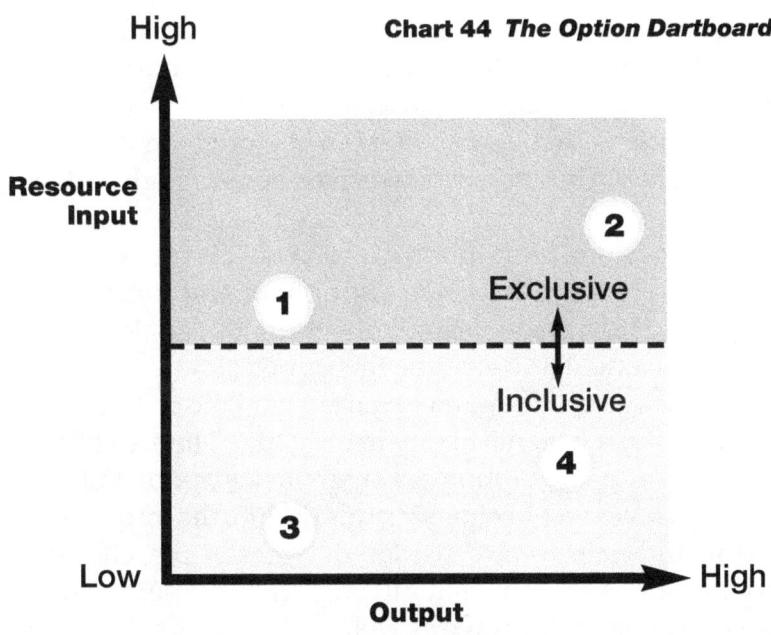

High

Resource
Input

2

1

Exclusive

Inclusive

4

3

Low

High

Output

Chart 45 *The Option Dartboard II*

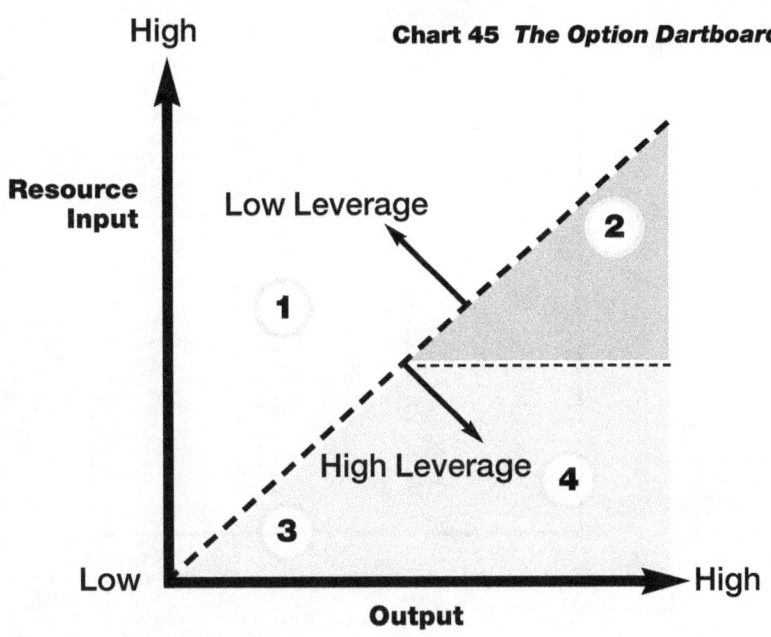

High

Resource
Input

Low Leverage

2

1

High Leverage

4

3

Low

High

Output

The dartboard can be dissected in another way (as represented in *Chart 45* on the previous page). Based on resource input and output, some options have a higher degree of leverage than others. A diagonal line can be drawn on the board to represent the boundary between options of high and low leverage.

Using the same four options, it becomes clear that Option 1 is definitely not a first-choice option for any company, as it requires a high resource input in return for very low leverage in the game. The only time this option should be chosen is when the rules of the game require it, and the company has *no other option* if it wants to stay in the game. The area of safety is a case in point. Option 2 is an exclusive option but does have high leverage. In choosing this option, the opportunity costs would have to be considered. For example, choosing options 3 and 4 combined might be a better bet because they both possess high leverage as well.

Chart 46 *The SHE Curve*

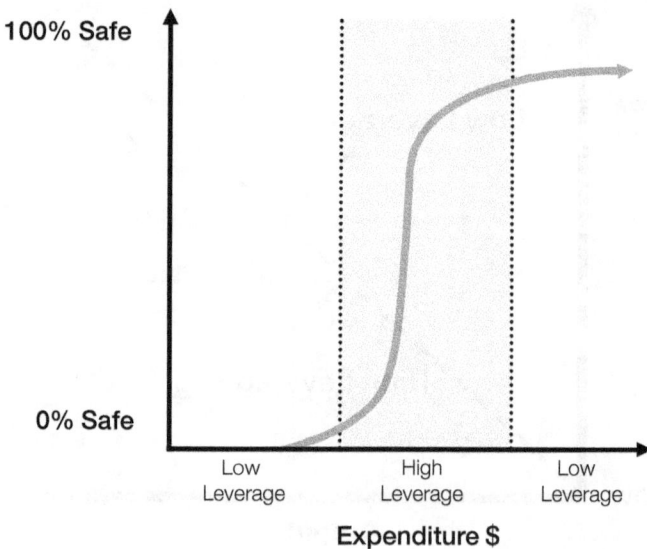

300

In companies where considerations of safety are paramount, a critical way to analyse options is in terms of the expenditure required to achieve an acceptable level of safety in the working environment. This relationship can be expressed as the SHE (safety, health, environment) curve in *Chart 46*.

In terms of the SHE curve, a minimum amount of expenditure is required to achieve any results at all. Below this amount, leverage is low to nil. There follows a band of expenditure within which options can produce a signi cant improvement in safety, the health of employees and conditions of the environment – up to as much as 95 per cent of what is possible. This is an area of high leverage. Beyond this, the remaining 5 per cent requires a huge amount of expenditure, with ever decreasing leverage. However, this last 5 per cent may be vital to prevent an accident which, even though it is extremely unlikely to happen, could result in a large loss of life if it does. Hence, an option should sometimes be chosen for reasons other than leverage. It's very hard, though, to take risk totally out of play, because it's more difficult to justify expenditure to stop something happening than to make something happen. Governments have the same problem with preventing terrorist acts. How much money and how many civil liberties are you prepared to sacrifice to make a country safe?

The nal matter we must cover in the option section centres on risk and return. In a game of chess, as each move is made new options become apparent. Some are entirely safe, but some are daring and might meet with an unexpected move by your opponent. The same is true in business where each incremental step in the decision-making chain unveils new options, each with its own risk/return pro le. In a way, it's like placing bets. Depending on the magnitude of the bet, there is a level of risk beyond which you normally wouldn't go unless the bet was small or you were a real gambler. Similarly, in business, when judging an option such as whether or not to go ahead with a new project, a key factor to weigh up is the magnitude of the bet the company would be taking (i.e. the percentage of the company's assets or market capitalisation it would be putting on the table) versus the chance of unintended failure. Prudence dictates that the greater the magnitude of the bet, the safer the option has to be in order for it to be exercised. This principle, however, is broken time and again in corporate bidding wars, where risk rises in direct proportion to increases in the amount bid. The price just goes on up. But then takeover battles are about power and pride, and pride invariably comes before the fall.

The relationship between risk and return is shown in the R & R Graph *(Chart 47)*:

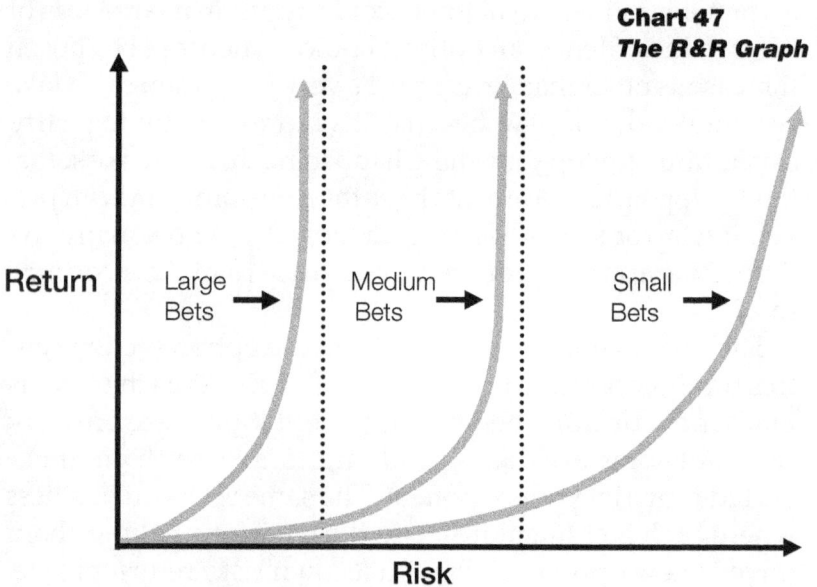

Chart 47
The R&R Graph

Return

Large Bets →   Medium Bets →   Small Bets →

Risk

Applied within a business context, the terms used in this graph can be de ned as follows:

1 The *magnitude of the bet* is the percentage of wealth you are willing to wager.
2 The *risk* is the chance of unintended failure due to market, cost, technical or political factors, or a combination thereof.
3 The *return* is the return on capital employed or the internal rate of return after discounting all future cash ows.

According to the R & R graph, there is a choke limit for options involving large and medium-sized bets (represented by the dotted line). No matter how high the anticipated return is, most companies will simply not go beyond a certain level of risk. For small bets, the risk is open-ended as long as the anticipated return rises in step with the risk. Obviously, choke limits vary from company to company, depending on how entrepreneurial the CEO and the board are. It is not unknown for a board to bet the entire company on a single project, but it's rare, and the company usually has to be in pretty desperate circumstances. In our conversations, we nd the R & R chart is used sparingly, since the vast majority of options raised in a strategic conversation individually represent small percentages of a company's overall wealth. Nevertheless, the risk of an option has to be taken into account.

All companies have a limited amount of top management time and cannot waste it. Time is, after all, money. Generating options through strategic conversation provides informed choices and takes the guesswork out of strategy formulation. The best possible paths forward become clearer as the false leads are unveiled. We are not for one moment saying that an executive team should slog through every one of the charts we've inserted in this section. But the principles behind them should be kept in mind at all times. All that is required now is to make strategic decisions to take the company on the path with the greatest chance of winning the game.

Decisions

No sensible decision can be made any longer
without taking into account not only the world as it is,
but the world as it will be.

ISAAC ASIMOV

Decisions! Decisions! We only say that when we are caught
between equally attractive options like which chocolate to

Chart 48 *The Conversation Model – Decisions*

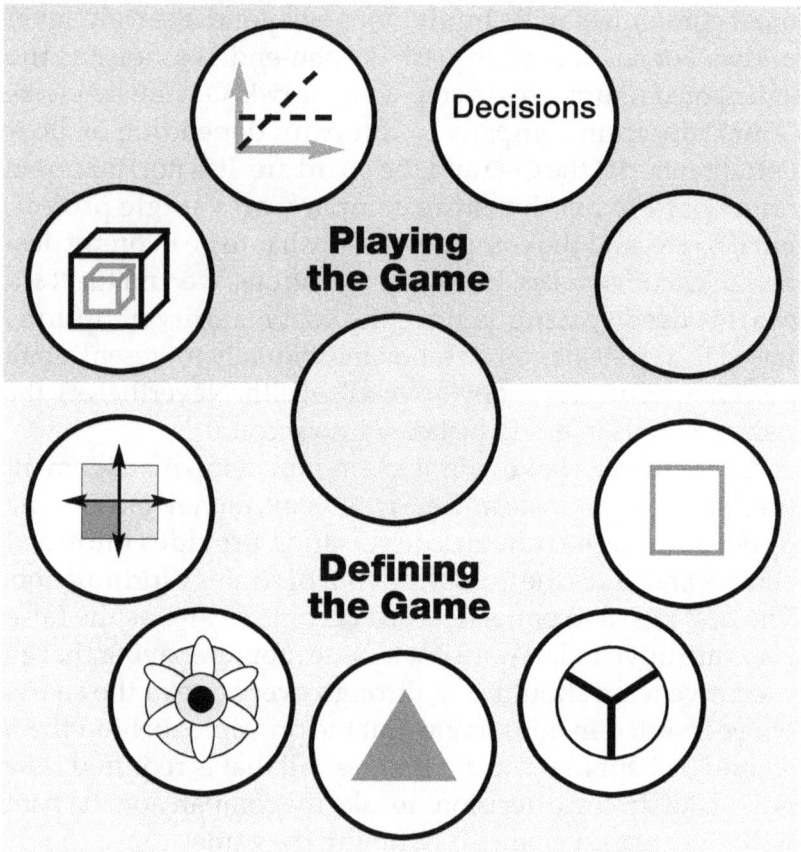

have in the box. Think about how many decisions we make in a day from the moment we open our eyes to when we close them. Life (when you're awake) is a continuous decision stream. And the difference between options and decisions is very simple. With options you can be as wild as you like because you are not making a commitment. With decisions you are committing yourself.

Nevertheless, the interesting thing is that you *only* have to make decisions when you *have* options. In prison, for example, you make very few decisions in a day, because you have very few options – dress, food and recreation periods are pretty much laid down. In the outside world, a routine job can mean you have very few options while you are doing it. You almost go into a decision-less mode, performing the routines like an unthinking robot. Sadly, the poorer you are, the fewer options you have. If you have one skirt or one pair of trousers, you don't have to make decisions when you dress. At the other end of the scale, if you're very, very rich, your options become endless. Want a candle-lit dinner in New York when you're shopping in Paris in the morning? Just ring up the pilots of your private jet and ask them to re the engines up because you'll be at the airport in the next hour. This all boils down to one inescapable fact: you should really only entertain options that you have the capability of turning into action. Otherwise, it's daydreaming. So check your span of control before making any decision.

In the context of this phase of the strategic conversation, we must return to another distinction we made at the beginning of the book – the difference between strategic and tactical decisions. Strategic decisions are ones which change the direction of your life; tactical decisions are the ones you make every day to stay alive. Your parents make some strategic decisions on your behalf – like having you in the first place! Seriously though, they decide on the neighbourhood where you're brought up, the school in which you are enrolled and to some extent the value system you take through life. Then you take over and start making strategic decisions on whether or not to attend university, which career to choose, where you are going to live and with whom you are going to hitch a ride in the longer run (the other option: staying single). The important thing to realise is that if you accept this de nition of 'strategic', you don't often make strategic decisions – maybe fewer than a hundred in your life. Some people will argue that this is too narrow a de nition. But we're into semantics. Sure, you may want to cast a wider net for classifying decisions as strategic, but the main point still stands: strategy is about direction, tactics is about how to get there.

So how do we transfer all the thoughts we've expressed about making decisions in our personal lives to the world of business? According to the de nition we've accorded to the term 'strategic', the only part of the conversation model around which decisions can be called truly strategic is the scope of the game. If your business significantly expands its product range or replaces existing products with new and different ones, that can be considered a change of direction and is often referred to as 'strategic repositioning'. If you take over another company (or start a business from scratch) in an entirely new field, that is likewise a strategic decision. Moving into a new country in a major way, same deal. By contrast, gradual organic growth of a business where internal research and development leads to a steady stream of new and upgraded versions of your existing product range would fall into the 'tactical' classification – innovation to keep yourself alive. Major decisions about organisational structure, human resource policies, nancial/IT systems and capital structure would also be tactical. Decisions about the business model can go either way depending on the magnitude of the decision.

Does this mean that strategic conversations should not embrace all these issues? Absolutely not. As we said at the outset, our conversation model should be seen as a prelude to the normal planning cycle. Thus, it must include both strategic and tactical decisions so that one segues in a logical fashion from the big picture of strategy to the more detailed arena of tactics. Moreover, the whole purpose of introducing key uncertainties and the scenario gameboard into the conversation is to explore how tactics need to be adapted in order to cope with possible changes in the environment. Added to which, radical external shifts may demand a revamp of strategy like redirecting your game, exiting part of it or closing up shop altogether.

Ultimately, the quality of strategic conversation is de ned by the calibre of decisions that are made as a result of it. But this is not the end of it. Some of these decisions then have to be converted immediately and some stockpiled in case there are changes in the environment. As in any game, players in business work strategically to create opportunities and to counter threats. Often though, there's no implementation of the decisions, i.e. no action, and then the opportunity is lost or the threat grows. It is therefore a vital step in our model that decisions from the range of options are banked for action today or possible action tomorrow. But which option is the right one to select? The secret here is to identify which of the scenarios is most likely to play out. This decision alone will form the basis of the company's ve-year plan and accompanying budget. Obviously, if the future changes within the realm of the scenario gameboard, the strategy will be revisited and adjusted accordingly. If, however, the future changes dramatically in a direction totally unexpected, the scenario gameboard, options and decisions will have to be re-examined in a new round of strategic conversations.

In today's business world where global connectivity punishes you very quickly for procrastination, there is an emphasis on policy execution. We are, in fact, entering an 'era of policy execution'. A company's success or failure in the global market can sometimes be measured within days of the execution of its strategy. If it wants to remain a player in the game, more than ever before a company has to update its understanding continually of the subtle shifts taking place on the eld. A foxy company adapts its execution of strategy in light of its opponents' tactics and other twists in the plot beyond its control.

In the fantasy world of action movies, the hero always ends up in a situation where he has to make one of two decisions: save the girl or save the world. And somewhere nearby there will always be a large bomb with a clearly visible digital timer ticking away. Whichever choice he makes he risks a negative outcome. It's obvious that, given the choice, the hero would clearly prefer not to be in the situation, and the suggestion is that the decision he has to make is forced onto him by factors outside of his control. Of course, we momentarily forget that our hero has superpowers and will therefore easily manage to save the girl (and everyone else), defuse the bomb and beat up the baddy, all without disturbing the parting in his hair.

In the real world, decision-making is a fundamental life skill and not simply an act of choosing the most appealing option; and unfortunately not enough emphasis is placed on this skill within the whole strategic process. Often a decision is made at the end of a strategic process that is out of the context with the whole game. It is frequently based on an arbitrary response to a situation, or is blurred by emotion and, especially in business, by power plays and personal attachments. Although these factors cannot be ignored, because they are, whether we like it or not, elements in any decision-making process; they can destroy value in the chain when they become too dominant. The effect is to steer the company in the wrong direction or in no direction at all. Jamaicans have a typically vivid expression for this predicament: "sitting on the one-one cocoa" – a wooden raft that cannot be steered but instead see-saws with the waves, moving backwards and forwards and not really going anywhere. How many company chairmen sit on their one-one chairs performing the same aimless role?

As we know, a philosophy of doubt and indecision doesn't work in business. Decisions need to be made, deadlines have to be met. Straddling the fence can lead to very painful results. Because effective decision-making relies on both intuitive and analytical thought, it is an art as well as a science. It is not simply about making a choice. It's about *creating* choice within your span of control and then deciding from that choice. And obviously with a little help from your friends, you can widen your span of control. Alliances and partnerships are formed on that basis. Whereas some decisions are no-brainers and therefore require very little exercising of any decision-making skills, most of the important decisions we make are complex. They will have outcomes, both expected and unexpected. In the game of business, strategic decisions made by any player in the game will have an impact on the game. Other players will react and the game will change.

Because companies are people organisations, decisions will also affect people within the company; and because people are sensitive and emotional they will react, sometimes illogically. No matter how much a company develops a team-playing ethos, every player within the team will eventually do whatever is necessary to protect his or her own interest. So, the bigger the company, the more complex the decisions and outcomes, and the more necessary it is to have the kind of strategic conversation we have outlined. It allows a company to look through the lens of complexity, understand the game better and make the most effective incremental decisions in a process that has a built-in mechanism for adaptation. By making decisions around scenarios, you can adjust gradually to a changing environment rather than having to make dramatic switches. Implementing our conversation model gives people the ability to learn how to make better decisions by interaction with their colleagues. The more the model is used and the more iterative it is, the greater the degree of mutual learning and frequency of breakthroughs.

By the time the application of the model has got to the decision phase, the correct problems have been identified and clearer objectives have emerged. Clarity on key uncertainties and alternative futures through scenario construction has instilled more flexibility in the nature of decision-making. It has also developed the mindset that mistakes are part of the learning process and that better decisions are made when creative thought to overcome a weakness is harnessed. Furthermore, the model discloses a company's appetite for risk. It compels consideration of where decisions might lead in the future and therefore provides a deeper understanding of any difficult choices and trade-offs down the line. Above all, the model encourages an examination of the potential outcomes of any decision.

Decision-making can lead to three types of outcomes:

- an intended outcome (IO);
- an unintended outcome (UO);
- a zero outcome (OO).

This is represented in *Chart 49*.

Even though a company's strategy is to get from A to B, the tactical decisions needed to steer it there will need to be broken down into do-able chunks, first to establish momentum and then to build upon that momentum. Each tactical decision is based on the outcome of the previous decision, which is either intended or unintended.

Should a decision have an intended outcome, the next decision made will simply be in line with the original, or planned, overall decision. It could be slightly different from the first decision, depending on the circumstances and the response to the first decision (hence the adjacent circles), but it will still be in line with the overall strategy.

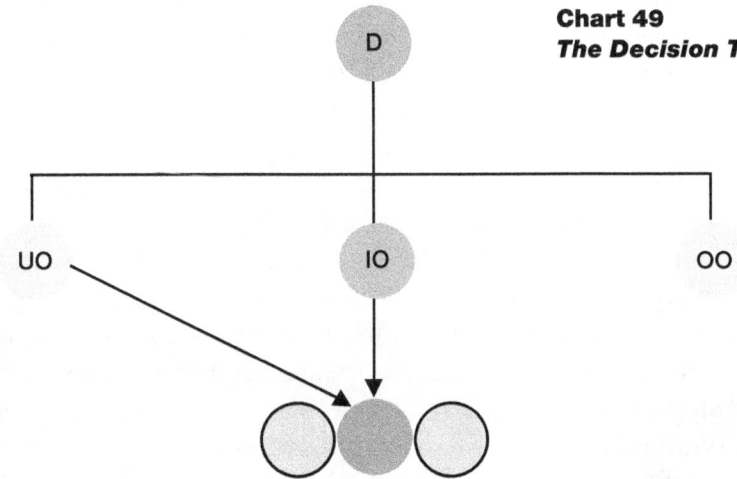

Chart 49
The Decision Tree

If, however, a decision produces an unintended outcome, it is crucial to examine *why* there was an unintended outcome if any degree of learning is to take place. Anyone who has hit their thumb with a hammer instead of hitting a nail will agree that it was an unintended outcome and that unless they examine a possible reason for this happening, it could very easily happen again. In another context, an iron shot that completely misses the green can be viewed as an unintended outcome in a game of golf. It could be the result of incorrect implementation – something within the player's control to rectify like an incorrect grip, stance or swing. If, on the other hand, a gust of wind deflected the ball in flight from its intended direction, it might be the fault of the player because

311

he should have checked the wind; or it might not be his fault because the gust happened out of the blue. Either way, his next shot is like the diagonal arrow in our diagram, a do-able thing to get back on track.

In business, the sign of a successful strategic conversation is one where an unintended outcome has already been worked through and the tactics are adjusted accordingly. Catch-up is easy. A zero outcome is the result of finger problems or lack of follow-through (as opposed to a decision to do nothing).

Unlike a game of chess where decisions can be turned into action very quickly by the player simply moving a piece on the board, the implementation of a decision in business requires a whole set of actions to be taken by management and staff working in concert. Because people tend to make more effort in getting things done if they know their results are going to be measured, a zero outcome is less likely in a situation where outcomes are being measured. Hence, the second last step in our conversation model is to establish measurable outcomes. Indeed, a measurable outcome of the decision phase of the conversation should be a ranking of decisions in terms of importance and urgency, as well as a list of options rejected or held over for later consideration.

Incidentally, a little known fact about the spectacular turn-around in the crime rate in New York is that it wasn't just due to the 'broken window' strategy of following up on the most trivial of crimes. It was also attributable to CompStat – a computer system which tracked all categories of crime on a weekly basis in each precinct. Where there was an increase in a particular category, in a particular precinct, the police chief was called to account. If he complained about lack of resources, he was given extra ones. If at subsequent meetings the statistic was still heading in the wrong direction, he was replaced. Simple, no nonsense stuff. It should be used in every city with a crime problem.

Measurable Outcomes

There are two possible outcomes:
if the result con rms the hypothesis,
then you've made a discovery.
If the result is contrary to the hypothesis,
then you've made a discovery.

ENRICO FERMI
Nobel prize-winning physicist

As we were at pains to point out earlier on, without measurable outcomes, conversations are social, not strategic. Asking attractive strangers at a function how they are is polite and sociable. Asking those same persons for their telephone number is strategic. It has a measurable outcome: they either give it or they don't. If the response is affirmative, it implies permission to make further contact with the promise of maybe a series of increasingly elevated measurable outcomes. We will introduce you to our incremental staircase in a minute.

Because of the interactive nature of the business game, the larger its scope and the longer its duration the less control a player can have over its outcome. For this reason, short-term strategy – which in our nomenclature may be more accurately described as tactics – can have clear measurable outcomes. It is easier to budget for, and easier to monitor. Suppose, therefore, you have chosen a strategic option. To get the show on the road, you need to identify a nice, easy, initial task and ask yourself: who is going to do what, by when, and how much is it going to cost? The answers to these questions can be inserted among the targets, milestones and key performance indicators normally included in the one-year operational plan against which progress is monitored on a monthly or quarterly basis. One of the commonest rst steps we have come across in our experience of facilitation is merely to evaluate

Chart 50 *The Conversation Model – Measurable Outcomes*

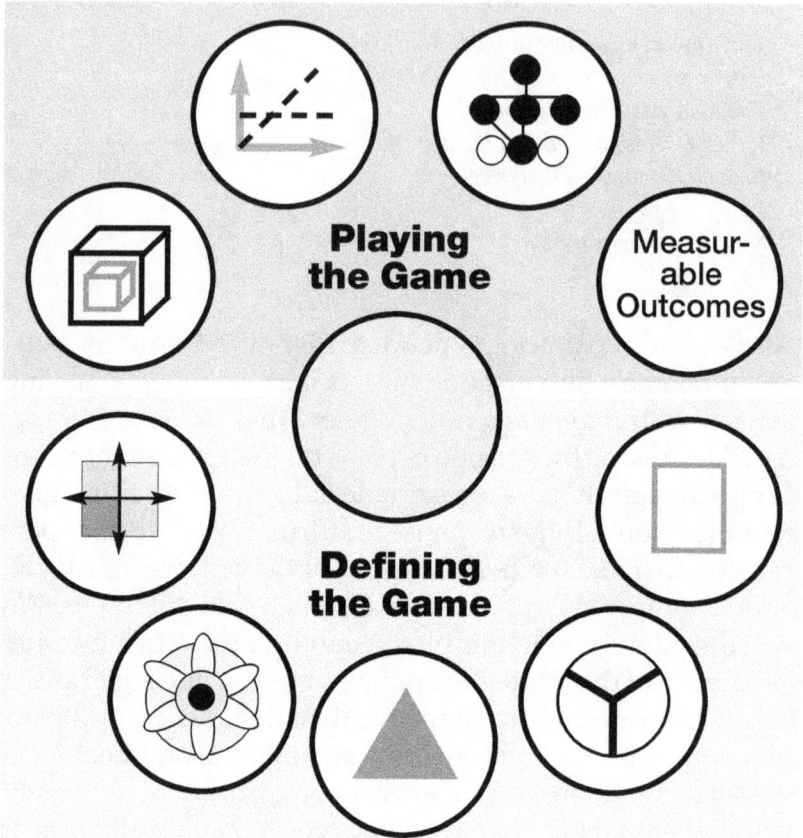

the option in more detail. That's ne. Reintroducing our cone of uncertainty, the conversation on short-term strategy falls on the left-hand side of the diagram *(Chart 51 opposite)*.

Over time, the cone of uncertainty widens as more and more factors beyond our control influence developments. More and more flags are needed to monitor developments and ensure some measure of control. Long-term strategy therefore is not as clear cut as short-term strategy. While there may be a grand, eventual outcome, getting there requires

Chart 51 *The Cone of Uncertainty II*

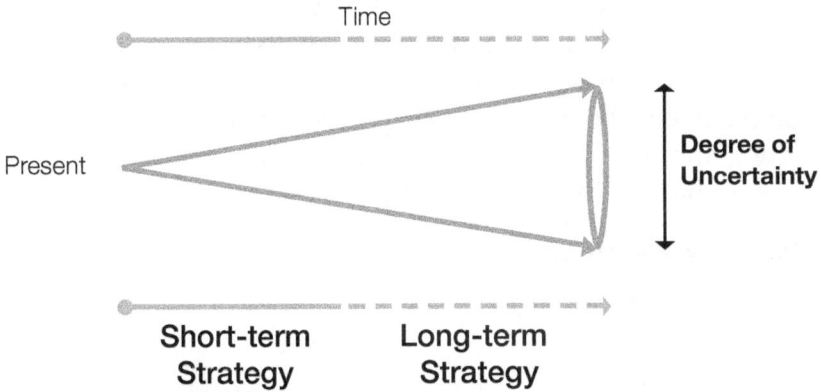

more flexibility. Therefore, true success can usually only come about by establishing a series of outcomes upon which the strategy is incrementally built. Detractors of incremental decision-making will argue that you can't cross a chasm with anything but a single jump. Our comment would be that if you are faced with a chasm, then you probably haven't strategised properly. Just once in a while, you have to take a mighty leap (preferably with a bungee cord attached).

Chart 52 *The Incremental Staircase I*

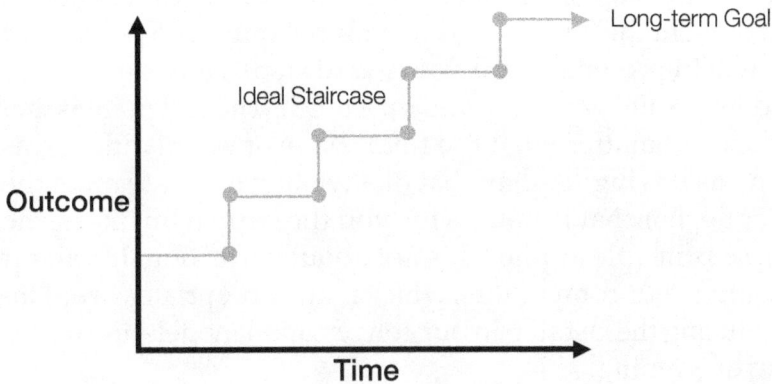

Thus, our recommended approach to long-term strategy is akin to climbing a staircase similar to the one in *Chart 52*.

However, this is an ideal staircase where each step propels you upward and is of the same height. In the real world, external events beyond the control of a company often change the shape and direction of the staircase. Victories and setbacks mean that it looks more like this:

Chart 53 *The Incremental Staircase II*

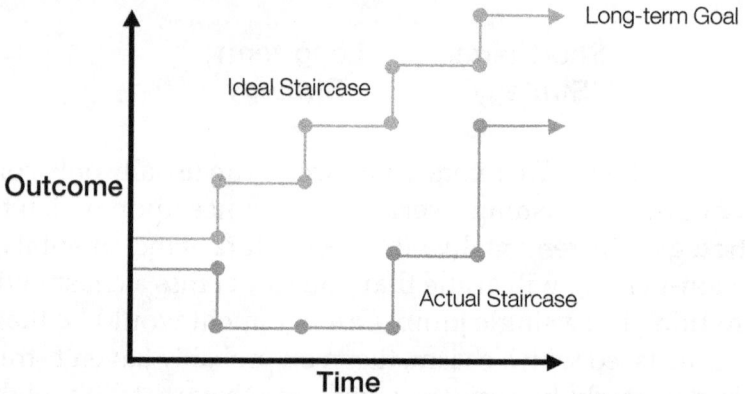

The objective is still to reach your goal. It just might take you a little longer to get there (although sometimes with the wind behind you, you arrive early). The best example we can quote you is the English Premier League for soccer. Unless you're Arsenal in the 2003/4 season, you're bound to lose the odd match (represented by a downward step). Draws move you sideways and wins take you up a notch. The real point is that it doesn't matter what the final shape of your ladder is, as long as it is higher than that of any other soccer team in the league. For that is what wins you the cup. In business, the same principle applies. It's not about perfection. It's about beating your competitors, which is an appropriate way of introducing the last step in our conversation model – the meaning of winning.

The Meaning of Winning

If the world be worth thy winning,
Think, oh think, it worth enjoying.
JOHN DRYDEN

The ultimate step in our conversation model is to make sense of what it means to win the game. If the meaning of winning for a company is purely about chasing targets, it has already

Chart 54 *The Conversation Model – Meaning of Winning*

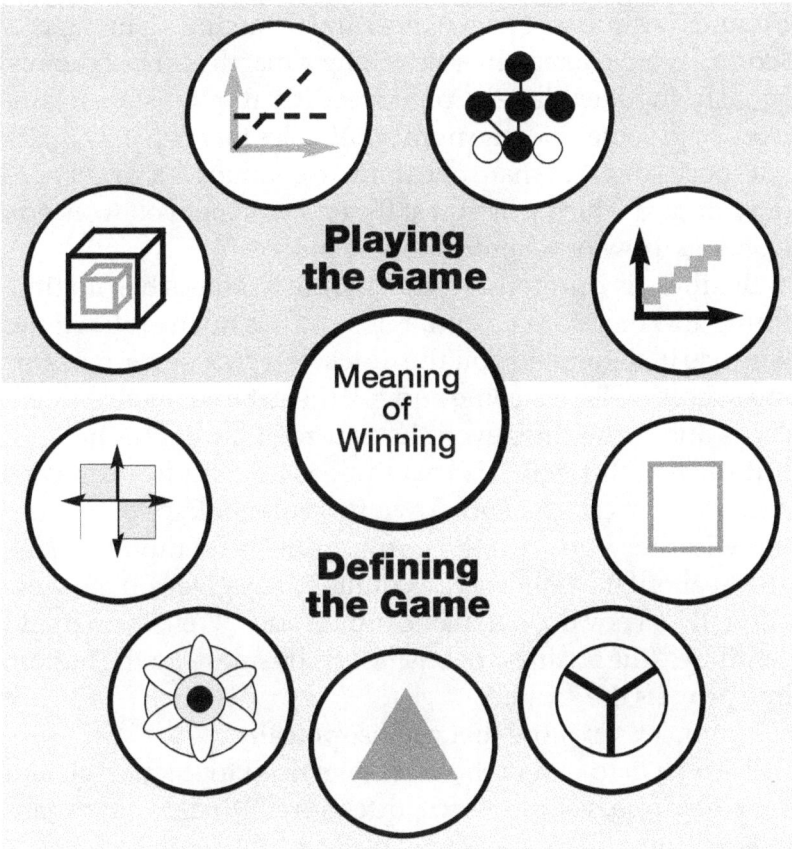

lost the game. Yes, measuring the performance of people against targets has its place (as we've already remarked), but dots don't mean anything if they're not put in context. Have you ever gone around the factory oor asking employees why the company exists and why they're doing what they're doing? You'd be surprised by the variety of answers, some of which would be revelations. People need a purpose, an end; and if you don't provide them with one, the vacuum will be completely taken up by their own purposes and ends.

A game of sport has a start and an end. It sometimes has a distinct time period (ninety minutes plus injury time for Premier League soccer matches) and sometimes a method of scoring which determines how long a match will last (tennis, squash, snooker, darts). Sometimes it's about distance (athletics) and sometimes the number of holes that you play (golf). All sports, though, share one thing in common – a scoreboard or scorecard which tells you at the end whether you won, you lost, you drew or where you were placed.

Business is different. A sustainable business has no time frame and therefore no end. Business has no overall winner because it all depends on the dates you choose for measuring success. Players come and go, the external environment shifts and sometimes even the nature of the game changes. But the real difference is that there is no definite scorecard and no exact criteria laid down in a rulebook for determining whether you won the game. "Oh," you might object, "what about the published accounts? They give you the score annually." They do, but in one dimension. "Well," you might continue, "the business of business is business. So the bottom line pro t *is* the score."

Hmm, let's explore that philosophically.

If we wish to win in the game, we need to ask ourselves a very obvious, yet powerful, question: "What is *our* meaning of winning?" For example, is it to:

- be the employer of choice?
- be the supplier of choice?
- be the most admired company by the public/customers?
- win the 'green' award for triple bottom-line achieve-ment?
- grow our earnings per share and share price ahead of our competitors?
- be the industry innovator?
- etc.

A hedgehog approach to the meaning of winning is equivalent to staring down a telescope – one lens offering one vision. Mine! So all we have to do is identify an optimal strategy in order to win the game according to *my* definition: Simple. You don't have to make any decisions in this regard because you have no option. There are plenty of CEOs turned astronomers out there who think this is the way to go.

Chart 55 *The Kaleidoscope of Winning*

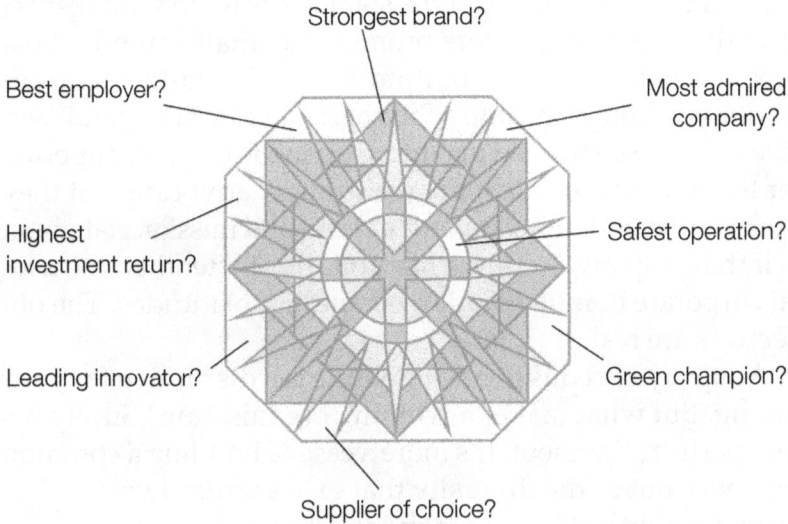

Strongest brand?

Best employer?

Most admired company?

Highest investment return?

Safest operation?

Leading innovator?

Green champion?

Supplier of choice?

In counterpoint, the games that foxes play present a variety of ways to win. They look at the meaning of winning not through a telescope, but through a kaleidoscope *(Chart 55)*. The mirrors create different views of an ever-changing picture of the future. Because a company is a social organisation, the different people that make it up have different wishes, different opinions, different strengths and weaknesses. There is no single meaning of winning. A successful strategy is articulated through a balance of each person's meaning of winning. A sustainable business therefore emerges not from seeking alignment of everyone's meaning of winning, but a *balance* between their meanings, i.e. achieving a win over a variety of fronts instead of aiming for a single win.

How do we go about extracting these personal views of winning at the tail end of the strategic conversation? We literally go around the table individual by individual and ask them where they'd like to see the company in five years' time. What prize would they want the company to win? It's amazing how everyone's eyes light up as they articulate their desire for the company. And the soft factors to do with respect and decency feature more prominently than you might expect (our answer to the bottom-liners). We faithfully transcribe what they say onto a flip chart and carefully hand over the sheets to be framed and hung up in the corridors of power for all to see. In addition, we strongly advocate that they form the basis of the company's vision and mission statement – if the company desires to have one. It's better than the usual corporate homily of hollow-sounding platitudes. The objectives are real.

You may find this final step a little too disruptive for your liking. But what makes a winning organisation? Surely it's not perfect alignment. It's more a case of building a common purpose out of the diversity that exists around you. A diamond would not be a diamond if it had only one facet.

Full House

The sleeping fox catches no poultry.
BENJAMIN FRANKLIN

There you have it. We have laid down our cards (except for three still up our sleeve). It's a full house. The diagram looks a bit like an Egyptian hieroglyph but there is no other like it in the world. Indeed, our model completely upends many of

Chart 56 *The Conversation Model – Full House*

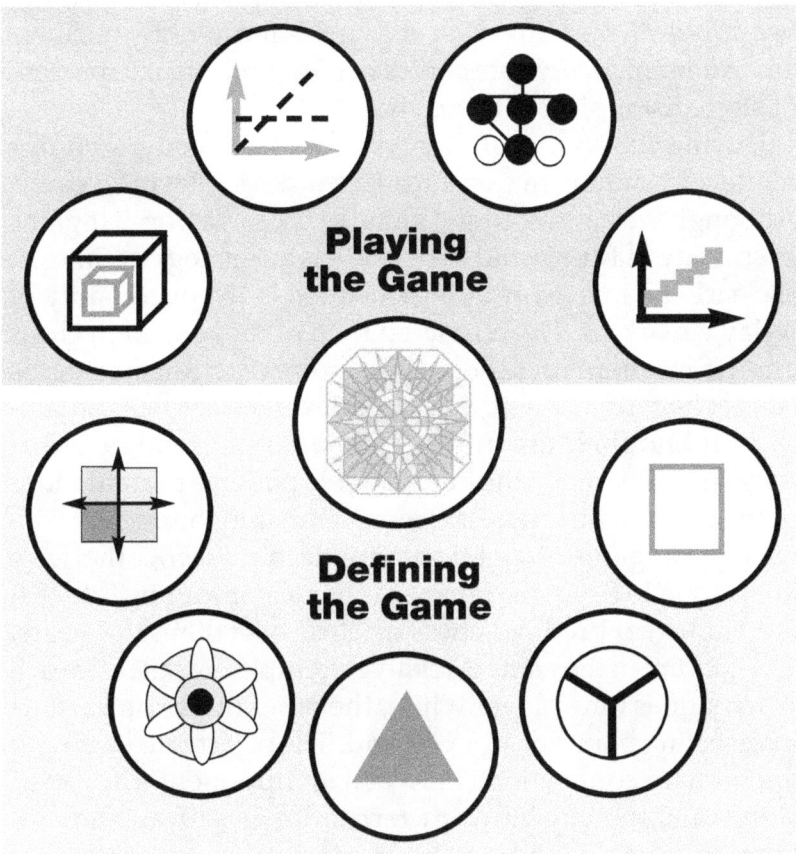

Playing the Game

Defining the Game

the models on display in academic circles. No doubt in the fullness of time, someone will come along with something smarter and take out our 'full house' with 'four of a kind'. Great – but we don't see our basic logic being disturbed. The transformation of global business is unfolding before our very eyes. Today's future is tomorrow's history. Over the past decade and a half, the explosion of the internet has added new impetus to globalisation and, paradoxically, the increasing connectivity has cast a growing shadow of uncertainty over the way we do business. Although increased access means that more is known now than ever before, uncertainties appear in the blink of an eye. In this hurly-burly business environment, many companies need a more exible process of strategising simply to survive.

During the course of this book, we have compared our model of planning in extraordinary times to playing a game. Although we have used the game of chess – a popular game of strategy in Russia and the West – as an analogy at times, it is clearly no match for doing business in the uncertainty of today's markets. The restricted field of movement in chess and its mathematically based action-reaction strategies cannot help us deal with the complexities of human organisations and their emotional and sometimes illogical drivers. In reality, given the innumerable possible permutations of the game of business, it is more similar to the ancient Chinese board game of Weiqi (pronounced *wai-chi*), otherwise known as Go (from the Japanese character meaning *battle*). It is a game that predates chess by close on a thousand years. The concept of the game is relatively simple: two players each place stones (one player white, the other black) on various intersecting points of a 19 x 19 grid. The object is to surround and isolate connections between an opponent's adjacent stones and thereby limit any territorial growth and advantage. Because it is a large board and rules are somewhat limited, it allows great scope in strategy. What's more, decisions in one part of the board are in uenced by situations that develop on other parts of the board, and moves made at the beginning of the game can have consequences hundreds of moves later on.

The scope of the game is too large to imagine. In fact, it's been calculated that, given the size of the board and the limited restrictions, there are approximately 2.1×10^{170} possible combinations of positions in a game of Weiqi as opposed to between 10^{43} and 10^{50} in the game of chess. To put things further into perspective, some physicists estimate that there are fewer than 10^{90} protons in the entire visible universe!

The emphasis in Weiqi is on the importance of balancing tensions at different levels within the game. To secure an area of the board requires moves that are close together; and yet to cover the largest territory possible a player needs to spread out. To ensure that you do not fall behind, you need to play aggressively; but playing too aggressively leaves weaknesses undefended that can be exploited. Playing too close to the edge secures insufficient territory and minimal growth; yet diversifying too far from the edge opens a player up to invasion. Does sound a bit like business, doesn't it? Western companies wishing to operate in China would do well to remember this. It's a whole new game that requires different strategic thinking and a different meaning of winning. Indeed, one of the differences between the concept of the future possessed by Chinese and Americans is that the Chinese think it will change whereas Americans think it will get better.

If we are to attempt to strategise in a game under such extraordinary conditions, the best we can do is acquire a detailed understanding of the game and its players, as well as to effect an honest self-appraisal; eliminate those elements which will have little or no impact on the future, and then prioritise what remains in the design of possible scenarios.

323

By doing so, it is possible to extrapolate a full range of options and then make decisions that can be constantly measured and assessed for their effectiveness.

Generally, executive teams spend too much time discussing tactics under the banner of strategy and not enough time on developing clear strategic direction for the company. The conversation model is an ideal methodology for allowing a high level of strategic conversation before moving into traditional strategic planning and tactical sessions. Furthermore, the process can take as little as five hours and at the most two days.

If a successful company is one that draws on the combined meanings of winning of all its signi cant internal players, it makes sense that its strategic direction should be formulated and driven by these same drivers. A strategic conversation should therefore be flexible enough to encourage the sharing of this diversity of insights and the nurturing thereof, and yet at the same time be sufficiently structured to facilitate its ow. We feel strongly that such a strategic conversation worked through the conversation model is an ideal tool for top and middle management to identify the direction in which the company and its workforce should travel if they wish to win the game.

Furthermore, the conversation, if cascaded down to the shop oor, provides a sense of purpose at every level. Because employees all take part in the process, it encourages buy-in. This in turn provides the necessary motivation to turn the plan into action. Out of the debate around the meaning of winning comes a feeling of common purpose. Anyone who has watched a children's swimming gala is well aware of the different ethos driving an individual and a house/team event. With the common purpose of the latter, there is a shared enthusiasm and energetic support from all involved, resulting in an increase in performance by individuals because they

324

don't want to let the team down. Additionally, people who normally wouldn't shine on their own, and are aware of that, have an increased opportunity of experiencing the meaning of winning as part of the team.

Now for the three cards still up our sleeve. It would be remiss of us in our concluding remarks if we did not include three more examples of gameboards that we have found particularly popular over the past couple of years:

HIV/AIDS in South Africa

We have both had the benefit of giving presentations to very knowledgeable people in the field of HIV/AIDS who in turn have influenced the shape of our presentation.

We are in a war situation in South Africa where the HIV/AIDS virus is our very own micro weapon of mass destruction. To try to get people to understand the seriousness of this war and to show that there is a path to victory, we developed the following gameboard:

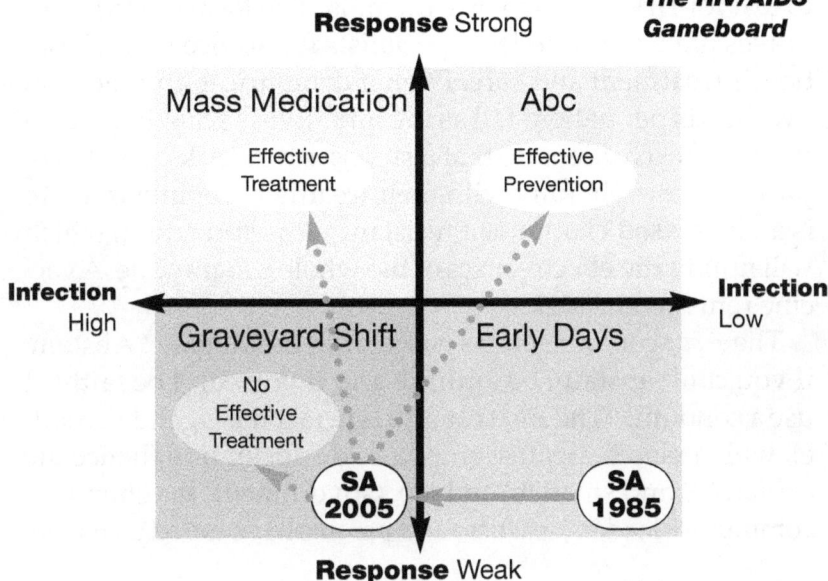

Chart 57
The HIV/AIDS Gameboard

Response Strong

Mass Medication · Abc

Effective Treatment · Effective Prevention

Infection High · **Infection** Low

Graveyard Shift · Early Days

No Effective Treatment

SA 2005 · SA 1985

Response Weak

In the *Early Days* scenario, the prevalence rate for HIV/AIDS is less than one per cent of the population. There are still isolated communities within South Africa that are in this scenario. But the bulk of the country moved out of this scenario by the mid-1990s.

Indeed, South Africa has just entered the *Graveyard Shift*, since the people infected in the mid-1990s are now dying of AIDS. The total number of registered deaths in the 30–34 age group is now higher than in any other age group for both males and females. This means that South Africa is losing its active working population as well as its parents, and leaving behind orphans and the elderly. If an effective treatment is not implemented, South Africa will sink deeper into the *Graveyard Shift*.

In the *Mass Medication* scenario, the government lives up to its promise of providing universal anti-retroviral treatment. An estimated five million people are eventually on medication, which makes it the largest programme of its kind in the world. Clinics are provided in every town and village to test for HIV and dispense the pills. The local doctors and nurses have access to HIV specialists for advice on each patient's treatment and care. Even if drug prices and medical overheads per patient fall as the initiative is scaled up, it is a very expensive scenario that also poses high risks. For if people don't comply fully with their treatment regimens, there is an increased chance of a resistant virus spreading, which will nullify the effectiveness of the whole programme. A vaccine remains a *wild card*.

The *Abc* scenario gets its name from the slogan: "Abstain; if you can't abstain, be faithful; and if you can't be faithful use a condom!" The *Abc* scenario is in fact the Ugandan model, which places greatest emphasis on abstention (hence the capital 'A' and small 'b' and 'c'). Government, the churches, community leaders, teachers and parents have urged teenagers to postpone their first sexual experience and then remain faithful to one partner. The programme, according to research conducted in Uganda, has achieved widespread behavioural change and lowered the teenage HIV prevalence rate.

The simple message of this gameboard for South Africa is that if it seriously enters the *Mass Medication* scenario (which we fully support), it must at the same time move into the *Abc* scenario. Otherwise, new infections could build the figure of five million to a much higher figure (assuming that anti-retrovirals slow down the AIDS death rate), which in turn will put even more strain on government financing of health care. However, for an *Abc* campaign to be effective, it will require a co-ordinated and passionate effort by all sectors of society, including the churches. Advertising agencies should be at the forefront of designing the campaign since it is their job to change people's behaviour.

The Ultimate Gameboard

It would be true to say that although HIV/AIDS dominates the scene in South Africa and many other developing countries, the developed world has other worries on its plate. Given the tempestuous nature of man, and his propensity for fighting, our world has been, and always will be, pockmarked with skirmishes, battles and wars that dictate the course of history. But there is one threat that is of global significance. It is well known that the current nuclear weapon stockpiles of the few nations who have them are enough to destroy all life on this planet many times over. The future of our existence hangs in the balance, because access to these weapons could dramatically increase over the next fifty years.

We have therefore constructed a gameboard which has peace and war as the horizontal axis and nukes and no nukes on the vertical axis.

This leads to four possible scenarios upon which we have

Chart 58 *The Ultimate Gameboard*

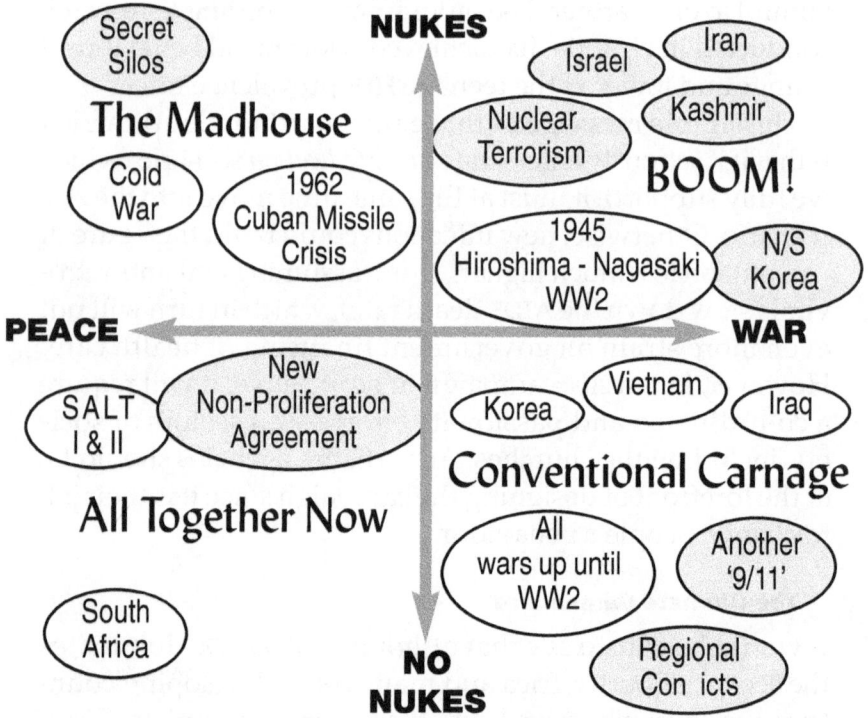

plotted past events (white ellipses) and possible future events (yellow ellipses).

Given, as we've mentioned, our proclivity for war, *Conventional Carnage* is a crowded spot and could see more regional con icts or 9/11s. The *Madhouse* scenario is where the world has been since 1945 (brie y irting with *Boom!* in 1962). The logic is that mutually assured destruction (MAD) will deter any nation from a rst strike. Obviously, the advent of stateless terrorism has knocked this principle on the head since terrorists who plant nukes need have no fear of reprisals in a specific spot. They could be anywhere. Meanwhile, in this scenario, new nations build up secret silos to have at their disposal if attacked.

The *Boom!* zone has only been entered twice – on both occasions by America in Japan. As our yellow ellipses indicate, there are enough trouble spots around the world which can go nuclear and pose a real danger of another nuclear exchange. On top of which you must now add nuclear terrorism, where some shady member of the arms trade passes on a nuke for $25 million to a terrorist outfit. It could have been manufactured in a private laboratory in some secret location. And James Bond does not come to the rescue.

All Together Now is obviously the desired scenario where the world is at peace with no nukes. We put the Strategic Arms Limitation Talks between America and Russia in this quadrant, as well as South Africa that voluntarily dismantled its nuclear capability. But what is really needed is a new nonproliferation agreement that tackles the issue in a completely neutral manner. Hence the name of the scenario. For how can America or any country that currently has nukes take the moral high ground by arguing that other countries shouldn't have them? The only rationale they can offer is that they are more civilised and therefore more responsible than the have-nots. Such reasoning is definitely out of kilter with the modern notion of people of all colours and creeds being equal and therefore being treated equally. Maybe the West can single out some rogue states as too irresponsible to be trusted with nukes, but it begs the question of what constitutes a rogue state. Thus for any new agreement to be sustainable in the long run and have teeth, the 'haves' will have to come to the party and disgorge some of their nukes. All together now! Definitely not the form of headstrong hedgehogs.

However, John Nash – the mathematician in *A Beautiful Mind* – would approve of this scenario. In the movie, he is in a bar with friends when a blonde and several brunettes walk in. He advises that, instead of competing for the blonde (first prize for each of them), they should ask the brunettes out on the basis that this is the best outcome for the team. Otherwise, all but one of them are going to lose out as the brunettes, realising they are second choice, walk off in a huff. In real life, Nash won the Nobel Prize for his idea that games played in a co-operative fashion can lead to a higher level of equilibrium than pure rivalry. Nuclear games are no different, particularly as the West no longer has the supremacy to impose its own solution but equally has the most to lose.

Speakers' Corner

We'd like to end up our gameboard trio on a lighter note. Giving a speech in public has been recognised as one of the most stressful events anyone can ever face. The traditional advice of imagining the audience without their clothes on is only helpful for speakers who are avowed nudists. As speakers who prefer to keep our clothes on, we feel it is our duty to leave you with a gameboard that, hopefully, you will find particularly helpful when you are under the spotlight. It may be making a speech at a friend's wedding or presenting the annual report to anxious shareholders. Similarly, as someone who no doubt finds yourself at the receiving end of countless speeches and presentations, you can use this gameboard to score speakers. With content and delivery as the variables, the scenario gameboard – called *Speakers' Corner* – looks like the one opposite.

If the content of the speech is good but is lost in delivery (should one say translation?) it is *Buried Treasure*. If the content is shocking and it is delivered with all the panache of a wet blanket, it is *The Pits*. A blisteringly good delivery with memorable content peppered with anecdotal wit and real value earns the speaker an *Oscar*.

And the *Alpha Gamma*? There's an interesting story attached to this name. Many, many years ago one of us handed in a paper to a professor at Oxford. It was summarily returned with

Chart 59
Speaker's Corner

Content
+

Buried
Treasure

Oscar

Delivery
−

Delivery
+

The Pits

Alpha
Gamma

Content
−

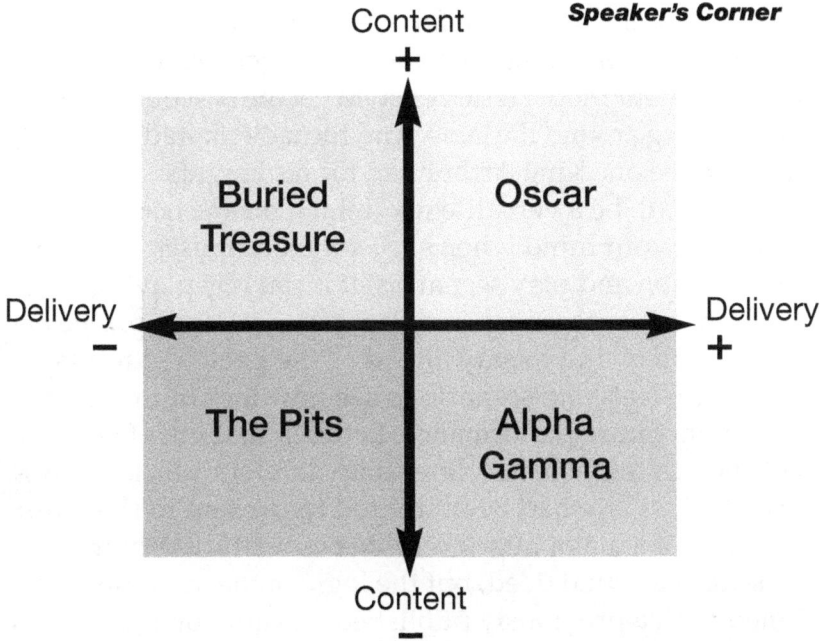

an alpha gamma grading. Not a top alpha, not an alpha minus, not even an alpha beta, but an alpha gamma. When challenged for an explanation, the professor simply replied the essay was "clever sh-t".

Here ends the lesson. You will have to judge for yourself the value and applicability of our conversation model. And the best way to do that is to test it in your own company. Do a reality check on your strategy; or evaluate your next project or takeover opportunity using our model.

Indeed, conversations are all the rage these days. Why do you think there has been such an enormous growth in personal executive coaches for CEOs? It's so they can have conversations on strategy and other things on a one-to-one basis. Not so much to learn new ideas from the coach, but to get their own ideas in order during the conversation. We just feel that it's equally important for executive teams to have these kinds of conversations so that they can get *their* thoughts in order too. Our model is designed to get the best out of everybody sitting around the table. And the table should be round, just like the one King Arthur had for his knights.

Above all, be a versatile fox, which means occasionally changing your mind when a *what if* materialises. Use your imagination and play scenarios. It is only by playing them that you will recognise a 'red flag' when it pops up. One organisation trying to stay ahead of the pack had to play a *Starving Greyhound* scenario to see how lack of cash might hinder its future performance. Better still, think of how the FBI and CIA might have followed up differently on leads, prior to 9/11, if we had been invited to present to them our scenario of a major attack on a Western city. It didn't come close to the actual deed, but the logic of the scenario, combined with a previously published warning on the serious challenge posed by fundamentalist Islam to Western lifestyle and values, might have opened their eyes to *possibilities* and *signs*. Fragments of the future contained in the present. It would certainly have sharpened their peripheral vision to the level of a fox.

Like Tilly Smith, the ten-year-old British girl who, because she had done a school project on tsunamis, recognised the abnormal withdrawal of the tide on Maikhao Beach in Phuket, Thailand for what it was – a 'red flag' for giant waves. According to Reuters, swift action by her mother and local hotel staff meant the beach was cleared before the tsunami arrived. It was one of the few beaches in Phuket where no one was killed.

So remember. Nobody is bigger than the game, especially when it involves Nature. And nothing, but nothing, can be discarded as a potential outcome. We live in extraordinary times. Let's talk about it and go on a strategic adventure.

Socrates & the FOX

A Strategic Dialogue

PROLOGUE

PROLOGUE

Socrates: A Brief History

The highest form of human excellence is to question oneself and others.

SOCRATES

"You are a traitor and deserve to die. And it shall be by your own hand."

Suppose you received an e-mail to this effect from your boss because you had dared to question his judgment on a strategic issue, and had persuaded some of your junior colleagues of the validity of your case. At the very least, you would consider his reaction to be over the top and ask for his decision to be reviewed by the human resources department. Yet this was the opinion of a public court of Athens that found the wisest man in Greece and the father of Western philosophy guilty of heresy and corrupting the youth. He posed an unacceptable threat to his Athenian bosses with his weapon of mass deduction: Socratic dialogue.

Yes, we are talking about Socrates. At the time of his death (399 BC), the once mighty Athenian Empire was recovering from defeat by Sparta following a destructive and protracted war between the two neighbouring Greek states. Socrates was highly critical of the Athenian strategy and debated the merits of alternatives with his students, many of them young aristocrats, and one of them Plato. He thus became the focus of the ire of a number of leading public figures. They declared that not only was he openly questioning the authority of the Athenian leadership, but he was involved in fomenting rebellion against it. It was commonly believed that a number of his former students might have betrayed Athens for Sparta, eventually leading to the overthrow of the Athenian government.

Furthermore, his teaching of philosophical enquiry encouraged his students to question the merits and even the existence of divine powers. This was not a good time to choose, as the citizens of Athens assumed that their defeat had come about because their protective goddess Athena had punished them for not believing in her. Decimated by decades of war and with its empire much reduced around it, Athens had no time for the ramblings of a grumpy old man. To the vast majority of the public, his continued questioning of that which had made the Athenian Empire great had seemingly contributed towards its downfall.

The Socratic Method

Of course, this was not true. Socrates was openly critical of the Athenian establishment – and the way it conducted itself – as a result of encouraging his students to go back to first principles and question all established norms. More importantly, he demanded that his students challenge contemporary definitions of key moral concepts such as 'justice' and what should be considered 'good'. This was not to promote 'injustice' or 'evil' but to understand things better. His method of enquiry, later called the Socratic method, embraced a dialectic form in which answers to questions were a prelude to further questions, which ultimately induced diametrically opposed answers to the ones given in the first place. In a back-and-forth debate on the truth of widely held opinions, Socrates managed to make his conversational adversaries meet themselves coming the other way in arguments.

However, he was convinced that this methodology helped people get closer to their underlying beliefs and the extent of their knowledge. In particular, it unveiled the limitations of their knowledge. By its nature, therefore, the Socratic method is a negative method of hypothesis elimination: as people steadily identify and eliminate those hypotheses that lead to contradiction, better and more resilient hypotheses emerge. During this process, the participants are invariably forced to examine their own belief systems – as well as their value systems – and where necessary revise them. As a result, a Socratic dialogue, once embarked on, becomes a rich and empowering form of conversation, leading to unexpectedly new and radical ideas.

It is highly unlikely that Socratic dialogue on its own posed a threat to the bitter remnants of the Athenian Empire. Nevertheless, it is undeniable that some of those who engaged in this form of dialogue became so adept at political debate that they could run rings around the unbending supporters of the status quo of the Athenian state. It is furthermore clear that, at a cruder level, the powers that be needed a scapegoat to answer for their downfall. "If you're not for us, you're against us", was their battle cry. All Socrates wanted was a better version of the truth. He wasn't so much a dissident as an asker of awkward and embarrassing questions. His reward for soliciting answers which were at variance with the official dogma was that damning description heard then, and now: enemy of the State.

And so it was that a public court found him guilty and he was sentenced to die by his own hand – a state-mandated suicide. He would ingest hemlock, a neurotoxin that disrupts the central nervous system. Death would be gradual as the poison crawled its way through the system, slowly robbing the extremities of the body of life and movement, turning it cold and rigid in its wake; and then eventually reaching the heart, insidiously crushing it, causing it to collapse.

It has often been asked why Socrates went to his death so peacefully; after all, he had other options, one being to escape. His followers had bribed the prison guards who were willing to assist in this regard. He could have then fled from Athens.

Yet instead he chose to drink hemlock knowing that it would kill him. His reasons, as he presented them to his followers, were, typically, philosophical in nature. He said that, as a citizen of Athens, he fully accepted that one should abide by its laws, even if they demanded an unjust punishment. Such an approach represented a 'contract' with the State. Should he break that contract he would harm society as a whole, something that was contrary to the Socratic code. He also said that true philosophers should not fear death, especially if in life they had achieved a measure of wisdom beyond their peers.

You have to hand it to Socrates for his conservative attitude towards the law and his acceptance of his fate. Given his disposition to argue the toss on everything, he must have harboured ambivalent feelings towards the people who had condemned him, and the fairness of his sentence. Yet he took it like a man – a remarkable man for any era and any generation. Fortunately for us, he passed on his methodology to Plato who laid it all out in his early works. And the torch still burns today, as you will see.

2 The Legendary Dialogue:
Socrates & the Fox

Really, Ischomachus, I am disposed to ask: "Does teaching consist in putting questions?" Indeed, the secret of your system has just this instant dawned upon me. I seem to see the principle in which you put your questions. You lead me through the field of my own knowledge, and then by pointing out analogies to what I know, persuade me that I really know some things which hitherto, as I believed, I had no knowledge of.

SOCRATES, as quoted by Xenophon in *Oeconomicus* (The Economist) as translated by H G Dakyns.

Legend has it that shortly before his trial Socrates uncharacteristically left his students and followers and walked into some nearby woods on the outskirts of Athens. He wandered awhile before finding a place where the sun trickled through the trees and created a swathe of dappled light around a fallen, mossy log. He sat upon the log, closed his eyes and breathed deeply.

Completely isolated from human contact, he searched deep within himself with the intention of finding the true wisdom that had eluded him for so long. At the point when he almost lost complete consciousness of his surroundings, he became acutely aware that he was not alone. He glanced up to see that a fox was nearby, watching him. The filtered sun bathed the fox in an incandescent light, its fiery red coat seeming to shimmer and its white underbelly looking rich and silvery. Its amber eyes were fixed upon Socrates. It displayed no fear. The fox was clearly unperturbed by his presence; in fact it seemed more intrigued than worried. It slowly cocked its head to one side and stared intently at the quiet man before it.

Socrates' inquiring eye examined the creature in return. It was lean and hardy, its athletic form forged from a life of continual quest. Yet it also commanded the grace and poise of pampered nobility. Its angular features had been honed through constant searching and foraging. It had a cold and piercing hunter's eye, and yet its soft fur gave it a gentle and caring demeanour.

For a while they both looked at each other, each seeking a reason for the other's presence. Socrates sensed that the fox was asking him something. Was it possible, Socrates asked himself. He slowly shifted his weight, leaned slightly forward, extended both his open hands and in a polite but firm whisper, asked, "Does my presence concern you?"

The fox seemed to smile. "Perhaps I should ask," retorted the fox, "does my presence concern *you*?"

Socrates smiled back, gently shook his head and said, "Not at all." Indeed, he felt a deep and fulfilled calm wash over him in the presence of an intellect that obviously matched his. "I have been continually questioning anything and everything, hoping to find answers, and that's what finds me here," he added.

"I, too, search continually, and sometimes, in the process of meeting paradoxes and contradictions along the way, I find what I am looking for."

"Then," said Socrates, "knowing your reputation for quick-witted and agile thinking, you may be the one finally to help me". As Socrates looked at the fox to confirm the seriousness of his intent to engage him, the creature slowly cocked its head once more and met his gaze. At that moment they both realised that just as they had stumbled across each other, so had they found themselves. There was much to talk about. And so started a dialogue between Socrates and the fox.

The Dialogue

FOX: Most philosophers start by asking: "What is the meaning of existence?"

SOCRATES: I don't. For whatever species you are, how can you define the meaning or purpose of your existence unless you fully understand the context in which you exist?

FOX: You mean in my case understanding how the forest works. For instance, the relationships between the various animals inhabiting it and the impact they individually and collectively have on the environment.

SOCRATES: Yes, but also the impact that the environment has on them. For example, my present surroundings have created a deep sense of tranquillity in me. However, when I'm in the busy streets of Athens, the hustle and bustle excites me. A rule of existence is that wherever you go, and whatever people you encounter, you leave something behind and take something away with you. We are all elements of a system in a continual state of interaction and mutual influence, as our minds are with our bodies.

FOX: So I'm leaving a lasting impression on you with this conversation, as I know you are now doing on me?

SOCRATES: Correct. But to get back to your original comment, my first question is always: "Why are you what you presently are? What mixture of natural-born qualities and experiences since birth has made you into the animal, or in my case the person, you are today?" It's a question of fact, because we are dealing with the past. I am asking you to trace the single unique line between the moment you came into being till now. Think about all the influences on your life so far – positive, negative, neutral – which have conspired to get you to this location at this point in time.

FOX: That question would take longer to answer than I have time for, given the necessity for me to be constantly on the move in daylight hours. But, yes, I was born a fox with all the strengths and weaknesses that go with the species. My choice of parents was beyond my control, as was my date of birth. But what has been within my control since then has been to use my strengths instinctively to cover for my weaknesses. I am small and therefore vulnerable, but I am agile and have keen senses. I know my limitations, I know the risks, but I also grab opportunities as they arise. I can adapt to the changes in the environment, and, man, have there been some big changes recently! As far as I know, you're the first person to have ventured into this grove. You have to accept change, and change with it. Call it foxiness that keeps me alive, call it cunning intelligence, but here I am and my wife has kids on the way.

SOCRATES: I wish I could echo your upbeat approach. My destiny line has been different from yours. I was born into a fairly well-to-do family and had a conventional upbringing in Athens. As you rightly say, I had no choice but to be an Athenian which, to begin with, was the most marvellous thing to be, since Athens used to be the leading city on Earth. I got married and had three children, but then my world was turned upside down when my nation went to war with its neighbour, Sparta. I joined the army as an infantryman, or 'hoplite' as we call it, and served in several campaigns. Basically I went with the flow until I realised how futile the war was and how corrupt our society had become. Then I started asking questions and gathered a set of young followers around me with whom to debate these questions. I've never written anything down, but the questions I ask have got to the ears of the ruling authorities and have made them very angry. I am about to be put on trial and I feel a sense of impending doom. But then it was my choice. I was in control.

FOX: So is there anything you would change about yourself now? In that respect, you have wider choices than me because my occupation in the animal kingdom will forever remain the same. All I can do is move to another place.

SOCRATES: Don't be so humble, because that was going to be

my second question: No, I would never contemplate moving out of the field of philosophy or change where I live. But it is the question that logically follows the first one. Having traced your destiny line from start to present, where should you go to now? But then the third question has to be: "Who is for you, who is against you and who is neutral?" In seeking to clarify the direction you wish to take, you have to return to the principle of being part of an interconnected system.

FOX: So you have to weigh up your friends and enemies and those who can go either way before deciding on your next move? I like that, because in the animal kingdom you very quickly learn who is out to kill you and who isn't. You avoid the places where the former may be and stick to potentially friendly territory.

SOCRATES: With human beings it's more difficult to judge, for we have the quality of deceit. But nothing really happens unless you have a few or many people on your side and you find ways around those whom you have identified as obstructing you. This makes the fourth question easy to ask: "What are the rules of the animal kingdom and how do they differ from those governing human society?"

FOX: Well, I can only speak for my world. The rule is simple and all-encompassing: you do lunch, or be lunch. Straight competition. Survival of the fittest.

SOCRATES: In our world, that rule exists too in commerce and war. Nonetheless, I have spent all my philosophical hours on enquiring about another set of rules that should co-exist with the rule of competition. These relate to morality and goodness, but everybody has a different idea about what they are. I doubt whether we will ever reach agreement, but the quest must continue.

FOX: Having acknowledged that each of us in our own way is an element of a complex system, and that we should have knowledge of the other participants and the rules that apply to all of us, there is one more thing. Life can surprise you and it is better to be aware of the surprises in advance, or have a very fast reaction time if they really do come out of the blue. Don't you agree?

SOCRATES: Of course; and that leads me to my fifth question: "What are the uncertainties that can radically change your destiny line?" Because, make no mistake, the majority of factors making up the future environment around you are uncertain and beyond your control. What you are does not determine what you will be. In my case, I have no power over the court that is going to sit in judgment on my future, and I have to be prepared for all eventualities. On a broader front, the defeat by Sparta came as a big surprise to most Athenian citizens since they believed that they were the most advanced society in the world with the greatest military might. They have reacted badly because defeat was unthinkable. But there again, they might bounce back if defeat has taught them to be more 'foxy' about the future. Which naturally leads on to my next question, which is one of the hardest to answer: "Where is your destiny line going to lead you? What are the possibilities? What are the consequences?"

FOX: My possibilities are to take my wife and travel north, south, east or west after this conversation. Each path will contain its own string of events and consequences, which will become part of my destiny line. And you?

SOCRATES: That depends on the outcome of the trial. I could be found not guilty of any crime and continue to debate the issues that intrigue me. I could spend the rest of my life in prison. I could be put to death. Three scenarios for which there will be one outcome, but I must be prepared for all three. Now in light of the fact that you ought to move on soon, we need to get to the crux of the matter. What are we going to take away from our conversation and do? For as we both know, actions speak more loudly than words.

FOX: Ah! You are rushing ahead in the conversation. As I said earlier, my whole destiny line to date has involved a growing understanding of my strengths and weaknesses. So the seventh question should be: "What *are* your strengths and weaknesses and where are your immediate opportunities and threats?" Unless you tackle this question, talk of possible action is academic, with due apology to you as a philosopher. Yes, I agree that what you are does not automatically determine what you will be or what you *can* be, but it sure as hell has an influence over your next move.

SOCRATES: I told you at the outset that I thought you were smart. You are! Well, my strength is that I have an enquiring mind, and I guess my weakness is that I do not suffer fools gladly. My opportunity is to leave a legacy of the importance of not accepting things at face value; and the threat is imminent death.

FOX: Well put. Which neatly dovetails into my next – and if I've counted correctly the eighth – question: "What options do you have?" I've outlined mine, which are pretty simple and relate to the part of the forest I want to sleep in tonight.

SOCRATES: Hmm, I could escape before the trial starts and come along with you. But that would damage my legacy. I could reconsider my public stand on the war and the way Athens is governed, but that would also damage my legacy. I can stand trial and stick to my principles, in which event I've already laid out the future possibilities.

FOX: So now we come to your question: "Which option are you going to exercise and turn into action?" Personally I've decided to head north and take my chances there.

SOCRATES: This dialogue has been delightful because it has clarified my mind. Of course, I will exercise the last option and take my chances in court.

FOX: Well, dear friend, best of luck. It is time to part.

SOCRATES: Not before the final and tenth question. Remember, at the very beginning you thought that I was going to ask about the meaning of existence. Now we have discussed the past, the present and the future, we must return to this issue with the extra knowledge we have gained. "What for you is the meaning of life?"

FOX: I suppose it has to do with the reproduction of my species. That is my legacy. I have to protect my wife and children so that someday in some far distant country my several times great-grandchildren will carry on the foxy tradition.

SOCRATES: Yes, that is the meaning of life for me too. But I also want my idea of enquiry to persist in the minds of future generations.

FOX: In all probability, that will happen if you suffer the worst of all possible fates. Premature death will ensure eternal life for your idea.

SOCRATES: Your final remark, my dear friend, is – whether you intended it or not – a Socratic outcome. You are a 'seer' in the true meaning of the word. Not only do you see things more quickly than other animals because of your peripheral vision, you see things differently – stripped of the assumptions and 'laws' we all like to lay down. You see things as they really are and, by doing just that, you see into the future. My life's work has been trying to give people a fraction of your talent by asking questions that reveal the truth behind the mask of appearances. Goodbye and good luck.

With that they parted company, never to meet again, but never to forget the wisdom and experience they had shared with one another. Both had given and taken something away from the encounter. Both their destiny lines had intertwined and changed.

348

3 The Conversation Model: Our Version of the Socratic Method

In every one of us there are two ruling and directing principles, whose guidance we follow wherever they may lead; the one being an innate desire of pleasure; the other, an acquired judgment which aspires after excellence.

SOCRATES, as quoted in Plato's *Phaedrus*

Little did the fox know when he responded to Socrates' question about the meaning of life that his wish to have several times great-grandchildren would be so spectacularly granted. For not only are there rural foxes in forests like his (but sadly even more encroached upon by man), his species are roaming around the streets of London, having adapted to living in an urban environment as well.

But the fox would have been even more amazed if he had been fast-forwarded to our den and met a pair of foxy, game-playing strategists who, in a small way, are the spiritual descendents of Socrates. We think that he would have totally approved of the methodology that we have designed to assist companies to have an effective strategic conversation about their future. It has a lot in common with the once-in-a-lifetime conversation he had with Socrates in the sunny grove. He might have viewed it as a coincidence. But then he might have reflected that he did leave something behind in the chance encounter – something passed down through the generations.

The Evolution of the Model

From our side, we could have said to the fox that our methodology is unique and independently crafted. It has come about through rigorous application, re-evaluation and fine-tuning in the course of facilitating countless sessions in plenty of boardrooms. We've paid our dues. The claim is partially true, and we would like to thank all the CEOs and their teams who have voluntarily subjected themselves to our version of the Socratic method. However, we would have had to acknowledge to our furry friend that the seeds of our first book, *The Mind of a Fox – Scenario Planning in Action*, published in June 2001, lay in the foxy dialogue that took place 2 400 years previously. The matrix we introduced in the book was based on two key questions about the future which asked what is certain and uncertain about it, and what you control and don't control in it. These two questions, as you will remember, were posed in the conversation in the woods. Nevertheless, we do go further by suggesting that you will not get a proper idea of what you do control unless you start by delineating what you don't control. In other words, we really do believe in applying the type of hypothesis elimination, much loved by Socrates, to the formulation of strategy.

We have found that these two questions open up a whole new way of strategic thinking. Most people operate in a constrained frame of mind, boxed in by certainty and control. This is quite understandable, because it creates a level of constancy and sureness within which most people feel comfortable. When push becomes shove, we don't like change. Extrapolate that into the business environment and it will explain why many companies' strategic vision involves doing the same thing but better; or, to put it bluntly, staying in the same rut. It may explain why every company we work with finish off their strategic conversation enthusing about the depth and clarity of the insight they have gained. It's almost as if Socrates himself had had a hand in guiding the discourse away from the rut to higher ground. As the father of Western philosophy, he was a champion of venturing beyond the constraints of conventional wisdom. Perhaps he would have made an ideal nonexecutive director in today's boardroom.

We have been fortunate to work with a diverse portfolio of companies throughout the world, operating in fields such as banking, pharmaceuticals, mining, financial services and asset management, legal services, the media, retail, manufacturing and agriculture – from giant multinationals to family-run businesses. We've done stimulating sessions as well with municipalities, schools, universities, churches and NGOs. One of us has even conducted an 'informal conversation' at the Central Party School in Beijing. In each case, we noted any observations made by participants on how we could improve our methodology and adapted it accordingly. The result was a model for strategic conversation that was the subject of our second book: *Games Foxes Play – Planning for Extraordinary Times*, published in April 2005. Again a vein of Socratic dialogue ran through the book in that a methodology of questioning and self-examination was presented to help companies arrive at a more lucid understanding of their strategic choices. This was all done in the context of business being a game.

That vein of self-interrogation is now at the heart of this book. The strategic conversation model has again been evolved into a series of specific questions and sub-questions in order to effect a higher level, and more robust form, of strategic thinking, with due allowance for the complexity of the system that any organisation finds itself in. The secret lies in the nature of the dialogue that is encouraged, and how this is done. Socratic dialogue allows for in-depth understanding of issues through a combination of rigorous enquiry and developing consensus. Preferably performed in small groups, it enhances individual self-confidence while at the same time encouraging the common search for truth in a question-and-answer pattern. The dialogue allows participants to reflect and think independently and critically; but at the same time it engages them as a group to search for collective answers, not as an end in itself, but as a means of deepening the investigation of long-held paradigms and their validity. By combining the philosophy of Socratic dialogue and the model of strategic conversation we designed in our last book, we have arrived at a core list of ten questions that, we believe, provide true strategic wisdom if answered sincerely and fearlessly.

Bear in mind that it was the common quest for this penetrating type of wisdom that brought Socrates and the fox together in the first place; after all, what other animal embodies the perpetually enquiring mind of Socrates better than a fox? It is a noble creature that projects a demeanour and knowledge beyond its ranking in the kingdom of life. More importantly, for our purposes, the fox is the most apt metaphor to embody the character needed by companies to outwit their competitors and remain world class in today's rapidly changing business environment. In nature, the fox is quick-witted, adaptable and resourceful and has an astute awareness of its environment and the forces and relationships at play within it. Expressed in more philosophical terms, a fox thinks of life as a system comprised of many parts and interdependencies; and that it is only through the knowledge of the system as a whole that decisions can be optimised about the future. In terms of strategy, a fox will stick to a strategic path, but will regularly check the environment ahead to see if there are any changes that would require the strategy to be amended.

The fox knows that just as there are those elements of its environment that present themselves as food, so it is presented as food to others. If it interacts correctly with these elements it should survive. If it interacts successfully with these elements it will thrive. Because a fox is omnivorous and continually applies its inquiring instinct, it doesn't follow a rigidly predetermined course in the search for food. Neither is it limited to a particular type of food. The result is an animal that carries with it centuries of inbred experience about its environment, and which can thrive under virtually any circumstances. It has learnt a great deal about the nature of enquiring, the processing of the information that is gathered and the effective and speedy implementation of ideas. Imagine what insight such an animal could offer if it could talk, and especially with one of human history's most experienced and influential thinkers.

Games and Strategy

Hence, the relevance of our 'record' of the dialogue between Socrates and the fox. The dialogue's value should resonate further with modern business by the inclusion of the metaphor of a game in our second book (and which we repeat here). Games and business have a lot in common. Both are subject to rules. Both involve competing teams where the winner is usually the team with the greater skill and more effective strategy and tactics. Both contain inherent risks and uncertainties; and both have definite outcomes – you win, you lose, you draw: you make money, you go bust, you barely survive. Moreover, the outcome can turn on factors that are beyond the control of any individual player, factors that are often seemingly minor at the time they first manifest themselves. Think of the clouds on the horizon that eventually wash out a game of cricket.

However, there are also some very important differences between the game of business and games, say, of cards and sport. In the latter case the rules are agreed upon and never change during the course of play. Any changes to the rules are made in advance and with input from, and full acknowledgement of, the various stakeholders. In business, as in life, the rules rarely stay the same, and when they do change they can do so spectacularly, without notice and even to the point where the game becomes unplayable. The only rules that never change are the moral rules of the game (but even then, there are some people who will either disagree or openly bend or break these rules!). The game of business is far more complicated than any sporting game, and therefore demands a greater degree of imagination. Those who stick rigidly to an established strategy without incorporating the potential for changing rules will soon find themselves playing a different game to everyone else. Any seasoned business campaigner, operating within such a continually changing landscape, knows that strategy is more of an intuitive feel than a rational science. But both are required.

Thus business is not a game to be directed by planners who believe that the future is simply a projection of the past. Although we can study the past and learn from it, we can't plan for the future around the past. Neither can we accept that the future can be encapsulated into a single forecast on which you can bet the whole shop. No matter how expert the opinion you've obtained is, it can be utterly wrong. The future is always changing, evolving, and creating different, new challenges. Any opinion on it is automatically subjective. As Socrates so aptly remarked to the fox: "What you are does not determine what you will be." It makes sense then that before any decisions can be made around how to *play* the game, a strategic conversation should start with a robust *examination* of the game itself, and the swathe of possibilities accompanying it.

It is particularly apt that our concept of a strategic conversation should be inspired by the insight and wisdom of Socrates, because the word 'strategy' is Ancient Greek in origin, specifically derived from his home city of Athens. The term *strategos* referred to a commander in chief (or chief magistrate) who was a leading figure of authority in the Athenian democracy. A military *strategos* was expected to possess the ability to project and direct the larger military movements and operations of a campaign. In fact it is a term still used today in the modern Hellenic army to denote the highest officer rank. At some stage the term *strategos* was expanded to include the decisions made by such a person – and not just the person himself. For centuries, therefore, *strategos* or its English equivalent 'strategy' has been a term employed in the planning and conducting of warfare, specifically the movement of forces on the ground, the allocation of resources in support of those forces and the deception of the enemy.

Given the notoriously competitive and aggressive campaigns of leading corporate players, it was only a matter of time before the word 'strategy' became embraced by the world of business. Indeed, Sun Tzu's *The Art of War* – that famous Chinese military treatise that inspired centuries of great commanders including Napoleon, Mao Zedong and Douglas MacArthur, and even those behind Operation Desert Storm – is a popular addition to many boardroom libraries! For example, compare the quote of the famous Prussian General Karl von Clausewitz: "A good strategy is the successful preparation of a tactical victory" with Jack Welch's quote, "Strategy is the evolution of a central idea according to continuously changing circumstances." The CEO has become the general.

In its shift from the battlefield to the boardroom, 'strategy' has often been confused with 'tactics' and the two terms are sometimes used interchangeably, albeit erroneously. Perhaps it makes sense then that at this stage we spend a little time clarifying the difference between the two terms, especially with reference to their implementation in business. If we were asked to summarise the difference in one sentence, we'd say: 'strategy' is the direction of the business and 'tactics' are how to get there. To expand a little bit further we could borrow from an old nineteenth-century saying: "Strategy differs materially from tactics; the latter belonging only to the mechanical movement of bodies, set in motion by the former." What this means is that a handful of strategic decisions determine all future operational decisions. We therefore don't believe that the 24-point strategic plan recommended by some consultants is useful. Unless the overarching strategy is to go off in 24 different directions, the result can only be to sow confusion (which the consultants then have to resolve in their next contract!).

It is our belief that, through a proper strategic conversation, what should emerge are one or two simple and clear decisions around *direction*, and a prioritised list of actions, or tactics, on *how* to get there. It is important, especially in view of typical time constraints and resource limitations, that such a list of tactics should not be so exhaustive as to paralyse their overall implementation. Ask any manager about the dangers of analysis paralysis or any politician about the crisis of implementation. Hence the need to prioritise the tactics to extract maximum leverage. The latter forms an essential objective of any complete strategic conversation.

And who should develop a company's strategy? Someone from outside the company? Why bring in external consultants to dictate a company's strategic policy, knowing full well that once they have dished out their opinion and their words of wisdom, they will leave the company to its own devices? It makes sense that the best people to paint scenarios for a company and then shape that company's strategic direction should be those who are expected to implement that strategy. However, internal strategy sessions often follow a set format which runs the risk of perpetuating traditional stereotypes and conventional solutions. These sessions, therefore, have to be restructured in a way that jogs executives into a more robust analysis of the company and the changing environment in which it operates. By its very nature, Socratic dialogue does this. It transforms the spirit of the conversation from the normal, dreary type of superficial analysis that companies go through nowadays to a full-blooded, back-to-basics debate. It thereby creates a richer picture of the game, breaks all sorts of moulds along the way and produces nuggets of strategic wisdom from deep inside the most reticent minds around the table (which would otherwise never be discovered).

But how do you set such a dialogue in motion, and how do you keep it on track? The answer lies in the nature and structure of the questions. Presented correctly and in the right order, the questions change the conversation within a team, which then changes their minds, which then changes their behaviour and ultimately influences their actions. This is the causal sequence upon which our methodology is based. Interestingly, the nature of this questioning encourages further questioning within the team, in that some of the questions have no complete answers, but instead they demand that the team critically evaluates preconceived perceptions of the company and the business, or game, it is in. These invariably unearth contradictions between what the company is doing and what it should be doing. Bit by bit these contradictions are stripped away until a more accurate representation of the truth is achieved. This is the very foundation of the Socratic method of dialogue.

The Seven Principles

To change strategy you therefore need a highly inclusive conversation amongst people who can implement that change, where the process is based on ordinary but sound common sense. Nobody should lose the thread or be compelled to put their hand up and say: "Why ask that question now?" It all has to flow smoothly and logically. We base the sequence on seven straightforward principles pertaining to strategy:

357

1 Strategy is direction. Tactics are how to get there.
2 Strategy formulated without first consulting the context will probably end up being bad strategy.
3 Strategy is as much about ruling in potential paths that fit your scope as ruling out others that don't.
4 Good strategy can be turned into bad strategy by a future change in the context. Scenarios are a way of exploring alternative futures, which might necessitate a change in strategy.
5 Bad tactics can destroy good strategy, but no tactic can rescue bad strategy.
6 Good strategy has a greater chance of being converted into good results if tactics are accompanied by a set of measurable outcomes to which people can aspire.
7 Above all, strategy is about understanding what you do and don't control, and what is certain and uncertain about the future – and knowing when to change direction to avert unintended, and possibly tragic, consequences.

Principle 1 has already been explained. You have to aim the gun before you fire. Principle 2 is based on a quote by Lee Kwan Yew – the prime minister of Singapore between 1959 and 1990 – that those who don't learn from history are doomed to repeat it, and his insistence that he preferred to learn from history than through trial and error. Context is very important. In one session we facilitated, a comment was made that most countries only learn from their own mistakes and not from the mistakes made by other countries. So true when we look at history repeating itself around the world. Hence, in the questions we put, we want companies not only to learn from their own experience but from the experience of others as well. A pinch of trial and error can then be added as an extra ingredient!

Principle 3 is based on the fact that we all have specific

competencies and limited resources and therefore our playing field has to be clearly defined as to what activities lie inside (and are core) and what lie outside (and are non-core). Principle 4 says that we are all human and even the best-perceived strategy at the time can fail and therefore should be constantly road-tested by reviewing the environment and where it can go.

Principle 5 is so often broken because companies will simply not back new strategies with the level of resources required to make them succeed. The initiative is seen as 'nice to have' as opposed to being a crucial link in the company's evolution. On the flip side of no tactic rescuing bad strategy, think of going on holiday with the destination as strategy and getting there as a tactic. If the destination is bad, getting there quickly will only make the experience worse. Principle 6 explains why we all have budgets, goals, targets, objectives, key performance indicators and scorecards in business, because nothing gets done without measurement of progress.

Principle 7 is last but by no means least. It is a fact that people in power prefer to feel that they are in complete control, but our principle demands acknowledgement that they're not. They feel that they have exceptional foresight, but our principle asserts that the future is inherently uncertain and unpredictable. Worse still, many CEOs and politicians will simply not change their minds because they see it as a loss of face. Even when it is obvious that they should reconsider, they don't. Call it emotional unintelligence or myopia due to their personal make-up. Unpleasant facts will not be countenanced. This is in marked contrast to the philosophy put forward by the fox to Socrates when he said, "You have to accept change, and change with it."

Stubbornness, moreover, can lead to unintended consequences, where the law of tragic choices kicks in. This law says that you should take the least tragic choice to limit the amount of pain involved and perhaps open up other opportunities. What you can't do is nothing because no decent option immediately presents itself. Think of the choices Socrates had – tragic to say the least. But as the fox so rightly said: "Each path will contain its own string of events and consequences." Victory *can* be snatched from the jaws of defeat. If you live on the edge, you will always make mistakes. Learn to retrieve the situation instead of dwelling on failure.

The Ten Questions

These seven principles on strategy underpin our conversation model. We have now developed the model into a series of ten strategic questions through which we steer the participants. As can be seen in the table after the questions, 'defining the game' is really the strategic part of the discussion and 'playing the game' the tactics and outcomes you wish to achieve.

Defining the Game

1 **Context**: How has the game in your industry changed, where is it heading and how have you fared as a player?
2 **Scope**: What is your playing field today, and how do you want to expand (or contract) it in light of the developing context and the resources at your disposal?
3 **Players**: Who are the players that can most advance or retard your strategy, and how should you handle them in future?
4 **Rules**: What are the rules of the game that are likely to govern your strategy under all scenarios?
5 **Uncertainties**: What are the key uncertainties that could have a significant impact on the game and divert your course either positively or negatively?
6 **Scenarios**: On your gameboard, what are the possible sce-

narios and where would you position yourself in relation
to them now?

Playing the Game

7 SWOT: What are your strengths and weaknesses as a
player; and what are the opportunities and threats offered by the game?

8 **Options**: Within your span of control, what options do
you have to improve your current performance and
longer-term prospects in the game?

9 **Decisions**: Which options do you want to turn into decisions right now, and what is the initial action associated
with each decision?

10 **Outcomes**: What is your meaning of winning the game
in five years' time, expressed as a set of measurable
outcomes?

The sequence of the questions can be explained in the following framework:

Question	Frame of Reference
1	Context
2	Strategy
3, 4, 5, 6	Testing the robustness of the strategy
7, 8, 9	Tactics, decisions, actions
10	Measurable outcomes

Straightforward though the questions may seem, they have
multiple layers to them because they explore both the game
as well as the player's relationship to the game. There are
sub-questions as well. As Socrates said to the fox: "We are all

361

elements of a system in a continual state of interaction and mutual influence, as our minds are with our bodies." To reflect this philosophy, the course of the strategic conversation continually weaves between internal questions about the organisation and external questions about the environment, the relationship between the two often evolving as the conversation progresses. Moreover, please don't treat the frame of reference as a list to which strict adherence has to be given. At any stage, an issue may be raised that demands that you revisit an earlier stage of the conversation. Or a bright idea comes up before its time. Brilliance is spontaneous, not ordered! So look at our ten questions as segments of a circle which can be rotated clockwise or anticlockwise as circumstances require.

Those familiar with business strategy will realise that the roots of our model and our thinking lie in scenario planning. What we have done through our ten questions is to integrate scenario planning into the mainstream process of strategic planning and decision-making. It allows top executive teams of companies to test the resilience of their strategies and tactics against alternative scenarios and, should the need arise, come up with other options faster and more effectively than their competitors.

And how successful is the model? Pierre Wack was the recognised master of scenario planning during the 1970s and 1980s. He used to say that the acid test for any successful scenario exercise was not that it captured an unusual future before it happened; rather it was whether the scenario penetrated the mindset of the relevant decision-makers and persuaded them to act ahead of time. We call this the 'Wack test'. The scenario itself did not have to be entirely accurate in its details, as long as, in retrospect, it modified for the better the course of action taken.

Many scenario exercises are brilliant intellectually, but fail the Wack test because they do not connect to the people who make the decisions. There are, however, three aspects to our conversation model which give the scenarios a good chance of passing the Wack test:

- We assist the decision-makers in writing the scenarios themselves instead of having external specialists presenting scenarios to them. The decision-makers are an intrinsic part of the scenario process;
- We have integrated options, decisions and measurable outcomes into the same conversation that handles the formulation of the scenarios. Thus the practical implications of the scenarios cannot be ignored; and,
- The scenarios sometimes feature the main decision-makers in the story. This makes them feel more committed to take appropriate action to ensure greater probability of the virtuous scenario materialising, and the worst-case scenario being avoided.

Of course our conversation can still fail the Wack test. If it does, it is often through the sheer inertia – or the resistance to change – of the team. This invariably brings about a crisis in implementation and a reversion back to old and defective ways that are out of sync with the new game. Equally, inertia can also be experienced when no effort is made to cascade the strategy through the ranks, and make effective use of all the players in a team. CEOs love to talk about motivating their players but often don't provide a clear direction. They rule by the mushroom method – keep the staff in the dark and occasionally pour manure over them. Never mind passing the Wack test, these CEOs need a whack!

Such inertia is one of the aspects that we address when we facilitate strategic sessions using our conversation model. We deal with this challenge towards the end of the dialogue by breaking actions down into easily manageable deliverables, and making very pointed notes of who is going to do what by when. It is then up to the team to monitor progress.

The Mechanics

Looking more generally at how we implement the model, we predominantly work with a company's top executive team but, at times, with middle management. Sometimes we take on individual divisions or business units. We have also worked with organisations that have multiple stakeholders from diverse backgrounds – where common ground needs to be achieved before any plan of action can be put in place. A shared perception of the game helps enormously in these circumstances.

The choice of venue for any session is important. We do not advise using a company's office premises, as it is far too easy to suffer temporary loss of participants during the conversation. There are few things more frustrating than people nipping in and out to return calls or deal with day-to-day business. On the other side of the coin, resorts that offer an exciting array of activities, especially golf, can prove just as much of a distraction. We insist in these instances on work, *then* play, so the conversation is not overly disrupted.

The venue also requires careful thought because conversation often continues outside the room out of official working hours. We recommend a venue that matches the culture of the company. We once held a session in a wine cellar that was arranged (not by us, we must add) for a company renowned for their maverick, expressive persona. We all found it quaint, but incredibly restrictive and claustrophobic. One of the most exotic venues was the main cabin of a paddle boat. As it forged down the river, you could not help feeling that it epitomised the calm and resolute manner in which the company was being guided into the future.

Strategic conversations with multinationals carry with them extra challenges, not least around logistics and different languages and cultures. A little more patience and sensitivity is all that is sometimes necessary. We once facilitated, using video-conferencing, a session on sustainable development with a leading multinational company that was spread over a number of countries. Although, with the digital delay, the session was a little more challenging, it was softened by the knowledge that we had produced fewer carbon emissions by not flying delegates to a single destination!

When planning a strategic session with a company, we suggest a venue that allows the executive team, or participants, to sit at a round table or in a horseshoe configuration so they can see each other. Socrates did this with his pupils. Conversation is as much about gestures and facial expressions as it is about what people actually say. A behavioural psychologist once said that if you see someone looking upwards to the left, he or she is about to tell you a huge lie! Sitting in a circle also means that nobody has superior status at the table because of position. It's important to create an environment that encourages the conversation to be as participative as possible, since the best strategists in a team are often the last people who want to speak up. Foresight is very different from charisma.

We also insist on zero paper except, if necessary, a flip chart upon which we record the conversation. Preferably, though, we like to capture the proceedings on a screen linked to a computer where we can move back and forth on points made. We want people to bring their minds, their experiences and, most of all, their imagination, to the meeting. Long documents on strategy tend to contain figures that are based on consensus forecasts and therefore kill the imagination, the very faculty that allows people to think outside of the box. Such documents also seek alignment before the conversation has taken place, when the whole point of the conversation is to obtain a diversity of views and then gain alignment. Above all, long papers on strategy normally confuse strategy with tactics.

In terms of the number of participants, this depends on what the session is trying to achieve. If the session is designed to develop a new strategy and identify a company's strategic advantage over its competitors, confidentiality is paramount. So it makes sense that the group is limited to the executive team and/or the most senior management. We have even facilitated a conversation with one person – this amounted to executive coaching. If a session is designed to promote buy-in across various levels within a company and to ensure inclusiveness of the conversation, then a larger group would make sense. However, too large a group runs the risk of becoming like a conference plenary session and destroying the intensity of the conversation. Our experience has shown that the optimal number is between 5 and 20 persons, with a maximum of 25; anything larger than that and the spontaneity of the conversation could be lost.

Should, however, for reasons of inclusiveness, the number of persons exceed 25, they can be divided into smaller groups, with the conversation being held within those groups. But a caution must be given. We do believe that our conversation model is holistic and cannot be broken down into parts, with each group, say, doing a different set of questions (such as one group working only through questions 1-6 and another questions 7-10). Hence, in such a case, we prefer each group to work through the entire conversation model and then report back to the rest of the groups, after which a synthesis can be done of the data. This allows the thinking to be subjected to the rigours of the ten questions while at the same time providing a diversity of perspectives and insights. Furthermore, it can also give an indication of whether the thinking and understanding of the business or game has some commonality across the diverse groups, or whether each group perceives the game differently. Breaking into smaller groups can work when discussing options, as long as everybody has participated in the section on strategy and scenarios, and contributed towards the SWOT analysis.

The next question we are often asked is: how long does a typical strategic conversation take? Well, how long is a typical piece of string? Some conversations are highly interactive and explore wide areas around the business or game, whereas others are intense, to the point and characterised by a high degree of agreement. The number of participants can also influence the duration of a strategic conversation, as can the logistics required for group work. Realistically though, a good strategic conversation should take not less than a day and, being sensitive to the time constraints of a typical world-class company, should take no longer than two days.

A post-workshop write-up is invaluable to the process as it provides an ongoing working document through which the conversation can continue. It also provides a frame of reference to look back on when participating in future conversations. The write-up can be done by the facilitator once all the data has been collected and assimilated; or someone within the group can process the data during the conversation and then disseminate it amongst the participants immediately afterwards, either by e-mail or internal post. However, during all workshops, data must be captured and displayed visually to the participants as a constant record of the conversation.

Two other practical questions we are often asked about the model are:

- How often should you conduct these strategic conversations?
- How far down the organisation should you go with these conversations?

The answer to both questions is that there is no set formula, and it is very much up to each person or company as to how to use our model. Some people like to have a one-off conversation on strategy and then only review it if and when the external environment changes to the point that it has to be reviewed. Obviously, any tactical decisions taken at the meeting along with their associated actions are regularly monitored. Certainly the scenario gameboard is reviewed at appropriate intervals to keep the team aware of its competitive position and possible changes to the environment. Other teams like to have a strategic conversation once a year before the next round of operational planning and budgeting begins. This is fine as long as it doesn't become a bureaucratic chore.

On the second question, some companies like to restrict the conversation to their top executive team, while others like to cascade it down through the different business units and service departments. Obviously, the lower one goes, the more restricted the scope of the game becomes. Nevertheless, it is still useful to consider the range of activities inside any production unit/service centre and whether these should be changed to accommodate the needs of other in-house departments, which are its clients. Equally, relationships with 'supplier' departments can be examined as well.

One company we worked with first held a strategic conversation amongst its executive team. Then each member of the team facilitated the conversation further with his or her region or department. We were not involved in the second step except as bystanders. Such a process developed the conversation into an important internal communication tool; and allowed the conversation to become a feedback mechanism to the executive. The whole company was thereby strategically empowered since all employees and management shared a common understanding of the game and the direction in which the organisation intended to go.

A word or two on the attributes of a good facilitator:

- It should always be borne in mind that the correct strategic combination to take a company forward is invariably within the minds and experience of the participants. It is simply the role of the facilitator to help the participants identify it. Therefore a good facilitator coaxes brilliance out of participants, rather than comes up with brilliant ideas himself or herself. Hence, the role of the facilitator is different from the role of a consultant.
- The facilitator should not be overly knowledgeable about the nature of the company's business. It sounds surprising, but there is a good reason for this. In helping the facilitator to familiarise himself or herself with the nature of the company's business, the participants are often forced to return to basics and examine the game from a fresh perspective – unlike anything they have done for years. Having said that, a facilitator should not go into a session completely ignorant of the game under debate since valuable time will be wasted.

Those with a knowledge of philosophy will find a resonance in the above two attributes with the founding principles of Socratic dialogue. In the dialogue between Socrates and the fox, each of them played a role as a facilitator in the conversation, just as they did that of participant and listener. The result was a conversation that flowed freely, where preconceived ideas were tested and where the participants felt sufficiently liberated to review their strategy.

The remaining chapters will take you through the ten strategic questions in more detail. A flexible set of sub-questions will be developed and examples provided to illustrate the relevance of these questions. The final chapter is the conclusion of our strategic conversation with you and a tribute to Pierre Wack.

But before you take the next step, we think it's necessary that you understand the impact it might have: our experience has shown that once people have been introduced to this methodology, the quality of their enquiry and the level of thinking about their future are permanently elevated to a new level. This will have an overall beneficial effect on your company's level of strategic skills, thereby reducing (or removing) the reliance on the opinions of external consultants and the regular transfusions of wisdom they try to inject into your corporate bloodstream. With our questions, we extract the innate wisdom residing in the minds of the executives around the table. We all learn at the same time – like Socrates did in his dialogues with his students, mutually exploring issues and mutually resolving them in the give-and-take of debate.

Furthermore, we give the executive team the 'quality of sight'. In today's age, where perception is often regarded as reality and spin merchants abound to provide convincing and sometimes contagious perceptions, seeing through the veil – or the 'mask of appearances' as Socrates described it – is vital to success. Whether you are looking at yourself or the world around you, the hype has to be filtered out to make good decisions about the future. You need X-ray vision!

Some comments made as a result of our sessions are:

It was a turning-point because we used the positive scenario derived from the conversation to establish a new set of values and practices throughout the organisation – all the way down to grass-roots level. CEO, BANKING GROUP

Normally I start a meeting by asking what the takeaways are likely to be. I note that, instead of answers, the takeaway will be some questions on strategy to keep me awake at night. I guess that's what Socrates had in mind. CEO, NATIONAL BAKERY CHAIN

As a small business, we are too busy doing business to take time out to think about the future. Nor can we afford to have a full-time strategic planner. So the conversation was an ideal way to take stock of our game briefly and passionately. Did you notice there wasn't a single interruption from a mobile phone? That has to be a first!   CEO, ATM SERVICE PROVIDER

We are all fierce individualists in our family. For the first time, we've had a conversation about the business which has brought us together as a team. No doubt in a few weeks time we'll be going our separate ways again, but at least we'll have the minutes of this meeting as proof of a fleeting moment of unity.

     CHAIRMAN, FAMILY FOOTWEAR BUSINESS

I'm looking at my watch. You said five hours for the conversation and we've done it. Unbelievable!   CEO, MINING CONTRACTOR

I like the game analogy because it will give us a better way to process information in the future. If there's a new player, a new rule of the game or the emergence of a new market scenario, we will be able to adjust faster than our competitors. That's the name of the game.

     DIRECTOR, ASSET-MANAGEMENT COMPANY

What is nice about your model is that it doesn't get in the way of discussing the business. It's invisible because it's so logical. I much prefer it to those methods with cheesy names where you spend half the time figuring out your next step.   CHAIRMAN, TIMBER COMPANY

I came in feeling paper withdrawal symptoms, but you've cured me of the habit. In future, I shall consign all thick strategy documents to File 13. I hope it doesn't get me into hot water!

     EXECUTIVE, MUNICIPAL WATER BOARD

DEFINING THE GAME

4 Context: How has the game in your industry changed, where is it heading and how have you fared as a player?

The unexamined life is not worth living.
SOCRATES, as quoted in Plato's *Apology*

Every organisation has a destiny line that can be drawn from its genesis through its current form and into the future. The line is jointly determined by two factors: the internal development of the organisation as expressed in its actions and results and the external evolution of the environment in which it is operating. "For every action, there is a reaction," said Sir Isaac Newton a few centuries ago in laying down a universal law of nature. Ironically there is no better example of this than in the relationship between man and nature. Each leaves its indelible mark on the other. The African philosophy of *ubuntu* expresses the idea perfectly: "I am because you are." Yet strategy sessions give scant attention to this fact. The organisation is treated almost as an island unto itself. Few of its surroundings are taken into account in plotting the next move. So we start with an in-your-face question that emphasises the historic and future interrelatedness between the industry (or whatever you like to call your immediate environment) and you.

Socrates talks about his 'destiny line' in his dialogue with the fox and in so doing gives context to his life. Our first question is all about context, for the very good reason that no strategy can be appropriate unless it is contextually valid. A strategy to hike northwards on the gently rolling green hills of England in ordinary gear is contextually valid, and therefore passes muster. On the other hand, a strategy to hike northwards through the Arctic waste to the North Pole in the same clothes is not appropriate, unless the objective is to satisfy the cravings of a foolish, extreme, adrenalin-driven junkie!

The opening question may seem simple on the surface, yet the insight from it sets the scene for the rest of the conversation. We need to know where we have come from before we can decide where we want to go; and we need to know what is going on around us at the moment. In brief, we need to understand the present state of the game as well as its history and where it seems to be moving into the future. We used to call this 'painting a rich picture' of the system you inhabited. But the question serves other purposes as well. It is a comfortable way to initiate the strategic conversation, to warm people up for the more difficult questions ahead. It explores familiar territory and coaxes the participants into presenting their interpretations of the past before venturing their opinions on the future. It makes them painfully aware that the vast majority of the changes that have happened in the game are beyond their control. It helps shift their mental models to the point that they begin to think like foxes about adapting their strategies to current realities. Indeed, the neutrality of the opening question precludes any attempt by individuals to be defensive about their previously stated positions. Instead, it provides a departure point for a new alignment on which the future of the business can be built.

The Viability of the Game

Once the question has been presented and answered, the extent of the changes to the game become significantly, and sometimes frighteningly, explicit. Often one of the first things that emerges is how many drivers of change there are. These may include technology, consumer taste, consolidation of customers or opposition players, the weather, political shifts, legislation, and the emergence of countries like China and India as serious contenders in the global arena. Sometimes there may be only one or two main drivers, but often there are many, and by grouping or clustering them it is possible to get a better picture of their impact on the game. Some games may be undergoing such a transformation that the initial decision may be that it's best to exit the game and try another one altogether.

This type of conclusion may emerge through reflecting on the last part of the question: ". . . how have you fared as a player?" It invites an examination of whether you have simply survived and kept up with the game or been in a position to influence the present outcome to your advantage – in which case you may be in the winning circle. If neither of these views resonates with you, then the best decision may indeed be to switch games; in which case the tone has been set for the rest of the strategic conversation. In judging your performance, though, a critical feature is whether you have merely responded passively to all the changes in the game or actually initiated some of them yourself. Obviously, it makes a big difference to your status as a player if you are a trendsetter as opposed to a 'dedicated follower of fashion'.

Often companies don't have a good understanding of their positioning in the game and survive from day to day on intuition. Some of the world's greatest leaders were blessed with intuition, and often had more than their fair share of luck. But intuition is a fickle companion, and if it lets you down it can do so disastrously and with a debilitating effect on your self-confidence and the confidence others have in you as a leader. Much better to have a healthy bout of introspection with your team and objectively consider your collective performance to date. Obviously, if a critical examination of the game shows that you are winning, the strategy going forward is not about enjoying the ride; it's about consolidating and enhancing your position. However, if you are in the losers' corner then the conversation will be more about changing strategic direction or, as mentioned earlier, changing games completely. Don't underestimate how hard it is to get a company to admit to being in the second situation. Once, it had to take a halving of the company's share price in the six months following the workshop to get the message through to management that fundamental change was essential.

When some businesses have examined the game and seen how they are faring, they feel a little concerned about their size in relation to other, larger players, as well as their measure of influence over the game that may be developing in complexity. This is important to note, but not a point to worry about. Smaller companies are often more agile than larger companies; they can change or adapt more easily, and they can manoeuvre around the gameboard more quickly. Size doesn't always matter; what *is* crucial in the game, though, is *momentum*. In physics, this is the product of a body's mass and velocity; so a larger company that is slow to innovate can have less momentum in the game than a smaller company that is continually hastening forward in accordance with the changes in the game. And the games of business are *always* changing.

It is the extent and speed of changes within a game that define its attractiveness or otherwise. Massive changes will contribute to the game's volatility and unpredictability. These can swallow up the most hardened players – whether they are large or small. Those remaining have to move into uncharted territory as they battle to reconfigure their game plan to deal with the changes. The answers to this first question in the strategic conversation bring such changes to the fore and demand that participants reflect on whether they are up to the challenge with their existing capabilities and experience, or need to start anew as pathfinders in a 'brave new world'.

Working with multinationals has its own special challenges. We have seen many such companies take a deep breath when the full scale of the game they are in is revealed to them. In the majority of cases their game is more a set of smaller games running concurrently. In some of them they may be a larger player with a dominant market share, and in some they may be a new, smaller player in the process of establishing their credentials. Each game has its own set of drivers for change.

But as a multinational, you have to take cognisance of how the global geopolitical game has changed as well; and perhaps how the game is changing in each of the countries where you are doing business. Ian Fleming in his book *From Russia with Love* made the best case we've seen for looking at the bigger picture. Imagine you're playing billiards, and the ball you've just hit is going into the pocket because you have obeyed the laws of the billiard table. However, a pilot in a jet above you faints at the controls, the plane crashes into the building and the building collapses on you and the table. The ball misses the pocket! End of story – even if you are James Bond. The big picture wins.

Finally, when presenting this first question in a strategic conversation, we've often heard that business follows set cycles and that "not to worry, things will pick up, they always do". If this is the case and these cycles are predetermined, why is it so few companies survive more than a few cycles? Resilient companies critically examine the nature of the ebbs and flows in the game and distinguish between the cyclical patterns and the changes that are permanent. They adjust to the latter.

Here are some examples of insights that have come to light in response to the first question of our strategic dialogue. They constitute preparation for the tough questions ahead:

The game changed in 1978 when Deng Xiaoping became leader and introduced the open- door policy. China's economy at the time was ranked around 100th in the world and now it is number 4. Not bad to rise 96 places in 28 years. We'll soon overtake Germany to be number 3. I wonder when the West will stop calling us an emerging economy!   CHINESE STRATEGIST, BEIJING

Thanks for the opening question. It has given me an unbiased perspective of my business. And, as the Irish would say, to get from A to B, you must start by knowing exactly where A is.

FAMILY BUSINESS OWNER

A few years ago, we had teenagers in the shops buying CDs. Now they download music off the internet onto iPods and the only customers we get are people in their 40s and older who can't. It's a middle-aged game now, so maybe we should only stock adult contemporary and gospel.   EXECUTIVE, MUSIC RETAIL CHAIN

Mining in the last century was a dull game of constant surpluses, where the company that won was the company that could cut its costs faster than its competitors. Now, none of us can keep up with Chinese demand, so we're all scrambling for resources; and the guy who wins will be the guy with the smartest geologists or the best relationship with the exploration juniors who discover big new deposits.   MANAGER, MINING MULTINATIONAL

Radio once was a 'lean forward' game where people listened to their favourite serials at any time of the day or night. Now it's a 'sit back' game with two peaks at morning and afternoon rush hours and relaxation stuff in between.   CEO, BROADCASTING GROUP

For the last 25 years, we've had below average rainfall and an increasing population. 2006 was the 'big dry' – an absolute stinker

for rain. We're constructing a desalination plant, but you feel there's been a structural shift in the game to the point where environmental constraints are going to dictate the outcome.

MUNICIPAL CEO, PERTH, AUSTRALIA

MBA programmes were for a long time the money-spinners for business schools and they're still seen as the flagship course by which status is judged. But advanced management programmes and short-term executive courses tailored for individual companies are where the real money lies nowadays.

DEPUTY DEAN, LEADING BUSINESS SCHOOL, USA

We used to have a Government Board selling our product. But it was abolished just when our customers – the retailers – were consolidating into larger groups. How have we fared? Terribly, because we're price takers with no negotiating clout and a falling percentage of the value chain. The game has become so unplayable that the definition of child abuse in agriculture is handing on your farm to your son.

SOUTH AFRICAN FARMER

My grandfather was a tailor in Munich in the early 1930s and ran an extremely profitable business. But when he saw Hitler changing the game, he decided to emigrate to America. If he hadn't read the signs and seen the possibilities, I probably wouldn't be around for this conversation.

JEWISH PROPERTY DEVELOPER

The British game has changed dramatically. We once mined coal, forged steel and built ships and cars. We were an industrial nation. Now, the Chinese have captured the manufacturing space and the British have had to adjust by moving into other spaces the Chinese can't yet replicate – like financial services. But judging by the performance of the economy and the low level of unemployment, we've done it rather well.

INDUSTRIALIST, WOLVERHAMPTON, ENGLAND

5   Scope: What is your playing field today, and how do you want to expand (or contract) it in light of the developing context and the resources at your disposal?

The nearest way to glory is to strive
to be what you wish to be thought to be.
SOCRATES

After answering the first question, you should be beginning to see your business as it really is. No blinkers on. When Socrates commended the fox at the end of the conversation, he said: "You see things as they really are and, just by doing that, you see into the future."

Now we're not about to turn you, the readers, into a bunch of professional 'seers', but it makes absolute sense for you to have no illusions about the game you're in and the shape of your business before you decide what you are going to do next. In other words, once you have judged the worth of your game and your current ability to play in it, you can move on to define your scope – namely the specific area within which you want to be a player in the future.

Inwards and Outwards

Nevertheless, we stress that, life being a continuum, you must consider it as a destiny line. Remember Socrates' question to the fox: "Having traced your destiny line from start to present, where should you go to now?" Of course, many individuals lead incredibly varied lives, starting out as soldiers and becoming pop singers (James Blunt) or moving on from selling avant-garde vinyl records to becoming the most famous British entrepreneur in modern times (Sir Richard Branson). You can do that as an individual because you don't carry the responsibilities that a company does. In the latter case, before you do anything radical, you have to face up to the looking glass and consider some – if not all – of the following: the expectations of your employees and shareholders, your culture, your core competencies, your organisational structure, your business model, the resources at your disposal, your location, your public reputation and brand, etc.

Succinctly, your DNA or corporate make-up – the glue that holds you together – plays a role in determining your future destiny line.

Sure, you can decide that the present game is unplayable and strike off in an entirely new direction. But, like the fox who admitted his options were limited to the four principal points of the compass, there are restrictions placed on organisations beyond a certain size. They're like supertankers that need plenty of space and time to turn. Yet again, when looking at future scope, you have to look inwards and outwards at the same time.

Moreover, defining a playing field isn't simply a case of plotting the addresses of your factories or your customers on a map. Business, unlike sport, does not have the clearly drawn lines of a football field or a tennis court. You can decide on your own boundaries, subject to the limitations we have just mentioned. But there *have* to be lines you don't cross, because focus is a key element of a successful strategy. Hence, it is important to define your current playing field upfront, and decide what you want it to be in the future. For this reason we have made 'scope' our second question after 'context'. It is a purely strategic question because it defines the direction in which you wish to go and towards which all the internal players in your business should be aligned. Once the scope has been agreed on, it is possible to start positioning your players, motivating their actions and rewarding their performance as individuals and as a team.

You may remember the fox describing his destiny line thus: "I was born a fox with all the strengths and weaknesses that go with the species. My choice of parents was beyond my control, as was my date of birth. But what has been within my control since then has been to use my strengths instinctively to cover for my weaknesses. I am small and therefore vulnerable, but I am agile and have keen senses. I know my limitations, I know the risks, but I also grab opportunities as they arise".

The fox makes an important point: understand what you can and cannot control and define your playing field accordingly. This is not a formula to be unambitious. You'd most probably be surprised at the potential scope of your playing field once you have acquired a genuine knowledge of yourself as a player. In this respect, the fox underlines another important factor: play to your strengths and employ them wherever possible to make up for your weaknesses. Nobody is superhuman, no company is perfect. People or companies that feel they are flawless or omnipotent lose the plot immediately. Sound business strategies juxtapose your capabilities with the requirements of the game. This does not mean that new capabilities cannot be built; it simply underlines the importance of having a proper understanding of what those new capabilities are and putting sufficient resources into developing them. Think back to school and the sports you chose (apart from those which were compulsory!). It was all about constantly matching your skills to the games chosen. 'Constantly' is a crucial word here, because strategy and tactics are dynamic, particularly in grudge matches with the competition. The side that innovates and adapts its game is usually the one that comes out on top. Thus, it's the ability to change your mind and transform yourself – as a person or as a team – that keeps you in the forefront of the game. Champions never stand still.

Nations and Cities

This concept is as applicable to countries and companies as it is to schools. Let's start with countries. The global playing field of the last century was divided up into segments, marked off from one another by barriers of language, culture and politics. A few, well-entrenched major-league players such as Western Europe, the us and, latterly, Japan, dominated the central field, occasionally teaming up with smaller players who came on as substitutes but who otherwise remained on the sidelines playing their own games. Some never came on at all, although continually in an expectant state of warm-up; they just couldn't make the grade into the main game. Others, meanwhile, chose to do their own thing on an isolated field with no intention of ever joining in.

Globalisation has changed all that. The field is flatter, the barriers to entry lower, the relationships between the players more interdependent. We still have losers (failed states), but significant new players have emerged who have their own ideas on how the game should be played. They've thrown out the old rulebooks, thus forcing a serious rethink on the part of the previously reigning champions: how can we be congruent with the new conditions and maintain our competitive edge? Well, like everybody else, they have to play to their strengths and develop new ones out of their old ones at the same time. The scope of their economies and their exports should reflect this, as David Ricardo (an English economist) first observed in his *Principles of Political Economy* published in 1817. His celebrated principle of comparative advantage stated that countries would most benefit by specialising in goods that they produced efficiently and trading these for other goods produced more efficiently by other countries. Ricardo was a foxy economist!

As we all know, China is dominating large chunks of the

manufacturing game, using its vast resources of cheap labour to make the 'China price' its key differentiator. Russia, Africa and South America are principal players in the resources game along with the Middle East, which has been there a long time. The West has moved on to the hi-tech and services sectors, while everybody plays some role in the agricultural and tourist games. Each country has come up with a scope or product offering that suits its natural advantages, whether it be minerals, climate, diversity of fauna and flora, spectacular features of nature, etc., as well as the skills of its citizens (which may have been acquired over generations). Moreover, a nation's economic focus changes over time. For example, the UK has progressed from agriculture through manufacturing to services but retains elements of all three.

What is true for nations is also true for cities and towns. Each city/town has its own character and location conferring certain advantages on it. Nevertheless, the really successful ones rejuvenate themselves with new industries, layouts and centres as they change with the times. Think of Glasgow and Barcelona and how their scope expanded to include culture and the arts, or new cities like Dubai which has established itself as an entrepôt in the Middle East.

Companies, Schools and NGOs

So, back to business. What type of sub-questions do we ask to define scope? Interestingly, we have found that the list applies equally to organisations of noncommercial kinds ranging from NGOs to schools to universities to municipalities and even churches. The principal sub-question is: what lies at the centre of the field, on the margin and outside its boundaries? That is, what is the absolute core of your business, what is the outer core that adds value to the inner core and what is non-core? Obviously non-core operations can be phased out or disposed of; or if the service is still required it can be contracted out.

A multinational estate agency we worked with provided a good example of the application of this sub-question. The core activity is selling houses. However, linked to this are other activities that may add value to the transaction, such as furniture removal and relocation and satisfying other lifestyle requirements associated with purchasing a new home. These are not core to the business, but they do add value. The more elements you have in your product line by cross-selling or acting as a one-stop shop, the more value you add to the business and the better your game. Where the estate agency lacked the competence to deliver the extra service, they outsourced the activity.

The second subsidiary question is: should the field be wider or more focused? One truck and bus manufacturing group we worked with offered 132 different models of trucks and buses, of which only eight were regular sellers. Basic business logic suggested the playing field needed to be more focused. Generally speaking, it became no longer fashionable during the 1990s to be a conglomerate. Hence the decade saw the dismantling of conglomerates with a greater emphasis on smaller playing fields where competencies were historically strong. One group sold off a bank, an insurance company, a property company and a whole range of industrial interests in order to revert to its traditional business of mining.

The converse must also be addressed by examining the scope in order to extend the field into new, profitable activities. Many supermarkets, clothing and lifestyle retailers now sell cellular services, handsets and airtime, something that used to be the sole concern of cellphone retailers. This represents the embracing of a whole new, and highly profitable, business for these retailers. At the same time cellular networks enjoy significantly higher sales because the retailers have the capability to reach consumers *en masse* – something that isn't a core competency of the cellular networks. Nevertheless, there is a major difference between the strategy of the old rootless conglomerates and what is now going on. Today, you expand into 'adjacent areas' where your competencies can be stretched or incrementally adjusted to make you a serious player in the new game. The only old-style conglomerate businesses left these days are family businesses run by founders with the Midas touch (and General Electric!). It requires a very special talent to play several games simultaneously where the culture and skills for each one are very different. Imagine alternating hands of bridge with hands of poker.

To achieve more clarity in the debate on scope, we divide the playing field into product range, product chain, market segment and geographical footprint.

Product Range

This comprises the *horizontal* range of goods and services offered by your company. In other contexts, it would be the curriculum and extracurricular activities of a school, the number of faculties at a university or the range of services undertaken by an NGO. Questions around your product range should include:

- Is there something new you should add?
- Is there something you should delete either because it is non-core or because it is consuming too many of your resources?
- Do you have something unusual in your product/service line-up which differentiates you from your competitors? If not, shouldn't you?
- Is your product mix correct or should it be shifted in line with changes in the demands of the market?

This last question is probably the most important one in the list to ask when facilitating the top executive team of a global multinational. Normally, such companies are broken up into business units, each of which has a mandate to do what is best for that area. Hence, the only place where decisions can be made to add other business units or apportion investment in a different fashion across the existing units is at that elevated level.

An example of insight gained from these questions came from a major food company we worked with. They had a product range that was limited to frozen foods. An analysis of global trends identified a growing demand for convenience foods – prepackaged meals aimed at people in the upper end of the market too busy at the office to get home in time to cook. After an examination of their capabilities, this company realised that they had the capacity to develop a new line to tap into this trend. They have since increased their product range, and very successfully too.

Another illustration concerns a boys' high school in South Africa that at the time of the conversation played cricket and rugby but not soccer. After much debate around a 'relevant product offering', it was decided to add soccer, with the consequence that the school now fields one of the top schoolboy teams in its province. Music has also become a much stronger part of their offering. Moving further afield to a middle-class suburb of Melbourne in Australia, the conversation among the municipal team revolved around the provision of more facilities for the elderly as the demographics in the area changed. For young and old alike, streamlining the product line to suit their needs is critical.

Product Chain

This is the *vertical* chain of processes from raw material extraction through manufacture and wholesale to retailing to customers. In some countries, it includes recycling as well, because legislation is demanding that companies are responsible for entire product life cycles. Questions aimed at unpacking the nature and value (or not) in your product chain include:

- Do you want to operate through the entire chain so that you have control from start to finish (like an oil company)? Do your competencies dictate that you should only operate in a particular link in the chain and try to dominate that link (like supermarkets)?
- If you are an upstream producer, are there opportunities to go downstream and add value to your product offering before selling it?
- If you are a downstream producer, might you wish to go upstream to control some of your raw material sources?
- Are there constrictions in the product chain that are negatively affecting your offering? Can they be obviated?

A good example of the value of an analysis of the product chain came to the fore during our work with the executive team of a global tobacco company. Like most other tobacco companies, they operate across the entire product chain from growing the raw material (agricultural game), through manufacturing the product, to its retail and even out into numerous hospitality end-points. However, increasingly restrictive legislation surrounding the consumption of their product, together with other changes in the tobacco game, meant that the company's marketing arm had lost valuable access to consumers. The executive team realised that they needed to focus more attention on the final link in the product chain, i.e. the retail and hospitality outlets, if they were to regain any measure of control over their ultimate destiny.

Concentrating on operations downstream for this company required a re-allocation of resources, but for many companies such a move downstream or upstream in the product chain often requires the acquisition of competencies they may not possess. Tactics to do so may therefore include the investigation and development of joint ventures/alliances with companies that do have competencies in the areas being targeted. An instance of where this fact became glaringly obvious was a gold-mining company that wanted to add value to its product by going downstream into jewellery manufacture and retail. The vast difference between digging the stuff out of the ground and turning it into something that women want became apparent as soon as the mining executives of the one company met the jewellery design team of the other. Their clashing taste in clothes gave it all away.

A further scholarly example is a nice way to round off this section. At a session with one of the most select private schools in South Africa, the issue was raised as to whether the product chain should be extended backwards from the existing primary/secondary configuration to kindergarten/pre-primary as well. This would ensure that potential pupils would be captured in the system at the earliest possible age.

Market Segment

As the name implies, this part of a conversation profiles the segment of the market towards which your products or services are targeted. This can comprise industrial clients in business-to-business trade, or consumers, in which case the debate centres around such things as age, gender, income and lifestyle. Market segment may be a factor that directly or indirectly influences your product or service offering. To this end, sub-questions that you should ask include:

- Have there been changes in the demographics of your market which may increase or reduce demand?

- Have there been advances in technology affecting consumer behaviour in your market, e.g. the shift to downloading music off the internet by young people, the shift to internet banking or the shift to purchasing airline tickets off the internet? Do these shifts necessitate a change in your product/service offering and/or create the need to exploit other markets?
- Are there shifts in the spending power between different layers of society which favour your products or mean you will have to capture completely new customer groupings?
- Have there been psychological shifts in the market segment that could influence consumer taste for your products and services?
- If you have one industry as a dominant client, what are the prospects for that industry in terms of future demand or regulation or anything else that might have a significant impact? Should you be looking elsewhere to diversify your risk?
- Does your brand still match the changing playing field? Is the message conveyed in your brand still relevant? Can you expand your market segment through rebranding or developing a new, associated brand? Think of BMW, a brand that was very niched in the upper income and slightly older group. When they wanted to increase their market segment, the company decided the best way was to capture a younger market with the same aspirational values that might lead them on to the BMW brand. So they released a new brand – MINI.
- Are the Chinese an existing player or a potential new entrant in your market segment? What is your game plan to compete with them if they regard your space as their space? It may be the moment to move on to another space or join up with them.

An interesting example of how shifting demographics within a market segment has impacted on a product is in play in South Africa. Focused policies by the government, changing regulations and a growing economy have produced a burgeoning sector of new homeowners, especially in the lower end of the market. People owning these homes need to paint their homes; but they don't own cars and instead use public transport, and paint is not the easiest thing to transport. So a re-examination of the packaging of paint products and route to market has become necessary for paint manufacturers.

One of the banks which used our conversation model recognised that their elite image at the time was out of step with the realities of the new South Africa and the rise of the black middle class. They have since rebranded themselves to offer wider appeal and be seen as a bank with all the nation's citizens at heart, especially the next generation of entrepreneurs. But what this case illustrates is the importance of involving the advertising agency at an early stage to ensure that their campaign reflects any changes in the company's strategic objective concerning market segment.

Geographical Footprint

The geographical footprint is defined by the following two questions:

- Where do you want your business to be located?
- Where do you want to market and sell your products or services?

The answers to these questions differ considerably, depending on whether you are a large or a small business. For a small business, geographical footprint is normally a question of whether you want to be a local business servicing a particular town or region or whether you want to go further afield and establish a national footprint or at least a footprint in all the major cities in a country. You may need to spread your production network to achieve this and open up multiple offices; or maybe there is a distribution network you can use which can be satisfied by one production source. The biggest difference between the past and the present for small business is the internet. You literally can market your product anywhere in the world off your website – something which would have been impossible to do twenty-five years ago.

For medium to larger companies which already have a national footprint, the issue is whether you wish to establish businesses in other countries. One of the principal reasons for spreading your wings in this fashion is to diversify economic and political risk. This can be done by having revenue-generating bases in a variety of countries or regions that act independently of each other. Of course, such a strategy does not take the risk of a global slump out of play, but it does protect you against specific national risks. Another reason obviously is to expand your market generally if you have a product or service you believe can be sold elsewhere. While exporting from your home country is a perfectly reasonable option, it often requires a physical presence in other countries to trigger sales (particularly if they are inclined to protect their home industries with quotas or tariffs). In our experience, one of the strategies that has to be considered by South African companies is to use home-grown competencies to push into selected African countries now that the continent to the north is opening up for business. An easy way to do this if you are a service company is to follow your client's footprint if that client is beating an expansionary path into Africa. One of the banks we did scenarios for has merged with a British bank in order to take advantage of the latter's African footprint (while the British bank wanted to re-establish its presence in South Africa).

Multinationals that operate across many countries often prefer to manufacture their products in countries with a relatively low cost of manufacturing (e.g. China) and then sell these products into developed markets. This may make business sense, but the cost and logistics of transporting products from point of production to the market is something that needs to be considered. What must also be borne in mind is the possibility of nasty geopolitical scenarios, which could disrupt international supply lines. Global warming could moreover mean higher freight charges as carbon emissions are figured into the cost of transport.

If you only dominate the market in one country, it is critical to understand who else may put their footprint beside yours (particularly if the foot belongs to a global giant). Look at South African Breweries in the 1980s. As a wholly South African operation, it had dominated the local market during a time when international companies were discouraged from investing in South Africa. As the country moved towards a more democratic status and was embraced globally, SAB was suddenly faced with the prospect of competing with international companies on its home turf. The company had two options – stay focused on a local market and fight tooth and nail to try and hold onto market share or, if it wanted to create sustainable growth, expand internationally. The company's decision was the latter with the first countries targeted being in Eastern Europe. Old and rusting breweries were acquired and upgraded to SAB standards. Then came the moves into the US and China. Now, as SABMiller, it is one of the top three brewing companies in the world by volume.

The one caveat that should be offered in the conversation around expanding one's global footprint is the fact that countries can have very different rules of the game. Socratic logic is different from Confucian logic! Hence, many well-managed companies have come unstuck when they have invaded foreign lands and found the rules of engagement with the competition (and the government) to be totally alien to their normal way of doing things. It requires local savvy to make up for ignorance, and that usually comes in the form of a trustworthy local partner.

Here is a sample of responses we have had to the second question on scope:

When our national airline carrier decided not to pay commission on airline tickets sold by travel agents, we knew that other airlines would follow suit. We realised that our business model was no longer valid and that our primary product was no longer the focus of the business. Customers could now book airline tickets directly with the airlines or on-line via the internet. We were about to be disintermediated from the chain! In order to survive and add value to the chain again, our primary product became the specialised advice we offered through our extensive knowledge of the travel industry. If we hadn't changed our playing field, we'd now be off the field completely.   CEO, NATIONAL TRAVEL GROUP

With the new regulatory laws in some countries around smoking coming into play, our initial thought was to look for new, emerging markets where growth could continue. This, however, was shortsighted because these laws are becoming accepted and implemented in more and more countries. Our primary focus is now to produce harm-reduction tobacco products, or new smokeless tobacco products. In order to do this, though, we will need to allocate far more resources to R&D than in our current model.

CEO, GLOBAL TOBACCO COMPANY

In many countries, beneficiation of raw materials before exporting them may become a rule of the game. Have we got the core compe-

tencies to move into this aspect of the product chain or will we need an alliance partner who does?　　EXECUTIVE, GLOBAL MINING GROUP

Today's schools need to strategise in order to attract pupils. Schools ought to offer a product that uniquely differentiates them in some form. Most schools become known as rugby, cricket or hockey schools, but we have chosen to define our playing field as offering a 'generalist education'. It fits with the community in which we serve, and offers a holistic, well-balanced approach to education.

PRINCIPAL, LEADING CO-ED HIGH SCHOOL

We were a property group known for its premium focus at the top end of the residential property market. With the recent shift in the demographics in the country and the rapid expansion of a middle class, we were losing sales in the mid-sector. We have since shifted our playing field and subtly redefined our brand. We now sell across nearly all market segments, but still offer a premium service.

CEO, RESIDENTIAL PROPERTY GROUP

Maize is a commodity, grown as a food source around the world for humans and for animals. However, rising energy demand, combined with the issue of global warming, have brought biofuels to the fore. Maize is a good source for ethanol. This has opened up a completely new market segment for us and will undoubtedly lead to higher prices. We will be feeding tanks as well as mouths.

MAIZE FARMER

We have changed the scope of our game completely from farming crops and animals to running a game farm. We don't have to rely on weather like we used to and we have lots of overseas tourists flocking to our place. We advertise in most European capitals with the by-line: "Come and see the Big Five without catching malaria." Hypochondria definitely works in favour of our new enterprise.

GAME FARM OWNER

We produce high pressure hoses for exploration companies to keep their drill holes clean. Somebody had the bright idea that another market segment could be fire stations and associated emergency services. With a small amount of capital to make the necessary conversions, we now supply a growing and highly profitable US market.

CEO, DRILLING EQUIPMENT COMPANY

Our playing field is divided into two halves. The one half can be explained by the fact that we are short of resources other than coal. So in that half of the field, the game is to do deals with all the countries in the world that have resources – particularly African countries. The other half of the field is focused on turning those resources into manufactured products at a competitive price using Western brands and Western technologies. We now have one of the most open economies in the world, a trillion dollars of foreign exchange and a growing capacity to move from replication to innovation. The next phase of the game is to create our own original products and global brands; and to establish a private equity fund to buy into foreign players of interest. CHINESE ACADEMIC, BEIJING

Obviously our core activity is teaching the Word of God and ministering to the religious and spiritual needs of those in the community that want to come to our church. But in our country, the scope of the church's activity has to be extended to cater for the social needs of people including those infected and affected by HIV/AIDS. The problem is we don't at present have the resources, the infrastructure and the skills to establish a social responsibility function. We must start addressing this problem at this workshop.

ANGLICAN PRIEST, JOHANNESBURG

Widening your scope into a 'one-stop shop' is a real fad at the moment, but you have to be careful about what consumers perceive as a reasonable addition to your offering. As an example, 'bancassurance' hasn't worked that well because customers put

398

banking and insurance into separate compartments and expect different service providers. On the other hand, preparation of a will can be part of a bank's bouquet.   MANAGER, RETAIL BANK

You must realise that academics by their very nature rule out 'ruling out'. Everybody at this session will fight their corner for the continued existence of their faculty and all the programmes contained in it. And they'll want new courses as well. So, the scope of universities, like the universe, will continue to expand.

UNIVERSITY PROFESSOR

I have been a dairy farmer beholden to the price of milk that, like the price of any commodity, behaves in a volatile manner. I have decided to go further downstream in the value chain, having just purchased two Spar Food franchises. I supply both my stores with my milk.   DAIRY FARMER

The scope of our town's offering to tourists is determined by the fact that we are an oasis in the middle of a desert. We are already testing the environment to its limits.

COUNCILLOR, ALICE SPRINGS, AUSTRALIA

For any urban renewal scheme to be successful, its scope should encompass four activities: making the inner city safe; keeping it clean; providing shops, restaurants and entertainment so that people can have fun in the city centre; and finding the right balance between offices and residential apartments to make it a 'mixed use' location.

URBAN PLANNER

If you want me as an environmentalist to take your product chain seriously, you must examine the energy needs and environmental impact of every single link in the chain from raw material input to disposal at the end of the product's life.

CANADIAN RECYCLING EXPERT

6 Players: Who are the players that can most advance or retard your strategy, and how should you handle them in future?

Bad men live that they may eat and drink,
whereas good men eat and drink that they may live.
SOCRATES, as quoted by Plutarch

Socrates recognised that our lives are affected by people whose influence can be positive or negative when he asked of the fox: "Having traced your destiny line from start to present, where should you go to now? But then the third question has to be: 'Who is for you, who is against you and who is neutral?' In seeking to clarify the direction you wish to take, you have to return to the principle of being part of an interconnected system."

Every game has players – otherwise it wouldn't be a 'game' – each of whom plays a different role in the course of the game in terms of its direction and outcome. The players are therefore more often than not the most interesting aspect of the game (think of the media coverage given to sports celebrities); and yet we generally don't spend enough time understanding an individual player's influence on the game. Business leaders are quick to talk about developing positive relationships with all stakeholders and seeking their views before decisions are taken. On the other hand, many haven't a clue about any of the other stakeholders' DNA – i.e. why they are what they are – which after all determines the latter's perception of the game. They gloss over the nature of the relationships required to be successful in the game on the grounds that they can meet their objectives without too much external assistance or interference.

Sometimes the absence of a critical examination of the other players is simply a consequence of being in a game for so long that everything is taken for granted. This runs the risk of ignoring or missing another player's repositioning within the game as it changes. For as we have already stressed, games are continually evolving and so naturally do the roles and behaviour of the players. Part of analysing how a game has changed is therefore assessing how the other players have fared or modified their function and what new players have emerged. Failure to do this means that you can lose out on opportunities to leverage relationships with those players who will most gain from your winning; and to come up with defensive strategies against those players who will most gain from your loss.

The Perfect Fit

Management and political theorist Mary Parker Follett, who first coined the phrase 'conflict management', said in 1940 of relationships with players who could influence your game: "The nut and the screw form a perfect combination, not because they are different, but because they exactly fit into each other and together can perform a function which neither could perform half or alone or any part of alone." The relevance of this quotation increases with the growing interdependence of the players in both the political and economic games of the world today.

So, in your game, who are these players that will provide a perfect fit? Are there enough of them within your organisation? Do they exist elsewhere in the game? How can you draw on their expertise to benefit you? How can you stop the opposition achieving a perfect fit before you do? Top coaches in a match of soccer, for example, know the attributes of all the players on both sides and how each person's play can contribute towards the outcome of the game. They know which individuals to draw on from the squad to get the best fit. They know which individuals shouldn't be picked together because they don't get along so well. They understand perfectly the influence a positive team dynamic can have on the result. Furthermore, they are not averse to adopting tactics which will sufficiently interfere with the other side to cause maximum discomfort and misalignment; and, importantly, working out how they can take advantage of such a reaction and score extra goals.

Each step, or move, you make in a game cannot be undertaken without thinking of the ramifications it will have on the other players. As the fox quite correctly remarks to Socrates: "So you have to weigh up your friends and enemies and those who can go either way before deciding on your next move? I like that, because in the animal kingdom you very quickly learn who is out to kill you and who isn't. You avoid the places where the former may be and stick to potentially friendly territory." Of course in the game of business, things aren't so clear. Socrates explains it thus: "With human beings it's more difficult to judge, for we have the quality of deceit. But nothing really happens unless you have a few or many people on your side and you find ways around those whom you have identified as obstructing you." Unlike sport, where the rules of straight competition apply (for me to win, you have to lose), business is about collective wealth generation. Yes, there is competition – but no, it is not a good thing to destroy all the other players in the game and then become a monopoly yourself, taking advantage of your pre-eminent position in the process. Society won't benefit from that result and consequently there are social and ethical rules of engagement covering the world of commerce, which we will describe in the next chapter.

While the influence that external players have on the game is often overlooked in traditional planning sessions, the same applies to ourselves as players. Successful companies tend to underestimate how much their presence may have changed the game. This is dangerous because it means they risk over-looking how other players see them and may wish to react to narrow the gap. As an example, a small company that grows into a major player that dominates the game can shift from being perceived as a worthy opponent to becoming a target for populist attacks. Microsoft is a case in point, but so is Google. Too much success changes your appearance from in-novative crusader to exploiting colossus in the blink of an eye. As the Chinese say, "Nail that stands up going to get ham-mered down."

Yet more worrying than being a dominant player who changes the game is being a player who is at the mercy of others. If it's not you influencing the game, then who is? Ana-lysing all the players in the game is important, but what is *essential* is to stand back and identify the few *key* players whose decisions and actions may be transforming the nature of the game. These players need to be carefully monitored because you have two choices – copy them or come up with some-thing different that is even better.

Referees and DNA

Where sport and business do coincide is in the fact that play-ers are never free from scrutiny by referees. After all, every game has rules and therefore requires constant supervision to ensure that players do not break the rules. Although in some countries business games are governed more closely than others, every country has its referees, whether they are government ministers, civil servants, regulatory bodies, state-appointed committees or ombudsmen. The function of these 'players' (because in our methodology we classify them as such) is to ensure that the game moves smoothly along, is con-tinually evaluated and, where it is in danger of going off the rails, restored to normality. Referees can play an important role in determining the outcome of the game because the job demands a balancing act of note. Too much officiousness (for that read bureaucracy) and the flow of the game is spoilt; too little and things can get out of hand with players adopting un-conventional (and sometimes unfair or illegal) tactics to gain advantage or create pandemonium. Consequently, referees require a thorough understanding of the game before they are appointed – or in the case of a government, elected.

Nevertheless, a critical difference between referees and gov-ernment is that the former are only there to interpret the rules whereas the latter in important aspects of the business game are rule-makers. They enact laws on commerce, fix tax rates, provide subsidies and other incentives, etc. Moreover, busi-ness games need an extra dimension of care and control, since they normally involve the livelihoods of a majority of a na-tion's population. The relationship between the key players is more complex than sport, and no business game is perfect in its design and outcome. As we've already mentioned, for a game to be sustainable, pure competition with a definitive end point of a victor and vanquished can never be the sole imperative. On the other hand, as soon as government starts protecting its players from foreign competition, other govern-ments will follow suit. So you have to rely on a balance, spe-cifically a balance between free markets (globalisation) and the societal objectives of individual nations (like a 'better life for all' in South Africa). This demands a level of co-operation between governments to stop the international game becom-ing distorted, either because some countries don't really under-stand the rules or deliberately cheat with an eye on short-term results.

Players can be prioritised according to their importance in your game. But for all of them, an understanding of their 'DNA' is critical – particularly if they are foreign players. Let us revisit this concept of DNA. Despite globalisation which has been accompanied by mass consumerism so that to some extent we all wear the same clothes, drink the same drink, watch the same TV programmes and go to the same movies, important and critical differences between national cultures remain. It's in our bones; it's in our blood; it's fundamental to the way we view the world. That's just the 'nature' side of the equation. On the 'nurture' side, our parents, our position in society (class), the schools we attend, the communities we live in – in short our environment – also affect our DNA. We can see Socrates and the fox figuratively nodding their heads in agreement!

Now in a sport like athletics, these differences don't really matter as it's all about physical prowess. Even in chess, a non-Russian sometimes becomes world champion. But in business if you wish to engage properly with all the other players in your game, you must acknowledge the differences and try to understand how the other side ticks. This applies equally to competitors and members of your own team. Only then will you be able to optimise your strategy and tactics. So we must now return to our original Socratic question: who are the players for you in the game that want you to win; who are against you and want you to lose; and who are neutral and liable to swing either way? Within this framework, a range of sub-questions can be asked in regard to a specific category of players such as competitors, suppliers, customers, employees, governments, communities and shareholders. Examples follow.

Competitors

Very few companies profile the competition during a strategic session. We insist that they do so by posing these questions:

- Who are your main competitors?
- What is different about their DNA compared to yours and in what respects are they stronger or weaker?
- In particular, how big are they in relation to you?
- What do you think their assessment is of you as a player?

By keeping your main competitors on the radar screen, you will be continuously aware of any changes they are causing to the game and you will note the entrance of new players and the exiting of unsuccessful ones. Such information brings with it insight into any changes in your position within the game in terms of relative size and influence. A big gorilla with greater economies of scale can just as easily kill you off as a swarm of bees with no overheads. Indeed, in our facilitations, we have come across so many examples of medium to small-sized businesses battling it out with the big guys. To continue the metaphor, if you are a mid-sized orang-utan up against a 400-pound gorilla, you have three options: exit the game; become a 'boutique orang-utan' and differentiate yourself from the gorilla; or marry the gorilla (or a group of other orang-utans to become a gorilla). As for the bees, best to leave them alone. You'll never beat the price of the honey they deliver in their own game.

Suppliers

Supply chain excellence is all the rage these days. It involves meeting your suppliers/subcontractors outside the normal negotiating period when the relationship is usually focused on price (and is naturally combative). The reason is to establish a rapport and develop a mutual understanding of each other's game and DNA. Much money can be saved this way as the parties adjust their practices to each other's realities. Because networking is about people, you should have a special contact person at each of your suppliers to whom you can pick up the phone anytime.

So the sort of questions we raise around suppliers are:

- Who are your key suppliers and are they assisting you in winning the game. Are you, for example, their sole client, or do they supply your competitors as well?
- When did you last have a heart-to-heart conversation with your suppliers about your respective games?
- What are their strengths and weaknesses and what significant risks if any do they face (remember you inherit all of these as you are downstream of them)?
- Are any of your suppliers malfunctioning and causing your business real grief? If so, what are the alternatives?
- What criteria do you use in choosing your specific suppliers? Is it pricing, quality, consistency of delivery, service excellence, treatment of their employees and ethical standards generally, track record on the environment, health and safety, or a combination of all these?
- Are some of your suppliers larger than you and taking advantage of it by using their negotiating clout to squeeze the extra cent? Do you treat the smaller ones well by paying them promptly and having simple tender procedures?
- What is the turnover rate of your suppliers? In other words, do you have long-term stable relationships built on trust or do you try to keep your suppliers on their toes by chopping and changing them?

Of course, an additional question that is put to suppliers in South Africa concerns the credentials they possess in the area of black economic empowerment. This counts towards the 'empowerment scorecard' of the company putting out the tender and procuring the goods. Interestingly, the strategy of

Chinese companies is to form long-term relationships with their key foreign suppliers (countries and companies), especially those providing raw materials. All in all, strategic negotiation has become an increasingly important skill for players in today's global game where the type of relationship you ought to cultivate with your suppliers is of the two-way, symbiotic kind (as opposed to the one-way grab-it-all variety).

Customers

There's a bit of role reversal going on here since, as a supplier to your customers, they are entitled to ply you with the questions of the previous section. Nevertheless, you ought to have questions for them and about them as well:

- Who are your major customers? If they are businesses, what do you know about their game? If they are end-consumers, have you worked out their DNA so that you can second-guess what they want next?
- Do you regularly vet your customer call centres since, as the front-line link to the public, they can do irreparable harm to your brand if they are inefficient and rude?
- When did you last do a customer survey to see what they think of you and particularly where they believe improvements can be made to your products or service?
- In the event that you are expanding or changing your market segment, what is the DNA of the potential customers in the new area (this question applies especially where a company is introducing a premium brand catering for high income/high net worth individuals)?
- Should you be an exporter, do you cater for the different DNAs of the different nationalities of your consumers in the design and promotion of your products?

Generally speaking, markets continually change and are one of the driving forces behind changes in the game. Demographics play an essential role in changing the customer base and should therefore be monitored for any shifts that could impact on the game. For instance, most European countries are experiencing a 'geriatric boom', which signifies a growing market for products and services for the elderly. If you are to build a sustainable relationship with your customers you need constantly to ask where your customer sees value and whether or not you are providing, and thereby tapping into, that value.

Employees and Unions

Internally, these are the most important players. As such, a trio of questions to kick off this section with are:

- Are your employees for you or against you or just plain neutral?
- Do they enthusiastically buy into your organisation's philosophy or do they just come to work in an uninterested fashion?
- Are you aware of how different the post-yuppie generation are to the young people recruited 10 or 20 years ago, and have you adapted your management systems accordingly?

It is amazing how many executive teams of companies we have facilitated put their employees in the 'neutral' category. How on earth can you expect to win the game if you don't have a positive team dynamic? After all, it is essential for victory in team sports. Tactics that can be chosen to improve employee morale and alignment include bonus and promotion schemes based on the company's meaning of winning the game; employee share-ownership schemes; regular briefings on strategy; and allowing them to have conversations like these and taking the results seriously.

It may be advisable to break this group down for further analysis into, for example, the young talent (novices, apprentices and new employees); older employees with long service; retirees who work as part-time consultants; the families and dependants of employees; top/middle management; shop floor staff; shop stewards and other union officials. In the end, they all have to get along and think the organisation is worthwhile. Otherwise, defeat by opposition companies becomes a genuine possibility.

The other really crucial question to ask about employees is: what type of culture do you have in the organisation, and does it match the game and how you want to play it? If you are a multinational operating in a variety of countries, the relationship between expatriate managers and local staff may demand particular care, given the different DNAs of the two groups.

To illustrate the pivotal nature of employees as players, we were called in to help a major bank which was dramatically losing market share. They realised the cause of their misfortune was obvious: all of the players in the game were neutral or against them. Their employees were situated in neutral, and so were their suppliers and customers. Their competitors were anything but neutral in gloating over their disarray! The bank's leadership knew they could never win until the 'neutral' were converted to 'for'. How did they achieve that? They walked the talk at all the branches with an inspirational message for employees, and cemented closer relationships with suppliers/customers.

It goes without saying that trade unions, where they exist, are critical players. The worst thing to do is treat them in a disparaging manner because they can seriously disrupt your organisation with strikes and go-slows. Better to keep them updated on your plans in a way that does not compromise their or your independence.

Government and Parastatals

Every organisation has to play by the rules of the country in which it operates. So, as we mentioned earlier, government is another key player that demands careful analysis. But, of course, government can be broken down into tiers and departments, all of which can affect your game in one way or another. There's national/federal government, provincial/state government and local/municipal government. Then there's the Department of Finance, Department of Trade and Industry, etc. It is essential to distinguish between the government players who indirectly affect your game and those who have a direct bearing on it. With the latter, you need an ongoing relationship because they can make your game unplayable if they are unreasonable.

Parastatals too have a major impact on the game. If they don't perform in crucial areas of the game involving infrastructure and services, e.g. ports and airports, railways, electricity, water, etc., the private sector player can be up a gum tree without a ladder. In a democracy, no one should underestimate how significantly and quickly a newly elected government can change the rules. They can facilitate a game by, say, encouraging international investment or removing barriers to trade. At the same time, and in similar ways, they can inhibit the game by erecting new barriers or being heavy-handed with legislation. The government is invariably a hard player to deal with and with which to build a relationship. It doesn't consider itself a business in a free-market economy; nor should it, because its agenda is not driven by profit, but by wider societal considerations. A word of caution, though, which should never be forgotten: politicians play a political game and business CEOs would be wise to have a grasp of what it entails.

Communities and NGOs

Even though some managers never look over the fence, businesses do not operate in a spatial vacuum. They are located within a geographical space, the communities around which are genuine players. Yet communities are so often ignored. Whether the physical unit is a factory or a mine or the head office of a business that is the hub of economic activity in the area, a friendly milieu in which to operate is a major bonus – the opposite a major liability. Think of how much difference the attitude of the fans makes to a team's performance in a game of soccer. That's why 'home' games are easier to win than 'away' games. Home for business is the community around it; they are the ones who pack the stadium. Best to have them as your fans cheering you on than cheering for the other side.

Communities can *inter alia* be classified into local residents living in villages/towns/cities near company sites, residents associations, chambers of commerce, schools and universities, hospitals, small businesses that are potential suppliers, NGOs and special interest/pressure groups. Of course, the local municipal authorities feature in this list too. Corporate governance (running your company ethically), corporate social responsibility (caring about the environment, health and safety) and corporate social investment (financially supporting worthy local causes) are becoming hot potatoes, given the increasing trend to look at business as more than an economic actor. Communities are beginning to wield more influence because they know this and how their actions can enhance or damage a company's reputation. They can actively shift some of the local rules of the game and the way business has to be transacted to be seen as responsible. In industries such as mining and agriculture that can have a serious impact on the environment, communities are becoming key players in the game since their approval has to be sought before the project is undertaken.

Whether one is looking at communities or NGOs, there are two real questions to ask above all others: who is the champion who gets things done and what can we do to assist? Where there is no champion, proceed cautiously, particularly when large amounts of money are being requested. The fox would heartily agree with this sentiment, since foxes are prone to action, not words. They respect like-minded types.

Shareholders

Despite the triple bottom line (profit, planet, people) being very much the phrase in vogue for all the reasons we've just cited, scratch the surface of many CEOs and you'll find a single-mindedness about the company's financial performance and growth in share price underneath. Consequently the shareholders are indisputably important players – especially as senior management are usually shareholders themselves through the award of either options or shares. The key questions are:

- Where do your shareholders in general stand? Are they for you, against you, or neutral? (Naturally, the answer depends very much on your performance as management.)
- Do you have a major shareholder/shareholders and what is your relationship with them? (They can frustrate capital expenditure plans by voting against them at meetings of the Board or shareholders.)

- Are there divisions between your major shareholders? If so, what are you doing to resolve the matter?

There can be few things more frustrating than having activist shareholders who don't share your vision. It makes playing the game extremely difficult. Are you communicating well or badly with them? It makes all the difference. Some companies we have worked with have been in the unenviable position of having shareholders who are competitors in the game. This presents all sorts of difficulties in terms of resource allocation and conflict of interest. Members of the public who are shareholders tend to be skewed towards short-term results, be it dividends or increase in shareholder value. They also wield considerable power over a business because they can vote to boot directors off the Board. Sometimes, it's hard to concentrate when such a sword of Damocles is hovering over your head! This partially explains the flurry of private equity deals that have recently been concluded, whereby companies are delisted and put into private hands again – friendly private hands (to begin with at least).

Other Players

Other players to identify and examine your relationship with include:

- *Nonexecutive directors* where you are the executive team. They wield considerable power over strategy these days. They appoint the CEO.
- The *media*, who are influential in shaping and swaying the perceptions of all other players, notably consumers. Specific media players are your own media spokespersons and columnists and reporters who specialise in your field. Questions you should ask include:

- Do you have a sufficiently open relationship with key analysts and role players within the media, and do they really understand your game (so that the reporting of it is accurate)?
- In case of emergencies and crises, do you have contingency plans in place for the media, bearing in mind that reputations are won or lost in the way you handle the media in the first 24 hours?

- The *investment community*: Here we are specifically referring to the pension funds/mutual funds, the stockbrokers, commercial banks and merchant banks – all the players in the money game. Are you on good enough terms to get new money when you need it?
- *Industry associations/representative bodies:* These bodies are vital in promoting the interests of the industry as a whole – it's the one opportunity of validly co-operating with your competitors! They also act as the interface with that crucial player – the State. Are they doing the job properly?
- *Advertising agencies:* Technically, these fall under 'suppliers', but they are so important because they are responsible for promoting your brands. As we've already implied, the agencies should be on the inside in terms of strategy so that brand campaigns are harmonised with it.

When facilitating a strategic conversation, we find companies often run through this section quite quickly. To them, it simply involves listing and clarifying the players in the game. The reality is that a thorough understanding of who the players are, and how they can influence the game, will feed into many of your strategic decisions. You should therefore take the time carefully to analyse the players, not only because your company is just one player in the game, but also because the rest will determine to a large extent whether you win or lose in the end. Of course, there are superstars who rely on no one but themselves, but most of us need 'a little help from our friends' (to quote the Beatles).

We have done sessions with many other types of organisations besides businesses; but we don't have the space to list all the players for all the different sorts of organisations. Nevertheless, two entities merit further consideration. We have worked on scenarios for a number of countries, facilitating strategic conversations with a diverse array of stakeholders, e.g. China, South Africa, Zimbabwe, the Democratic Republic of Congo and Jamaica. Here the players look a bit different. Hence, we suggest that they are divided into internal players (those within the country) and external players (those operating on the global playing field). The list then looks something like this:

- Internal players including government, opposition parties, business and the private sector, NGOs and civil society, communities, etc. Obviously, a vital player is the individual citizenry and whether they are in harmony or at war with one another. Manchester United are a winning side because they are 'united'. Is your nation the same?
- External players including other countries, regional trading blocs, global bodies such as the WTO, UN and IMF and international business, etc. Does your nation get the support it should?

A strategic imperative for a country to succeed in the global arena is to have an aligned and winning team that can contribute something unique as an international player. It boils down to developing the requisite variety of expertise to match the natural strengths of the country concerned, while satisfying some niche in the demands of the world economy. Healthy growth in GDP does not necessarily depend on size of economy or population; but it does depend on how responsibly the economy is managed by the government. The Head of State and Finance Minister are principal players in this game; and they have the intelligence agencies to keep watch on the other players!

On the other end of the spectrum to a country lies the family unit. They have a totally different set of players in their game, even if there's no family business involved. In terms of internal players, just ask yourself:

- Does my family operate as a team; or are we totally dysfunctional, with each member going his or her separate way and positively acting against the interests of the others?
- If it's the latter, is there no room for a conversation at the kitchen table?

As far as external players are concerned, these can stretch all the way from relatives, friends and work colleagues to your banker, doctor, employer, teacher, what have you. As in business, you should examine all relevant players and make up your mind whose side they're on and where the imbalances in your life are! How the players at home interact with you, and you with them, will certainly shape your personal game and influence the direction of your destiny line. It's a known fact that Socrates did not get on well with his wife. Perhaps she didn't appreciate the Socratic method of dialogue. His sons, though, supported him during his trial.

Now for some of the comments made in our workshops on players. Any sporting legend will tell you how important this phase of the conversation is:

Our major shareholders are a problem. Two of the three are actually our competitors and one has no interest in our industry. Strategically we need to address this situation urgently.

CEO, BEVERAGE GROUP

Our biggest competitor is the pharmaceutical industry. They are supporting the antismoking lobby because it gives them the opportunity to promote their own products that claim to help smokers give up smoking. However, they wouldn't want us out of the game; otherwise there'd no longer be any demand for that particular product segment. It is an interesting balance in the game.

EXECUTIVE, MULTINATIONAL TOBACCO MANUFACTURER

In the healthcare industry, the general practitioner used to be the gatekeeper. This has shifted and now it is the medical aid companies that hold the cards in the industry. This is where we need to build our relationships.

EXECUTIVE, HEALTHCARE AND PHARMACEUTICAL COMPANY

Looking at the future of the nonferrous metals industry in the European Union, two players are key to our future, and they both pose a threat – China because its industrial policy is different to Europe and it considers itself an independent player at all times; and the developing world which, as our key raw material supplier, are currently 'for' us. However, they are all on a beneficiation drive and could therefore soon be competing directly with us.

OFFICIAL, EU BODY REPRESENTING THE NONFERROUS METALS INDUSTRY

The government has become a player that seems to be firmly against us. It no longer understands the pharmaceutical industry and the need to make profits to fund research on new drugs. Instead, it is creating great uncertainty by intervening inconsistently in our affairs. You feel like quitting the market.

EXECUTIVE, GLOBAL PHARMACEUTICAL COMPANY

International banks are now moving into our country and it is incredibly difficult to compete against them. Their resources and infrastructure are much bigger. We will need to marry a gorilla just to stay in the game or alternatively look towards niche markets.

CEO, INVESTMENT BANK

Our relationship with our current advertising agency is weak. We need to improve their strategic understanding of the shift in our business and the new products we are launching, or else we should consider a new agency. These guys are key players in our lives.

EXECUTIVE, INTERNATIONAL FOOD GROUP

We are a parastatal. Our main competition funnily enough comes from other parastatals. We are overlapping our offering of services to the market, with the result that we are now competing. Our mandates are not clear and abided by.

EXECUTIVE, SOUTH AFRICAN PARASTATAL

There are four players in our game: the West, because they supply the brands, the technologies and the lion's share of the overseas markets for our products; the developing world because they supply the natural resources and some of the markets; the Communist Party because it runs China; and the Chinese citizenry who are the hardest-working, most disciplined people you could hope for when growing the economy. A Chinese riddle explains why people work so hard here: "Why is porridge better than love? Nothing is better than love, but porridge is better than nothing."

CHINESE HONOURS STUDENT, BEIJING

We have three players of note in our game: our donors, our permanent staff and our volunteers. Of the three, donors are the most fickle, giving us more than we expect one year and nothing the next. We try and take this uncertainty out of play by widening the donor base.

CEO, NGO FOR CARE OF SICK CHILDREN

419

My restaurant is only as good as my suppliers. If they don't supply me with Grade A meat and vegetables, there's not much the kitchen can do about it. So I visit them often. RESTAURANT OWNER

Given that some of our chemical inputs come from unregulated overseas markets, we are under much greater pressure to vet the upstream players in the fertiliser game. One incident of food poisoning due to our sprays could put us permanently out of business.

EXECUTIVE, FERTILISER COMPANY

High net worth housewives are the most important players in our game. They are the ones we want to attract to our food shop and pamper once they're inside. So we have to offer products of the highest quality and with impeccable environmental credentials. Price is also a factor but it doesn't beat a tantalising selection on the shelves. We even throw in some really exotic items that you can't buy anywhere else in the city to tickle their fancy.

MANAGER, RETAIL FOOD OUTLET

For years we have supplied the charts used to log the performance of equipment in the factory and even the progress of patients in ICU. But the advent of the paperless society brought on by advances in IT has changed all that. Simply put, you can't be an analogue player in a digital game. MD, GRAPHICS COMPANY

The Chinese are the best team players in the world because of their spirit of collectivism. They can construct suburbs, roads and rail systems at a rate we just dream of in the West. Ideally, they should build 20 Londons in 10 years to get 200 million people off the land into new cities. That's a tall order even for them.

URBAN PLANNING CONSULTANT

7 Rules: What are the rules of the game that are likely to govern your strategy under all scenarios?

Could I climb to the highest place in Athens, I would lift my voice and proclaim: "Fellow citizens, why do you turn and scrape every stone to gather wealth, and take so little care of your children to whom one day you must relinquish it all?"
SOCRATES, as quoted by Plato

Every game has rules. They define the game and provide a framework through which, and within which, the game is played. Any parent of a teenager will know that the foregoing statements go completely against the grain of teenagers' thinking. Fortunately for teenagers, though, one of the rules in life is that they inherit what we have accumulated ahead of them (unless we go skiing – spending the kids' inheritance). We also say 'fortunately', because in the absence of rules there is only anarchy and, in an anarchical state, freedom is diminished. "Rules," teenagers might counter, "are meant to be broken." Well, if you break rules in sport, you are liable to get a red card and be sent off; break the rules in business and bankruptcy probably awaits you. However, unlike those in sport, the rules in business change over time and vary in space, i.e. from country to country and, even within the same industry, from culture to culture. Teenagers are wrong: the challenge is not so much to try and break the rules, but to try and understand them and keep up with the changes.

Changes in business rules are driven by the evolution of social, political and regulatory conditions surrounding the game. Technological advancement, disintermediation and intensifying competition can act as permanent change agents too. For our definition of business rules is wider than the normal legal definition. In our methodology, they also represent the 'driving forces' or 'predetermined elements' that we are fairly sure will govern the game under all scenarios. Like good strategy rules in and rules out certain activities relating to scope, good rules of the game rule in and rule out possible futures. It's of real value to narrow the 'cone of uncertainty' when looking forward. This the rules are supposed to do in a Socratic manner by eliminating all futures which contradict them. Having 360-degree vision is all very well, but in the context of formulating strategy such an approach merely serves to create confusion. It brings to mind the old saw: "Give me a one-armed economist, so he can't say on the one hand and on the other."

Written and Unwritten Rules

To make things even more challenging for the players within the game of business (as well as that of life), some of the rules are to a large degree subjective. They are, in a way, parameters as perceived and set by each player. Selection of the rules is, therefore, more of an art than a science. You must deduce the other players' rules as well. Expressed differently, just as there are rules that are determined by forces or factors outside of the control of any player, so there are rules decided by the participants themselves. The forces of nature and the principles of science are examples of the former, whereas laws laid down by governments and corporate codes emanating from the directorate are examples of the latter.

On a personal level, self-regulation (or self-control) is something we learn from our parents if they are wise enough to teach us. These rules, together with our DNA, help define the limits or bounds of acceptable behaviour. Such internal rules are supplemented by ones imposed externally by adults in authority over us. Flout the latter and we soon learn that punishment is the consequence. It is no different for a nation playing the global game or a company playing the business game. Both types of rules apply and lead to reward or punishment, depending on the level of compliance.

A further categorisation of rules can be into those that are written down in the statute books and those that appear nowhere. Seeking to identify the second type gives you the advantage, whether they happen to be your own rules to win or rules dictated by external changes in the business environment. They usually do not form a multitude. Just a few, unwritten rules can swing your destiny line either way in the short and longer term. It is therefore vitally important to uncover these rules faster than your competitor, especially in light of the dynamic nature of markets and the fact that changes in the rules fundamentally change the game. As we have often seen, many companies continue to play according to the 'old rules' only to realise too late that they are now defunct. This would be inconsequential if such misjudgments had minimal effect. But in the dog-eat-dog world of business, losing a competitive edge because of an unnoticed shift in the game can be the difference between success and complete failure.

Our line of argument is not far removed from the explanation given by the fox, that in his world "the rule is simple and all-encompassing: you do lunch, or be lunch. Straight competition. Survival of the fittest." The similarity with certain elements of human endeavour was not lost on Socrates, who replied, "In our world that rule exists in commerce and war." This would suggest that the only rule of the game in business is that of competition. To a large extent this is correct, but true strategic advantage does not hang on the single thread of a dogged determination to win. It comes from a more intricate understanding of the game. Indeed, Socrates then went on to say: "Nonetheless, I have spent all my philosophical hours on enquiring about another set of rules that should co-exist with the rule of competition. These relate to morality and goodness, but everybody has a different idea of what they are. I doubt whether we will ever reach agreement, but the quest must continue."

And then there are the ecological rules – three of them according to Captain Paul Wilson, co-founder of Greenpeace International in 1979:

- The rule of diversity. The strength of an ecosystem lies in the diversity of species within it. Weaken diversity and the entire system will be weakened and will ultimately collapse;
- The rule of interdependence. All of the species within an ecosystem are interdependent. We need each other;
- The rule of finite resources. There is a limit to growth because there is a limit to carrying capacity.

He quotes Albert Einstein who wrote: "If the bee disappeared off the surface of the globe, then man would have only four years of life left. No more bees, no more pollination, no more plants, no more animals, no more man." And then Wilson adds that around the world bees are disappearing in a crisis called Colony Collapse Disorder. So there you have it: the rule of the disappearing bumble bee. It gives us "just enough time to get a college degree to discover that everything you learned is relatively useless when sitting on the doorstep of global ecological annihilation". It kind of makes it a very important rule that trumps all others.

Based on Socrates' avenue of philosophical investigation and the sentiments of Paul Wilson, we have identified three kinds of rules that you need to inquire about in order to understand the DNA of the game you are in: namely, descriptive, normative and aspirational rules. They cover all aspects of engagement, whatever you do.

Descriptive Rules

These rules describe the game you're in and the constraints you are under. They include the laws of the land and the regulations or charters relating to your industry. In addition, cultural norms are among the unwritten, descriptive rules that need to be taken into account.

If complied with, the descriptive rules are what grant you a licence to operate in the country or countries in which your businesses are located. As explained earlier, these rules can differ from country to country, which emphasises the severe problems multinationals can run into when they think one optimal strategy exists for all markets. Strategies (and tactics) should differ from country to country according to the descriptive rules of the game within each country. For the corporate head office to strategise more effectively, the underlying business units or divisions operating in different end-markets should feed their strategies back into the corporate team instead of the typical top-down approach of the centre dispatching plans to operations in the end-markets, thereby constricting or confusing them.

How often have you heard from people in the field: "We are limited in our game because our corporate strategy dictates . . ."? Clearly the local companies cannot be extracting full value from their markets if such an attitude prevails. An example of this kind of miscalculation is found in the number of exceedingly well-managed South African companies – particularly in the retail sector – which have foundered in overseas markets. They just don't get it: the local rules are different, consumers are different, just about everything in the game is different. Another demonstration of this principle concerns companies looking to expand into Africa, with its extremely diverse set of national rules, traditions and cultures. Unless companies have a clear understanding of the descriptive rules of a specific country in which they wish to operate, they risk getting burned. There is no single set of rules for 'operating in Africa' outside of the fact the government is always a key player!

The second type of descriptive rules which need to be explored are those that set out the long-term forces governing your market or industry. They constitute the near-certain trends which you may have already uncovered in the opening section on context. They relate to demographics, technology, shifts in consumer preferences, changes in the competitive environment, in other words all the nonlegal, noncultural stuff which can be classified as 'givens' in the game in the foreseeable future.

Questions that need to be asked at this juncture in the conversation are the following:

- Have there recently been any changes in the descriptive rules that could seriously affect any part of your business?
- Are there likely to be further changes?
- What unique descriptive rules apply in the countries where you are doing business?

Normative Rules

These rules cover ethics, corporate governance, care for the environment, health, safety, general working conditions/wage levels of employees and corporate social investment, i.e. all the things your company *ought* to do. Normative rules should be universal for all countries (although in reality they are flouted in some). Should a company apply different standards in this sphere they risk their inconsistency being picked up by the media – society's moral watchdogs – and then being publicly castigated. Instances of this are the intense moral pressure put on global companies not to do business with South Africa during the days of apartheid and, today, pressure not to operate in the sad list of 'failed states' in the world which continue to violate human rights.

Normative rules are becoming more important in a world that is increasingly interconnected, has issues like global warming and boasts more socially aware consumers. Indeed, some normative rules are almost classified as licences to operate, along with the descriptive rules of the game. And yet for many companies driven solely by the quest for bottom-line profit, these normative rules are, at best, tolerated. This is a risky game to play because minimal compliance can encourage individual employees to flout the rules, often with dire consequences. Sometimes all it takes is a minor accident to turn the spotlight onto the entire operations of the company in question – something management would far rather do without!

Questions that should be asked around normative rules are the following:

- Is your track record in relation to safety, health and the environment improving or deteriorating?
- Are there any new normative rules in the pipeline in host countries?
- Have you got a 'code of conduct' and are all your employees aware of it?
- Is there anything you are doing which is in conflict with your professed values and how are you going to stop it?
- Is your level of corporate giving in line with international norms?
- Which countries in the world should you rule 'out of bounds' because their rules of the game clash with the (stricter) normative rules your company has laid down

for itself? This is a dilemma that faces a number of mining/exploration companies that want to operate in certain countries but cannot because of the skewed value systems of the regimes there. Such countries are then classified as 'no-go' areas – unless, to be cynical, the treasure trove is just too inviting. As they say in business: everything has a price!

An interesting shift in the interpretation of normative rules has come about through the activities of certain major players entering the global game, such as China. They have altered the global playing field in such a spectacular fashion that many Western players view the normative rules they currently apply as a real handicap to remaining competitive. For decades the global game was dominated by the West and underpinned by normative rules that reflected the prevailing cultures of the countries that made up the West. Now the game has moved East where the normative rules – despite their universality – are applied differently. The cost implications are huge and have already created considerable tension between the players. Ultimately, though, both sides will see the sense in levelling the playing field because no game is sustainable without a sufficient degree of harmony over what constitutes fair play.

To summarise, a company's values should be unpacked and explored at this point of the strategic conversation. They should be given teeth by conversion into the internal rules of the game that determine how the company operates. On every notice board should be displayed statements such as: 'We do not hire child labour'; 'We pay a living wage'. Think of the normative rules as the corporate equivalent of the Hippocratic oath, i.e. a private contract, not a legal one. Incidentally, Hippocrates – the most famous of Greek physicians – was a contemporary of Socrates.

Aspirational Rules

Aspirational rules are based on *your* understanding of the game and what *you* believe are the golden rules to *win* the game. They are usually few in number but critical for the sustainability of a company. For example, in the mining industry an aggressive acquisition policy and quality/longevity of ore deposits are rules to win – especially with the growth in global demand caused by China and India as they move through their respective industrial revolutions. Throw the scarcity – or the concept of scarcity – of commodities into the pot and mining suddenly becomes a very different game to what it used to be. The winners will be the companies that first instigated a modification to their aspirational rules in line with the new developments in the industry.

In many service industries, on the other hand, the rule to win revolves around the establishment of long-term relationships with clients based on trust and value for money. In one company that has just introduced a premium brand in its product range, the rule to win is to keep that brand separate and distinct from its other brands in the public consciousness. One of the better rules to win came from a bishop in the Anglican Church. "Entertainment rules even in the church," he said, adding for good measure, "pepping up our services is the only way to attract the youth back into our congregations."

In business, we all want to be world class and win the game. Some common aspirational rules seem to apply across the board, like the need for focus; strong branding and other forms of differentiation to make your product/service unique; benchmarking yourself against the other players and adopting global best practice; maintaining an entrepreneurial flair and a capacity for improvisation (difficult as a company gets bigger, but jazz concerts can still take place in large structures like the Royal Albert Hall in London); having a perpetual spirit of innovation (both incremental innovation to achieve operational excellence and radical innovation leading to a change in the game you play), and being fanatical about attracting, developing and retaining talented people.

Questions to be asked here include:

- What set of golden rules to win should your business adopt?
- How are you going to communicate these rules to all your staff?
- What key performance indicators should you introduce to measure progress towards complying with these rules?

American companies appear to be much better at articulating the golden rules than their counterparts in Europe or South Africa. Go into a McDonald's restaurant and every member of staff knows the rules on hygiene, service delivery and quality of product which will ultimately win them extra customers.

Conclusion

All the rules of the game – descriptive, normative, aspirational – should be taken into account when developing the options later on in the strategic conversation. In fact, the operational planning sessions that annually follow the strategic conversation should include tactics to lead you towards closer compliance with the rules. It has to be said that how you act in accordance with the rules is wholly within your control, whereas the rules themselves are part and parcel of the game.

Comments made when discussing the rules of the game comprise the following selection. Notice the diversity of games covered in terms of industries and countries:

In South Africa, the government has introduced black economic empowerment as a new rule. You have to have a BEE *in your bonnet or you must go and play the game elsewhere. Initially it was an aspirational rule but now we have charters which have turned it into a descriptive rule. The aspirational rule therefore is to go beyond the level of minimum compliance, and be a leader in the industry.*

CHAIRMAN, TRANSFORMATION COMMITTEE, MINING COMPANY

Even better to have bees with bonnets! FEMALE BANKER

In the property game in South Africa, a new descriptive rule is a higher set of qualifications for estate agents. Its intention is to lift the level of the game and to recognise that selling property should be conducted in a thoroughly professional manner.

CEO, LEADING PROPERTY GROUP

Our key aspirational rule is to understand our clients' needs and to build sustainable relationships with them.

EXECUTIVE, INVESTMENT BANK

An aspirational rule in supplying retail chains is to get the shelf space. Big suppliers use every means to get it, which gives them an unfair advantage. In addition, a descriptive rule some chains have introduced is that our products should carry the chain's brand name because they don't want customers to know that the produce is coming from different countries at different times of the year. It makes it difficult for us to differentiate ourselves. APPLE GROWER

Our diamonds are not forever! This is a rule of the game we must take cognisance of, seeing that our economy is reliant on diamonds. If we are to be viable in the future, we need to diversify into a whole range of other activities that have nothing to do with the diamond business. PUBLIC SERVANT, BOTSWANA

Europe adheres to high environmental standards and is committed to addressing issues around climate change. These normative rules put all European corporate players at risk by increasing their costs relative to companies in countries where the same conditions are not enforced. EXECUTIVE, EU INDUSTRIAL GROUP

The last man still standing in the resource game will win it!
EXECUTIVE, MULTINATIONAL MINING GROUP

Professionalism, ethics and integrity are the DNA *of our game. So all three types of your rules are in play all the time.*
SENIOR PARTNER, INTERNATIONAL LAW FIRM

There's a new rule of our game that can have potentially devastating consequences. As an account officer I am now accountable for any books I sign off, irrespective of who the client is. This means if there are any signs of wrongdoing on the part of the client, it is I who risks going to jail. So now our firm has to reassess our client base, be very sure of new clients, and understand their business well.
SENIOR PARTNER, LEADING ACCOUNTING FIRM

We have three rules of the game. The first is guanxi, which in Chinese means connections. You are who you know. We were the first networking nation. The second rule is one child per couple which has been in operation for nearly 30 years. This is to stop overpopulation. The third rule we call 'Chinese baseball'. In American baseball the rules never change, but in our baseball the rules change during the game. CHINESE ENTREPRENEUR, SHANGHAI

In the motor vehicle industry, economies of scale and cost competitiveness are the aspirational rules of the game for the mass manufacturers. However, as a premium brand, we realised we could not compete in this arena; so we decided that our aspirational rule should play on the social aspect of owning/driving a car. We differentiated ourselves by promoting a lifestyle experience. The car becomes the vehicle to achieve this.

SENIOR EXECUTIVE, EUROPEAN MOTOR VEHICLE MANUFACTURER

There are two rules of the game associated with holding a successful conference these days. The first is a prohibition on all overpaid foreign gurus. Most of them have passed their sell-by date in any case. The second is to avoid what we call the 'conference sluts' – speakers who will do anything to be put onto next year's list. I mean anything. CONFERENCE ORGANISER

We have six golden rules to clinch a transaction. All the sales people within our organisation know those rules and apply them. You watch! Before you've completed the facilitation of this session I'll have sold you a complete range of my company's cosmetics. And I'll have convinced you – even though you're a man – that you look much better with my products on than au naturel.

REGIONAL MANAGER, DIRECT MARKETING COSMETICS COMPANY

One of the rules of the game reigns supreme over all the others. Even if the rest of the grid goes down, never interrupt supplies to an aluminium smelter. The stuff freezes over before you can even say 'abracadabra'.

CUSTOMER CARE MANAGER, ELECTRICITY PARASTATAL

I quickly realised that a rule of the game in fighting organised crime in New York is to think like an Italian. That was no problem for me because I am of Italian descent. As a result we got serious crime down to levels last seen in the late 1940s. I hope you can do the same here in Johannesburg by putting yourself in the criminals' mind in order to defeat them. EX-MAYOR, NEW YORK

8 Uncertainties: What are the key uncertainties that could have a significant impact on the game and divert your course either positively or negatively?

Remember that there is nothing stable in human affairs; therefore avoid undue elation in prosperity, or undue depression in adversity.
SOCRATES

As the fox so wisely said to Socrates: "Life can surprise you and it is better to be aware of the surprises in advance or have a very fast reaction time if they really do come out of the blue."

In business, the saying goes that 60 per cent of a company's bottom-line profit comes from how quickly and effectively it responds to things outside of its control. Obviously, the basic idea of the business has to be well thought through and profitable; but it's how the idea is modified in light of changing market conditions that separates the sheep from the goats. For example, in the automobile industry Toyota is ahead of the game with its hybrid petrol/electric car called the Prius. It recognised before its competitors that people's attitude towards conservation of the environment has grown much stronger. And this was before *An Inconvenient Truth* starring Al Gore! Speed of response is the essence of competitive advantage in today's business world. Failure to respond quickly and effectively means that, at best, a company will be continually playing catch-up or, at worst, soon find itself knocked out of the game.

Thus a question we often ask of a company's executive team is the following: "Does your company have a sufficient degree of flexibility in its decision-making process to adapt quickly enough to significant changes in its circumstances?" We then follow this up with what is, in reality, a rhetorical question: "If your company could somehow foresee these changes, surely it would have an even greater competitive advantage?" Yet conventional strategic thinking often takes place around the assumption that the future is unknown and unknowable; or – the exact opposite – that with enough experts it can be captured accurately in a forecast.

The Wisdom of Wack

Pierre Wack, whom we have already mentioned in this book, had a different view. It was somewhere between these two extremes. He believed that the future could be known, albeit with vagueness and difficulty, if it was approached with a 'sufficiently searching gaze'. Think of peering intently ahead in a fog and, by interpreting the indistinct shapes, you can make out what particular objects they are. He suggested that if we were to highlight the key uncertainties that may impact on us in the future, the logic of working through the consequences of these events or circumstances would allow for more clarity of thought, and create a natural instinct for future possibilities. He honed the technique by going East to visit Indian gurus, spending long periods of time studying their art of meditation and how they contemplated the world around them. He would have had a fascinating debate with Socrates, because intuitive inference arising from meditating on the possibilities is not as satisfactory or as precise as rational deduction, but it is the most appropriate tool when dealing with the future.

Here's an example of what Wack was trying to get at. Someone we know was driving down the main road in a suburb of Cape Town when she heard the sound of firecrackers and looked out of the side window to see puffs of smoke accompanying the sound. She thought how odd it was to mount a firework display in the middle of the pavement. Then she saw

435

four men running down the street to a getaway vehicle and realised that she was in the middle of a gun fight. She quickly turned the corner into a side road, having remembered the licence number of the vehicle that sped away. She wrote it down and handed it to the police who were by then at the scene of the crime. "What value would a scenario planner have added?" you might ask. The answer is that, by having such a person play the possibility in advance to her, she would have *immediately* recognised the danger of being hit by a stray bullet and taken evasive action a split second sooner. As it happened, it didn't matter and, to her great credit, she had the presence of mind to get the licence number. But things could have turned out differently. It's all about reading the signs correctly and putting an event into its proper context. That needs practice.

This explains why, when conducting a strategic conversation, we feel it is vital to examine key uncertainties, i.e. those uncertainties that will have a major impact on the business and affect the outcome of the game. This means that if and when a key uncertainty plays out it has already been considered; its potential impact has been evaluated; options and decisions have been identified to address the effects, and the necessary resources are allocated almost immediately to implement those decisions. The result? The very real chance of maintaining a proactive and influential position in the game. The alternative? Continually operating in a mode of crisis management, with short-term tactical skills to keep the boat in an upright position while negotiating the rapids.

Socrates makes an important point about uncertainty, which links into our argument, when he mentions: "What you are does not determine what you will be." The reality is that as uncertainties unfold they will affect us – just as we will affect them – and we, and the outcome of the uncertainties, will change accordingly. If we can consider these uncertainties from different perspectives and perhaps play them out in our minds or conversation, we may be empowered enough to move our destiny line in a direction which we would prefer above all others. As the Chinese say: "Every crisis is an opportunity." Remember, though, there are 'known unknowns' – things you know you don't know – and 'unknown unknowns' – things you don't know you don't know and never can prepare yourself for. The latter have to be handled with a mixture of gut feeling and instant reasoning.

The Radar Screen

When considering key uncertainties, it is important for one to prioritise their 'key-ness' by plotting them on the business equivalent of a radar screen. Such a screen serves as a continual frame of reference to assess whether or not an uncertainty is indeed turning into a reality and, if so, whether proper contingency plans have been put in place to mitigate the consequences or adapt to them.

One of our favourite quotes in this regard comes from A A Milne's *The House at Pooh Corner*, that famous children's book full of adult wisdom. Piglet asks Pooh a very pressing question whilst they are in the Hundred Acre Wood during a roaring gale: "Supposing a tree fell down Pooh, when we were underneath it?" After careful thought Pooh replies, "Supposing it didn't." Piglet is comforted by this. Clearly Piglet has the uncertainty on his radar screen whereas Pooh doesn't!

So how does a company capture possible changes in the environment and itself on a radar screen, and have an idea of the consequences should they materialise? We use two axes on a piece of graph paper, the vertical one representing the probability of an event and the horizontal one its potential impact. 'Blips' close to the origin (bottom left) are improbable and are considered to have a relatively low potential impact. They can hardly be described as 'key uncertainties' at this point in time. 'Blips' on the top right of the paper are quite probable and could have a major impact. Blips elsewhere on the chart are somewhere in between on both counts. We like to call the result a 'PI chart' because we are measuring probability and impact. Of course, as a company proceeds into the future like a battleship slicing through the ocean, the executive team can – like the officers on the bridge – review the chart to see whether any of the blips have moved and become more dominant in relation to the company's future. Sometimes a key uncertainty can become so 'certain' that it converts into a rule of the game.

Types of Uncertainties

Our primary classification of key uncertainties is into three types:

- *Shock events* such as a stock market meltdown, a flu epidemic or the disruption of oil supplies due to a terrorist attack; or, closer to home, an unwelcome takeover bid for your company;
- *Gradual threats* such as global warming or HIV/AIDS (the human species is not programmed to handle these as effectively as shock events, preferring fight-or-flight situations instead); and,
- *Volatile parameters* that are critical to the business such as swings in commodity prices, exchange rates or interest rates.

Superimposed on these three types of uncertainties are the areas from which they can emanate. External uncertainties can play out in the global, national or local arenas, and they can

438

be financial, political, social, technological, legal or environmental. They can arise because of shifts in the market that
make your industry obsolete or uncompetitive (think of how
many games become unplayable and how many new ones
open up as nations move from a manufacturing-based to a
service-based economy). They can relate to excessive dependence on a single customer; or they can stem from competitor
strategies. A dramatic example of the uncertainties we have
in mind is that San Francisco and Japanese businesses face
the constant threat of an earthquake. We would describe it as
an 'environmental shock event'. A shock event but of a man-
made kind is an electricity black-out. They are happening more
often these days as infrastructure around the world ages and
does not get replaced. Of course the contingency plan is buying your own generator! The development of blog sites on
the internet, the advent of 24-hour TV news channels and the
capabilities of the latest PCs/cellphones to capture any type
of data constitute a gradual technological or market-related
threat to the printed newspaper industry.

In addition, smaller companies may have *internal* uncertainties relating to CEO succession, lack of controls in the back
office, shortage of technically qualified staff or other factors.
Some of these should be picked up by the internal or external
auditors if they are doing their job properly, since risk evaluation forms an essential part of their service offering.

Moreover, risk evaluation shouldn't just be seen in the narrow context of health and safety and the financial accounts.
Actually, risk evaluation is about understanding the systemic
risks to the business and how they may be interconnected,
and overlap with one another. For instance, an uncertainty in
consumer preferences can influence or lead to an advancement
in technology which makes another technology or process
obsolete. Political and economic uncertainties are usually
interrelated. Hence, all uncertainties need to be identified,

unpacked, debated and discussed before they can be correctly plotted on the radar screen. However, given the scope of key uncertainties that could affect a company, especially a large one, if every uncertainty was played out in a set of scenarios it would lead to analysis paralysis. By logically focusing on those with the highest potential impact (whatever their level of probability), it is possible for management to see where the real strategic issues lie and paint the scenarios accordingly. One point bears repeating: whereas external uncertainties are normally beyond your control, your response to alleviate the impact of these uncertainties *is* within your control and constitutes tactics.

Among the sub-questions that should be asked are the following:

- Is the uncertainty something you can tolerate or does it make the game unplayable? For example, Russian roulette for most people is an unplayable game because the possible downside of oblivion, by a bullet through the head, is too much to bear. It is an unacceptable risk. Is there a chance that in your game your company can experience oblivion, in which case it might be best to change the game now?
- What are the positive as well as the negative consequences for you if an uncertainty materialises into actual fact? Remember that many uncertainties affect all players equally, and the quality of your response can elevate your position in the game.
- What shock events, if any, would put you out of business altogether? Is there any probability whatsoever of an occurrence of any of these events? If so, what are the signs you should watch for, and what will you do about it if the signs start blinking red?
- In terms of gradual threats, is the cost of adapting to the

threat more or less than the cost of taking action to mitigate it or even eliminate it?

■ What is the current range of values from highest to lowest that you think is possible for a volatile parameter (e.g. the future price of a commodity)? When you have previously experienced such ranges, has the actual value of the parameter in the period specified ever risen above or fallen below the estimated range? (If it has, you'd better widen your current range.)

Here are some of the key uncertainties raised in our strategic exercises. The list is quite long because we want to show you how much the conversation changes gear at this stage. Imagination takes flight!

We have a mandate from the national government to replace shacks with proper housing units throughout the country by 2014. Ironically, it is also a key uncertainty as we have not yet formulated a clear strategy nor mustered the resources to achieve this.

PROVINCIAL GOVERNMENT SPOKESPERSON ON HOUSING, SOUTH AFRICA

A worrying uncertainty we face is energy supply from Russia as well as future access to raw materials (mainly from Africa).

PARTICIPANT, EUROMETAUX WORKSHOP ON NONFERROUS METALS

Being in the wine industry, one of the longer-term uncertainties we have to factor into our plans is climate change or, at the very least, a shift in rainfall patterns. Another uncertainty for us, because we are a global player, is the image of South Africa as a wine-producing nation around the world. MANAGER, WINE ESTATE

One of our major uncertainties is future government policy and pronouncements on obesity. Will it be treated like smoking?

EXECUTIVE, GLOBAL FROZEN FOOD MANUFACTURER

441

The future relationship of China with us and the rest of Africa is a key uncertainty, since China is emerging as the largest bidder for resources and land on the continent. In fact, you could say that Africa is up for sale; and we could all go under the Chinese hammer (never mind the sickle) in a scenario called 'Going, Going, Gone'.

PARTICIPANT, SCENARIO WORKSHOP ON SOUTH AFRICA

Given the level of economic hardship in Zimbabwe, is widespread internal unrest an uncertainty? I am not sure, because people have an incredible capacity to suffer in silence there. Nevertheless, everybody has a tipping point.

PARTICIPANT, SCENARIO WORKSHOP ON ZIMBABWE

We have always talked of 'above-the-line' and 'below-the-line' activities in the advertising industry. The former relate to the formulation of TV, radio or print ads and the latter to packaging, event promotion and point-of-purchase display. Now that we live in such a fragmented world where people are distracted by so many choices, is such a distinction relevant? This is creating great uncertainty among agencies about what their core functions are.

EXECUTIVE, ADVERTISING AGENCY

Political factors and traditional forms of land ownership in Africa sometimes make the securing of development rights and land tenure a hazardous business. In other words, property rights can be a key uncertainty, which is pretty fundamental to the success of any transaction. CEO, LEADING PROPERTY DEVELOPMENT GROUP

The price of gold is, without a doubt, our main uncertainty. In terms of what makes it move, it's like a guard's van. You never know which freight train it's going to be hitched to next. That's what makes it such an exasperating, yet alluring metal. It does the exact opposite of what you would normally expect it to do.

MARKETING DIRECTOR, GOLD-MINING COMPANY

There has been a dramatic shift in our industry towards greater uncertainty. The impact of China and India, especially if they start dumping products, the upsurge in popularity of generics and the regulatory behaviour of governments are all new ingredients in the broth. The result could damage our health!

CEO, GLOBAL HEALTHCARE COMPANY

In the legal industry, the ability to retain talent has become a key uncertainty, especially in light of the new rule of the game in South Africa – black economic empowerment. Black lawyers are in huge demand from all quarters. SENIOR PARTNER, LEADING LAW FIRM

Our competitiveness in the future has become our greatest uncertainty. New prohibitive regulation, shifting market perception and counterfeit cigarette sales in some of our markets all feed into our future ability to compete.

CFO, LEADING INTERNATIONAL TOBACCO COMPANY –
EUROPEAN END-MARKET

Our key uncertainty revolves around the tactics which our biggest competitor in the US will employ to reduce our market share. They go beyond the reasonable. MANAGER, GLOBAL BREWING COMPANY

We've discovered all the 'big easies' – easy to find, easy to mine, easy to treat deposits. Now we're into the 'big toughies' – tough ore bodies in tough countries. It's a rule of the game that you can't move an ore body, so any ore body has associated with it all the uncertainties that go with the country in which it is located.

CEO, GLOBAL MINING COMPANY

The future role of synthetic diamonds is a key uncertainty in my business. Will they become the equivalent of cultured pearls and start displacing natural gems? Nobody knows.

OWNER, DIAMOND JEWELLERY MANUFACTURER

443

When we enter the 21st century in ten years' time, fundamental Islam will be the definitive uncertainty facing the West. The extent of its influence and ultimate consequences are unknown. Should the spreading of an idea turn into a war of beliefs, a nuclear jihad *is possible.*   MIDDLE EASTERN EXPERT, GLOBAL SCENARIO SESSION, SEPTEMBER 1990

In June 2001, when you published an open letter to George Bush citing a massive terrorist strike on a Western city as his primary threat, why was nobody in the security agencies listening to you? I know you were referring to nukes, but you were spot on in highlighting the enhanced capability of international terrorist organisations to hit the West on Western soil. I guess that's what the role of scenario planners is – to shake people's trees and rid them of deadly misperceptions. After all, there was the tip-off (which was ignored at the time) of Arabs learning to take off but not land at one American flying school. You'd have provided a new slant to this information which might have resulted in it being processed differently.

DEFENCE INDUSTRY ANALYST

In terms of sustainable development and preserving the global environment, the key uncertainty is not so much the world's total population growth but rather how many more people are going to enjoy an American lifestyle now that China and India are experiencing phenomenal economic growth. At present the figure is 900 million out of 6.5 billion; but the number could easily double in the next ten years.   CLIMATE-CHANGE EXPERT, SCENARIO SESSION, LONDON

We have six major uncertainties that could derail the Chinese game. The first is an American recession because we export so much to America. The second is a general rise in international terrorism and turmoil which could disrupt our supply lines and marketing channels. The third is a growing scarcity of raw materials and rising commodity prices created by our own growth in demand as well as

India's. The fourth is increasing social unrest in China should the economy start slowing down. The fifth is the rate of environmental degradation in China itself limiting our prospects, and the sixth is global warming which would necessitate a movement away from the one resource we have – coal.   CHINESE STRATEGIST, BEIJING

A bubble is only a bubble when it is no longer a bubble. Otherwise it is a trend. Such is the uncertainty that always plagues my game.

PARTNER, STOCKBROKING FIRM

If a change in the jet stream caused by global warming was responsible for the recent flooding in England, the unprecedented could become precedented or, in your terminology, a wild card could turn into a rule of the game. Think of the consequences for households in the absence of enhanced flood barriers. We would become the 'Isle of Mud'.   OFFICIAL, ENVIRONMENTAL AGENCY, UK

As America's gambling capital, uncertainty is embedded in our way of life. But if the summers here get any hotter, the tourists will go elsewhere. And that, my friend, is the end of the game.

DELEGATE, TRAVEL CONFERENCE, LAS VEGAS

I've never attended a strategy session where the 'black swan' which lurks in the shadow of the rushes has been so convincingly revealed. By black swan I mean the dark future – full of slit-wrist uncertainties – that can capture you unawares and take you down. Not that I've got anything against the white swans swimming gracefully down the centre of the river. It's just that we all see them coming, because it's how we want the future to pan out.

SITE SUPERVISOR, CONSTRUCTION COMPANY

Life is so uncertain here, I constantly feel like an impala at the waterhole.

PARTICIPANT, CRIME-PREVENTION WORKSHOP, JOHANNESBURG

Scenarios: On your gameboard, what are the possible scenarios and where would you position yourself in relation to them now?

I realised that it was not by wisdom that poets write their poetry, but by a kind of nature or inspiration, such as you find in seers and prophets; for these also say many beautiful things, but do not know anything of what they say.
SOCRATES, as quoted by Plato in *Apology*

When replying to the fox's question as to where his destiny would lead him, Socrates responded: "That depends on the outcome of the trial. I could be found not guilty of any crime and continue to debate issues that intrigue me. I could spend the rest of my life in prison. I could be put to death. Three scenarios for which there will be one outcome, but I must be prepared for all three."

Every game we play, whether in life or business, will more than likely have a potential set of different outcomes. These possible outcomes are based on the key uncertainties that play into the game we are in. We call these outcomes 'scenarios', and, in keeping with the metaphor of the game, these scenarios interconnect to form a scenario gameboard. At any time and point in the game we are positioned somewhere on the gameboard, specifically in one of the scenarios. Depending on the external forces that drive the game and on how we choose to play the game, we can move on the gameboard to where we want to be; maintain our position; or, if we allow it, be moved by other players or forces to a less desirable position. Scenarios offer multiple pathways to the future – both good and bad.

Instead of 'outcomes', scenarios are also often defined as different 'plausible future environments'. For example, when Socrates questioned the fox about his future destiny line, and what possibilities and consequences that destiny line might present, the fox replied: "My possibilities are to take my wife and travel north, south, east or west after this conversation. Each path will contain its own string of events and consequences, which will become part of my destiny line." The fox was simply alluding to a set of scenarios that could play out as a result of his interaction with other animals (particularly those that represented a threat) as well as the state of the forest around him. This interplay could still lead the fox to a complex array of possible outcomes, or plausible future environments. For instance, he could start by 'zigging' to the north and then 'zagging' back south if a river blocked his progress.

The Eyes and Ears

For us, of course, given the intense convolution of human emotions and patterns of decision-making, the complexity of outcomes is magnified, and cannot be simplified or ignored, as is often the case in traditional strategy development where a strategy is established, a course is plotted, tracks are laid and the command given to move forward. Ordinary life is anything but rational in the sense of everyday events and actions being propelled by pure reason. Passion is an element of most scenarios, whether we're talking nations, companies or individuals. It takes more than deduction to figure out the possibilities in a non-Platonic world. Moreover, because every scenario is shaped by the interplay between the players, as well as between the players and the environment, the potential for change is high. Such an interplay demands that an examination of oneself and the environment remains an ongoing exercise. We believe this can be achieved by diligently questioning assumptions and debating issues through our conversation model, and referring back to it at any time.

Scenarios help to depict what future environments will look

like, as well as define the capabilities required in order to succeed in any scenario. That's where you hold the mirror up to yourself to see if you do indeed possess those capabilities – and, if not, what you are going to do about it. Scenarios are a crucial tool in the decision-making process in that they help set out the best options for a successful course into the future in the face of significant uncertainty. This may explain why scenarios should be the core of any strategic conversation. They help crystallise the group's strategic thinking and, more often than not, provide the group with an 'aha' moment that acts as an accelerant to the pace and direction of the strategic thinking. Scenarios often allow people to *re-perceive* the future and re-contextualise it, rather than just fixate on a part of it as a predetermined focus point, which is the trend in general strategic thinking. Scenarios provide not only a clearer definition as to where we would like to be in a future state, but also an insight into the paths we do *not* want to follow because the outcome will turn out to be negative for us.

Building and developing scenarios is not an exact science. They are instead a way of tapping into and developing our more intuitive and creative thinking, which is then manifested through the logic and plausibility of each scenario. In essence, scenarios open our thinking and provide us with a window of insight into our future (and into ourselves); and with insight comes clarity of choice. Because we tend to view things through a lens determined by our own DNA, different people have different perceptions of an event. The point of scenarios is to provide a shared window of insight and allow different people to debate the world as it really is – in a more transparent framework – instead of talking past each other as a result of perceiving the world through their individual lenses. Ultimately, a decision will also be enhanced by the fact that scenarios provide a powerful context for our choice, since we never play a game alone or out of the context created by our environment.

Hence, in a group situation, it is wise to form a consensus on which scenario is in play before deciding about the action to be taken. You may still be collectively wrong, but at least you will have been consistent.

Through constant questioning, Socratic dialogue allows us to construct the logic of a scenario via the unveiling of the interplay between cause and effect: if this were to happen, what would be the result and how would the other players react? As already mentioned, the power of doing this also builds a refined awareness of both our capabilities and the environment within which we operate. This is a skill that, as individuals and organisations, we require if we are to observe and anticipate changes, synthesise information around us and give it meaning. The scenarios may never play out in the exact form in which they were constructed, but the very process of constructing the scenarios provides an awareness of our environment that would otherwise have been missed through standard planning techniques. Consequently, this awareness becomes an in-built quality of the organisation, giving it eyes and ears it never had before. Perceptions of new data can be converted into knowledge, i.e. meaningful information in context, at a faster rate with a scenario gameboard than without it.

Finally, at the risk of overplaying the importance of their construction in our strategic thinking process, scenarios also help us develop longer-term perspectives. This is an essential tool for strategy, and yet something that is often glossed over because, naturally, human thinking is more comfortable in the short-term arena. This means that when most organisations are developing strategies for the future (the next 5-10 years), their thinking more often than not remains in the current reality, with short-term actions generally being the desired outcomes. This can lead to a blurred big picture of the 'what's it all about?' kind – or, as one Enron employee put it, "why?". Confusion reigns within the company as management run around the playing field issuing instructions amounting to short-term tactics. Meanwhile the team has no clarity as to where the goalposts are positioned! By using scenarios, however, the long-term purpose of the business can be articulated in a positive story, which can then be cascaded throughout the organisation and serve as a motivational tool.

The Scenario Gameboard

A common misapprehension is that, for scenarios to be effective, they need to be highly detailed and go through a process of many iterations involving lots of workshops. This is not true. If scenarios are overcomplicated, they can lose their appeal and thus their usefulness. What must be done is to assure a degree of differentiation between the scenarios such that each of them registers clearly in the minds of the participants. The last thing you want is someone saying: "I can't see the difference between your first and your third scenarios." When facilitating strategic conversations, we therefore continue with the game analogy and design a one-page *scenario gameboard* – like any other gameboard such as that used in Monopoly. It features catchy and meaningful names that have been suggested and embraced by the participants. These gameboards then become platforms for understanding the future. Obviously, for each scenario displayed on the gameboard, a text or a series of bullet points accompanies it.

Each gameboard is developed by considering a list of principal variables that can affect the topic chosen for the scenarios, be it the future possibilities for the world economy, for the industry you're in, or for your organisation. The two pivotal uncertainties that will have the most influence on the game, or impact on the organisation, are then selected. It is these two pivotal uncertainties that, represented as intersecting axes, create the framework for the gameboard: a 2 x 2 matrix containing four scenarios, namely a best-case scenario, a worst-case scenario and two intermediate scenarios. In game parlance, these would respectively be called a 'win' scenario, a 'loss' scenario and two 'draw' scenarios. Developing worst-case (or loss) scenarios is an essential part of understanding the future, as it provides a greater consciousness of the signs indicating impending danger. There is also as much strategic insight to be gained in discussing ways of steering the organisation away from worst-case scenarios as there is in pointing the helm towards the desirable one.

The variables for constructing a gameboard may both be external, i.e. outside of the control of the organisation (such as that for the global geopolitical or national economic game); or they may consist of one largely outside of and one largely inside the control of the organisation, e.g. having the state of the market as the horizontal axis and the competitiveness of the organisation – relative to its competitors – as the vertical axis. This is possibly the most popular matrix we have used for businesses. There is an alternative business gameboard, where an organisation can plot a possible change in strategic direction on one axis and competitiveness on the other, in which case both axes are pretty much within its control. This gameboard is particularly useful when a change in strategic direction is contemplated. Whichever model of gameboard is used, as long as the variables represent the parameters by which you want to measure the environment or yourself or both, you'll have a lot of fun pinpointing your current position on the board. By considering two gameboards – the international economic and specific business ones – the interdependencies and connectedness between the two provide a strong overall picture of the whole game. It always does an organisation good to put its own strategic path within the context of the bigger game.

To illustrate the method of construction of these different

models of gameboards, we have developed three different examples: an international, a national and a business
gameboard.

The Global Gameboard

The best example we can give of the first type of matrix (where
both variables are external) is the one we are currently using
to demonstrate the different possibilities for the future state
of the world, politically and economically. The vertical axis
relates to whether globalisation continues to be the grand,
unifying force it is, or whether the world enters an era of
fragmentation driven by national and religious rivalries. The
horizontal axis is simply based on the global economic growth
rate and whether (on the right) it can be sustained at over
5 per cent per annum; or whether (on the left) it falls back
into the zero to 3 per cent range. The middle part of the gameboard represents a rate somewhere between 3 and 5 per cent.

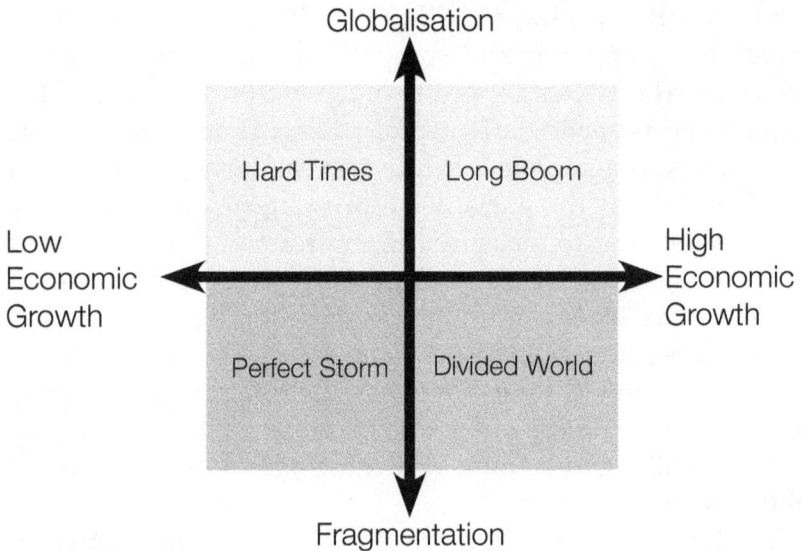

Globalisation

Hard Times   Long Boom

Low   High
Economic   Economic
Growth   Growth

Perfect Storm   Divided World

Fragmentation

Going clockwise from the top right, we have the following scenarios:

Long Boom

The world was located in this scenario for most of the 1990s, and remained so in the opening years of the new century. The *Long Boom* is driven by the conversion of most countries to free-market economics and the spectacular rise of China and India. The party continues, with inflation and interest rates remaining low, the Chinese and Indian economies continuing to defy gravity and stock markets continuing to boom. The world still has conflict zones, but the impact of these is completely overridden by the unstoppable force of globalisation. One day either global warming, a growing scarcity of raw materials, the latter causing a general rise in inflation rates, or a new global health epidemic could moderate the boom.

A *Long Boom* scenario envisages the centre of gravity of the world economy moving East, meaning that Western institutions like the IMF and World Bank will have to revise their mode of operation. The scenario also brings other players onto the global playing field, such as Africa. African countries have many of the raw materials required for China and India's growth. The focus on Africa comes from these two countries as well as companies whose purpose is to supply them. This in turn implies that African nations will have more influence to negotiate their long-term future so that it comes to pass in a sustainable manner. Nevertheless, they need to build the necessary negotiating skills to compel the counterparties to add value to the raw materials *before* they leave the national borders. With this one proviso, *African Sunrise* – the continent's equivalent to the global *Long Boom* scenario – becomes a distinct possibility. An incidental consequence of the *Long Boom* is that the G8 will eventually become the G10 with the addition of China and India as new members.

Divided World

The world develops into a more hostile place as regional conflicts intensify and trading spats/cases of protectionism multiply. In this scenario, the anti-globalisation lobby grows stronger while an increasing number of countries reject the 'Washington consensus', revert to old-style Socialist policies (some in South America) and become more nationalistic about the resources they possess (Russia). Nevertheless, just as no terrorist incident or war in the recent past has been a show stopper (not even 9/11), the global economy shrugs off all these problems because of the sheer momentum caused by the two most populous nations on earth simultaneously going through an industrial revolution. Whereas in the *Long Boom* companies can invest virtually anywhere in the world because the tide is rising everywhere, they have to be more circumspect in *Divided World* because of the emergence of more 'failed states'.

Perfect Storm

As the name suggests, this scenario represents a confluence of negative events in both the political and economic arenas, which could lead to a huge change in the fortunes of the world. It is a reprise of the 'roaring' 1920s, which was followed by the depression of the 1930s and the rise of Nazi Germany. The party ends just as spectacularly – only the script and the actors are different. Potential triggers could be nuclear terrorism in a Western city, a major war between Iran and Israel/the West over its nuclear programme, a new Cold War as Russia reverts to authoritarianism, or a financial meltdown in China followed by widespread unrest. Recovery from this scenario proves to be agonisingly slow, as business confidence has to be rebuilt from scratch. Remember that leading Wall Street stocks only recovered their peak 1929 value over 25 years later (having shed 89 per cent by 1932). It was a 'long drop'!

This is a scenario of conventional global recession, probably initiated by a US economic downturn and the knock-on effect it has on the other economies. India and China are not spared, as the interdependencies created by globalisation and international trade turn against them. Asset prices (property and equities), the improvement of which has over recent years allowed consumers to borrow more to spend, suddenly reverse. The downward spiral is reinforced when commodity prices plummet, except for gold that does well in light of the uncertainties around paper currencies and paper assets. Eventually the blood-letting ends, green shoots start springing up in the burnt landscape and a recovery gets under way, which returns the world to the top right-hand quadrant. The length of the recession is relatively short, i.e. it is more like a 'V' than a 'U', but the depth of the 'V' is unknown. The crucial difference between *Hard Times* and *Perfect Storm* is that globalisation remains intact in the former scenario, while it is seriously compromised by political and military events in the latter one. The rebound in the second case therefore takes much longer.

These descriptions or 'short stories' paint a brief picture of the suite of scenarios, and allude to their different characteristics. As we've already intimated, the differences can also be expressed in a series of bullet points. However, it must be remembered that the object of interest of the scenarios – in this case the world economy – is not static. Every news bulletin means a dynamic reappraisal of the situation as events unfold; and because the name of the game in business is to acquire knowledge and truth faster than your competitor, any business that notices a shift in the commercial environment before its competitors do will always have the upper hand. The secret is to know what signs, or leading indicators, to look for that herald a shift in the game, or more fundamentally announce that you are about to cross into a different part of the game-board (i.e. enter a new scenario). We have registered some of the indicators in the narrative of our international scenarios.

Equally important is to work out in advance what the consequences of the new scenarios are for your strategy, so you can immediately exercise other options if need be. Moreover, over time the scenarios themselves will lose relevancy if they are not updated. So even the gameboard is dynamic!

National Gameboard

For a country, the two pivotal uncertainties are its competitive-ness on the global playing field as well as, from an internal perspective, the state of its society, i.e. whether it is charac-terised by harmony or conflict.

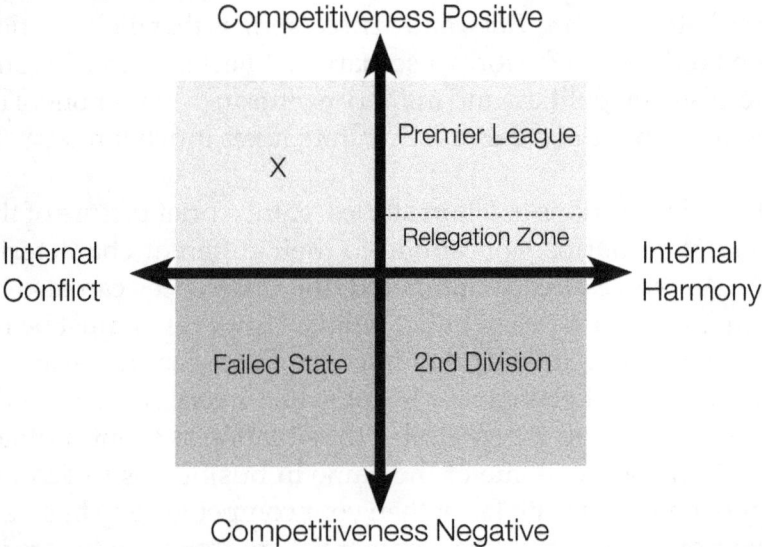

You will note that the top left-hand quadrant of the gameboard has been marked with an 'X'. It signifies that we rule out this scenario altogether on the grounds that it is not sustainable.

A country cannot be riven by internal conflict and still be competitive. Hence, there remain three scenarios and again we start in the upper right-hand corner:

Premier League

To be in the *Premier League* scenario, a country should enjoy a high level of social harmony and act as a cohesive team. The economy is 'inclusive', with a low unemployment rate and acceptable income differences between the classes. At the same time, the country is competitive because it possesses the attributes of a 'winning nation' which include quality education; a strong working ethic; a high savings rate and an adequate infrastructure to cope with economic expansion. It positions itself as an export-oriented global player by exploiting its strengths to differentiate itself from other nations. It develops a dual-logic economy where world-class global businesses combine with a thriving small business sector to create synergies between the two. Tax rates are competitive, the environment for foreign direct investment is attractive and above all government is efficient (particularly regarding health services).

Countries fall into the 'Relegation Zone' when they decline in competitiveness for whatever reason. This is a dangerous area to be in, because relegation means that the country will no longer enjoy the privileges of being a member of the top league – and it's very hard to get back into it. The *Long Boom* scenario has conferred Premier League status on quite a few developing countries – particularly resource-rich ones – that have taken advantage of the positive economic climate.

2nd Division

This scenario is for countries that are poor but peaceful. They remain *2nd Division* players either because they have no ambition to move up to the *Premier League*, or they are quite bereft of mineral resources, or nature is harsh in terms of climate or soil. But they get by and, the human spirit being what it is, the people lead relatively contented lives. The *2nd Division* also contains ex-Premier League nations that once were rich but whose income per head has declined for any number of reasons including bad leadership. They don't wield much influence in global affairs and seldom obtain anything prestigious like a seat on the UN Security Council. They may even possess some of the attributes of a 'winning nation', but somehow they simply cannot get their entire act together.

Failed State

This scenario is characterised by high levels of unemployment, gross inequality of income and appalling human rights abuse including routine torture. 'Government' is either a malevolent dictator living in a palace among the ruins of the country around him, where conflict is kept in check through intimidation; or it is a shifting alliance of warlords, each with a private army or militia. Here, conflict can range from a low-intensity to high-intensity civil war, depending on whether the informal coalitions are holding together or falling apart. Those with the means and skills in a *Failed State* are the first to emigrate, taking their capital with them. Thereafter, ordinary citizens become refugees, fleeing for their lives when the situation becomes really desperate.

We have purposefully omitted to put names of countries into any of the three scenarios because we want you, the reader, to decide where you would allocate your own country, and other countries as well. Moreover, the national gameboard shouldn't be examined without reference to the international gameboard. For example, should there be a global move from a *Long Boom* towards a *Hard Times* or *Perfect Storm* scenario, it is quite possible for a country that is in the 'Relegation Zone' of the *Premier League* to slip into the *2nd Division* scenario, with the chance of then sliding into a *Failed State* if conditions appreciably worsen. The converse is also true: should the world remain in a *Long Boom,* the consequential flourishing of international trade could help some countries that are in the *2nd Division* to be promoted into the *Premier League* (obviously because they have succeeded in developing a comparative advantage in specific areas which are in demand).

The Business Gameboard

This is the scenario gameboard that in our facilitations has proven the most popular among companies. If you really concentrate on what drives a company's long-term profitability, it boils down to two factors: the attractiveness of the game that it chooses to play and its competitiveness in that game. Let's use a sports analogy to buttress this point. If you are the reigning world champion at squash, you will never earn a vast amount of money since it does not draw mass audiences. Hence, from a financial point of view, it is not an attractive game. In contrast, if you are the world's premier golfer or Formula One driver, you will earn a fortune. Even if you are past your best and declining in competitiveness, you will still earn a lot of money. A squash player will earn nothing!

The same principles carry through to business. This is why we've chosen the horizontal axis of the business gameboard to denote the state of the market in which the company is selling its goods and/or services, and the vertical axis its competitiveness in the market. Both areas have features which are within and beyond the control of the company. Taking the market axis first, what is inside a company's control is to choose which market, or if it has a variety of business units which markets, it should be in. Clearly, once a market has been chosen, there are plenty of factors beyond the company's control, such as the general level of demand for the product; whether it is outstripping supply or whether the market is constantly saturated because of the number of other suppliers of an identical or similar product; the availability of substitutes in the event of price increases the public don't like; the possibility of product obsolescence due to technical advances; and the stability/economic growth of the countries in which the revenues are being derived. On top of this is the general state of the global economy and whether it is in a boom or a recession.

Relative competitiveness, on the other hand, depends on how effectively the company is being managed in areas such as cost containment and service delivery (inside its control), but also on the relative performance of existing competitors, the advent of new competition and the movement of currency exchange rates which may affect its ranking in the international cost league (all outside of its control).

In considering these two axes, some executive teams like to keep their definition fairly general and intuitive, while others unpack the meaning using key performance indicators.

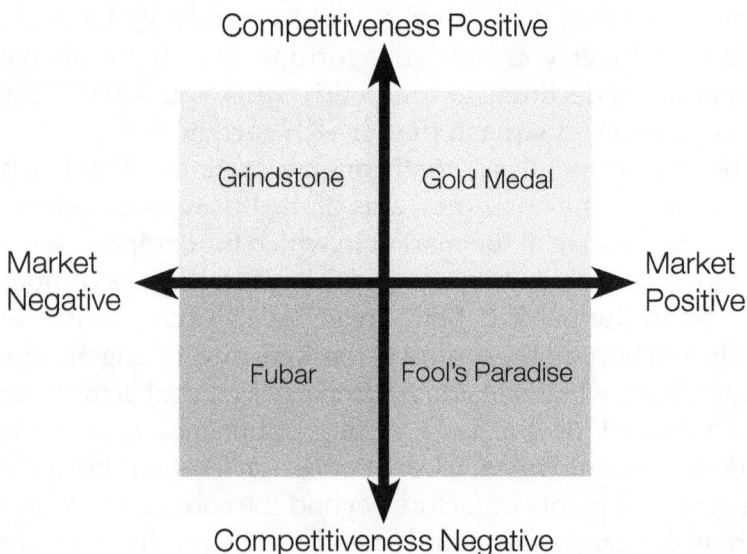

One of the reasons for the popularity of this gameboard is the effectiveness of the names in projecting the image of the scenarios. Contrary to the other two gameboards, we normally start with the bottom left quadrant, move to the bottom right, then top left and finally top right. This means that the scenarios are presented in ascending order of desirability.

Fubar

This is obviously the worst-case scenario, where your competitiveness is declining in a poor market. The stark reality is that you're uncompetitive in an unattractive game. Incidentally, the name of this scenario first arose during a strategy session one of us was facilitating for a leading South African company. Those familiar with military slang will know that *Fubar* is an acronym for something a little more desperate than simply 'mucked up beyond all recognition'! Suffice it to say that the scenario is now well established in the oral tradition of the company. No company wants to be in this scenario, because it is the last stage before bankruptcy and death. Best to change the game or conduct major surgery.

Fool's Paradise

As the name suggests, this is a nonsustainable position where all the company's faults are covered by a booming market. Should the market turn and the company does nothing, it will go directly into *Fubar*. Time to jack up the efficiencies.

Grindstone

We've all been here – a scenario where you put your nose to the grindstone and grind out better efficiencies than your competitors in a hostile market. Not a bad place to be since an improvement in the market can put you in *Gold Medal* territory. It's also a quadrant where you can launch a takeover bid for a competitor because the tough market makes its shares cheap. Inevitably, some of your product range or business units may lie in this quadrant and will continue to do so. But they are an essential part of your product offering, so you have to live with the 'grind'.

Gold Medal

This is where you want to be. Your competitiveness is growing in an attractive market. As the title suggests, you're winning the game. The challenge is to maintain your competitive streak despite being showered with success. However, if you become complacent and take your foot off the pedal you could slip into *Fool's Paradise.* The big issue is whether you're putting enough resources behind the products or businesses that belong to you and are in *Gold Medal* territory.

During the conversation around the scenarios, the questions to ask are: where is the company on the gameboard at the moment, and where have you come from during, say, the last five years? But the fun really starts when you drill down and ask where each of the business units should be positioned and, even further down, where each of the products resides. The gameboard gives you a very good pictorial feel of your portfolio of businesses and products and immediately suggests strategies for each of them.

Other sub-questions that may be asked include:

- Where would you place each of your major competitors on the gameboard?
- Do you think that your business or product mix should change as a result of reviewing the gameboard?
- How do the international and national gameboard scenarios impact on your positioning on the business gameboard?
- Do you have any second thoughts on the scope of the

business that you discussed earlier as a result of the insights gained from the gameboard?

Of course, a company must feel absolutely free to design its own business gameboard with its own variables, should it wish to do so. Moreover, NGOS, for example, use different parameters such as relevance of service offering and financial sustainability as the two key parameters in constructing the board. But whatever you do, please remember to come up with intriguing names for the scenarios – ones that the team are unlikely to forget. A certain amount of humour and irreverence also comes in handy. It's a great way to get across serious themes in a non-threatening way and keep the creative juices flowing.

Here are some of the memorable comments made during the scenario section of the debate (and again we've listed a considerable number for illustration):

When considering our position as a country on the global playing field, we should construct scenarios using GDP per capita in US dollars as one axis and exports as a percentage of GDP as our other axis. Three scenarios come to mind. We have a 'Grounded' scenario with low GDP per capita and a low export percentage. Like an aircraft stranded on the runway through mechanical problems, the country goes nowhere. The second scenario is 'Take Off', where a country uses its strengths – which in our case include our minerals – to raise the export percentage to a point where the economy starts rolling. The third scenario, which we all want to be in, is 'Flying High', with high GDP per capita, high exports, an attractive environment for foreign direct investment and an efficient government. Right now, we are grounded, but the turnaround time for take-off is shorter than people think.

PARTICIPANT, SCENARIO WORKSHOP ON ZIMBABWE

463

Our scenarios are 'Survivor' where, despite increasing regulation, we manage to grow our revenue by increasing cigarette sales in Third World markets; 'Crime and Punishment', where excessive regulation starts driving us out of business; 'Barbarians at the Gate', where we get taken over; and 'Brave New World', where we seriously promote nonsmoking nicotine products as part of our product range. Not only are the latter less harmful, but people will be able to consume these products in public places while enjoying a smoke at home. EXECUTIVE, GLOBAL TOBACCO COMPANY, UK

We have just won the largest number of global awards that an advertising agency could win. I guess that would put us in the 'Gold Medal' scenario. Is that a good thing? Well, it scares me in that we now have to try and maintain our position. This will require a review of our strategy and a new set of tactics in light of changing trends in the market. EXECUTIVE, GLOBAL ADVERTISING AGENCY

As a member of the nonferrous metals industry in Europe, a very likely scenario is high global economic growth, but a low ability on our side to compete. An appropriate name for this scenario is 'Chinese Water Torture'.

PARTICIPANT, EUROMETAUX SCENARIO WORKSHOP

Our best-case scenario has been cascaded throughout our organisation and is now deeply embedded in all of our actions and decisions. It is called 'Deep Green'.

SENIOR EXECUTIVE, MAJOR BANKING GROUP

Finding names for our scenarios helped us to build a strong understanding of the strategic options available to us. We used the weather as our theme and called the scenarios 'African Sky Blue', 'Scattered Thundershowers', 'Gale Force' and 'Perfect Storm'. They helped us to decide whether or not to split our auditing business from our consulting side. SENIOR PARTNER, LEADING ACCOUNTING FIRM

Four scenarios can play out in the gold market:

- *'Bull Run', where growth in jewellery demand, especially from China and India, takes place against a background of a scarcity of new mines. This combination sees the gold price hitting $1 000 an ounce;*
- *'Mellow Yellow', where new demand is balanced by new supply and the price hovers between $500 and $800;*
- *'Big Dipper', where a world traumatised by an escalation in terror speculates on gold and the price fluctuates between $400 and $900; and*
- *'Golden Bear', where some major new gold field is found, investment demand falls because of continuing low rates of inflation and the price slumps to between $300 and $500.*

Take your pick! CEO, GOLD-MINING COMPANY

The wine industry is definitely in the 'Grindstone' scenario because of the wine lake across the world. In order to move towards 'Gold Medal', we will need to differentiate ourselves with a wine in the ultra-premium category.

MARKETING DIRECTOR, INTERNATIONAL WINE MAKER

Post 2012, when the Kyoto agreement comes to an end, four policy scenarios on climate change are possible, depending on the level of political will and degree of co-operation between nations. The worst is 'Dirty Dancing', where everybody goes their own way with no restraints on carbon emissions. Slightly better is 'Different Dances', where at least some nations seek to limit their emissions in an uncoordinated way. 'Dances with Wolves' is where a new agreement is achieved but several parties immediately cheat on it. The best-case scenario is 'Strictly Ballroom', where all countries fall into step and waltz together under a new dispensation. But will they, given the level of rivalry and antagonism that exists in the world today? We'll have to wait and see.

PARTICIPANT, CLIMATE-CHANGE WORKSHOP, LONDON

Essentially, there are two scenarios for China. The positive one, 'Harmonious World', is where China achieves a significant level of harmony on three levels:

- harmony between the rural poor and the urban elite inside China, by putting greater emphasis on rural development and at the same time building new cities to take people off the land into higher-paying urban jobs;
- harmony between man and nature by re-orienting the economy from heavy industry into services and by improving energy efficiencies; and
- harmony between China and the rest of the world by ensuring that other countries prosper as a result of China's success and China is seen as a beneficial force in world affairs.

The negative scenario for China is 'Polarising World', where exogenous shocks to its economy – either through an escalation in the war of terror, increasing protectionism by European countries or a recession in the US – cause economic growth to fall by at least five percentage points. This could cause widespread social upheaval in China as people's expectations are no longer met, which in turn could mean a new clique in the Communist Party emerging to take over the reins of power.　　　　CHINESE ACADEMIC, BEIJING

Australia could experience two scenarios: 'On Golden Pond', where the country gradually subsides into an old-world economy, but the decline is quite graceful; and 'Matilda Changes Step', where a whole raft of new industries are created to replace the resource sector.

PARTICIPANT, SCENARIO WORKSHOP ON AUSTRALIA

Our current reality in Cape Town has been described in a scenario-planning exercise as 'Southern Comfort'. This is something akin to the early days of the south-eastern states of America, where the few live in grand style and great comfort, while the many struggle to eke out a living and suffer great hardship, oblivious to the natural beauty that surrounds them.　　　　CEO, ACCELERATE CAPE TOWN

We have decided to use key performance indicators to locate our position on your business gameboard. For competitiveness, we are in the top half of your chart if we hold the No. 1 or No. 2 ranking in the national survey of asset managers. That also applies to the funds under our supervision. We are on the line if we are No. 3 and, anything lower than that, we are below the line. For the market, the right-hand side of the gameboard represents a bull market for the period under review, and the left-hand side a bear market. Simple! And we'll do a scattergram on your gameboard of all the funds we manage to get a feel for who's who in the zoo when it comes to bonus time. CEO, LEADING ASSET-MANAGEMENT COMPANY

We are entering a new era for the mining industry and there are four scenarios depending on whether or not demand will continue to outstrip supply, and whether or not over time Eastern mining companies will challenge the might of Western mining companies. The first scenario, which we are in at the moment, is 'Rational Exuberance', where the mining boom continues and the existing multinationals hold sway and prosper. If the market reverts to normal, we will be back to 'Classical Rules', where the costs of the marginal producer determine the commodity price. High-grade mines will still make plenty of money. If the centre of gravity of the mining industry moves East, the scenario changes to 'Chinese Chess' because of the number of new Chinese, Indian and Russian mining companies entering the market with lots of deals being done. The last scenario is 'Hard Ball', where the negotiations turn nasty because the market goes flat just as all these new players have entered it. They battle for business on their own terms.

EXECUTIVE, GLOBAL MINING COMPANY

With the level of multitasking in this organisation, the downside scenario is 'Empty Wheels'. It's when the hamsters quit because they're so exhausted! STAFF MEMBER, LEADING BUSINESS SCHOOL

467

PLAYING THE GAME

10 SWOT: What are your strengths and weaknesses as a player; and what are the opportunities and threats offered by the game?

Whenever, therefore, people are deceived and form opinions wide of the truth, it is clear that the error has slid into their minds through the medium of certain resemblances to that truth.
SOCRATES, as quoted by Plato in *Phaedrus*

SWOT? So what?

We've heard that comment a number of times from people who have worked through a SWOT exercise at their organisation's annual strategy session. SWOT is a well-known process in business strategy and, being quite straightforward, its popularity up till now has been relatively assured. The basic assumption is that a quick whiz through an organisation's strengths, weaknesses, opportunities and threats will somehow throw out deep insights. Opinions as to the next step forward are then drawn from the analysis in the belief that the result will contribute towards moving the organisation in the correct strategic direction.

Sometimes it does, sometimes it doesn't. But the limitation of a SWOT analysis lies in the way it is normally done as an isolated exercise and repeated over and over again – until people suffer from SWOT fatigue. Thereafter, it's a case of going through the motions with little follow-through, other than someone being allocated the task of turning it into a nice graphic for the strategic document. It is amazing how often participants in our sessions wheel out the previous year's SWOT analysis without conviction or enthusiasm. They expect nothing from a revisit. Consequently, unless SWOT is given its proper place in the strategic conversation, its value as a tool will continue to decline in the 'appreciation stakes'.

A Lesson in DIY

We believe that we have discovered the right place. SWOT should form the link between *defining* the game and *playing* the game. If a strategic conversation was, say, a DIY (do-it-yourself) task, defining the game would be ascertaining what had to be done, playing the game would be doing it, and SWOT would be examining the tools you had at your disposal and what tools might still be needed. In the world of DIY, running through your list of tools *before* you have established the nature of the job to be done would not be particularly helpful. In a similar vein, doing a SWOT exercise on its own is pretty pointless, whereas doing it as part of a strategic conversation – after establishing the nature of the game – immediately places your abilities in context and provides a valuable reference point for what is still required. In other words, SWOT becomes a powerful tool for probing your skills gap.

Furthermore, anticipating the dynamic changes in a game is only halfway to winning it. Not great odds at 50/50! It is often said that knowing is one thing; doing is another. One of our greatest weaknesses as humans lies in our limited ability to bridge that knowing-doing gap. Performing a SWOT analysis at this stage of the strategic conversation provides that bridge between knowing the game and playing the game. In essence, a SWOT analysis provides the most realistic assessment of your profile and situation before you start investigating the strategic choices and tactics in the game.

In the conversation between Socrates and the fox, Socrates – after hearing the fox's story – was determined that they both should have some measure of insight into its practical implications. He asked the fox: "What are we going to take away from our conversation and do? For as we both know, actions speak more loudly than words." The fox explained that his whole destiny line to that point had involved a growing understanding of his strengths and weaknesses; and that unless they tackled the question of their strengths, weaknesses and immediate opportunities and threats, any talk of possible action would be purely academic. In the fox's words: "What you are does not determine what you will be or what you can be, but it sure as hell has an influence over your next move."

Perhaps we should examine more closely how the fox's interpretation of strengths, weaknesses, opportunities and threats applies in the milieu of commerce. Strengths and weaknesses are inner dimensions that relate, among other things, to the quality of leadership at the top; the existing competencies and prevailing ethos among employees; the financial resources at the organisation's disposal and even its business model, brand and internal structure. Opportunities and threats are external dimensions – lying outside of the office walls – and relate more to changes in the rules of the game as well as to the uncertainties associated with the external environment. However, as we have stressed on several occasions in this book, while the appearance of an opportunity or threat may lie outside of an organisation's control, the seizing of the opportunity or response to the threat is definitely within the remit of management.

The Gameboard Connection

The last point brings to mind the gameboard of the previous chapter. For, consider this: your strengths and weaknesses (and how you modify them) move you up or down the competitiveness axis; whereas opportunities and threats (and your response to them) move you left or right depending on how they influence the attractiveness of the game. It all ties in and gives the SWOT analysis the logical foundation it lacks when done as a stand-alone exercise. But don't forget that the definition of competitiveness can change as the game changes.

Different strengths will make you competitive at different times. For example, one small process-control company told us that they used to rely on developing long-term relationships with clients to win contracts. It was their strength. Now with higher staff turnover in client companies, personal contacts are a thing of the past. Their bids are handled by faceless tender committees who only look at price and not at the quality of service which accompanies the installation of the equipment. Their strength has been effectively neutralised.

By contrast, in another arena altogether, war games have also changed to such an extent that different capabilities are required to be a first-rate military force. As Major General Les Rudman of the South African National Defence Force puts it: "The South African Army needs a force that is able to wage both war and peace at the same time." You need a 'big-stick' warrior force backed up by a 'baton-stick' constabulary force. He quotes Josephus' words in 100 AD: "The Romans are sure of victory. For their exercises are battles without bloodshed and their battles bloody exercises." But in the end the Roman Empire fell apart because all their strengths became weaknesses. They did not recognise the changes in the game – nor did they really care.

In light of the fact that an organisation's SWOT should always be examined within the context of the game, its true value emerges with sub-questions such as the following:

- If you now were to examine the SWOT of your rivals in the game, how do you measure up? Are what you thought were your 'strengths' really so? The answer to this question will very much depend on your points of differentiation from your competitors.
- If events in the commercial environment were to bring about a shift in your position on the business gameboard,

474

how would you cope in relation to your competitors (bearing in mind your SWOT and theirs)?

- In what way does your SWOT change in the different quadrants of the international and national scenario gameboards? Does, for example, one of your strengths come to the fore under a particular scenario? Could one of your weaknesses prove potentially destructive in another scenario? How resilient are you to the slings and arrows of global or national misfortune?
- Is it perhaps time to invest more in the game or get out of it altogether (SWOT is the 'last-chance saloon' to discuss this issue)?

A Different SWOT

A SWOT analysis, as suggested by the fox and modified by us, therefore falls into line with the critical concept that underpins our strategic thinking: the key to success in any game is understanding the interplay between yourself and the environment. Just as the scope of the game must be defined within the context of looking at one's reflection in the 'looking glass', so should a SWOT analysis be a combination of introspection and gazing at the horizon. But SWOT can go beyond merely crystallising your capabilities to play the game and enhancing your powers of perception. It can actually provide a formula for winning the game. This requires a subtle redefinition of SWOT's different components, as follows:

- **S** for 'Start' – In order to *start* playing the game and be a viable player, you need to know the *strengths* that set you apart. Do you have any distinctive competencies in areas like research and development, one-of-a-kind product design, locking in distribution channels, strong branding or being a low-cost producer? Distinctive competencies are usually a basket of strengths that together are hard to copy. They raise the barrier to entry. Without them you will in all likelihood be a nonstarter, unable to pass 'Go' on the gameboard. These strengths should set you apart from your competitors and, should the game change, be re-examined for their future validity.

- **W** for 'Winning' – When you enter the game it must be done with the end-point of *winning* the game in mind. As in the game of tennis, this often means simply making fewer mistakes and therefore not losing. In golf you don't necessarily scrutinise your game when you win, but you do scrutinise your game if you lose. By identifying and then obviating your *weaknesses,* you can reduce the chances of playing a losing game.

- **O** for 'Outmanoeuvring' – In order to play a game to its fullest and continually maintain a competitive advantage, a player needs to *outmanoeuvre* his or her competitors. Identifying *opportunities* before competitors do will enable you to seize those opportunities first, and then build your organisation's skills around those opportunities.

- **T** for 'Thriving' – Thriving in a game relies on eliminating or, at least, minimising risk, and ensuring that contingency plans are in place for those risks that are out of your control. *Threats* are external risks and should therefore be identified and managed in order to achieve long-term sustainability and viability, i.e. to thrive over the long run in the game. Above all, *thriving* means having fun on and off the court!

swot, so what? I think we've managed to show that in the proper context the what becomes 'so, this is your reality check', an invaluable step in strategy design. Furthermore, at this particular stage in our conversation model, swot acts as a funnel for all the data which has been amassed in defining the game to be consolidated into a punchy tabulation. Armed with this information, you are ready to enter the next stage of the conversation, that of realistically entertaining the options you have for *playing* the game. SWOT has produced some marvellous comments from participants, which we reproduce below:

Our biggest threat in light of the latest marriage in our industry is that someone else we know follows suit, but we remain a wallflower.

EXECUTIVE, RETAIL BANK

As an island in the Caribbean, our greatest strength is offering an attractive destination for tourists. We also have the added leverage of a reggae culture made famous by Bob Marley – and you can't get a stronger brand than that. However, our biggest threat is on our doorstep: Cuba. It is a beautiful country with many unique characteristics. If it should open up to international tourism, the effects could be devastating for us.

PARTICIPANT, SCENARIO WORKSHOP ON JAMAICA

An opportunity for us is to become another state of the US. On reflection, that would possibly translate into a weakness over time because of the security hassles our tourists would encounter at our airports. PARTICIPANT, SCENARIO WORKSHOP ON JAMAICA

One of our key strengths is our size. We are a highly profitable radio station with a very large listenership firmly concentrated in the highest-earning segment. This has also, strangely enough, been our biggest weakness, because it has brought about complacency and left us with a lack of focus. We're also in an industry where the success of one's product is there for everyone to copy. New competition is therefore a threat that may necessitate a tighter positioning around the competencies that made us great in the first place.

CEO, LEADING SOUTH AFRICAN RADIO STATION

Talent retention (especially young talent) is one of our critical areas of weakness. We recognise loyalty but not specifically talent. We will need to develop performance indicators for this area of human resources. We are also a highly risk-averse company, which in today's world is a weakness. We cannot afford to lag behind our competitors. EXECUTIVE, LEADING ALCOHOLIC BEVERAGE COMPANY

The 2010 Soccer World Cup will be South Africa's grand opportunity to position itself as a brand in the global market. The spotlight will be that much brighter, as it will be the first time that this – the world's biggest event – will be staged on the African continent. At the same time, this occasion brings with it all measures of threats in the event of non-delivery.

TOP SOUTH AFRICAN BUSINESS EXECUTIVE, WORKSHOP ON 2010

Our principal opportunities and threats lie in our relationship with America. The latter is as good and as bad as it can reasonably be.

PROFESSOR, CENTRAL PARTY SCHOOL, BEIJING

Our opportunity is to capitalise on the expansion of South Africa's two largest ports (Durban and Richards Bay) as well as the new airport. The reason is that we own prime land in the corridor between the two ports and the airport. PROPERTY DEVELOPER

A fire raging out of control in one of our suburbs is now our biggest threat. MUNICIPAL CEO, SYDNEY, AUSTRALIA

Copper is our strength. Corruption our weakness.

PARTICIPANT, SCENARIO WORKSHOP ON THE
DEMOCRATIC REPUBLIC OF CONGO, KINSHASA

Our CEO is our strength because he is a legend in our industry and initiates most of our business. But he is also our weakness because of our huge dependency on him (with no clear succession plan).

DIRECTOR, ADVERTISING AGENCY

Despite our success, our only shareholder is about to dispose of our shares because we are considered non-core to their business. The threat is that we don't get on with the new owners.

EXECUTIVE, PRECISION ENGINEERING COMPANY, GERMANY

The big opportunity for us is to hang on to the coat-tails of our clients and follow them into Africa.

CEO, SUPPLIER TO MAJOR RETAIL CHAINS

Our opportunity is to use our brand and expertise to expand our global footprint (or should I say roadprint!), since the market at home has become a zero-sum game.

EXECUTIVE, TARMAC COMPANY, UK

Preservation of the cold chain is fundamental to our business, so the rising frequency of power failures is one of our biggest threats. It will subject our products to greater thermal abuse at the retail level.

EXECUTIVE, GLOBAL FROZEN FOODS COMPANY

Given the shortage of technical skills in South Africa, the opportunity is to provide a 911 service where our electronics engineers act like paramedics. When clients experience equipment breakdowns, our guys will quickly arrive at the scene and sort out the mess – for a fee. CEO, ELECTRONICS COMPANY

The point you make about looking inwards and outwards certainly applies to me. I taught children in secondary school, and then quite by accident I moved to a primary school. I've never looked back, because the strengths in my character obviously suit the needs of the kids I now teach. Fortuitously, the external world and I have achieved a perfect state of harmony. PRIMARY SCHOOL TEACHER

11 Options: Within your span of control, what options do you have to improve your current performance and longer-term prospects in the game?

The hour of departure has arrived, and we go our ways –
I to die and you to live. Which is better, God only knows.
SOCRATES, as quoted by Plato in *Apology*

Having arrived at this point in the conversation, you should have a realistic understanding of the game and its nuances. You have also established a realistic assessment of your own profile and the situation in which you find yourself, and therefore are conscious of how you are faring as a player. This means that when you consider your options, you can do so from a more robust starting point. It also means that options become clearer and easier to flesh out; in fact at this stage the options are often obvious. What still remains something of a challenge is how to convert those options into decisions.

In order to extract the ones of greatest value, options need to be dissected and positioned in the correct perspective. Some options are simple, others more complex in their potential outcomes. For example, the fox asked of Socrates, "'What options do you have?' I've outlined mine, which are pretty simple and relate to the part of the forest I want to sleep in tonight." Socrates explained his options: he could escape before the trial started, but that would damage his legacy; he could reconsider his public stance on the war and the way Athens was governed, but that would also damage his legacy; or he could stand trial and stick to his principles and face possible death. A tortuous array of outcomes indeed!

Sometimes it is a set of options working together that produces the most effective result; at other times a single option can create huge leverage in the game. Whatever their nature, options should as far as possible be played out to their end-point in order to fully understand their consequences, both intended and possibly unintended.

Choosing options relates back to your DNA, and your DNA defines the way you play the game. Of course, good leaders can change the DNA of the organisation they run, but it takes time. Moreover, while business has its mavericks, most of us are risk-averse and err on the more cautious, or conservative, side. This is why so few players really stand out in a game, and why most form the bulk of the peloton (the main body of cyclists in the *Tour de France*). They breeze along in other people's slipstream. Accordingly, participants in any strategic conversation should preferably be as diverse as possible (within the parameter of being at the correct management level) in order for all the options to be explored effectively.

Strategic and Tactical Options

Options to improve the scope of your game as well as your performance in it broadly fall into two categories that should be considered side by side. The first set draws on your *external* perspective of the game, whereas the second set relates to the *internal* perspective you have of your organisation as a player. The external perspective focuses on the business portfolio – what the product/service offering of the organisation is – and throws light on the most promising direction for the organisation, given the different scenarios. This is pure strategy. The internal perspective looks at organisational capability and builds options to help the organisation meet the needs of the game. This constitutes tactics.

Options are therefore classified as either *strategic* or *tactical*. There should be fewer strategic options than tactical options, and these should be debated first in the conversation because they relate back to the scope. Obviously, if the rules of the

481

game have changed drastically or the uncertainties/scenarios offer huge challenges, a significant amount of time may be spent on these options.

Strategic options can be ranked as follows:

- If your SWOT shows that you are a strong player in your current game, you may embark on an *organic-growth* strategy using options that tap into your core competencies, or go for a *stepping-out* strategy that will take the organisation in a new direction;
- If you're aware that you are a competent player but your future hangs in the balance, you should examine options for a *turnaround* or *survival* strategy. It's resurrection time.
- If your weaknesses and threats are overwhelming and you clearly have no future in the game, you should be designing the most economical *exit* strategy. This is just as important as other forms of strategy, and is often more difficult to execute. However, as we point out in one of our seven principles of strategy: "Above all, strategy is about understanding what you do and don't control, and what is certain and uncertain about the future; and *knowing when to change.*"

It's not necessary for an organisation continually to change its strategy – although it should be regularly reviewed – and so in many strategic conversations the options that are identified are generally tactical options, i.e. the 'how' and the 'what' of achieving the strategic direction that is chosen. These often vary or change as the game evolves due to the divergent tactics of existing or new players; or because of changes in the business environment. As a result, the range of tactical options considered may simply amount to a slight change in the overall game plan. Yet, however slight, that change may be essential. After all, the consistency of a player's game plan can make it vulnerable on account of its predictability to competitors. Then that player loses a measure of competitive edge, and the advantage swings in favour of the other side.

The tactical options formulated in this phase of the strategic conversation should still be somewhat broad, or high level, because if too many smaller, nitty-gritty options are generated they could obfuscate the conversation. Only once these broader options have been explored at the higher level and then converted into decisions, should the 'options within options' be identified. These more practical issues can be addressed at a later stage in an operational planning meeting; or as the conversation model is cascaded through the organisation to departmental level.

The Ethical Compass

Options can however be narrowed down and unpacked further to determine things that can realistically be done within your control. Sometimes options may sound impressive and the answer to an organisation's predicament, but on further analysis they may not be the smartest choice. This is where the interplay between DNA, scope, rules, scenarios and SWOT come back into play. Because descriptive rules of a game are the basic licence to operate. and the normative rules of the game are the moral rules to which any organisation aspiring to be world class should adhere, it makes sense that, for any option to be effective, it must not fall foul of either type of rule. So the direction in which you should point yourself should take cognisance of routes you should avoid just as much as those you ought to follow. We have therefore developed an 'ethical compass' as a guide to action, particularly for those managers who are inclined to check in their values at the office turnstile in favour of power and glory – and money. Think of our compass instead!

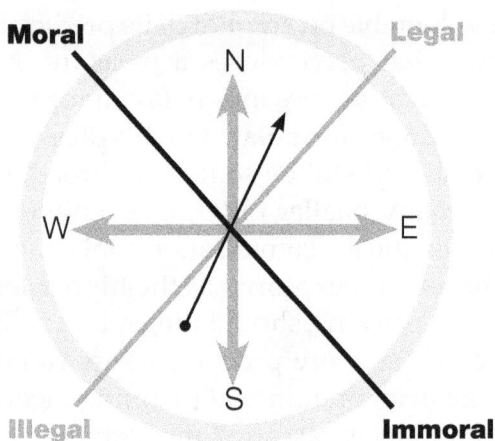

Any option between 'NW' and 'NE' has a reasonable chance of propelling the organisation towards long-term sustainability. However, an option that falls between 'SW' and 'SE' is both immoral and illegal, and will sooner or later prove the undoing of the organisation. We don't like to name any country, leader or organisation in particular that operates in this area, but we all know some that do! The fact is that how you select your options through the ethical compass will unveil what your meaning of winning the game really is.

Given that any organisation has finite resources, options also need to be prioritised on the basis of urgency or importance, leverage (output-to-input ratio), and risk versus reward. Options can sometimes be *exclusive,* meaning you can do either this or that. Normally, the greater the magnitude of resources required the more exclusive the option becomes. Options that provide marginal leverage in the game but do demand high resource input are not great options to choose, and should rather remain in the drawer unless they change their status. Sometimes, though, in order simply to stay in the game in a particular scenario, an option is a prerequisite –

whether or not it provides any leverage at all. In this case it must be converted into a decision, and actioned for defensive reasons.

Choosing exclusive options means refusing others. For an organisation this demands that the opportunity cost of 'the others' must be assessed. Yet, even though life is full of trade-offs, we don't always have to play the trade-off game. Sometimes options are *inclusive* of one another and it's just about choosing the correct set. As long as you design the programme of action in such a way that you're not overstretching your human or financial resources, there are times when you can have it all.

The Treatment of Risk

Often in business, given its similarity to a card game between various players, each incremental step taken in the decision-making chain elicits a change in play and thereby unveils new options, each again with its own risk-reward profile. Hence, playing out the consequences of an option is a critical part of the analysis. Questions should be asked about how the game will change should an option be followed and how the competitors will react. Will it influence the overall business environment? Are there possible hidden risks that could emerge? From a risk-reward perspective, it is like taking bets. It all depends on the magnitude of the bet, the level of risk and your choke limit as a gambler. Very seldom – if ever – in a business situation should an organisation go beyond that magical threshold where too much of the company's destiny is being put on the table. It really doesn't matter how attractive the potential return is, a sensible executive will walk away.

So why take the risk in the first place? Surely if an organisation has been successful in the business offering there's no reason for it to risk changing its strategy? In such a case surely the best option is to do nothing? However, let's not forget that business is a game. Retaining the status quo does not mean that an organisation may continue from here to eternity. Sometimes, on the contrary, continuing to play the game the same way incurs the greatest risk. External factors and a change in the competitors' game plans may suddenly shake the gameboard and topple the organisation into a worst-case scenario. Standing still makes you an easy target.

The final remark we wish to make on risk concerns the 'cautionary principle'. This basically states that where you face a threat, it is wise to take precautions even though the threat may not materialise. It all sounds simple, but the devil is in the detail. We go back to our PI chart because the option of doing something to prevent a nasty thing happening turns on its probability and its potential impact. Nobody disputes taking preventative measures against a terrorist attack (shock event), but the world still does not agree on the measures to be taken to stop climate change (gradual threat). In the end, there is no perfect formula for knowing when to invoke the cautionary principle, how much you should spend and how far you should reduce the odds. It's all about feel. Nevertheless, in areas like the environment, health and safety, options to minimise adverse environmental impacts, reduce the chances of occupational disease and stop accidents that could cause injury and death are receiving much greater attention than before.

It's clear that option generation is on occasion no easy task. Sometimes options are fairly pedestrian, with little risk attached. They just become obvious during the conversation. At other times options are more intricate and perplexing, and may need to be brainstormed in more detail before a decision can be made. They are then held over for further discussion at a subsequent meeting, with an individual or team within the strategy group being tasked to produce draft recommendations by a specified date.

To summarise, the sub-questions we specifically ask to help identify, group and prioritise options are the following:

- What are your strategic and tactical options (i.e. things that you can realistically do within your control) to take the negative scenarios as far as possible out of play, and to thrive in the good ones?
- What options do you need to consider to achieve greater compliance with the rules of the game, specifically the ones to win?
- In relation to the key uncertainties, you have two options: live with them or take them as far as possible out of play. Which choice is realistic for each uncertainty?
- How will the other players in the game react if you pursue the options identified to be the best?
- Are your options in line with your swot? In other words, do they add to your competitiveness by exploiting your strengths and reducing your weaknesses; and do they embrace the challenges posed by the opportunities and threats inherent in the game?

We conclude this section with a warning: the process of formulating options may seem a little clearer now, but this stage of the strategic conversation should not be entered into lightly. The most frequent trap for an organisation is to select a change in scope (i.e. strategic direction) and then, because it falls outside the comfort zone of 'business as usual', *not* allocate sufficient resources to make it happen. Business is a complicated and unforgiving game. Clearly identifying the most effective options is one thing. Putting the ones you choose into practice with the intended results is another, especially when you are setting off in a new direction.

Here are some comments which we noted down during this stage of our conversation. Remember that we follow the heuristic method where people are encouraged to discover the best options for themselves in a question and answer mode:

One of the rules in our game is an acute shortage of artisans and other skilled craftsmen, which looks set to continue. A tactical option must therefore be to look at various ways to attract, develop and, especially, retain people of this ilk in our organisation. This demands an overhaul of our personnel policy where such people have up till now been given scant regard compared to, say, recruiting accountants. SENIOR MANAGER, CONSTRUCTION INDUSTRY

Radio as a stand-alone medium is losing ground. The global trend is a shift towards multimedia offerings. If we are to attract new listeners, it is now clear that we need to consider the synergies between the different media platforms. Thus our strategic options are to stay on familiar ground or broaden our offer so that we're seen as a multimedia news and entertainment group, not just a broadcaster. EXECUTIVE, RADIO GROUP

Up till now, we've just given money away to good causes, chosen by our trustees. But, with the advent of public/private partnerships, we must explore the strategic option of partnering with the appropriate level of government to fund desirable projects on a rand-for-rand basis. This represents a major change in direction for the fund with all the risks and complexities associated with having to establish steering committees and the like.

CEO, SOCIAL RESPONSIBILITY FUND

As a provincial law society we play a pivotal role in promoting the legal fraternity within the context of the country's imperatives. A tactical option that has come to the fore, which could give us greater leverage in the game whilst requiring a relatively low resource

488

input, is that each legal member within our province provides 24 hours' worth of pro bono *work a year to the State (with cases that have been prepared beforehand). Collectively, this allows people who cannot afford legal counsel to receive the service they desperately need; and, at the same time it gives the legal fraternity a different image in the eyes of both the community and, importantly, the government. We may not be as callous as people think!*

HEAD, PROVINCIAL LAW SOCIETY

In the passenger airline industry, routes are critical. Until now we have been beholden to the standard view of maximising the number of routes to give ourselves the greatest reach. It's now increasingly obvious that routing options should be seen from two different angles; one, whether or not they provide long-term strategic advantage; and two, whether they are financially viable. It will be a massive shift for us if we accept the second philosophy, bearing in mind that, when you lose a route, it is very difficult to secure it again. But the state of the market compels us to examine the latter as a strategic option. AIRLINE EXECUTIVE

Our options are to become more transparent in the way we do business; or go on being seen as a secretive tax haven where rich folks can stash their cash. The international net is closing in.

ASSET MANAGER, ISLE OF MAN

We have two strategic options: provide electricity as cheaply as we can to all Indian citizens, or install expensive technology to reduce carbon emissions and raise the price of electricity accordingly. Guess which option wins if America with the highest carbon footprint per citizen in the world refuses to lead the way!

UTILITY EXECUTIVE, NEW DELHI

Your options are limited when the enemy wants to annihilate you.

ISRAELI BUSINESSMAN, JERUSALEM

One option is to do absolutely nothing. Just kidding!

EXECUTIVE, STATIONERY COMPANY

Is it an option for China to evolve into a multiparty democracy as it gets richer? Of course, but let me answer the question with a question: does your company – for which you have worked your entire career in the belief that it is a worthwhile institution – tolerate an official opposition to the Board? No? I rest my case.

CHINESE ACADEMIC, BEIJING

Do you think the option outlined in the 'High Road' scenario of negotiating a settlement with the real opposition leaders is viable? Yes, it is the only road.

INTERCHANGE BETWEEN TWO CABINET MINISTERS, SCENARIO SESSION ON SOUTH AFRICA, NOVEMBER 1986

Given our diversity as a nation, we need to develop a South African-ness to transcend our differences. Americans are diverse too, but their spirituality, respect for the flag and undoubted economic success have bound them together. They have real national pride – even the minorities. We have the 'High Road' option of fostering our pride or the 'Low Road' option of falling apart.

PARTICIPANT, SCENARIO SESSION, JULY 2007

Thank heavens you put a $70 scenario on the table when the price of oil was $25 a barrel. It scared the living daylights out of us, given that we consume as much energy as a small European country. It made us consider energy-saving options throughout the business and implement solutions where we could. In retrospect, a very wise thing to do. ENERGY HEAD, GLOBAL RESOURCES COMPANY

12 Decisions: Which options do you want to turn into decisions right now, and what is the initial action associated with each decision?

If I am to live longer, perhaps I must live out my old age,
seeing and hearing less, understanding worse, coming to learn
with more difficulty and to be more forgetful, and growing worse
than those to whom I was once superior. Indeed, life would be
unliveable, even if I did not notice the change. And if I see the
change, how could life not be even more wretched and unpleasant?
SOCRATES as quoted by Xenophon in *Memorabilia IV*

Free as air. That's what you are in the previous section when reviewing your options, with the obvious rider that you should be reflecting on your capabilities at the same time. Now comes the sharp end of the conversation when decisions are made, commitments given and actions taken.

Every point, or cross, on our destiny line, and every step we take along it, represents a decision – a moment of action that either keeps us on track or changes our tack. If no decision is made, the result is a hovering moment of indecision, or hesitation, where we are bogged down, remaining in limbo, whilst the game continues unabated around us. The fewer decisions we make, the more uncertain we become. And yet, not making decisions because we feel we do not have sufficient information to make them seems a perfectly rational thing to do. But what is 'sufficient information'? Sometimes, too much information can create such a profusion of possible paths ahead that you are simply too spoilt for choice. Perhaps, like Goldilocks, you don't want your porridge too hot or too cold. You just want the right amount of information.

As you must recognise from our text by now, a decision is never taken in isolation. As a point on your destiny line it represents the convergence of your DNA (which dictates your predisposition to act) with the external events happening in your proximate environment (which are normally outside of your control). Of course, in your imagination and dreams this is not an issue, because you create and control your environment. However, in the real world, decision-making entails juggling the controllable with the uncontrollable and has very real consequences. It should therefore be considered a life skill and not simply an act of choosing the most appealing notion. This is captured wonderfully in a snatch of verse from Dr Seuss's *Oh, the Places You'll Go*. It is one of the few books he wrote for adults as well as children. The extract goes: "Simple it's not, I'm afraid you will find, for a mind-make-upper to make up his mind." The book remains a favourite gift from parents to their sons and daughters upon leaving school and embarking on adulthood. It explores, in entertaining storybook fashion, the very real life skills they must develop in etching out their individual destiny line; in writing their own individual story as a 'mind-make-upper'.

Transferring this line of thinking to the busy and crowded world of business, where decisions often impact significantly on the lives of many, it is critical that companies strengthen their decision-making powers as far as they can. It is only by doing this that they can remain the central character in their own story, the lead player in their own game. Wrong decisions will place companies at the mercy of other players who have taken control of the game; and then such companies will have no alternative but to watch their destiny line being drawn by people who do not have their interests at heart (quite the opposite!). They will be reluctant characters in their own story. Avoidance of the possible pitfalls of incorrect decisions, by engendering a philosophy of covering all eventualities and then waiting to see how a story pans out, won't work either. Straddling a fence can prove very painful! No, this is business; if a profit is to be made, deadlines have to be met and bets placed before the race begins.

The Fall of the Axe

So how do we make the most effective decisions? How do we get to a point where the correct decision becomes clear, where possibly incorrect decisions are discarded and where indecision is a nonevent? We'll try to sketch out the answer, but we have to be truthful and admit that there are no guarantees: you can still make a bad decision through misreading the future or just plain bad luck. At this point of our strategic conversation, keeping an open mind becomes positively counter-productive. Confusion has to be stripped away and a plot of your future destiny line must emerge. Granted, the debate on key uncertainties and alternative futures through scenario construction will hopefully have instilled flexibility in your nature. Granted, challenges to your destiny line may well have been considered and possible contingency plans put in place to change course. But ultimately, the axe has to fall one way or the other for progress to be made and the integrity of your story line to remain intact.

The drama of this moment was expressed towards the end of the conversation between Socrates and the fox. The latter says to Socrates: "So now we come to your question: 'Which option are you going to exercise and turn into action?' Personally I have decided to head north and take my chances there." Socrates enthuses that the conversation has clarified his mind, and unveils his decision to exercise the last option of taking his chances in court. We'd hazard a guess that plenty of people reading this book wouldn't have taken the route of Socrates and risked death. But then, as we now know, Socrates had his reasons; and for him the decision was final.

Some decisions in business are 'no-brainers' and require very little exercising of the grey matter. The key word here is 'some', for the complexity of the game of business inevitably makes most decisions associated with playing the game pretty complicated. Every decision made by management has its outcomes, some expected, others unexpected. But all of them incur reactions to the decision from, on the one hand, the company's own staff playing to their individual needs and acting in their own interests; and on the other hand, from competitors protecting their corners as well. In a way, each decision an organisation makes generates a ripple effect that unsettles a game's status quo and prompts reactions from all sides present on the field. Using the metaphor of 'locker-room talk' before a game, any coach who unveils an unbreakable master plan down to the last detail – thus leaving no room for unanticipated responses from the opposing team – risks losing the game. Taking command of the game demands that players have Plan Bs which can be activated should the reactions of the opposing side demand alternative strategies and tactics. The side's game plan can be adjusted accordingly, keeping the game firmly within their control, but at the same time fluid and unpredictable to the opposition.

Innovative Swans

Applying this metaphor to the game of business, this means, especially in bigger organisations, the more complex the decisions and potential outcomes, the more it is necessary to have the kind of strategic conversation we are outlining – the kind that embraces uncertainty. However, at this point, we must revert to our distinction between strategy and tactics. Strategy, being direction, cannot be chopped and changed at will. One has to be decisive and allow a strategic decision time to bed down and time to validate itself. Tactical decisions, on the other hand, are incremental. Each one can be reviewed to see if it is having the desirable result, and if not the next one can be changed. This bipolar approach to strategy and tactics allows the organisation to have a strategic end-point in mind, while retaining a built-in mechanism for adaptation of tactical decisions as the future unfolds. The incremental philosophy underlying the latter means that an organisation can adjust to a changing environment intuitively and gradually, rather than rashly and overdramatically. Picture a swan gliding serenely through the water. Strategy is what you see on the surface, while tactics are the energetic paddling underneath.

As an added benefit, our process also has innovation built into it. Because the scenario gameboard explores the edge of the envelope in terms of possibilities and opportunities, it promotes innovative thinking and allows new and creative ideas to surface. The thing we find somewhat puzzling is that many major organisations we have worked with treat innovation as a separate entity cloaked in the guise of an 'innovation hub'. It then lives a half life on the outskirts of traditional corporate strategy and every now and then is tapped for any nuggets of creativity that can be moulded into the organisation's official mindset. Unfortunately, when innovation floats around as a disconnected entity from the main decision-making body, most of its ideas are dead in the water.

Innovation doesn't have to be earth-shattering. When Steve Jobs posed to his Apple colleagues the question "Why should all computers be beige?" he wasn't asking for a cataclysmic "Oh wow!" response. It was simply a subtle challenge to the existing state of affairs in the design of personal computers. Yet it proved to be a transformational moment. Moreover, the insights from innovation are not the sole reserve of so-called 'creative thinkers' such as Steve Jobs. In order for an idea or option to be 'innovative', it simply has to offer a departure from an established line of thought. Our conversation model, by going back to basics, encourages such lateral thinking, provided that there is a thoroughness in the depth and scope of its implementation. The more the model is used throughout an organisation, the more inclusive it is, the more iterative it is and the greater the degree of mutual learning and frequency of breakthroughs. It tends to capture the innovation that simmers below the surface of the workforce, which would otherwise go to waste.

The Strategic Statement

As we have just observed but wish to expand on, strategic decisions vary from tactical decisions in that the former define your direction, and relate predominantly to the scope of your game or the definition of your playing field; whereas the latter improve your competitiveness and thereby your organisation's position in the game you have selected. A strategic decision can therefore lead to a change in range of products or services; repositioning within the product chain; an entry into a new market segment and/or an expansion of the geographical footprint. Sometimes it can lead to a change in the game altogether, should the current one be unplayable. Sometimes, it confirms that there is no need for any shift in direction, in which case the decisions made are exclusively tactical.

Given the critical importance of an organisation's strategic direction, we become somewhat alarmed if it becomes evident early on in the conversation that an organisation's strategy is not fully written up in one particular place. All too often the strategic model is fragmented, its elements scattered about in different forms and in different parts of the organisation. This naturally undermines the purpose and results in limited buy-in. No defined goalposts mean no clear playing field and no nets to aim the ball at. It is therefore paramount that the first decision should take the form of a synthesis of the outcomes of the strategic conversation concerning the organisation's future scope. The latter should be expressed in a pithy statement which has a dynamic ring about it so that it can be presented as the vision of the organisation – an internal communication tool to rally the troops. At least each business unit or department can then build its strategies and tactics in line with the organisation's central strategy. The playing field is clearly marked and the goalposts are upright for all to see. It also gives the strategic process a simple, clean end-point that enables effective activations along the way.

Incremental Tactics

Once this strategic statement had been formulated, it is easier to go back to the options and convert them into decisions. Indeed, we often juxtapose options with decisions, because frequently the only decision that can be made at the time is to explore the option more fully. On other occasions, the decision may be to defer the option until resources become available or circumstances warrant its pursuit. Where a decision is taken to implement an option, the initial action to get the show on the road must be described and assigned to whoever in the team is considered most suitable. In this sense, the process should be incremental, with further steps being agreed upon after the first step is complete. This keeps everyone on the ball and allows continual monitoring of the implementation programme. The concept we are advocating is evident in the game of golf, where many a professional will invariably answer the question as to how he or she is going to play the game with "One shot at a time". You'll be surprised how enthusiastic people can be in ensuring the implementation of their actions when they're being measured incrementally and they have a deadline for each incremental step! Any excuse about the complexity of the task delaying the project sounds pretty lame in these circumstances.

In summary, sub-questions we often ask when going through the decision-making stage of our model are the following:

- What is your strategic intent and direction?
- What are the preferred options that, right now, are 'go' and can be turned into decisions and actions?
- What is the initial action associated with each decision; i.e. who is going to do what by when and how much is it going to cost? (Sometimes there is no additional cost because it is just extra workload for an existing team member.)
- What options do you want to defer, either because they are lower priority or will only be triggered by other scenarios coming into play?
- Which options are too risky or unethical and should therefore be rejected as possible decisions?
- Where an option is exclusive, has the decision to take it been weighed up against the 'opportunity cost' of refusing all the other options?
- What, if any, are the potentially unintended and undesirable consequences associated with the decisions?

At this point in the book you should realise that you have two options: write your own story and determine your own destiny line, or let others do it for you. Although Socrates' decision to place his life in the hands of the courts was made with the full knowledge of what the outcome might possibly be, he never abandoned his destiny line; and although he left it to others to write his story, he had an inkling of the theme and the finale. But then he was Socrates – the father of modern philosophy. Meanwhile, the fox took his chances in the forest. For the rest of us, if we are to write our own stories, the next decision should be to finish the book and learn how to identify the outcomes we desire.

Here is a sample of the decisions made by companies and other organisations for which we have worked:

Because the game has become increasingly difficult, our decision is to niche ourselves and focus on the ultra-premium sector. The logic is that this sector is less vulnerable to economic cycles because the rich will always have money to drink. We in turn will have more control of our destiny.   WINEMAKER

As a clothing retailer supplying the lower-to-middle income market we have access to, and knowledge of, consumers with whom other industries can create huge marketing opportunities. Our decision is to move into selling 'pay-as-you-go' airtime for mobile telephones, which will open up a whole new, and highly profitable, business unit for us. In fact, it should surpass our core business. Our ambition is to become the single largest customer for the cellular service providers. Their decisions around this market will come from our knowledge base and customer understanding. Of course the next decision will revolve around how to play in two games at the same time.   DIRECTOR, MASS-MARKET CLOTHING RETAILER

Currently, my raw materials cost more than the landed cost of a Chinese suit or shirt. I could pay my workers nothing and I still couldn't compete. This conversation has convinced me to go to the higher ground of tailoring suits and shirts for the individual needs of customers. And I'll import the rest of my requirements from China.

CEO, CLOTHING MANUFACTURER

As a result of the attention given to auditing firms following the Enron scandal, many professional firms made the decision to split their services. We have decided to keep all our services under one brand, but we will erect 'Chinese walls' between them.

CEO, FINANCIAL SERVICES FIRM

After your session, we decided to marry a foreign gorilla to expand our African footprint. What a good strategic move!

EXECUTIVE, LEADING BANKING GROUP

Our sales team are losing ground with our customers because they are playing a traditional marketing game. However, marketing now demands a more strategic focus and closer alignment with the operational side of the business. Having decided to change the internal rules of the game, our key decision is to build new competencies into the sales team. Training and internal communication are critical for us. These decisions are purely tactical because we want to keep our scope the same. DIRECTOR, PRINTING COMPANY

The first thing we shall do after this session is articulate the golden rules to win the game and brief all our staff. We shall also introduce key performance indicators (KPIs) for each of the rules and measure performance against them. Finally, we'll make the KPIs an integral part of our remuneration system by attaching financial incentives for the staff to achieve them. In other words, we'll take the golden rules as seriously as any American company and thereby sharpen our competitiveness. It should keep us in the top half of your business gameboard. CEO, SOFTWARE HOUSE

We're definitely going to introduce a talent-management system in light of the rule about attracting, developing and retaining talented staff. It means hiring a human resource person, but that's no bad thing since we've always given that discipline short shrift.
MD, ASSET-MANAGEMENT BUSINESS

Our decision has to be that we should be seen as the best head-hunting outfit in Africa. We will need a database containing the names of all CEOs and CFOs in every African country, as well as the names of all expatriates from the continent in those positions wherever they may be around the world.
SENIOR PARTNER, HEAD-HUNTING BUSINESS

Our decision is to go into Africa and brand ourselves as African rather than South African. It will produce some interesting reac-

tions from our global competitors. However, our decision on which countries to enter will be based on careful analysis of each country's market and prospects. DIRECTOR, FAST-FOOD COMPANY

The decision has already been taken to re-integrate Taiwan into the Middle Kingdom. The only question is on what terms and when. We can wait a hundred years. CHINESE STRATEGIST, BEIJING

Definitely the biggest takeaway from this session is that we need to expand our donor base and retain the services of a full-time professional fundraiser in order to make it happen.

DIRECTOR, HIV/AIDS FOUNDATION

The most important issue raised in this workshop is the level of intellectual leadership we should be giving on the major environmental issues of the day – such as global warming, marine conservation and management of elephant herds in game parks. We are already involved in a number of projects in these areas, but we need to be more visible in championing the causes and educating the public on viable solutions. Let it be so.

CHAIRMAN, GLOBAL ENVIRONMENTAL AGENCY

We got the young talent in the company to sit around a table and use your conversation model to give their views on the company's future. Boy, were their recommendations different to our decisions!

CHAIRMAN, EXECUTIVE COMMITTEE OF ENTERTAINMENT GROUP

Today's conversation has convinced me that we need to get a better handle on the long-term trends in recidivism (relapse) of our patients in order to judge the effectiveness of our treatments. I think we would be pleasantly surprised by the results in regard to alcohol abuse, but mortified by the lack of success with drug addiction.

CEO, LEADING REHABILITATION CLINIC

501

13 Outcomes: What is your meaning of winning the game in five years' time, expressed as a set of measurable outcomes?

Our purpose in founding the city was not to make any one class in it surpassingly happy, but to make the city as a whole as happy as possible.
SOCRATES, as quoted by Plato in *The Republic*.

If we are guilty of a presumption in writing this book, it is that ordinary human beings play the game to win. Only masochists prefer to lose. But here's the key question: what, for you, is 'winning'? What is *your* 'meaning' of winning the game? To make as much money as possible, as quickly as possible? To beat the other guy? To be number one in the game for as long as possible? To be a legend? To lead an anonymous but happy life, balancing your career with family and recreational pursuits? To make a difference in *other* people's lives? To be a hedonist and seek pleasure for pleasure's sake? In today's world, the last question would attract a host of affirmative answers with which Socrates would definitely not agree.

If you think winning is only about chasing targets then you've already lost the game. It's easy to circle a point on a graph and say: "That's our end-point, that's where we want to be: now, team, let's get there." Indeed, we made just this assertion in the last chapter when advocating that management draw up a strategic statement before getting down to tactics. But if the chase becomes too blinkered, you will invariably lose sight of what else is happening around you and of the shifts in the game that can throw you off course. The true meaning of winning should be bigger than merely chasing a collective target. It should be about each individual identifying his or her real purpose in the game; why he or she has chosen the game and what he or she wants the outcomes to be. Not for one moment are we suggesting that this marvellous diversity of human nature be reflected in the strategic statement. It would become too long and too nuanced. But what we are implying is that the conversation will be the poorer for not permitting the diversity of opinion about the yardsticks for success to be revealed before the conversation closes. Those around the table must have their say on this matter.

The Meaning of Success

We have intentionally left the question of winning until last on the grounds that it can only really be answered once you have understood the game, and your role in it. Being contrarian like Socrates, we have gone against the grain of contemporary thinking in doing this. Most strategic methodologies demand that an organisation's purpose and meaning of success should be addressed first in order to set the agenda for the rest of the discussion. We, on the other hand, want to keep the debate as open-ended as possible for as long as possible, with the first moment of alignment coming with the strategic statement of the last section. The latter constitutes a perfect stepping stone to a deeper discussion on the game's proper meaning and direction. One of the chief objectives of this final session is to construct a series of indicators to tell you whether or not you're on course for a desirable future – as *you* desire it.

In their dialogue, Socrates asks the fox what he considers to be the 'meaning of life'; to which the fox replies: "I suppose it has to do with the reproduction of my species. That is my legacy. I have to protect my wife and children so that someday in some distant country my several times great-grandchildren will carry on the foxy tradition." 'Legacy' is also foremost in Socrates' mind when he concurs with the fox

503

about leaving something behind. In his case, his fervent wish was that his idea of enquiry persisted in the minds of future generations. The fox's next observation highlighted the paradox for Socrates: "In all probability, that will happen if you suffer the worst of all possible fates." Eternal fame for Socrates was linked to his premature death.

Luckily for us, the chances are that we will never be called upon to leave our mark on the world through the dilemma that faced Socrates. Emerging battered and bruised is probably the worst possible fate for most of us! Business is a tough game, as is life, but for many human beings it constitutes a major dimension of their existence. Although their respective DNAs impinge on the way they play the business game, it is the unpredictable nature of the game itself that gives it complexity, and shapes their experiences. This complexity is not so common in the game of sport where 'winning' is clearly expressed on a scoreboard or scorecard at the end of a finite period of play. Someone wins, someone loses, or there is a draw; or (as in golf) there is a list of who came where when the event is over.

By contrast, the changing nature of business is relentless and unforgiving; sustainability has no time frame and no end; therefore there's no clear moment when you can announce an overall winner. If a corporate competitor falls, another will be there to pick up the baton, and their very presence will change the game. Therefore, should you wish to 'win' in the game, you have to determine what it *means* for you to win; within your time frames and according to your own personal criteria for success. Coming third in a race, for example, could be a win for you if the previous year the best you could do was seventh; and provided that coming third falls in line with your sequential plan for improvement.

Let's shift the analogy for a minute. Imagine you've seen your reflection in the mirror, winced and made the decision to lose a little weight. You're going to play the 'weight' game. In order to measure your progress you naturally think it best to set a target weight and keep an eye on the scale. Is this an accurate measurement of winning? Not really. It is in fact quite disempowering at times because it only measures short-term shifts in your body weight. It also relies predominantly on tactics. It is, after all, quite possible to lose weight quite dramatically using extreme tactics, but at the expense of good health. The true meaning of winning the weight game would therefore have to include assessments of body tone and overall health. These would provide the necessary components of a longer-term, more sustainable win than simply the loss of weight as measured by the scales. It's all about seeing the bigger picture of the game (not of yourself, hopefully). Otherwise, you will put it all on again!

A Measured Balance

Defining a well-balanced meaning of winning is both an empowering and uplifting experience, and a nice way to end the conversation on a positive note. This applies in every sector of business. We have chosen five years as a suitable period to focus the mind – anything less being too short and anything beyond beginning to appear too long. Who knows what the world will be like in ten to twenty years' time? Although it is undeniably the collective responsibility of the executive committee/board of directors to determine strategic direction, the organisation that is expected to embrace it will always be a social organisation made up of different people with different wishes and opinions, different strengths and weaknesses, different aspirations and values. There is no single meaning of winning. A successful strategy is one that is articulated through a balance of the different meanings of winning. Instead of one person placing one point on the graph and saying "right, let's get there", a more meaning-ful expression of intent for the organisation would be one where the strategic statement of the last chapter is supple-mented by a series of agreed outcomes which map out the organisation's destiny line in the foreseeable future. Such outcomes represent a composite of the individual ambitions of the executives for the company, i.e. where they would per-sonally like to see it going. And that brings substance to the purpose of the game.

We achieve this objective by posing the question at the start of the chapter to each member of the strategy team – perhaps rephrasing it thus: "What is your personal criterion by which you will judge whether the company has won or lost the game in, say, five years' time?" Predictably, each member of the team will have a different answer. For example, the director of human resources may well state that the meaning of win-ning for him consists of being the employer of choice in the industry, and thereby one to which the top graduates in the field will turn first when looking for a job. Indeed, he may add that one of the rules to win is about developing talented people to the point where they act as key differentiators. Having the pick of graduate talent is therefore a good foun-dation for a sustainable victory. From another perspective, the technical director, with an eye on retaining the company's profile as an organisation on the cutting edge, will probably want at least three revolutionary breakthroughs in product design during the five years. And so on. The 'meaning of win-ning' for the company is thus balanced in the sense that no one meaning of winning predominates over another to the point where the 'whole meaning' is impaired. Of course, all this somehow has to fall into line with the CEO's passionate desire to elevate the share price (because he or she inevitably has more share options than anyone else!).

We know what you're thinking: surely working with too

many meanings of winning can very well prove confusing and diffuse the value of the process? The point has validity, but balancing these meanings of winning is not impossible. The secret is to work with four or five *key* meanings of winning by clustering the answers from the strategy team. In this way, by the end of the process, each member of the team feels that they have contributed their money's worth, and the result is a *balanced scorecard* which, with the strategic statement as a precursor, can be treated as the overall mission statement for the company for the next five years. It represents a concrete expression of the purpose and subsidiary goals of the entire company, and incidentally serves as a much more useful tool than the biblical homilies which usually pass for the corporate 'vision' in the annual report.

As far as possible, meanings of winnings should consist of measurable outcomes. So instead of recording your wish as: "To be a company people want to work for" (perfectly healthy but unmeasurable), the statement should read: "To be included in the Top 10 of so-and-so's published list of companies to work for." The obvious advantage of having a measurable outcome is that it is a definitive goal which demands accountability on the part of the person or persons who are entrusted with the challenge of championing that element of the organisation's purpose.

Having such a balanced meaning of winning recognises that business is a considerably more subtle pastime than sport. As already intimated, there is no ultimate winner, no outright victory, because the game never stops. Yet another dimension is that, although the purpose of business is to win, it should not necessarily be to make other people lose. Sometimes an organisation must accept a 'draw', on the grounds that an outright victory would have repercussions that could scupper the game completely, taking the organisation down with it. Monopolies are frowned upon! Equally, a balanced game is one in which the impacts of certain uncontrollable factors are, to some degree, shared by all the players and perhaps mitigated by their collective influence. For instance, what is the purpose of business chambers other than to do this? Upsetting the balance of a game can mean opening it up to the unchecked ravages of alien factors and alien players. In practice, business is therefore a combination of pure rivalry and cooperative games which requires a very delicate balance between the two. We like to think of it as a touch of von Neuman with a dash of Nash (the two mathematicians who excelled in the field of game theory).

Summing up, we are well aware of the argument that if you chase two rabbits you will catch neither. This is often used to justify why it's a good idea to focus on one target at a time and go for it. We argue that if you're clever in your use of lettuce, both rabbits will *come to you*. Defining your organisation's purpose upfront limits the richness of the debate by constricting thought, discouraging new insights and narrowing the options. It is only satisfactory if your organisation is intent on spending a short time in the game, taking a short cut to success. But if your organisation is looking towards a more epic journey, where its presence as a business leader will be felt far and wide and its legacy will be experienced long after it may have left the playing field, it needs constantly to reinvent itself as the game changes. This requires open debate of the highest order, with maximum participation.

Socrates debated issues throughout his life without ever abandoning his characteristic humility. The fact that his non-acceptance of things at face value is still the guiding philosophy of many of the world's greatest scientists and philosophers, so long after his death, is the result of the balance he achieved in his meaning of winning. His choice to accept the worst possible fate so that his idea of enquiry would warrant sufficient respect to be remembered by future generations was a defining moment. There are many great philosophers, but Socrates will always stand alone because of that. As humans, our attention is drawn to the point in any story that defines it, that gives it purpose, and that ensures its longevity in the minds of those who have been absorbed by it. So, we must ask you now: what is your innermost thought on the purpose of your organisation? What is the story you would like to see unfold? What is the 'win' you desire?

We conclude this chapter with some provocative definitions on the meaning of winning the game:

The meaning of winning in our business would be to achieve the following measurable outcomes in the next five years:
- *to have a supply chain excellence programme in place whereby we have forged closer and more productive links with our key suppliers;*
- *to be considered the 'supplier of choice' in our annual customer survey by at least eight out of our top ten customers;*
- *to have opened businesses in at least three other African countries and to be generating at least 20 per cent of our revenue from these sources;*
- *to continue to grow our bottom-line profit at 25 per cent per annum, the rate we have achieved over the last five years; and*
- *to be voted by our employees as the best company to work for in the published survey of our industry.*

EXECUTIVE TEAM, COMPONENT MANUFACTURER

Our meaning of winning in five years can be expressed in three simple outcomes. Just to have made progress will be good enough. The outcomes are:
- *to halve the HIV/AIDS prevalence rate in the community in which we work by the introduction of effective prevention programmes;*

- *to have full coverage in terms of home-based care for households affected by the epidemic; and*
- *to ensure that the clinical capability exists to test all those that want to be tested and to provide antiretroviral drugs to all those who need to be treated.* DIRECTOR, HIV/AIDS NGO

We will have won the game in five years if we can do at least two things:
- *continue to be as competitive as the best New Zealand dairy farms by adopting global best practice and even improving on it where we can; and*
- *turn the business into a model for black economic empowerment that can be used elsewhere in the farming industry.*

DAIRY FARMER, EASTERN CAPE, SOUTH AFRICA
(who subsequently won the award for the empowerment deal of the year from a major bank)

My contribution to the meaning of winning is to create an environment within which the majority of our employees become our brand champions because they are so proud of working for our company.

MD, CLOTHING MANUFACTURER AND RETAILER

For me, the meaning of winning is when the human resources division is recognised by line management as a strategic business partner in this company. HEAD OF HUMAN RESOURCES, MULTIMEDIA GROUP

In this game, one of the critical meanings of winning is to triple our current reserves within five years. Another is to improve our health and safety statistics by at least 20 per cent per annum.

EXECUTIVE, GOLD-MINING GROUP

The reality is that we can't begin to win the game if we don't achieve our objective of raising R500 million over five years. But it's not just about the money. We need to use that money to make huge inroads

into providing tertiary education for thousands of people in Africa who would not otherwise get it. We want to be the biggest and best distance-learning institution on the continent, however that is measured. HEAD, UNIVERSITY FOUNDATION

For me, winning means each agent selling on average 1.5 houses per month and the company having the largest waiting list of agents because it is seen as the market leader.

SENIOR MANAGER, LEADING RESIDENTIAL PROPERTY GROUP

For the people of China, the meaning of winning is to become the largest economy in the world (again) by 2040. But we can't do that at the expense of the environment; which is why in our latest five-year plan we have a target of reducing energy consumption per unit of GDP by 20 per cent. CHINESE ECONOMIST, BEIJING

Our preparatory school has been established for almost a hundred years; but our high school is new. Our meaning of winning is to see the two integrated into a well-respected educational institution spanning the most important years of a child's life. We would also like to be seen as representative of people from every kind of background, which means establishing a significant bursary/scholarship fund and having active alumni who participate fully in our development programmes. HEADMASTER, INDEPENDENT BOYS' HIGH SCHOOL

In a nutshell, our meaning of winning is to get through the next five years without any major incidents of power outages or voluntary/involuntary load-shedding. We want to be seen by our prime customers as a strategic partner of choice. EXECUTIVE, PARASTATAL

If ever we introduce a container deposit system in Western Australia, the criteria for judging whether we've won the game in five to ten years' time will be that:

▪ *an improvement in container recovery rates to a level of*

511

80 per cent is achieved within two years of inception and maintained thereafter;
- *manufacturers significantly redesign their products so that they are better suited to recycling;*
- *the system is cost-effective and self-funding;*
- *state government and industry begin to work together to solve the problem of waste avoidance; and*
- *the mindset of consumers towards the environment changes because they feel empowered to do something about it.*

PANEL OF EXPERTS, WASTE MANAGEMENT WORKSHOP,
FREMANTLE, AUSTRALIA

A measurable outcome which would indicate we're winning our game is to be the organiser of 15 large-scale events a year – ones that repeat themselves either because the topic is evergreen or because it's an annual industry conference. CEO, CONFERENCE ORGANISER

My meaning of winning? Hmm. Like your fox, I treat life incrementally – one day at a time. I guess being the man in the White House in five years' time would be nice! If not, I'll find other ways to win the game. EX-US MAYOR, AFRICAN HR SUMMIT, JOHANNESBURG

The meaning of winning for a goalkeeper is to stop the other side from scoring goals. The meaning of winning for a striker is to score goals. Stopping something happening is not nearly as glamorous as making something happen. That's why strikers are much better known than goalkeepers. But I suppose the same applies to anybody in the prevention game. Heaven forbid you should let something through. The sky falls on your head. EX-MANCHESTER UNITED
GOALKEEPER, CO-PRESENTER, AUDITING CONFERENCE

In defining the criteria for South Africa to become a 'winning nation', I'm sure the people around this table will give you quite different answers. After all, we are a democracy. But for the 'meaning

of losing', you only have to look north to Zimbabwe. It is our 'cautionary tale'.

PARTICIPANT, SCENARIO WORKSHOP ON SOUTH AFRICA

We had a memorable session at which all the players in the game bird industry – the conservationists, the farmers, the shooters and the safari operators – were present. Not only did we achieve a better understanding of the overall game, we also clearly defined our respective roles in winning it. It also made us realise that to play a leading role as a research organisation, we needed a full-time CEO. One of the participants at the session applied for and got the job and we've never looked back.

CHAIRMAN, GAME BIRD RESEARCH NGO

For us, a yardstick for winning is to continue to be voted the second-best managed port in Africa – or even the best. We also want to maintain our status as a principal gateway for trade into southern Angola.
CFO, NAMIBIAN PORTS AUTHORITY, WALVIS BAY

Winning is Living with a capital 'L'. Losing is Dying without Living.
DEEJAY, LEADING HIP-HOP RADIO STATION, JOHANNESBURG

We're about to be hit by a tsunami of cash arriving from the exploitation of our oil and gas fields. Billions upon billions of extra dollars rolling into the government exchequer every year. Like the winner of the largest lottery on earth, we can spend the money wisely or foolishly. Winning is the first option.

OFFICIAL, GOVERNMENT OF AZERBAIJAN

The meaning of winning is catching the fox.
MEMBER OF BRITISH ROYAL FAMILY, AWARDS CEREMONY, CAPE TOWN

EPILOGUE

From Socrates to Wack: Looking Forward and Looking Back

Often when looking at a mass of things for sale, he would say to himself, "How many things I have no need of!"
DIOGENES LAERTIUS on Socrates in *Lives of the Eminent Philosophers*

Traditional ways of formulating strategy have their place, but they also have their weaknesses; and in the face of growing uncertainty in the world, those weaknesses are not the foundations upon which organisations should plan for the future. However, many organisations seem reluctant to change their linear approach towards strategy, and are attracted instead to the seductively easy conclusions that such an approach brings.

Imagine if strategy could be so straightforward that data could be fed into a computer model and then a future would pop out of the other end for every one to digest and plan around accordingly. Such a model existed for the oil industry as far back as the early 1970s. After crunching data involving 120 variables, the model produced the seemingly unassailable prediction that the world would run out of oil within twenty years. It was clearly wrong.

East Meets West

But someone did get it right. Incontestably so in fact. His name was Pierre Wack, and he was anything but typical. He was a French economist with a flair for Indian mysticism. He had studied under George Gurdjieff, a religious philosopher who brought to the West a mystic tradition within Islam known as Sufism. Amongst other things Wack learnt from Gurdjieff was the value of 'seeing' as performed by mystics, and that the true secret of the martial arts was the ability to 'see' when an opponent was about to strike and therefore when and where to strike or retaliate with maximum effect. As Wack described it: "Naturally, we 'look' with our minds – with interpretations, inferences, perceptions, comparisons, expectations, and through all our previous experiences. Actually, to 'see' is a function of a pure consciousness. It is an enchantment." In other words, cut out all those filters that cloud your everyday observations and judgement. Link your senses directly to your soul.

Later Wack would travel to Svamiji's ashram in India to learn more about this practice "of not believing, imagining, speculating, but seeing". He admitted that he was not 'predisposed' to see but was more inclined to give himself over to 'interpretation' and 'mental constructions'. As such he likened the challenge of his conversion to splitting an old, tough tree trunk with an axe, the tree being 'knotty' and with 'lots of curious difficulties'. "Svamiji", he said, "was without equal when it came to discovering the right angle of attack, coming up with an adequate axe and inspiring his disciple with the will to use it, because in this case, the disciple was both the trunk and the one who has to use the axe."

Wack's affinity for Indian mysticism seemed out of place in the early 1970s in the dour corporate corridors of Royal Dutch/Shell in London where he was part of a new division called Group Planning. But it helped him separate himself and the group from the traditional forecasting techniques used at the time, and move towards a new approach of handling the future called 'scenario planning' – or, as Wack preferred to call it, 'scenario thinking'. The latter, as he explained, "demands, firstly, the identification of the forces at work and the chain(s) of cause and effect behind the development of a market; and, secondly, information about a chain that is much wider than global statistics, a ladder where significant differences appear". He did not invent scenario planning. That accolade belongs to Herman Kahn, an American genius who served as a consultant to the US armed forces and even wrote a bestseller on military scenarios with the title *On Thermonuclear War: Thinking About the Unthinkable*. Indeed, Wack was a student of Kahn. Yet his achievement is still monumental, for he took a discipline which was created in a military setting and adapted it to commerce.

Under Wack's guidance, Shell designed scenarios through which they managed to 'see' possible futures for the price of oil and what forces could affect it; and when the seemingly 'unthinkable' oil price shock came in October 1973, only Shell had captured it in a scenario. But as Wack was wont to say on many occasions afterwards, that was not enough. "Svamiji had made it very clear to me that it wasn't only important to see, but also to make others see. Without this, scenarios which went so much against the ruling expectations of the day would be nothing but 'water on the stone', that would dissipate without leaving a trace." Indeed, he was bitterly disappointed that the scenario did not penetrate the 'microcosm' of Shell decision-makers to the point that it changed their minds on strategy. They did nothing.

He then spent the next few years plying each senior executive with questions in order to understand how to connect to them and what language to use. When the second oil price shock happened in the late 1970s, he anticipated it with a scenario that captured their imagination because of the homework he had done. This time they acted by building up their oil stocks in advance; and almost overnight Shell moved from being one of the smaller of the seven large oil companies in the world to becoming the second biggest. The Gallic guru had passed the Wack test!

Just as Socrates is widely considered as being the 'father' of Western philosophy, so is Pierre Wack thought of as the 'elder statesman' of scenario planning; and he is widely credited for laying the foundations for scenario thinking in business, still one of the most successful (though alas not yet mainstream) forms of strategising for the future. Wack's distinctive approach to scenarios was a fascinating combination of deep perception and intellect, often resulting in profound insight. He believed that this acute perception of the future – or 'reperception' – came about by freeing oneself from old perceptions and prejudices. "Taking off the blinkers", he called it, "and taking on the peripheral vision of a racehorse." You could then pick up the 'strong tendencies' of the present which acted as constraints on the future in important ways. An alternative name he gave to these forces was 'predetermined elements', and the example he often quoted was the monsoon rains that subsequently cause floods on the plains of the Ganges downstream. It has to happen. By sheer concentration, backed up by systematic application of logic or reasoning, he felt that you could peel away the layers of uncertainty and move from uncertainty-based – or, as he called them, 'first-generation' – scenarios and create 'second-generation' scenarios that were a lot more than an imaginary projection; they were a window onto the future.

The Socratic Link

Sound familiar? Even though Pierre Wack was considered a visionary, his driving philosophy was hardly new. Over two thousand years before Wack, Socrates was explaining to his students that true wisdom could only come about by returning to first principles and vigorously questioning them. Any answers that were provided were not the real answers but were masked by the influence of established beliefs and norms and should be considered preludes to further, deeper questioning. By steadily identifying and eliminating those hypotheses that led to contradiction, Socrates

520

gave his students the ability to reperceive the world around them.

Wack also spoke of hypotheses, and often quoted Roberta Wohlsletter, the famous historian of military intelligence who attributed the failure of the US forces to anticipate an attack on Pearl Harbour to their lack of considering a variety of hypotheses outside the realm of contemporary thinking. We sympathise with this view, having had our analysis of a massive terrorist attack on the West fall on deaf ears prior to 9/11 (see the letter to the US president in *The Mind of a Fox* published by Human & Rousseau and Tafelberg in June 2001). Furthermore, Wack believed that the formation of scenarios encouraged participants to sharpen their focus on the key environmental considerations surrounding any business, aided by a deeper and richer language system through which ideas and data could be exchanged.

The similarities between Socrates and Wack don't end there. Both provided a way of thinking that produces an empowering conversation amongst those tasked with creating policy. Limits are tested and radical departures from the norm countenanced. For Wack, this opened up new possibilities which he considered the driving forces behind entrepreneurial flair and foresight. In a similar vein, Socratic dialogue forces participants to re-examine their own belief and value systems and, where necessary, revise them. Wack spoke of an 'inner space', where participants are obliged to question their assumptions about how their business world works and, where necessary, re-organise or change their inner models of reality. This he contrasted with the 'outer space' beyond the control of the participants and subject to rigorous scenario analysis (and possible reperception).

Both Socrates and Wack rocked their worlds. Through his relentless pursuit of virtue and truth, and as a social and moral critic of the Athenian status quo, Socrates challenged not only the city's authority but also its whole way of life. By irritating the establishment with his interrogations of the common man's meaning of justice and goodness, he suffered the ultimate injustice of being tried for supposedly corrupting the youth, and was sentenced to death. Pierre Wack fascinated the establishment with his hooded eyes, goatee beard and the incense he liked to breathe in before uttering something controversial. He actually looked quite like Socrates (or rather what we believe Socrates looked like). But above all, it was his appeal to mystical philosophy that rattled the grey suits together with his uncanny ability to 'see' things they didn't.

Just as Socrates' thinking attracted a dedicated core of deep-thinking, dynamic intellectuals; so it alienated him from mainline popular thought. To a lesser extent, Pierre Wack's approach to business strategy was cold-shouldered by established business thinkers; but his unrivalled success in the field earned him the respect and following of some of the most original and insightful minds in business. In fact, the team that followed in his footsteps at Royal Dutch/Shell and developed his work foresaw the rise of Mikhail Gorbachev and the collapse of Communism years before these events were on anybody else's radar screen.

But in a world where business leaders demand quick-fix solutions based on computer models and quantified predictions, the embracing of uncertainty as recommended by scenario thinking proved too unfamiliar to take off as a tool for business strategy. Consequently, only the exceptional and more forward-thinking companies followed Pierre Wack's philosophy of strategising. Moreover, it was only towards the end of his life that scenario thinking really got its second breath, most notably in South Africa where it is not an exaggeration to suggest that his methodology influenced a nation's destiny. As he remarked to one of us at the time: "Changing the mindset of a company is one thing: changing the mindset of a nation – *c'est magnifique.*" Tragically, it took his death in 1997 to make it clear to the world that it had lost one of its least-known but most remarkable business thinkers.

Coincidentally, the true power of Socrates' philosophy was only fully appreciated after his death (like the paintings of Vincent van Gogh). Yet little is known of him directly from his own words, as he never wrote anything. Instead, what knowledge we have of him comes from the testimony of others. Even as death approached, he never lost his moral integrity. His last words were reputed to be a request to settle an outstanding debt: "Crito, we owe a cock to Aesculapius; please pay it and don't let it pass." Both he and Pierre Wack have often been described as 'remarkable' men. But they were humble too.

The End of the Beginning

And so it is that, as active and passionate proponents of scenario thinking, we have embodied the principles of both Socrates and Pierre Wack into our work. Like the fox, we have been *resourceful* and adapted our model with experience. We have used the Socratic method in a deep and rigorous process to challenge the basic beliefs of the important decision-makers; to integrate intuition with logic; to demand that participants look both inwards and outwards; to use scenarios to create windows onto the future; and finally to make people *act* on the practical implications of the scenarios.

In addition, we have also tried to steer the thinking of participants in our sessions towards the sometimes unpalatable realities of change and to address the often tumultuous world of intensifying competition, unstoppable advances in technology, abrupt turnarounds in economic cycles, and shifting allegiances between nations. Our process is succinct; and it uses a time frame for the conversation that is acceptable in today's world, where pressing issues from all quarters demand the effective use of time. It deals with facts as well as perceptions. It enables continual additions and updates as the future turns into the past. Yet, it steadfastly remains true to the philosophy of scenario thinking, which is to provide a unique competence to the players in today's uncertain game of business.

Pierre Wack said of scenarios that they serve two main purposes. The first is proactive – anticipating and understanding risk; the second is entrepreneurial – discovering strategic options of which we were previously unaware. For many people in business and other activities, the kind of game-playing which underlies our model is something which they may find strange. But as most of the executive teams whose sessions we have facilitated will attest, it is not that difficult to master. Our questions do not intrude on discussing the real business. Quite the reverse.

Socrates said of education: it is the kindling of a flame, not the filling of a vessel, that counts. We hope that we have stoked a fire within you, and that you are ready to adopt our approach by answering our ten questions. We have said our bit. The rest is now up to you. Or, as the fox would say: "Now that the conversation has ended, so may the journey begin." Your destiny line stretches ahead.

About the authors

Chantell Ilbury is an independent strategist and facilitator whose work with corporate teams has taken her to the UK, the US, Europe, Australasia, the Middle East and Africa. She lectures on strategy at a number of top business schools and is an accomplished speaker on effective strategy in times of uncertainty. Chantell holds a BSc in Chemistry, a Higher Diploma in Education, an Executive MBA from the University of Cape Town, and has studied Strategic Negotiation at Harvard Business School in Boston.

Chantell is married to Daryl and they have two children.

Clem Sunter studied at Winchester and New College, Oxford. He joined Anglo American in 1966, eventually heading up the Chairman's Fund from 1996 to 2008. He has written numerous books on scenario planning, some of which topped the national chart. In 2004 he was awarded an honorary doctorate from the University of Cape Town for his work in this field. He was also voted by leading South African CEOs as the speaker who has made the most impact on local best practice.

Clem married Margaret Rowland in 1969 and they have three children.

Other books and ebooks by
Clem Sunter and Chantell Ilbury:

The Mind of a Fox
Designed by Jürgen Fomm
First published in 2001

ISBN: 978-0-7981-4169-7
ISBN: 978-1-920-32354-7 (e-Pdf)
ISBN: 978-1-920-32353-0 (e-Pub)
ISBN: 978-0-7981-6007-0 (mobi)

Games Foxes Play
Designed by Jürgen Fomm
Diagrams based on original designs by Daryl Ilbury
First published in 2005

ISBN: 978-0-7981-4509-1
ISBN: 978-1-920-32354-7 (e-Pdf)
ISBN: 978-1-920-32356-1 (e-Pub)
ISBN: 978-0-7981-6005-6 (mobi)

Socrates & the Fox
Designed by Nazli Jacobs
First published in 2007

ISBN: 978-0-7981-4905-1
ISBN: 978-1-920-32354-7 (e-Pdf)
ISBN: 978-1-920-32358-5 (e-Pub)
ISBN: 978-0-7981-6006-3 (mobi)